Assessing the Reagan Years

Assessing the Reagan Years

edited by David Boaz

Library of Congress Cataloging-in-Publication Data

Assessing the Reagan years.

   1. United States—Politics and government—
1981–   . 2. Reagan, Ronald. I. Boaz, David,
1953–   .
E876.A777   1988   973.927   88-25820
ISBN 0-932790-68-2
ISBN 0-932790-69-0 (pbk.)

Cover illustration by Keith Dana, Design Consultants, Inc.

Printed in the United States of America.

CATO INSTITUTE
224 Second Street, S.E.
Washington, D.C. 20003

Contents

Introduction   1
David Boaz

PART I: TAXING AND SPENDING

1.   Reflections on Reaganomics   9
   William A. Niskanen

2.   How Tight Was the Reagan Administration's   17
   First-Term Fiscal Policy?
   Laurence J. Kotlikoff

3.   The Tax Reform Act of 1986: Revolution or   29
   Counterrevolution?
   Norman B. Ture

4.   Origins and Effects of the Deficit   45
   Mickey D. Levy

5.   Supply-Side Success   71
   Richard Rahn

PART II: FOREIGN AND DEFENSE POLICY

6.   The Reagan Defense Budget and Program: 83
   The Buildup That Collapsed
   Lawrence J. Korb

7.   Requiem for the Reagan Doctrine   95
   Christopher Layne

8.   Two Cheers for SDI   113
   Ted Galen Carpenter

9.   Reagan's Failed Restoration: Superpower   125
   Relations in the 1980s
   Earl C. Ravenal

10.   Making Friends in the Third World   143
      Doug Bandow

PART III: MONEY AND BANKING

11.   Monetary Policy: Monetarism to Fine-Tuning   157
      William Poole

12.   Weakening the Dollar: The Tax No One Has to   175
      Vote For
      Jerry L. Jordan

13.   Financial Services Regulation: Driven by Events 187
      Catherine England

PART IV: TRANSFER PAYMENTS

14.   Social Security: Look at Your Pay Stub   201
      Peter J. Ferrara

15.   Social Welfare Policy: A Failure of Vision   211
      Kevin R. Hopkins

16.   Health Care: The Tyranny of the Budget   223
      Roger D. Feldman

17.   Agriculture: Growing Government Control   243
      Robert L. Thompson

PART V: DOMESTIC POLICIES

18.   International Trade: Better than Congress   253
      Murray L. Weidenbaum

19.   Antitrust: An Incomplete Revolution   261
      James L. Gattuso

20.   What Ever Happened to Deregulation?   271
      Robert W. Crandall

21.   Educational Schizophrenia   291
      David Boaz

22.   Energy Policies: A Few Bright Spots   305
      Robert L. Bradley, Jr.

23.   Labor Reform: A Blip on the Radarscope   321
      Morgan O. Reynolds

24.   What Environmental Policy?   333
      Fred L. Smith, Jr.

PART VI: LAW AND THE COURTS

25.   The Endangered Branch: The Judiciary Under   353
      Reagan
      Stephen Macedo

26.   Civil Liberties: What Ever Happened to   367
      Limited Government?
      Barry W. Lynn

27.   One Cheer for the Reagan Years: Economic   379
      Liberties and the Constitution
      Randy E. Barnett

28.   Civil Rights as a Principle Versus Civil Rights   391
      as an Interest
      Clarence Thomas

PART VII: THE REAGAN LEGACY

29.   A Record of Success   405
      Malcolm S. Forbes, Jr.

30.   The Intellectual Debate   413
      Paul H. Weaver

31.   Who Will Lead?   423
      Edward H. Crane

      Contributors   429

Introduction

David Boaz

No president in this century has come to Washington with a clearer policy agenda than Ronald Reagan, or so the story goes. The months between his election and his inauguration were marked by manifestations of terror on the part of the Washington establishment, generally voiced in the *Washington Post*. On February 8, 1981, a headline in the *Post* warned, "Epic Political Struggle Looms: Official Washington Realizing Reform Crusade Is Not Business-as-Usual."

Among the more outrageous charges made in the early days of the administration was that Reagan was appointing people to jobs in agencies whose basic purposes, or even existence, they didn't support. Apparently it had never occurred to those critics that in a democracy, the purpose of an election is to give the people a chance to change public policy. Of course, because many of the critics were members of the House of Representatives, that oversight is understandable; House members don't even recognize that an election should result in a change of officeholders.

In any case, the critics needn't have worried. As the months wore on, it became evident that the dreaded Reagan reform crusade *would* amount to business as usual. Federal spending would keep rising; federal agencies would keep regulating.

There were exceptions, of course, and the real achievements of the Reagan years deserve recognition. In two landmark tax bills, President Reagan reduced the highest marginal tax rate on Americans' personal incomes from 70 percent to 28 percent (and the rate on upper-middle-bracket incomes to 33 percent, an interesting case of regressive taxation)—a success that could hardly have been imagined in 1980 and that outweighs a multitude of failures. It was good news not just for Americans but for the citizens of major industrialized nations around the world, from Great Britain to Australia, from Japan to France. It has pressured their governments to reduce their own tax rates in order to prevent a flow of brain power and capital

1

to the United States, once more the land of opportunity where people can keep (a substantial part of) what they earn. That remarkable accomplishment is explored in this volume by Richard Rahn and Malcolm S. Forbes, Jr.

However, that achievement is balanced by what is perhaps the administration's greatest shortcoming: its failure to reduce federal spending, discussed in this volume by William A. Niskanen and Mickey D. Levy. If the actual burden of taxation is neither the stated tax rate nor tax revenues but the total amount of money taken out of the private sector by the government, then taxes weren't reduced during the Reagan years; they were increased. Real federal spending, as Niskanen notes, increased by 2.7 percent annually.

The size of the federal budget, of course, is not the only measure of an administration's effectiveness, and this volume is perhaps the most comprehensive assessment of the Reagan administration's policies to date. The topics of its 31 essays range from the deficit to education, from foreign aid to the selection of judges, from international relations to antitrust law. The contributors are an interesting mix; some were in the highest echelons of White House policymaking, others were administration appointees in various departments and agencies, and still others were not part of the administration.

A term that recurs throughout these essays is "Reagan Revolution." Was there a Reagan Revolution? If so, did it end at some point? Did it nonetheless have permanent effects? It may well be that the term Reagan Revolution, and some would say even "Reagan administration," falsely suggests a sense of purpose on the part of the administration—the same illusion that so terrified the Washington establishment in the bitter winter of 1980–81. In most agencies and most programs, the Reagan Revolution turned out to be a paper tiger; the bureaucracy and the iron triangle had mobilized for a blitz that never came.

Indeed, it is astounding that there were so many issues on which, as Peter Ferrara observes in his essay on social security, the Reagan administration "never even showed up" for battle. Education is a classic example. As noted in this volume, the administration's rhetoric on education policy went from Reagan's 1980 campaign promise to abolish the Department of Education in order to keep education in the hands of local governments to his 1981 proposal, to

2

change the department in form but not in substance, to a 1988 boast by the staunchest Reaganite in his cabinet that "largely because of me" the department would never be abolished.

The illusion of commitment can largely be traced to Ronald Reagan himself, as Edward H. Crane has argued in this volume and elsewhere. For 16 years before his election to the presidency, Reagan gave stirring speeches about individual liberties, the free market, and the evils of big government. It is thus understandable that despite his failure to act on those principles as governor of California, both critics and defenders of big government expected President Reagan's arrival in Washington to be like Carrie Nation's in a saloon.

Yet after the passage of the 1981 tax bill all signs of the long-awaited Reagan Revolution seemed to fade away. David Stockman related that Reagan never had the stomach for real budget cuts. Conservatives continually defended Reagan's "detached" style of administration, arguing that he kept his eye on the big picture and avoided getting bogged down in the kinds of details that had consumed President Carter. But the "details" that bored Reagan turned out to include the selection of cabinet officers, White House staffers, and other key personnel as well as the federal budget. Perhaps the most revealing anecdote in Donald Regan's book *For the Record* is his report of presenting a detailed economic agenda for the second term to the president and getting no reaction other than "It's good, Don"—no questions, no areas of disagreement, no discussion.

President Reagan's detachment from the process of governing may explain the disjointed policies of his administration and the gulf between rhetoric and reality. Some of his appointees successfully carried out the policies widely believed to be his; others ignored them or pursued policies that were clearly antithetical to them. But the successes seem almost random rather than the result of careful presidential attention to the agencies or policies involved.

Now, far be it from me to advocate a vigorous government. Like Thomas Jefferson, "I am not a friend to a very energetic government. It is always oppressive." I have always admired Calvin Coolidge, who took a nap in the White House every afternoon—in his pajamas. It is the pajamas, I think, that signify an admirably restrained presidency.

Nevertheless, in our time there is much for a president to undo.

3

A systemic bias toward government growth is evident in Washington. Because every government program grants benefits to a well-informed few that are paid for by the unaware many, our capital city has come to harbor a huge concentration of special interests, each with its own small portion of the federal budget or regulatory apparatus to preserve, protect, and defend. A president who lacks a strong commitment to reduce the size of the government and expand the civil and economic liberties of Americans—and the energy to follow through on that commitment—will be swept along by the inertial force of government growth. Milton Friedman called it the tyranny of the status quo, but it is important to remember that the status quo is not simply all the government we have now but all the government we have now and then some.

A president who appoints cabinet officers that are on record as opposing his professed goals, who never bothers to tell his secretary of the treasury what his economic policy goals are, who avoids making tough decisions on spending programs, whose aides are so concerned with photo opportunities and spin control that they lose sight of substance—such a president will soon find himself rolled by the Washington establishment.

Perhaps the greatest mistake advocates of limited government could make is to conclude that "if Reagan couldn't do it, nobody can," a theme that will be popular with the establishment. In other words, if the most conservative president of the 20th century couldn't get rid of program X, then the American people must want it and it must be here to stay. As I think this volume makes clear, a president with a more consistent approach to reducing the size of government, a better understanding of the values expressed in his speeches, and a greater willingness to provide firm leadership to his administration and not shrink from battle could make far more headway than Reagan did.

A second mistake is to conclude, as David Stockman did, that the American people want big government. In his younger days, Stockman understood that "the solid entrepreneurs of southern Michigan's hamlets" were willing to give up their subsidies in return for a smaller federal government, but when their voices were heard in Washington it was through the interpretations of trade associations lobbying for pet spending programs.

Later, depressed by his own failure to get government spending under control, Stockman forgot that home truth about the political process. "We have had a tumultuous national referendum on everything in our half-trillion-dollar welfare state budget," he wrote in *The Triumph of Politics,* so the persistence of "lavish Social Security benefits, wasteful dairy subsidies, futile UDAG grants, and all the remainder of the federal subventions" was not "solely due to weak-kneed politicians or the nefarious graspings of special-interest groups."

What Stockman failed to recognize is that "we" did not have a national referendum on spending; Congress and the White House did. In a mixed-economy democracy, the government's actions reflect not the will of the majority but the pressure of interest groups. Congress hears from the beneficiaries of every program, whereas those who pay for it are silent. Stockman's economic agenda, as he acknowledged elsewhere in his book, "was utterly repudiated by the combined forces of the politicians"—not by the people.

Obviously, a definitive assessment of the achievements and the lessons of the Reagan administration must await the fullness of time. If journalism is indeed the first rough draft of history, the essays in this volume may constitute a second rough draft. The Reagan administration changed some public policies, though fewer than the conventional wisdom acknowledges. It also changed the tone of debate in Washington, though it is doubtful whether that achievement will endure. Unlike the Roosevelt Revolution, which ushered in a half-century of expanding government, the Reagan Revolution will likely prove to be, in Doug Bandow's term, only the Reagan Interlude.

PART I

TAXING AND SPENDING

1. Reflections on Reaganomics
William A. Niskanen

Reaganomics represents the most serious attempt by any administration since the New Deal to change the course of U.S. economic policy. It has been a program guided by a common belief that, in Ronald Reagan's words, "only by reducing the growth of the government can we increase the growth of the economy." Its common direction has been to reduce the role of government in the U.S. economy by reducing the growth of government spending, tax rates, regulation, and the growth of the money supply.

It is too early to write the full history of Reaganomics, for there is usually some time lag between changes in economic policies and changes in economic conditions. And, most importantly, ideas cast an even longer shadow. It is not too early, however, to reflect on the major lessons of the first six years of this ambitious program. These remarks summarize my reflections on six of these lessons.

The Growth of Real Government Spending Proved Very Difficult to Reduce

This was so despite Reagan being the most conservative president since the 1920s and the Senate having a Republican majority through 1986. From FY 1981 through FY 1987, real federal spending increased at an annual rate of 2.7 percent, lower than the 5 percent annual increase during the Carter administration, but, until recently, higher than the growth rate of the economy. Moreover, the growth of real federal spending would have been somewhat higher if Congress had approved the administration's full defense budget requests. Some calculations that I made in 1985 suggest that the pattern of total federal spending during the Reagan administration was not significantly different from the pattern of the prior postwar years.

The continued high growth of real federal spending was the major failure of the Reagan economic program. Moreover, the deficits that were caused primarily by the continued growth in real spending threaten to undermine the major accomplishments of this program—specifically, the reduction in tax rates and inflation. There is plenty of blame to go around.

First, the initial Reagan budget plan severely constrained the potential for budget restraint. A substantial increase was proposed for the defense budget, equal to 25 percent of total outlays in 1981. The initial program also promised to preserve and maintain the core social safety-net programs, which took 35 percent of total outlays in 1981. Interest payments on the outstanding debt were another 10 percent of 1981 outlays. To reduce the growth of total outlays, therefore, the budget plan required a substantial reduction in the level of spending for the many domestic programs constituting the remaining 30 percent of the 1981 budget.

Another part of the problem was that contemporary campaign politics undermines the potential to govern. At no time during the 1980 and 1984 campaigns, for example, did Reagan acknowledge that a substantial reduction in domestic programs was necessary to permit both a defense buildup and a tax cut without an increase in the deficit. The 1980 solution to this budget problem was to reduce "waste, fraud, extravagance, and abuse." The 1984 solution was to increase economic growth. Both of these solutions to the budget problem proved to be illusory. There is plenty of waste in the federal budget, but most of this waste is there for the same reason that the programs are there—because someone wants it. Cutting waste proved to be no easier than cutting programs. An increase in economic growth (discussed later) proved difficult to achieve. In the absence of any campaign commitment to reduce domestic programs, therefore, substantial election victories did not provide a sufficient mandate to reduce these programs.

Another part of the problem was that Reagan's agenda included a number of controversial proposals that required congressional approval, usually obtained by administration support for other spending proposals favored by members of Congress. Consequently, the total budget cost of such proposals as the sale of weapons to Saudi Arabia, the MX missile, additional funding for the International Monetary Fund, and aid to the contras was often much higher than the direct budget cost.

A major problem, I now believe, was that the phased tax-rate reductions approved in 1981 were not made contingent, at least in part, on subsequent budget restraint. The initial budget proposals were not sufficient to offset the revenue loss of the tax cuts, and not all the initial proposals were approved. Once the tax cuts were approved, the only case for budget restraint was the rather vague general benefit of lower deficits—a benefit that became increasingly implausible after inflation and interest rates declined and the economy recovered. The political problem of reducing the deficit was due to a developing recognition that the deficit did not lead to substantial economic problems in the short term.

The most important problem, as David Stockman documented, is that there are very few consistent advocates of spending restraint in the administration or in either party in Congress. Almost every self-styled fiscal conservative strongly supports some part of what Stockman called "the social pork barrel." Stockman may be wrong that the public also supports these programs, but there is now no doubt that the contemporary welfare state is broadly supported in Congress.

A related lesson of this period involves the relation between spending and taxes. For many years, Milton Friedman has argued that an increase in taxes would increase spending, a view shared by President Reagan. James Buchanan maintains the directly contrary view that an increase in taxes, by increasing the perceived current price of government services, would reduce spending, a view apparently shared by Prime Minister Margaret Thatcher, Chancellor Helmut Kohl, and, more recently, Prime Minister Brian Mulroney. The developing evidence has only confused this issue. A careful 1986 study concludes that changes in taxes do not appear to have any effect on changes in spending.[1] Spending restraint, according to this study, must be addressed head-on, without much effect from whatever is happening to taxes. Several later studies, however, are more consistent with the Friedman-Reagan view. These findings may be only small comfort to those who share either view, in that the costs of the several experiments with this relation have been very high, and the lessons are not yet widely understood.

[1]See George von Furstenberg, R. Jeffrey Green, and Jin-Ho Jeong, "Tax and Spend, or Spend and Tax?" *The Review of Economics and Statistics* 68, no. 2 (May 1986): 179–88.

The Growth of Real Domestic Output Proved Very Difficult to Increase

Real gross national product increased at a 2.8 percent annual rate during the Reagan years, compared to a 2.9 percent annual rate during the Carter administration. The slower growth of real GNP, however, is entirely attributable to a slower growth of the adult population. On a per-adult basis, the growth of real GNP and other measures of domestic output was slightly higher than during the Carter administration.

The growth rates did not change much, despite policies that most economists regarded as stimulatory. For the Keynesians, the record peacetime deficits should have increased demand. For the monetarists, the record rate of money growth since mid-1982 should also have increased demand. For the supply-siders, the reduction of tax rates and some deregulation should have increased output. As it turned out, economic growth did not appear to have been much affected by the combination of these policies. There was reason to expect that the growth rate might increase after inflation was stabilized, but the growth rate during Reagan's second term to date has been only slightly higher than during his first term.

The most interesting effect of the Reagan policies has been that despite a slightly slower growth of real GNP, the growth rate of each major component of real domestic purchases—consumption, domestic investment, and government purchases—was higher than during the Carter administration. How can this be? The answer is that net imports grew very rapidly, allowing the United States, for a limited period, to use more goods and services than it produced. The magnitude of the current account deficit, now equal to 3.4 percent of GNP, is not sustainable. As this deficit is reduced, we may experience the opposite pattern—an increase in the growth of real GNP and a lower growth rate of each major component of real purchases.

The Reduction in Inflation Was Much Less Difficult than Expected

The last *Economic Report* of the Carter administration estimated that each percentage-point reduction in inflation would cost about $100 billion (in 1980 dollars) in lost output. In fact, the inflation rate was reduced about 7 percentage points by 1986 without reducing

12

the growth of real GNP per adult. The temporary loss of output relative to this trend was less than half that implied by the Carter estimates. The substantial decline in inflation was the one economic condition that is superior to the initial Reagan forecasts.

It is much less clear why the inflation rate declined as much as it did. The most obvious reason was the reduction in money growth from late 1979 through mid-1982. The rest of the story is much less clear. Since mid-1982, M1 has increased at the highest sustained peacetime rate without reigniting inflation, due to a corresponding reduction in the velocity of money, a condition that was not anticipated and is not yet broadly understood. The most probable reasons for the decline in velocity were the combination of lower market interest rates, the higher interest rates on deposits permitted by bank deregulation, and the substantial increase in the real value of financial assets.

A third condition contributing to the decline in inflation was the sharp increase in the real foreign-exchange value of the dollar through early 1985, a condition that was primarily the result of the reduction of the effective tax rate on domestic business investment approved in 1981. A fourth condition was the growing excess supply of oil, in part a result of a higher real exchange rate. My own judgment is that the earlier reduction in money growth contributed only about one-third of the reduction in inflation, an important contribution but not the dominant contribution for which Paul Volcker is credited.

On Such Issues as Regulation and Trade, a Good Defense Is Not Enough

All too often, those of us responsible for reviewing regulation and trade issues faced a no-win situation. On numerous occasions, often with considerable effort, we managed to defeat or defer some new regulation or trade restraint. On other occasions, we lost. The net result of this process was that we ended up with more regulations and more trade restraints than at the beginning of the administration. The reason for this is that most regulations and many trade restraints do not automatically expire, and most of the new proposals are for more such restraints.

An aggressive strategy of deregulation is the only way to avoid a net increase in regulation. The total amount of regulation increased during both the Carter and Reagan administrations, but for different reasons. Under Carter, there was a substantial reduction of the regulation of prices and entry in the airline, trucking, railroad, and financial industries, as well as a substantial increase in the regulation of health, safety, the environment, and the uses of energy. Under Reagan, there was little deregulation and less new regulation; the only deregulatory legislation approved so far involves banks, intercity buses, ocean shipping, and the uses of energy.

Similarly, an aggressive strategy of reducing existing trade barriers is now necessary to avoid a net increase in protection. Average U.S. tariffs are now about 5 percent, and the automatic reductions in these tariffs are correspondingly smaller. There is no automatic mechanism, however, to relax many of the nontariff barriers. For the first time in many decades, the new trade restraints exceeded the automatic reductions. For several years, the administration proposed a new General Agreement on Tariffs and Trade (GATT) round of multinational trade negotiations, but the prospects for the new Uruguay round are not promising. The omnibus trade bill approved by Congress in 1988 would end a half-century of U.S. leadership of the world trading system.

For the most part, the convictions of the president on these issues are admirable. My disappointment is that the administration did not have the vision and political commitment to follow through on these convictions.

The Experience of the 1980s Has Been, or Should Have Been, Chastening to Economists of All Persuasions

Only an econometrician could love this period, in that it produced such a high variance of the key policy variables. Keynesians, for example, may wish to reflect why the record peacetime deficits did not apparently increase total demand, inflation, or interest rates, and, until recently, did not reduce domestic investment. Monetarists, for their part, need to explain why the record sustained peacetime rate of money growth since mid-1982 has not (yet) increased inflation. Supply-siders, not to be left out, should consider why the reduction in tax rates has not (yet) increased economic growth.

None of these schools has yet offered a coherent explanation of the most unusual and unanticipated economic conditions of this period:

14

- the combination of strong domestic investment through 1984 and high real interest rates;
- the strong increase, and later sharp decline, in the exchange value of the dollar;
- the rapid increase in the trade deficit; and
- the unusual decline in the velocity for money.

For economists, one of the more important lessons of this period may be that we need to rebuild our understanding of macroeconomic phenomena. A little more humility would also be appropriate.

The Major Lesson of Reaganomics Is That Those of Us Who Share the Jeffersonian Vision of Limited Constitutional Government Have Not Yet Much Changed the Wondrous Ways of Washington

Only one significant program has been terminated, and the federal budget share of our national output has continued to increase. The net amount of regulations and trade restraints has increased. Monetary policy still operates without any rules. The basic motives, constraints, and institutions of government have not changed. The Reagan administration may prove to be only a temporary pause in the increasing politicalization of American life.

The future, however, will be of our own making. We can continue to accept a progressive loss of liberties, usually in the name of some other value. Or we can restore a constitutional republic that is limited by rules that reflect the broad consensus of the American community. We need a better understanding of the actual effects of government activities and the process of government—a task in which the foundations, universities, and policy institutes will continue to perform an important role.

We may need a new Reagan to articulate a vision of an American community of both opportunity and caring, one in which the federal government has an important but limited role. Some one or more constitutional amendments may be necessary to limit the government's authority to borrow and tax and to preserve a viable federal system. Most importantly, we need to sort out in our own minds the rules by which we expect the government to operate, and we need to hold our political officials accountable to these rules. Reaganomics was a first, halting step in this direction. No one of us can avoid a responsibility for the direction of the next steps.

2. How Tight Was the Reagan Administration's First-Term Fiscal Policy?

Laurence J. Kotlikoff

I am particularly pleased to have this opportunity to review the Reagan administration's first-term fiscal policy because I think I can offer a new perspective. This perspective is grounded neither in the fantasies of supply-side economics, nor in the myopia of Keynesian models, but rather in mainstream neoclassical economics. In contrast to ad hoc models of the Keynesian or supply-side variety, a proper neoclassical analysis doesn't let one ignore major components of the fiscal policy. The neoclassical model also provides a nonarbitrary metric for comparing the potentially offsetting impacts of alternative policies.

The neoclassical perspective indicates that the first-term fiscal policy was, on net, fairly tight—indeed, much tighter than the fiscal policy of the 1970s. This statement may strike most of you as ludicrous. Surely, anyone with eyes can see the enormous run-up in government debt between 1981 and 1985 that was unprecedented during peacetime. Indeed, during those years, the government debt in the hands of the public increased from $794 billion to $1.5 trillion, or from $3,452 to $6,310 per man, woman, and child in the country. How can one acknowledge this sea of debt and argue that fiscal policy was anything but horrendously loose?

The answer is that in addition to the first-term tax cuts, there were two other very significant first-term fiscal policies that, by and large, have been totally overlooked in discussions of the general stance of fiscal policy. The first is the shift in the effective tax base from income taxation to consumption taxation resulting from the introduction of the accelerated cost recovery system (ACRS). Consumption, of course, equals income less investment; hence, if the government wants to tax consumption it can do so directly by calculating each household's consumption and taxing that consumption, or it can do so indirectly by taxing income less investment—that is, by allowing a deduction for investment. While ACRS did not explicitly provide 100-percent expensing of all new investment, it effectively came close. As a consequence, it greatly altered the underlying tax structure.

The second overlooked first-term fiscal policy is the 1983 change in social security legislation that dramatically reduced the future benefits of members of the baby-boom generation. This cut in the baby boomers' benefits arises because of the scheduled increase in social security's normal retirement age and the scheduled income taxation of essentially all of the baby boomers' social security benefits.

Is the Deficit a Meaningful Measure of Fiscal Policy?

These two overlooked fiscal policies—the shift in the tax structure and the change in social security legislation—represent very tight fiscal policies. But if introducing ACRS and changing social security were tight fiscal policies, why didn't they show up in the deficit numbers, and why were we running a deficit? The answer is that the official debt numbers are not measuring what most of us think. Indeed, from a neoclassical perspective, official government debt is a totally arbitrary accounting construct that has no necessary relation to the basic stance of fiscal policy. This is a very strong statement and is worth rephrasing in the following manner: According to neoclassical economics, the government can run any real economic policy while at the same time announcing any size deficit or surplus it wants.

Many of you have doubtless heard comments about the government's bookkeeping suggesting that it can be improved by adjusting for inflation, government assets, and the unfunded liabilities of government retirement programs. You may think you are hearing more of the same here, but that's not the case. Rather than suggest that the deficit numbers can be improved, I'm arguing that they should be thrown out entirely because they don't measure what needs to be measured. Unfortunately, using the deficit to measure fiscal policy is akin to using an excellent road map of New York City for navigating in Los Angeles. One is guaranteed to get lost.

The deficit is an inherently arbitrary concept for the very simple

18

reason that the government is free to label its receipts and payments any way it wants, as well as to choose the timing of its receipts and payments. For example, rather than label social security contributions from workers as "taxes" and social security benefit payments as "spending," the government could call social security contributions "borrowing" from workers, and it could label benefit payments as "the return of principal plus interest" on that borrowing. As demonstrated in the 1982 *Economic Report of the President*, this alternative labeling would have produced reported deficits to the tune of $600 billion in the 1970s. Had we gotten used to $600 billion deficits, $200 billion deficits would be a welcome sight.

Here's another example. Suppose the government takes the dollars it says it's borrowing this year and simply relabels these dollars as taxes. Let it also relabel the future repayment of principal plus interest as transfer payments. Clearly, this relabeling should have no affect on the economy. If you are giving the government money today that it will return to you in the future with interest, you don't care how it labels the payments; all you care about is how much you're giving up today and how much you'll get back in the future. While it makes no difference to you, the relabeling of this year's "borrowing" as "taxes" enables the govenment to report a deficit of zero.

Here's a third example. Suppose the government permits the public to prepay its future "taxes" by providing a future tax credit equal to the additional "taxes" paid today plus interest. Alternatively, the government could simply mandate higher current "taxes" and lower future "taxes" such that the present value of "taxes" is unchanged. These policies would not change the present value of anyone's lifetime "tax" payments, but they would change, in a potentially dramatic fashion, the government's current reported deficit.

Your response to these examples may be "Yes, the government can play labeling games and change the timing of its receipts and payments without altering their present values, but, with some exceptions, it doesn't play such games. Furthermore, it basically uses the same labeling conventions through time." My response is, How do you know? If labeling is entirely arbitrary, how do you know what the government's labeling convention is? Return to the social security example. Was there anything fundamental that led to the "tax/benefit" labels as opposed to the "borrowing/repayment of principal plus interest" labels? If you agree that there really was nothing fundamental, then did we really run $600 billion deficits in the 1970s or did we really run rather small deficits in the 1970s? If you are determined to stick with the deficit as a measure of fiscal policy, you are totally free to take your pick and argue that the policy in the 1970s was tight, loose, or anything you want.

How Should We Think About the Stance of Fiscal Policy?

If our official debt numbers are inherently arbitrary and provide no real guide to the extent and nature of fiscal policy, what numbers should we be looking at according to neoclassical economics? The answer depends, in part, on the neoclassical model one is using, but let us focus on the celebrated life cycle model of Nobel Laureate Franco Modigliani and his collaborators. The life cycle model is particularly relevant to this discussion because it is the model that raises the greatest concerns about government policies that crowd out capital formation.

According to this model, fiscal policies have real effects on the economy, not because they are labeled one thing or another but because they (1) alter economic incentives, (2) redistribute within generations, or (3) redistribute across generations. It is this third issue, intergenerational redistribution, that underlies the concern about deficits from the perspective of the life cycle model.

Intergenerational redistribution occurs whenever a government policy lowers the present value of receipts-less-payments it takes from some generations at the expense of raising the present value of receipts-less-payments it takes from other generations. According to the life cycle model, government policies that redistribute to older generations at the expense of younger and future generations will crowd out saving and capital formation. The explanation is that older generations, because of their shorter remaining lifespans, have larger marginal propensities to consume than their contemporaneous younger generations, and they certainly have larger marginal propensities to consume than future generations, whose marginal propensities to consume are zero because they are not yet born. The differences in marginal propensities to consume mean that a transfer to older generations from young and future gener-

20

ations will increase total national consumption and lower national saving.

In the life cycle model, a tax-cut policy, to the extent it is a real policy rather than an accounting subterfuge, will crowd out capital formation because it lowers the present value of net lifetime payments to the government from older generations and raises the present value of net payments to the government from young and future generations. But a tax-cut policy is only one of several mechanisms the government uses to redistribute intergenerationally. A second, fairly well-known mechanism is pay-as-you-go social security. In the social security Ponzi game, every generation pays for the retirement benefits of the previous generation—with one exception: At the initiation of the program, the first generation of elderly receives benefits without having had to finance the retirement of its immediate predecessors. This generation receives a windfall at the expense of younger and future generations, which receive, on average, a lower rate of return on their social security contributions than they would if they had invested their funds privately.

Another, but more subtle, intergenerational transfer mechanism is a change in the tax base that shifts the burden of taxation from older to younger generations. For example, shifting the tax base from income to consumption redistributes toward young and future generations and away from current older generations. If this shift in tax bases is done explicitly by calculating each household's consumption and levying a tax, it will be clear to older people that they are paying more to the government than would have occurred under the income tax. But if the shift to consumption taxation is effected by increasing investment incentives, the transfer away from initial older generations arises in a very subtle manner. An increase in investment incentives redistributes away from initial older generations by lowering the market value of capital, which is primarily owned by older generations.

The reason for this government-induced drop in the stock market is that investment incentives are effectively restricted to new investment. Old capital—capital that has been fully or partially depreciated for tax purposes—sells at a discount relative to new capital, reflecting the preferential tax treatment available to new capital. An increase in investment incentives for new capital means a bigger discount on old capital, that is, a decline in the value of old capital.

21

Hence, by using investment incentives to shift the tax base, the government redistributes away from the initial older generations by effecting a decline in the value of their capital assets. This reduction in asset values benefits younger and future generations, which can now buy old assets at a lower price.

How Should We Measure Fiscal Policy?

According to the life cycle model, if one wants to measure properly the government's intergenerational redistribution, one needs to examine the lifetime present-value budget constraints of current and future generations and see how the government's policy has affected these constraints. More specifically, one needs to calculate the present expected value of payments-less-receipts paid to the government by each generation and examine how a change in policy has changed the level and distribution of these generation-specific net-present-value payments to the government. Such present-value calculations of payments to the government will be unaffected by accounting labels since each payment to the government or receipt from the government will be included in the calculation regardless of how the government labels that payment or receipt. In addition, these generational accounts would be invariant to pure changes in the timing of government payments and receipts since they are present values.

One property of these present-value statements of what each generation owes on net to the government is that the sum of these accounts over all generations equals the present expected value of government consumption. This is the condition of intertemporal budget balance; it simply reflects the fact that what the government consumes in present value must be paid for in present value by current and future generations. With a set of generational accounts, one could see at a glance what the government intends to consume in present value and which generations will have to pay for that consumption. By establishing generational accounts that satisfy the intertemporal budget constraint, the government would be forced to disclose how it intends to finance any reduction in the net present value of payments of current generations; that is, would the reduction be financed by reducing the present value of government consumption or by increasing the present value of net payments of other generations.

22

First-Term Fiscal Policy: The Perspective of the Life Cycle Model

Unfortunately, the generational accounts needed to assess fiscal policy have not yet been constructed. But one can use related information and analyses to consider how these accounts were affected by the first-term fiscal policy. First, the Economic Recovery Tax Act of 1981 provided for an across-the-board reduction in income-tax rates of 23 percent over a three-year period.

To get a sense of the importance of this provision, consider the level of income taxes per adult in 1985. This was $1,983. Had the 23 percent tax cut not been implemented, taxes per adult in 1985 would have been roughly $600 higher. Consider now what this $600 reduction would mean in present value to a typical middle-income household with a household head aged 30. If we assume no future offsetting increase in tax rates and use a 3 percent real interest rate, we arrive at a figure in the neighborhood of $18,000. Given the hysteria about the "deficit," a reasonable assumption is that most households in 1985 anticipated a future offsetting increase in income-tax rates. If we assume that households believed that a third of the tax cut would be offset in the future, we arrive at $12,000 as an admittedly extremely rough measure of the reduction in a typical 30-year-old household's present value of net payments to the government arising from the tax-cut policy.

This $12,000 figure can be compared with the reduction in the net present value of social security benefits arising from the 1983 social security amendments. According to estimates developed by Gordon Goodfellow and Anthony Pellechio for the typical middle-income household headed by a 30-year-old, the present-value increase in net payments to the government resulting from the change in social security ranges between $10,000 and $15,000.[1] Hence, it appears that the social security legislation roughly canceled the tax cut for the typical younger household.

For older households, the present-value gain from lower income taxes will be larger because they are more likely to avoid the future tax increase through death or retirement. On the other hand, because they are older, the tax cut will apply for fewer years. Turning to

---

[1]Gordon Goodfellow and Anthony Pellechio, "Individual Gains and Losses from Social Security, Before and After the 1983 Amendments" (U.S. Department of Health and Human Services, 1984, mimeographed).

social security, since the 1983 legislation pertains primarily to younger generations, the reduction in net-present-value benefits to older households is much smaller. In sum, the income tax and social security policies probably reduced the lifetime net present value of payments of older households to the government.

While older generations may have been made better off by these two policies, the shift in the effective tax structure toward consumption taxation is an offsetting consideration. The predicted impact of ACRS is a 1981 value of the business capital stock that is $233 to $292 billion lower than would otherwise have been observed.[2] If we use the $233 billion figure and divide by the population aged 45 and older in 1981, we arrive at a capital loss per person over 45 of $3,291. Now clearly, not everyone over 45 owned business capital and many under 45 did own business capital. But even this crude calculation gives a sense of the order of magnitude of the effect of the change in the tax structure on the present value of resources of older generations.

In sum, for younger Americans the gain from the income-tax cut may have been largely offset by the loss from the social security amendments, while for older Americans the gain from the income-tax cut may have been largely offset by the loss due to the change in the tax structure.

Simulation Analysis

Another way to gauge the impact of these simultaneous fiscal measures is to simulate their joint impact. The Auerbach-Kotlikoff life cycle simulation model can be used for this purpose.[3] The model is composed of households, firms, and the government. Household heads live from age 20 to age 75. They are assumed to have rational expectations. The structure of preferences and production is given by conventional constant elasticity of substitution functions. The government finances its consumption through taxes on total income, capital income, wage income, or consumption. The government

[2]Alan J. Auerbach and Laurence J. Kotlikoff, "Investment Versus Savings Incentives: The Size of the Bang for the Buck and the Potential for Self-Financing Business Tax Cuts," in *The Economic Consequences of Government Deficits*, ed. L. H. Meyer (Boston: Kluwer-Nijhoff, 1983).

[3]Alan J. Auerbach and Laurence J. Kotlikoff, *Dynamic Fiscal Policy* (Cambridge: Cambridge University Press, 1987).

can also set the rate at which new investments may be expensed. Finally, there is an unfunded social security system. The model is capable of simultaneously analyzing changes in the tax structure, conventional deficit finance, and changes in social security.

To analyze the first-term Reagan policy, I have simulated an economy that initially has a 30 percent income tax, an unfunded social security system with a 40 percent benefit-wage replacement rate, and a zero rate of expensing of new investment. The initial effective tax rate on capital income in this economy is 30 percent. The simulated policy is an eight-year (two-term), 25 percent cut in the income-tax rates, coupled with (1) a reduction from 40 percent to 30 percent in the social security benefit-wage replacement rate for all individuals younger than 40 at the time the policy is enacted and for all generations born after the policy is enacted, and (2) the introduction of a 40 percent rate of expensing. The cut in the replacement rate is intended to roughly approximate the change in retirement age. At a 30 percent income-tax rate, a 40 percent expensing rate lowers the effective tax rate on capital income to 20.4 percent. In the simulation, the changes in the social security replacement rate and the rate of expensing are permanent; but after the eight years of the income-tax cut, the income-tax rate is raised to restore conventional budget balance.

In the first eight years of the simulation results, the economy displays quite sizable deficits as conventionally measured; the annual deficit during this period is over 6 percent of gross national product. The debt-to-capital ratio, which is initially zero, ultimately rises to .27. The model also predicts an increase in short-term interest rates at the beginning of the policy transition; in the first year of the transition, short rates jump from 9.5 percent to 11.0 percent. This increase in interest rates is not due to the deficit finance, but rather to the investment incentives; the firms in the model are forced by competition to pass on the investment incentives in the form of higher interest rates paid to their investors.

Notwithstanding the significant annual deficits and long-run increase in officially reported debt, the combined policy produces only very minor crowding out of capital in the long run. The long-run capital stock is only 1.6 percent smaller than its initial value. The reason is that the crowding-in associated with reducing social security benefits and the crowding-in associated with the effective change in the tax structure outweigh the crowding out arising from the 25 percent, eight-year income-tax cut.

Yes, future generations have a slightly smaller capital stock, and they face a 35 percent, rather than a 30 percent, income tax because of the need to meet interest payments. But the investment incentives lead to a 12 percent fall in the market value of capital at the beginning of the policy, which hurts initial older generations. In addition, the cut in social security benefits of middle-aged and younger generations alive at the time of the policy change lowers, in the long run, the payroll tax by one-fifth of its initial value, which benefits generations born after the initiation of the policy. Finally, the investment incentives mean a larger after-tax rate of return to saving than prevailed prior to the initiation of the policy. In the initial economy, the after-tax return to saving was only 6.6 percent, but following full implementation of the combined policy, the after-tax return is 7.2 percent.

On net, the policy somewhat hurts initial older generations, which lose more from the loss in the market value of their capital loss than they gain from the income-tax cut. The policy is also slightly detrimental to generations born after the policy is enacted. Initial middle-aged and young generations are slightly better off because of the policy; their loss in social security benefits is somewhat more than offset by their gain from the eighth-year income-tax cut and the reduction in the effective tax on capital income.

In considering these results, it is important to bear in mind that the Auerbach-Kotlikoff simulation model is as conventional a neoclassical model as exists. The parameters used in the model with respect to preferences and production are very conservative; that is, they are biased away from getting large responses to tax incentives. The model, which is written down in equations rather than drawn on a napkin, certainly displays nothing akin to the whimsical Laffer curve. The crowding in rather than crowding out occurring in the simulation is not due to supply-side magic but rather to the inclusion in the analysis of two previously neglected but very powerful policies—namely, the change in the effective tax structure associated with increased investment incentives and the change in social security.

Conclusion

In discussing the general stance of fiscal policy in the first term of the Reagan administration, I have adopted a neoclassical perspective. The neoclassical perspective suggests that popular discussion of fiscal policy has missed both the forest and many of the trees. Seeing the trees means not ignoring major fiscal policies. Seeing the forest requires throwing out cash flow accounting constructs, such as deficits, and constructing generational accounts that can shed real light on the stance of fiscal policy.

3. The Tax Reform Act of 1986: Revolution or Counterrevolution?

Norman B. Ture

Introduction

The Tax Reform Act of 1986 (TRA–86) has been widely heralded as the most important and far-reaching tax legislation in the history of the contemporary U.S. federal income tax. TRA–86 sharply reduced statutory income-tax rates for both individuals and corporations; when these rate reductions are fully effective, the top individual income-tax rate will be lower than at any time since 1931. The act drastically reduced graduation of the individual income-tax rates. It made a far greater number and far more significant changes in the delineation of what is to be taxed as income than were made in any single preceding tax act. The legislation altered the tax treatment of virtually all of the principal categories of both personal and business expenses. It is difficult to identify any category of economic activity in the business sector, and, indeed, to a substantial extent in the household sector as well, that will not be significantly affected by these tax changes.

Should we identify TRA–86 as the crowning achievement of the Reagan Revolution or should the legislation be seen as unmistakable evidence of the abandonment of the Reagan program?

The overall goal of the Reagan economic policy program, the very essence of the Reagan Revolution, was to lighten, if not completely remove, the deadening hand of the federal government on the nation's economy. The motto of the revolution, reflecting its truly new populism, was "Give the economy back to the people." Achieving this core objective called for seeking out and eliminating those elements and features of government policy that impair the free market's allocative functions, or at least mitigating the distortions of economic outcomes that result from the government's intrusions.

29

As applied to tax policy, the pursuit of this goal specified two requirements. One was to reduce marginal income-tax rates and the steepness of their graduation. The other, equally important, was to revise those statutory provisions defining taxable income that distort relative costs and prices. Of particular importance in the latter respect was reducing the inherent income-tax bias against saving and in favor of current consumption, and moderating the numerous tax-induced distortions of the relative costs of differing forms of saving and of different kinds of capital.

The same basic goal of cutting back the government's presence in our economic lives called for tax revisions to reduce the costs of tax enforcement, administration, and compliance. It also generated a more meaningful standard of tax equity, at least one that would be less of a policy will-o'-the-wisp, calling for elimination of provisions that discriminate against risk taking, innovation, and entrepreneurship.

Insofar as TRA–86 furthered the attainment of these objectives, even if only feebly, it should be deemed to have advanced the cause of the Reagan Revolution. Unhappily, save for its dramatic rate reductions, TRA–86 must be characterized essentially as the enactment of much of the longstanding, conventional tax-reform agenda, the central objective of which is egalitarian income and wealth redistribution. As such, most of its major provisions (again, except for the rate cuts) tend to increase the cost of saving relative to the cost of current consumption. A great many of its provisions generate artificial differences in the cost of capital in differing uses. TRA–86 gives truer and deeper meaning to the phrase "lawyers' and accountants' full employment act" than any prior legislation; it adds nightmarish complexity to a tax system that had long been beyond the ken of ordinary citizens. It adds blatantly inequitable, anti-affluent provisions to the Internal Revenue Code—provisions for which the sole justification is "they got it; let's get it."

Contrary to the hyperbolic rhetoric of some Reagan-right-or-wrong zealots, the individual and corporate income-tax rate reductions, wholesome and welcome though they are, are not sufficient to outweigh the counterproductive and unwholesome changes in the definition of taxable income made by the great preponderance of the provisions in the legislation. Rather than an achievement of the Reagan Revolution, TRA–86 is the culmination of the disorderly retreat from the Reagan program that began with the "revenue enhancers" of late 1981 and that turned into a rout with the ludicrously misnamed Tax Equity and Fiscal Responsibility Act (TEFRA) of 1982.

Why, it is reasonable to ask, did this sharp policy reversal come about? What are the conceptual origins of TRA–86? The answers to these questions should help us to decide whether the damage that TRA–86 has done to the Reagan Revolution is permanent or may be overcome by a renewed commitment to the fundamentals on which the original Reagan program was based.

The Political and Conceptual Origins of TRA–86

The TRA–86 that emerged from the congressional legislative process and wound up on the president's desk differed in no basic respect from the set of tax-reform proposals that the president had forwarded to the Congress a year and a quarter earlier. The act he signed into law is the outcome of his legislative initiative. It is his statutory baby, conceived in his State of the Union Message in January 1984.

Why?

Why did the president take this initiative? The answer cannot be found in any need for tax reform that was newly discovered in 1983 or the first few days of 1984. Against the conventional standards, the federal income tax, bad as it was, had not significantly deteriorated in recent years. TEFRA—the enormous 1982 legislation—was supposed to have made the income tax fairer, albeit considerably more complex, by repealing or restricting the alleged giveaways to business and affluent individual investors enacted in the Economy Recovery Tax Act (ERTA) in 1981. Since TEFRA, the income tax had not become noticeably more unfair; nor had policymakers in the administration or Congress suddenly uncovered previously hidden inequities. No new urgency for tax reform, in terms of making the tax system conform more closely with the criteria of neutrality, equity, and simplicity, impelled the president to identify tax reform as one of his top policy priorities for 1984.

Rather, the president's initiative was intended to achieve two things. One was to preempt tax-policy issues for the president and Republican candidates in the 1984 election campaigns. This objec-

31

tive was fully realized. The Democrats' nominee for the presidency found it virtually impossible to claim that he was more concerned about the tax system and more determined to do something about correcting its faults than the incumbent, who had got there first. Walter F. Mondale was driven, instead, to promising the nation a large tax increase, a prospect that obviously was not well received by the electorate.

The second objective of the Reagan tax-reform initiative was to leave a legacy of much reduced statutory tax rates, particularly a much lower top rate in the individual income tax. When President Reagan was inaugurated in 1981, the top individual income-tax rate, applicable to so-called "unearned" income, was 70 percent. What greater testimonial to the success of the Reagan Revolution could there be than for the president to leave the White House with a top individual income-tax rate of only 35 percent? As the tax-reform drama played out, the congressional policymakers went considerably further than President Reagan might well have thought possible, legislating a top individual tax rate of 28 percent. If one disregards the very high price that had to be paid to achieve so drastic a drop in the top statutory tax rate, one could claim that in realizing this objective, President Reagan had indeed stayed with his program and substantially achieved its goals, at least in the tax-policy area.

Significantly reducing the top marginal tax rate in the individual income tax was the central objective to be served in the design of the income-tax-reform proposals. Achieving that objective, however, was to be subject to important and severe constraints.

One of these constraints was the perceived requirement to be evenhanded with respect to the income-level distribution of personal income-tax reductions. Low- and middle-income individuals had to get tax reductions that were proportionally at least as large as those of upper-income persons if the rate cuts at the top were to be politically defensible. For low- and middle-income taxpayers, however, feasible reductions in tax rates could not provide reductions in tax burdens of a magnitude proportional to the cut in upper-bracket persons' tax liabilities resulting from reducing the top rates. To avoid shifting relative tax burdens, tax reduction for lower-income persons was to be provided by very nearly doubling the personal exemption and by substantially increasing the standard deduction.

Another constraint was thought to be the need to avoid opening an untoward gap between the top individual and the top corporate income-tax rates. A top individual tax rate substantially below the top corporate rate was deemed to afford inducements for tax-impelled shifts in the form of business organization that would not be warranted on the grounds of sound business practice. If the top individual rate were to come down to 35 percent, the top corporate rate would have to be reduced from 46 percent to something very close to, and preferably less than, 35 percent.

A third constraint was that the tax-reform program had to be revenue-neutral. The reduction in individual and corporate tax rates, along with increases in the personal exemption and the standard deduction, would result in staggering revenue losses, as measured on a static revenue basis (that is, ignoring the revenue consequences of behavioral responses to the proposed tax changes). The prevailing and prospective budget deficits made these revenue losses politically unthinkable. Revenue gainers of equally staggering proportions had to be found as an essential part of the tax-reform effort.

A final constraint was that no new revenue source was to be relied upon to provide any significant part of the enormous revenue additions required by revenue neutrality. This meant, in effect, that the bases of both the individual and corporate income taxes had to be broadened. Most of the large gaps in the tax base, conventionally identified as loopholes that should be closed, were products of efforts by businesses and savers/investors to mitigate the income tax's escalation of the cost of capital in their particular activities. With few exceptions, these loopholes served to moderate the income-tax bias against saving and the capital to which the saving was committed. To be sure, the effect of the various loopholes in this regard was far from uniform among differing kinds of capital; their effect, however, was to reduce the overall cost of capital. Broadening the tax bases by closing these loopholes, therefore, necessarily involved increasing the cost of capital in varying degree, in use after use and in activity after activity, and in raising the overall cost of capital.

The politically feasible individual income-tax-base broadeners fell far short of providing the revenue gains needed to make up individual income-tax revenue losses. Draconian revisions in the corporate—more generally, the business—income-tax base were required, not only to offset corporate income-tax-revenue losers but also to help offset losses of individual income-tax revenues. These changes, in turn, resulted in a huge shift in the assignment of tax liabilities from individuals to corporations and among corporations, as well. As ultimately enacted, individual income-tax liabilities are estimated to fall by $122 billion over the five fiscal years from 1987 to 1991, while corporate income-tax liabilities are estimated to increase by $120 billion over the same period.

The mere fact that a very large shift in the assignment of tax liabilities from individuals to corporations and from some corporations to others was made to finance the revenue losers to TRA–86 doesn't mean that the legislation was at odds with the spirit or substance of the Reagan Revolution. It is, instead, the very nature of the severe changes in the income-tax bases that might well cause one to wonder whether the president's tax-rate-cut legacy and his 1984 campaign maneuvering came at an excessively high price. With regard to most of these base changes, it was asserted that they were needed to equalize effective tax rates among differing kinds of capital in differing uses by differing taxpayers. In fact, ignoring the reduction in statutory tax rates, most of the base changes had the effect of increasing effective tax-rate differentials while raising their overall level. If one believes that the principles of the Reagan Revolution were embodied in ERTA in 1981, one must also believe that those principles and the Reagan Revolution were abandoned in TRA–86.

Whence?

The most striking thing about TRA–86, apart from the reduction in statutory tax rates that it affords, is the extent to which it embodies the traditional liberal approach to tax reform. The conceptual origins of the act certainly are not to be found in the supply-side economics that was the hallmark of the Reagan Revolution's approach to public economic policy, particularly tax policy. The supply-side tax agenda emphasized removing, or at least moderating, the excise effects of the income tax—that is, its distortions of relative costs and prices. Although TRA–86 gave lip service to this goal (remember the dreary and repeated references to the level playing field?), it did little to implement this objective and, indeed, significantly aggravated these excise effects.

34

The conceptual origins of TRA–86 are to be found, instead, in the work of Henry C. Simons, one of the true titans of public finance, whose work had an unparalleled influence on thinking during the last half-century about the requirements of a "good" tax system. As delineated in his seminal *Personal Income Taxation*[1] and other writings, Simons's views on this score have dominated much of the work of economists and lawyers in this field and have long provided the context for tax-reform agendas. Not until TRA–86, however, had any such agenda actually constituted the substance of a legislative enactment.

Simons's work in this area derived from his vigorously asserted conviction that the raison d'etre of an income tax is to reduce inequality in the distribution of income and wealth, a goal to which he gave considerably higher priority than to other tax-policy objectives. The priority given this goal, in turn, depends not on any construction of social welfare functions or utility maximization, but, as Simons candidly avowed, "on the ethical or aesthetic judgment that the prevailing distribution of wealth and income reveals a degree . . . of inequality which is distinctly evil or unlovely."[2]

Attaining the redistributive objective, Simons recognized, is not merely a matter of tax rates; even more essential, he believed, is a concept of income for tax purposes that adequately measures economic status and allows the imposition of progressively heavier tax burdens on those with superior economic position. Simons was well aware that an income concept that he found suitable for measuring economic status rather than claims on currently produced income involved a compounding, if not confusion, of stocks with flows, and necessarily entailed significantly adverse incentive effects. Although Simons did not deal at length with these adverse incentive, or excise, effects, he clearly was aware of them, even if not much concerned about them.[3] His intellectual disciples, however,

[1] Henry C. Simons, *Personal Income Taxation* (Chicago: University of Chicago Press, 1938).

[2] Simons, pp. 18–19.

[3] Simons asserted that gains in more nearly equal distribution of income and wealth achieved through taxation must necessarily be at the expense of reductions in the nation's total output and income. However uncertain the conclusions about the effects of progressive income taxation on other economic activity, he asserted that the consequences with respect to saving and capital accumulation are certain to be

35

have either seldom avowed these excise effects or have attempted to show that they are so slight, if not indeed figments of some supply-sider's imagination, that they may safely be disregarded in the tax-policy pursuit of equity.

Among those disciples, some of whom may not be aware of their intellectual heritage, are many of the cadre of the Treasury Department's Office of Tax Policy and the staffs of the congressional tax-writing committees. To them fell the job of spelling out the tax reforms that the Reagan initiative appeared to call for. Their job was made easier than it might otherwise have been by the availability of the volume *Blueprints for Basic Tax Reform*, produced in 1976 by the Office of Tax Policy staff under the able direction of David Bradford, then deputy assistant secretary for tax policy.[4] This volume presented detailed specifications of the basic structure of an income tax that (apart from statutory rates) conformed closely with a Simons-pure income tax; it also laid out an alternative model tax based on consumption, a so-called cash flow tax. The Treasury tax staff's efforts in 1984 were also facilitated by the accumulation, over many years, of a hit list of tax avoidance devices—that is, provisions of the then present law, regulations, case law, etc., that were deemed to be deviations from the treatment called for by a model income tax, cast in the Simons image, and of an inventory of proposals for dealing with those loopholes.

When the president's call for tax reform came, the Treasury's tax staff was ready. It delivered a tax reform package, "Tax Reform for Fairness, Simplicity, and Economic Growth," that closely conformed with the redistributive Simons paradigm.

Use of the *fisc* to redistribute income and wealth certainly was not part of the game plan to achieve the Reagan Revolution's goals. On the contrary, the redistributive cast of prior fiscal policy was identified as a major source of the economic malaise of the 1970s. In 1981, the Reagan administration rejected considerations of the distribution of tax liabilities in designing ERTA and fought off most congressional efforts to reshape ERTA along redistributional lines.

---

adverse. Simons argued that the adverse effects of progressive taxation on saving should be corrected by government saving rather than by moderating progression. Simons, pp. 19–29.

[4]The first edition was published by the Treasury Department in January 1977. A second edition was published by Tax Analysts (Arlington, Virginia) in 1984.

In 1984, on the other hand, the top policy officials in the Treasury Department and the White House appeared to have forgotten the valid reasons for the earlier stance. Perhaps they failed to recognize the redistributive thrust of the reform package delivered to them by the Office of Tax Policy staff. Or they might have been convinced, mistakenly, that the individual rate reductions in the package offset the base-broadening provisions, leaving the distribution of tax liabilities unchanged.

Although it included a number of modifications of the Treasury program, the proposal submitted by the White House to the Congress in May 1985 was very much in the same spirit and substantially the same in content. Much the same can be said of the tax bill (H.R. 3838) as it struggled to enactment in the House and went to the Senate, and, indeed, much should also be said of both the Senate version and the act as it emerged from conference, was passed by both chambers, and went to the president for his signature. A number of details had been altered or modified from the original November 1984 offering, most especially the rate reductions, but when all is said and done, Henry Simons's legacy had at long last been made the law of the land.

To be sure, an ardent reformer may very well find a loophole here or there that TRA–86 overlooked or treated with insufficient severity. Noises about restoring more and higher rate brackets continue to be heard in the Congress, particularly in connection with tax increases to reduce the federal budget deficit. Notwithstanding, tax reform has been substantially relegated to a back burner as far as urgent public economic policy issues are concerned. Wittingly or not, President Reagan's tax initiative as presented in his 1984 State of the Union Message not only preempted the tax reform ground for his administration, it may very well have also substantially eliminated any plausible tax reform issues in the national elections in 1988.

The Economic Consequences of TRA–86

The core of the Reagan program as it pertained to public economic policy was to reduce the federal government's intrusion into the nation's economic life and to ensure that the government's participation contributed to, or least impaired, the efficient functioning of the market system. In this context, the acid test of TRA–86 is whether, on balance, the principal excise effects of the income tax were moderated or aggravated by the tax reform. Does it reduce the tax bias against effort and in favor of leisure? Does it reduce the income tax bias against saving and investment and the tax-induced distortions of the allocation of capital?

The drastic reduction in the number of individual income tax rate brackets and the reductions in both individual and corporate income tax rates must be counted as huge advances toward the attainment of the Reagan Revolution's goals. In terms of initial impact, the individual rate reductions and restructuring significantly reduce the excise imposed by the income tax on using one's time and resources in activities that give rise to taxable income rather than in so-called leisure uses. They also moderate the increasing excises that statutory income-tax rate graduation imposes on efforts to increase one's productivity.

These rate reductions, taken by themselves, also significantly reduce the income tax bias against saving and investment. So, too, do the corporate tax rate cuts, which also moderate the misallocation of capital and other inputs between incorporated and unincorporated businesses. Individual and corporate rate reductions also erode the benefits afforded by tax shelters and diminish the incentive to seek out tax avoidance devices.

The changes in the statutory provisions delineating both the individual and corporate income tax bases, unhappily, must be counted as enormous setbacks in the efforts to obtain a more nearly neutral tax system, a major goal of the Reagan program. The assessment of TRA–86 against the Reagan Revolution's goals, therefore, depends on whether the beneficial effects of the rate reductions outweigh the adverse effects of the base changes.

Few of the base changes involve any significant increase in the extent to which compensation for labor and professional service are included in the individual income tax base. In fact, as measured by static tax revenue estimates, the single largest income tax base change enacted in TRA–86—the increase in the personal exemption, together with the increase in the standard deduction—will remove substantial amounts of wages and salaries from the tax base; these provisions will take more than 6 million persons, most of whose income consists of wages, off the income tax rolls.[5]

[5]Revenue estimates are from "General Explanation of the Tax Reform Act of 1986,"

38

The overwhelming proportion of the base broadeners in TRA–86 are additions to the individual and corporate income-tax bases of current saving formerly sheltered in part from current income taxation and of larger amounts of the gross returns on assets in which saving is embodied.[6] For the five fiscal years 1987 to 1991, the aggregate increase in tax liabilities generated by these base broadeners is close to $387 billion, averaging roughly $77 billion a year. This increase in taxes implies that something in the neighborhood of $250 billion of saving and the gross returns thereupon were added to the income tax base.

It isn't possible to draw reliable inferences from the static revenue estimates about the effects of the base broadeners on effective tax rates or the cost of capital. Nonetheless, it is virtually certain that increases in tax burdens of the magnitude noted above must involve substantial increases in real, as opposed to statutory, marginal tax rates; hence, they must increase the relative costs of acquiring, holding, and using capital.

If this stunning increase in the amount of saving and returns to capital included in the income tax base had been produced by the elimination of true tax subsidies in the prior law, one might well find substantial justification for the implied increase in the overall tax burden on capital. If it could be established that the scores of base-broadening provisions in TRA–86 mitigate differentials in effective rates of tax on the returns to capital in differing uses, the gains from more efficient allocation of capital in response to this more nearly neutral tax might be perceived as at least a partial offset to the investment-shrinking impact of the enormous increase in the income-tax burden on saving and investment. This, of course, was the rationale relied on by both the Congress and the administration to justify tax "reforms" that must so drastically increase the cost of capital. With few exceptions, however, the rationale is mistaken. The base broadeners, taken by themselves, enhance disparities in effective tax rates among different kinds of capital, used by differing groups of taxpayers in differing kinds of production. Efficiency

---

prepared by the staff of the Joint Committee on Taxation, U.S. Congress, May 4, 1987, pp. 1359 ff.

[6]With a few significant exceptions, the latter base-broadening provisions involve accelerations in the timing of the recognition of income for tax purposes, hence increases in the present value of the taxes on this income.

39

losses in the allocation of capital are much likelier than gains to result from these tax changes.

Neutral income tax treatment of saving and investment requires that the present value of allowances for the recovery of the capital in which the saving is invested must just equal the amount of the saving or the capital outlay. The easiest way to satisfy this requirement is to allow expensing of the saving or the capital outlay for tax purposes. However, if this front-loading of capital recovery is deemed to be too expensive, neutrality can also be achieved by extended period write-offs, as long as the aggregate amount of such write-offs is not limited to the amount of the saving or capital outlay.

Tax neutrality demands either expensing or an extended-period capital recovery system that affords tax deductions with a present value equal to the saving or capital outlay. This satisfies the second (inter-asset) dimension of tax neutrality as well as the first dimension (neutrality in the tax treatment of consumption and saving). First-level neutrality was rejected out of hand by the administration at the outset of the Treasury effort to respond to President Reagan's call for a tax reform plan. The basis for doing so, apparently, was that the Treasury and White House policy advisers had considered a consumption-based income tax or a value-added tax, but rejected this route to tax reform as politically unacceptable; strangely, first-level tax neutrality was deemed to be incompatible with efforts to achieve a more nearly pure income tax. Notwithstanding, inter-asset neutrality could have been provided by an extended-period capital recovery system affording allowances with present values that were the same per dollar of all capital outlays.[7]

The prior law's capital recovery system—the accelerated cost recovery system (ACRS) and the investment tax credit—provided a rough approximation of inter-asset neutrality for most kinds of machinery and equipment, although it fell substantially short in the case of most structures, for which the investment tax credit was not available. The front-loading of ACRS deductions, along with the investment tax credit, resulted in the deferral of substantial amounts

[7]See Norman B. Ture, "Pluses and Minuses (Mostly) in the President's Capital Cost Recovery System," *IRET Economic Report*, no. 29, July 8, 1985, for an arithmetic illustration of one such capital-recovery system. Complete inter-asset neutrality would require similar treatment for all kinds of capital, not merely depreciable property.

of taxes. Elimination of these provisions, therefore, would generate huge near-term revenue increases. Their repeal proved to be politically irresistible.

ACRS and the investment tax credit could have been replaced by an extended-period, rear-loaded capital recovery system that afforded inter-asset tax neutrality. Any prospect of achieving inter-asset neutrality, however, was forfeited by the effort to devise a cost recovery system that would approximate so-called economic depreciation. The new depreciation system that was at last incorporated in TRA–86 falls quite a bit short of realizing that impossible dream, for which we should all be grateful. It does, however, result in many of the disparities in effective tax rates and costs of capital among differing types of capital and capital uses that would have been an inevitable consequence if anything like economic depreciation had been adopted.

The repeal of the investment tax credit and the replacement of the ACRS by the new capital-recovery provisions are estimated to expand tax liabilities by more than $155 billion during the five-year projection period. The increase in the tax burden on saving and capital formation suggested by these revenue gains is substantially augmented by numerous other base broadeners. Prominent among these are the expansion of the scope of the alternative minimum tax and the increase in its rate; the new, severe limits on personal saving plans such as individual retirement accounts (IRAs) and 401(k) plans; the repeal of the net long-term capital gain deduction; and the limitation on the deductibility by some taxpayers of so-called passive investment losses.

These additional tax burdens on capital will not fall evenly throughout the private sector of the economy. It seems highly likely that the brunt of these additional burdens will be felt principally in manufacturing, natural resources, and construction. In these industries it is plausible to assume that additions to the stock of capital will be smaller than they would have been under prior law and that the pace of capital formation will slow compared to that elsewhere in the economy. In those industries in which the production technology involves heavy reliance on depreciable property, unit production costs are likely to be higher than they would have been under prior law. Because much of our exports originate in such capital-intensive businesses, the increase in the cost of capital they confront as a result of TRA–86 will erode their profit margins and inhibit growth in production for export markets. TRA–86, in short, erected an additional policy barrier to improving the merchandise trade balance.

As TRA–86 was pushed through the legislative process, much was made of the incentives provided by the proposed rate reductions for innovation, risk taking, and entrepreneurial activity in general. The rate reductions surely are important in this respect, but the TRA–86 enthusiasts conveniently ignored the adverse effects on these activities of the repeal of the deduction for net long-term capital gains while retaining stringent limits on the deductibility of capital losses.

Implementation of the entrepreneurial zest for starting new businesses and for risky, innovative ventures requires the infusion of capital, very often supplied by outside investors. For both outside investors and entrepreneurs, the reward sought is primarily an increase in the value of the equity interest in the venture. For outside investors, in particular, it is important to be able to realize the appreciated capital and to transfer it into promising new ventures. Raising the tax on capital gains blunts the inducement for undertaking these ventures in the first place. The 40 percent increase in the top rate on capital gains, along with the other tax changes that increase the cost of capital, represent a significantly anti-entrepreneurial set of tax "reforms."

Conclusion

The answer to the question posed earlier is that substantial though they are, the statutory tax rate reductions enacted in TRA–86 are insufficient to offset the intensification of the income tax's anti-saving excise effects resulting from the base-broadening provisions in the act. Even though the individual income-tax reductions will substantially mitigate the income tax's distortion of the labor/leisure choice, the benefits therefrom are very likely to be significantly offset, if not more than offset, by other, adverse consequences of the new tax law. Ultimately, the net effect is likely to be a lower ratio of capital to labor for the economy as a whole and a less productive allocation of that capital than would otherwise have prevailed—hence, a lower growth path of labor productivity, real wages, and total output and income than otherwise would have been achieved. The economy is likely to be smaller and less efficient in its operations. Such results are the very antithesis of those sought by the Reagan program.

Changes in federal tax policy are certainly likely to influence the performance and growth of the economy. Tax policy, however, is no more an ultimate determinant of economic outcomes than any other government policy or institutional arrangement. For toilers in the field of public policy, there is an unfortunate inclination to identify every policy twist and turn as altering the shape of the world. More realistically, the U.S. economy, as vast, complex, and dynamic as it is, cannot be viewed as a marionette dangling at the ends of public policy strings.

The economy will survive TRA–86, will grow and progress despite the policy retrogression that TRA–86 embodies. The defenders of the Reagan Revolution can take pride in the very substantial modification of individual income tax rate graduation and the substantial reductions in statutory tax rates that TRA–86 achieved. Indeed, these are achievements that may set the pattern for tax policy developments in many other nations. Overall, however, TRA–86 is far more of a counterrevolution than an advance toward achieving the economic policy goals of the Reagan program. The Reagan Revolution has not been irretrievably lost, but TRA–86 created a significant barrier to its recovery.

4. Origins and Effects of the Deficit
Mickey D. Levy

Unprecedented high budget deficits and mounting federal debt have dominated the economic policymaking debate during the Reagan administration. Even before enactment of President Reagan's pathbreaking tax- and spending-cut initiatives in 1981, fears arose that the administration's forecast of a balanced budget in 1984 would not be achieved. Deficits, which averaged less than 3 percent of gross national product during 1975–80, jumped to 6.3 percent of GNP in 1983 and remained above 5 percent through 1986.

Following Reagan's initial political successes, the administration joined Congress in efforts to reduce the deficits while trying to maintain its earlier tax reform and defense buildup. Attempts to cut deficits have been prolonged and controversial, and have yielded results inconsistent with good public policy. Much of the controversy about reducing deficits has arisen because of confusion and disagreement about the economic effects of deficits. Although there is general agreement among economists that the rapidly mounting federal debt will adversely affect long-run economic growth, there is substantial disagreement about nearly all other potential impacts of deficits. Even the causes of the deficits remain controversial. Consequently, policymakers lack a deficit policy that is a consistent part of broader macroeconomic policy.

Earlier allegations that formed the basis for the initiative to cut deficits by whatever means possible, including raising taxes—such allegations as high deficits are inflationary, that they drive up interest and exchange rates, and that they would choke off economic recovery—have been proved incorrect by subsequent economic performance. Despite the string of record-breaking deficits, infla-

The author wishes to acknowledge helpful discussions with Allan Meltzer, Jacob Dreyer, Bill Haraf, John Makin, Rudy Penner, Jean Cooke, and Joel Naroff. However, the opinions expressed in this paper are the author's.

tion has declined and remained low, interest and exchange rates rose sharply and have subsequently fallen to close to pre-Reagan levels, and the economic expansion has been surprisingly durable. Also, a growing body of economic research has emerged to challenge these earlier alleged impacts of deficits. However, the preconceived notions persist and are the source of misguided macroeconomic policies.

This analysis stems in part from my role as an economic forecaster and my assessment of various hypotheses about the economic effects of deficits in terms of their internal consistency and their ability to forecast major trends in economic performance and financial markets. My general conclusions are:

- Long-run trends suggest that the rise in deficits in the 1980s is largely the story of rising federal spending, as revenues as a percentage of GNP have not changed from recent decades. These deficits reflect the revealed preferences of policymakers to spend more—in the 1980s, to allocate more resources to national security while maintaining the earlier rise in real entitlement spending—and to prevent taxes from rising faster than economic activity.
- During President Reagan's first term, deficits rose to unprecedented levels, and the projected rise in the ratio of federal debt to GNP was alarming. Since 1984, a series of revenue-enhancing initiatives, the abrupt halt to the defense buildup, and declining interest rates have lowered deficits as a percentage of GNP and will stabilize the federal debt-to-GNP ratio.
- The Reagan administration deficit (fiscal) policy in the 1980s has been confused and hampered by disagreement about the short-run economic consequences of deficits. Although the stimulative impact of deficits is uncertain and the ability of policymakers to smooth aggregate demand fluctuations through changes in the deficit has proved ineffective, the widespread concerns of the early 1980s about the depressing impacts of high deficits on economic expansion have turned out to be unwarranted. Importantly, the alleged positive correlations between deficits on the one hand and interest rates and exchange rates on the other have not been supported by empirical analysis. If such linkages exist, they are significantly weaker than

46

generally presumed, and their recent influences have been overwhelmed by other factors.

- Analyzing the impacts of deficits per se is difficult and misleading because deficits are a residual of federal spending and taxes and they impart only limited information about fiscal policy. A major lesson of the 1980s is that the economic responses to specific tax and spending structures that underlie deficits have overwhelmed the impact of deficits on aggregate demand. Looking through the persistently high deficits of the 1980s to the allocative effects of shifts in President Reagan's tax and spending policies is crucial to understanding the macroeconomic effects of fiscal policy. In particular, the shifting tax burdens imposed by the Economic Recovery Tax Act of 1981 (ERTA) and the Tax Reform Act of 1986 (TRA–86) have significantly affected economic activity and rates of interest and exchange.

- Economists generally agree that the mounting federal debt will lower long-run economic growth, although they are uncertain about the timing and magnitude of the effect. However, reducing the deficit by raising taxes is not good fiscal policy. The proper goal of fiscal policy—creating an environment conducive to long-run economic growth—requires reducing deficits primarily by cutting spending for consumption. Since the potential adverse effects of the federal debt buildup bear on capital formation, any tax increases to reduce the deficit should avoid disincentives to save and invest.

A Brief Review of Budget Trends

The rise in federal deficits, which began in the mid-1970s and jumped in the 1980s, can be explained by continuous increases in outlays as a percentage of GNP without matching increases in tax revenues (see Table 4.1). In the early postwar period, taxes and spending were fairly evenly matched; from 1947 to 1960, the federal budget was in surplus in as many years as it was in deficit. Deficits remained low in the 1960s and early 1970s, but then, as spending growth accelerated, deficits jumped appreciably in the mid-1970s and again in the 1980s. Federal spending as a percentage of GNP rose from 14.5 percent during 1947–51 to 22.8 percent in 1980 and 24 percent in 1985. Spending averaged 23.6 percent of GNP from

Table 4.1

FEDERAL REVENUES, OUTLAYS, AND DEFICITS AS PERCENTAGE OF GNP

Period	Revenues	Outlays*	Deficit
1951–55	18.1	18.4	−0.3
1956–60	17.7	18.0	−0.3
1961–65	17.9	18.7	−0.8
1966–70	18.8	19.7	−0.9
1971–75	18.1	20.0	−1.9
1976–80	18.5	21.4	−2.8
1981–85	18.9	23.6	−4.7
1986–87	18.6	22.6	−4.0

SOURCE: Executive Office of the President, *Budget of the United States Government, Fiscal Year 1987.*
*Measures on- and off-budget revenue and outlays.

1981 to 1986, up from 20.4 percent in the 1970s. The story of rising spending is similar in inflation-adjusted and real per capita terms. Tax revenues as a percentage of GNP did not rise materially after the early 1950s. They averaged 17.6 percent in the 1950s, 18.3 percent in the 1970s, and 18.8 percent during 1981–86.

This rise in spending has stemmed in part from the unresolved conflict between defense and nondefense priorities. Spending rose in the late 1960s with the Vietnam-related defense-spending build-up and the concurrent sharp expansion of nondefense programs. Through most of the 1970s, defense spending receded in real terms and fell sharply as a percentage of total federal outlays and GNP. This partially offset the explosion of nondefense programs (See Table 4.2). The largest dollar increases occurred in social security, Medicare, and other non–means-tested transfer entitlements. From 1970 to 1980, outlays for entitlements and other mandatory spending programs more than quadrupled, and their share of GNP jumped dramatically, from 6.8 percent to 10.5 percent. During the same period, outlays for defense receded from 8.2 percent of GNP to 5 percent, its lowest share since 1950. In a sense, the sharp decline in defense outlays in the 1970s offset the massive expansion in nondefense spending programs.

As President Reagan assumed office, the budget outlook for the

1980s pointed to continued rapid spending growth and a sharp acceleration of tax revenues. In President Carter's last submitted budget, spending was projected to rise at a 10.3 percent annual rate during 1981–84, and to remain above 22 percent of GNP in each year.[1] Projected rapid growth of nondefense spending was accompanied by a renewed rise in defense spending based on increases in budget authority beginning in 1978. A whopping 54.9 percent budgeted rise in revenues from 1981 to 1984 (15.7 percent annually), driven by inflation-induced bracket creep, was expected to eliminate the deficit and generate a large surplus in 1984. This would push taxes above 22 percent of GNP, a significant jump from its 18.5 percent average during 1976–80.

Reagan's Initial Tax and Spending Initiatives

The Reagan administration's initial fiscal program sought to reverse budget trends of the 1970s by substantially accelerating the rise in defense outlays, slowing the growth in real nondefense outlays, and cutting taxes from current services projections so as to offset the higher actual and expected tax burden due to inflation. Reagan proposed a balanced budget by 1984, with both taxes and spending at approximately 19 percent of GNP.[2]

The president's tax proposal included large cuts from projected current services tax revenues, featuring a phased-in 30 percent rate reduction for individuals and reduced taxes on capital through an investment tax credit (ITC) and an accelerated cost recovery system (ACRS). Reagan recommended tax receipts be reduced 7.4 percent from current law in 1982 and 15.2 percent in 1984; this effectively lowered projected taxes in 1984 to 19.3 percent of GNP from 22.9 percent estimated under existing law.

The administration's spending-cut initiative included a massive increase in defense budget authority and spending, offset by even larger cuts in nondefense outlays. The administration requested increases of nearly 9 percent annually in real defense outlays, along with declines in real outlays for nondefense programs. Most of the recommended nondefense cuts were in grants to state and local

[1]Executive Office of the President, *Budget of the United States Government, Fiscal Year 1982* (Washington, 1981), pp. 8, 22, 65.

[2]Executive Office of the President, *America's New Beginning: A Program for Economic Recovery* (Washington, 1981), pp. 7–9.

Table 4.2

CHANGING TRENDS IN THE COMPOSITION OF FEDERAL SPENDING, 1950 TO 1987

Category	Fiscal Year								
	1950	1955	1960	1965	1970	1975	1980	1985	1987
Defense									
% of GNP	5.1	11.0	9.5	7.5	8.2	5.7	5.0	6.4	6.2
% of Outlays	32.2	62.4	52.2	42.8	41.8	26.0	22.0	26.7	28.4
Nondefense									
% of GNP	10.8	6.6	8.8	10.0	11.5	16.1	17.2	17.6	15.8
% of Outlays	67.7	37.6	47.8	57.2	58.2	74.0	77.3	73.3	71.6
Human Resources[a]									
% of GNP	5.3	3.8	5.2	5.4	7.6	11.4	11.7	12.0	10.8
% of Outlays	33.4	21.8	28.4	30.9	28.5	52.1	53.0	49.9	49.3
Physical Resources[b]									
% of GNP	1.4	0.7	1.6	1.7	1.6	2.3	2.5	1.4	1.1
% of Outlays	8.6	4.0	8.7	9.5	8.0	10.7	11.2	6.0	5.0
Net Interest									
% of GNP	1.8	1.3	1.4	1.3	1.5	1.5	2.0	3.3	3.3
% of Outlays	11.3	7.1	7.5	7.3	7.4	7.0	8.9	13.7	14.9

Table 4.2—(Continued)

CHANGING TRENDS IN THE COMPOSITION OF FEDERAL SPENDING, 1950 TO 1987

Category	1950	1955	1960	1965	Fiscal Year 1970	1975	1980	1985	1987
Other[c]									
% of GNP	3.0	1.7	1.5	2.5	1.7	1.8	1.7	1.7	1.4
% of Outlays	18.7	9.8	8.4	14.5	8.8	8.3	7.6	7.2	6.3
Undistributed Offsetting Receipts									
% of GNP	−0.7	−0.9	−0.9	−0.9	−0.9	−0.9	−0.7	−0.8	−0.8
% of Outlays	−4.3	−5.1	−5.2	−5.0	−4.4	−4.1	−3.4	−3.5	−3.8

SOURCE: Executive Office of the President, *Budget of the United States Government, Fiscal Year 1987.*

[a]Human resources includes social security; income security; health; veterans' benefits; and education, training, employment, and social services.

[b]Physical resources includes energy, natural resources and environment, commerce and housing credit, transportation, and community and regional development.

[c]Other includes international affairs; general science, space, and technology; agriculture; justice; general government; and general-purpose fiscal assistance.

governments, payments to individuals, and other discretionary spending. Only minor cuts were recommended for social security and Medicare, two of the fastest growing budget programs in the 1970s.

According to administration projections, with these tax cuts and spending cuts, the deficit would recede from $59.8 billion in 1980 and a balanced budget would be achieved in 1984. These projections were based on assumptions of strong real economic growth, a gradual slowdown in inflation, and double-digit nominal GNP growth through 1984 (see Table 4.3). What is more, these economic assumptions projected a large surplus in the current services budget.

The rapid enactment of ERTA in 1981 and the Omnibus Budget Reconciliation Act were considered stunning political successes for the president. The cut in individual income taxes was modified to a phased-in 25 percent cut, but ERTA also included indexing the individual income-tax system beginning in 1985 (which Reagan strongly supported), and included larger cuts from current services

Table 4.3

THE REAGAN ADMINISTRATION'S ORIGINAL PROJECTIONS AND ACTUAL ECONOMIC PERFORMANCE

	1981	1982	1983	1984
Real GNP (% change)				
Administration	1.1	4.2	5.0	4.5
Actual	1.0	−1.1	3.0	4.4
Nominal GNP (% change)				
Administration	11.1	12.8	12.4	10.8
Actual	11.7	3.7	7.6	10.5
CPI (% change)				
Administration	11.1	8.3	6.2	5.5
Actual	10.4	6.1	3.2	4.3
Interest Rate, 3-month Treasury-bill (%)				
Administration	11.1	8.9	7.8	7.0
Actual	14.0	10.7	8.6	9.6

SOURCE: Executive Office of the President, *America's New Beginning: A Program for Economic Recovery,* February 18, 1981, pp. 25, S–1; Council of Economic Advisers, *Economic Report of the President,* January 1987, pp. 245–46, 312, and 324.

revenues than Reagan had requested originally. The initial phase of the president's proposed defense build-up, plus many of the recommended cuts in nondefense programs, became law.

As the Reagan tax and spending initiatives were being enacted, the onset of recession, rising real interest rates, and an unexpected sudden deceleration of inflation and nominal income growth drove up actual and projected deficits. In sharp contrast to the administration's projections, the deficit reached a then-record high of $128 billion in 1982 and surged to $208 billion in 1983 (6.3 percent of GNP).

Despite the tax increases and spending cuts of the Tax Equity and Fiscal Responsibility Act of 1982 (TEFRA), the Highway Revenue Act of 1983, the social security amendments of 1983, and the Deficit Reduction Act of 1984 (DEFRA), the deficit outlook deteriorated continuously through early 1985.[3] In February 1985, the administration projected no decline in the current services deficit, with deficits remaining above $220 billion through 1990.[4] The baseline budget developed by the Congressional Budget Office was even more pessimistic.[5] It projected spending to remain above 24.1 percent of GNP through 1990, with the deficit to rise continuously and reach $296 billion (5.3 percent of GNP) in 1990. This generated an alarming projected rise in the federal debt-to-GNP ratio from 37 percent in 1984 to 50 percent in 1990.

Three pieces of deficit-cutting legislation—the Consolidated Omnibus Budget Reconciliation Act of 1985 (COBRA), the Budget Reconciliation Act of 1986, and the initial sequestration under the Balanced Budget and Emergency Deficit Control Act of 1985 (Gramm-Rudman-Hollings)—plus larger-than-expected declines in interest rates, prevented deficits from rising. This budget legislation abruptly halted Reagan's earlier defense build-up (budget authority for defense declined in real terms in 1985–87), made further cuts in nondefense discretionary programs, and raised tax revenues. As a consequence, budget trends in Reagan's second term have been in stark contrast

[3]Revenue estimates of these tax-policy changes are given in Executive Office of the President, *Budget of the United States Government, Fiscal Year 1986* (Washington, 1985), pp. 4–5.

[4]Ibid., p. 2-2.

[5]Congressional Budget Office, *The Economic and Budget Outlook: Fiscal Years 1986–1990* (Washington, 1985), p. 48.

to those of his first term, as defense spending has receded as a share of total outlays, while shares for social security and non–means-tested entitlements have risen. Presently, without further legislation, deficits should gradually recede as a percentage of GNP and the federal debt-to-GNP ratio should peak at approximately 45 percent.

Sources of the Deficits

Measured from current services budget projections and official economic forecasts of early 1981, the sharp rise in deficits may be attributed arithmetically to President Reagan's tax cuts and defense buildup, and even to the Federal Reserve's tight monetary policy. However, attempts to blame the large deficits on specific components of the budget typically stem from differences of opinion about whether the Reagan administration's tax and spending initiatives have been good or bad.[6] Additionally, many of these assessments fail to recognize longer-term budget trends. For example, the 1981 tax cuts are often singled out as the source of high deficits. However, tax revenues actually rose modestly as a percentage of GNP in the 1980s (from 18.5 percent in 1975–80 to 18.8 percent in 1981–85), which conflicts with this assertion. Reagan's tax cuts merely prevented the sharp projected rise in taxes under existing law. Similarly, blaming the deficits on Reagan's defense buildup fails to recognize that even after the Reagan initiative, defense outlays constituted a lower percentage of GNP than in earlier decades. Identifying the proper allocation of resources to national security involves considerations other than budget accounting.

Another alleged source of recent deficits is the Federal Reserve's tight monetary policy in the early 1980s that temporarily suppressed economic growth, reduced inflation, and temporarily drove up real interest rates. This argument has little merit. While arithmetically correct, failure to tighten monetary policy, accommodating high inflation and double-digit nominal GNP growth, would have been unacceptable, regardless of the deficit impact. Moreover, deficits rose sharply in the 1980s, even if they are adjusted for economic cycles, net of interest expense (the primary deficit), and also adjusted for inflation.

6See Herbert Stein, "Controlling the Budget Deficit: If Not Now, When? If Not Us, Who?" *AEI Economist* (December 1983).

A more accurate interpretation of the rise in deficits stems from the revealed preferences of budget decisions and outcomes. In the 1970s, deficits were a clear result of the combined preferences of policymakers and the public to radically expand nondefense spending programs. During the first Reagan term, the outcome of the political process was to restore resources to defense, reduce the growth of nondefense outlays, and cut taxes from existing law to prevent taxes from rising substantially faster than economic activity. Reagan's preferences clearly strained the unresolved conflict between defense and nondefense spending. Crucial to this conflict is the preference to protect the earlier sharp increases in real outlays for social security and non–means-tested entitlements, in the face of the recent budget "crisis." Although subsequently the administration has grudgingly allowed its defense buildup to unwind and taxes to increase, the conflict between spending priorities remains unresolved.

Whether Reagan placed a lower priority on controlling the deficit is uncertain, since his initial projections called for a balanced budget in 1984. In addition, the administration contended that lowering taxes would pressure Congress to lower spending. This contention, however, is unsupported by experience.[7] Certainly, ex post analysis reveals a huge forecasting error in Reagan's early balanced-budget projection. However, an ex ante assessment makes those projections seem less outlandish, although still open to criticism that the administration forced economic assumptions to meet budget goals. The prolonged recession from July 1981 to November 1982 was unanticipated, as was the speed of inflation deceleration and extent of rise in real interest rates. The unexpectedly sharp rise in unemployment and slowdown in nominal income growth suppressed tax revenues while the higher real rates on mounting federal debt pushed up net interest outlays.

Noteworthy, the Carter administration and CBO proved no better in their economic or budget projections. In its final budget, issued one month before President Reagan's *America's New Beginning: A Program for Economic Recovery*, the Carter administration forecast above-average economic growth through 1984 and a balanced bud-

[7]See George von Furstenberg, R. Jeffrey Green, and Jin-Ho Jeong, "Tax and Spend, or Spend and Tax?" *Review of Economics and Statistics* 68, no. 2 (May 1986): 179–88.

get in 1984.[8] A CBO forecast with President Reagan's tax and spending initiatives also projected above-average economic growth.[9] However, it assumed substantially higher interest rates than did the administration, and it projected a $50 billion deficit in 1984.

Nevertheless, President Reagan's economic projections and budget forecasts are open to criticism. First, they were inconsistent with the administration's call for the Federal Reserve to slow the growth of money and credit "to levels consistent with noninflationary expansion of the economy."[10] The administration recognized the Fed's restrictive monetary policy as a cornerstone of its overall economic program and wrote the policy into its own budget. Despite this, the administration projected double-digit nominal GNP growth through 1984 and only a gradual decline in inflation (see Table 4.3). In addition, the administration significantly underestimated the rise in interest rates that would be necessary to achieve the monetary policy objectives. In 1981–82, the three-month Treasury bill averaged 2.4 percentage points higher than the administration projected. A second criticism centers on the very large elasticities assumed for labor supply, savings, and investment with respect to the proposed tax changes. Although these assumed economic responses were substantially larger than historical experience, Reagan administration economists contended that parameters derived from historical relationships were inappropriate standards for evaluating responses to the new economic program.

These criticisms should not obfuscate the point that President Reagan chose to test the long-standing conflict between defense and nondefense spending priorities, and what emerged from the political process was a preference to increase spending and limit tax increases. Facing this budget outcome, understanding the eco-

[8]See *Executive Office of the President, 1981*, pp. 3–5, 22. President Carter proposed minor spending and tax cuts and projected a balanced budget by 1984. The economic forecast underlying this budget was surprisingly similar to the ensuing Reagan administration forecast. It included modestly slower real GNP growth (1.7 percent in 1981, 3.5 percent in 1982, and 3.7 percent thereafter); gradually declining inflation (the consumer price index receding gradually from 12.6 percent to 7.5 percent in 1984), and short-term interest rates that would decline gradually from 13.5 percent in 1981 to 8.5 percent in 1984.

[9]See Congressional Budget Office, *The Economic and Budget Outlook: An Update* (Washington, 1981), p. 5.

[10]See Executive Office of the President, *America's New Beginning*, chap. 6.

nomic impacts of the deficit is necessary to avoid policy mistakes in dealing with the imbalance.

The Economic Effects of Reagan's Deficits

Most of the short-run effects of high deficits expected in the early 1980s have not occurred, and a growing body of economic literature has emerged to challenge empirically and conceptually the basis for the earlier assertions. Although there is widespread disagreement about many of the short-run effects of large deficits—on economic cycles, rates of interest and exchange, and role of deficits in the macroeconomy in general—there is a growing consensus that a mounting federal debt is potentially very dangerous and eventually will impinge on economic growth.

The Uncertain Short-Run Economic Effects of Deficits

Standard Keynesian analysis postulates that a rise in deficit spending stimulates aggregate demand, which generates an increase in the demand for money and higher interest rates. But the stimulative impact of deficits, plus the ability of policymakers to smooth aggregate demand fluctuations through changes in the deficit, proved ineffective in the 1970s, and they are now being challenged on several counts. Even if deficits (government bonds) add to net wealth (a proposition denied by the controversial Barro-Ricardian equivalence hypothesis),[11] or generate an intertemporal redistribution of wealth that causes a temporary addition to consumption,[12] measuring the economic responses to discretionary fiscal policy changes is exceedingly complex. The responses depend on whether discretionary fiscal policy changes are perceived to be temporary[13]

[11]The Barro-Ricardian equivalence hypothesis posits that economic activity and interest rates are independent of whether government spending is financed by taxes or borrowing because, in response to deficits, saving will rise in anticipation of higher future taxes, leaving consumption and interest rates unchanged. See Robert J. Barro, "Are Government Bonds Net Wealth?" *Journal of Political Economy* 82, no. 6 (1974): 1095–118.

[12]See Alex Cukierman and Allan Meltzer, "A Political Theory of Government Debt and Deficits in a Neo-Ricardian Framework," unpublished manuscript, 1987. Cukierman and Meltzer use their assumptions of uneven bequest motives of different households and intertemporal wealth redistribution to explain the combined public preference for deficit spending.

[13]See Milton Friedman, *A Theory of the Consumption Function* (Princeton: Princeton University Press, 1957); Robert Eisner, "What Went Wrong," *Journal of Political Economy* 79 (May/June 1971): 629–41.

or whether they may be influenced by a change in policy regime.[14] Moreover, it is very difficult to predict the time profile of the fiscal multipliers and the amount of real discretionary change that actually occurs when the policy is implemented,[15] in part because the economic response involves an adjustment among stocks of assets. With these uncertainties, previous failures of fiscal fine-tuning in the 1970s are not surprising.

This focus on fiscal fine-tuning was replaced by the sizable shift in monetary policy in October 1979, the breadth of change of Reagan's tax and spending initiatives in 1981, and the unprecedented magnitudes of the deficits. Beginning in 1982, concern that deficits would drive up interest rates and choke off economic recovery led many economists and policymakers to recommend a tax increase to stimulate the economy. This line of thinking called into question the direction, as well as the magnitude, of standard fiscal multipliers.

Much of the recent confusion about the effects of deficits stems from the overemphasis on deficits, the underemphasis on the tax and spending structures underlying the deficits, and the assumed positive linkage between deficits and interest rates. As residuals of tax revenues and spending, deficits provide only limited and ambiguous information about fiscal policy. Failure to recognize this has tended to oversimplify and mislead fiscal policy analysis, in part by focusing only on the aggregate demand impact of deficit changes. Instead, specific tax and spending structures generate significant economic impacts, aside from any change in the deficit. A tax assessed on capital has a distinctly different economic effect from one imposed on labor. It is particularly important to realize that the large interest elasticity of investment implies that a tax policy change that alters the rate of return on capital significantly influences investment.

The potential stimulative impact of spending varies by program, depending in part on the substitutability of goods and services among the federal government, state, and local governments and private sector providers. For example, lower defense purchases

[14]See Robert Lucas, "Econometric Policy Evaluation: A Critique," in *Studies in Business Cycle Theory* (Cambridge: MIT Press, 1981), pp. 104–5.

[15]See Robert Eisner and Paul Pieper, "A New View of the Federal Debt and Budget Deficits," *American Economic Review* 74 (March 1984): 11–29.

tend not to be replaced by private-sector provision. In contrast, the economic effect of a cut in federal revenue sharing tends to be offset by an increase in provision of goods and services by state and local governments and the private sector.

In assessing the effects of fiscal policies during the Reagan administration, it is essential to emphasize the allocative effects of changes in the structures of tax and spending programs, rather than the aggregate demand effects of changes in deficits. Tax and spending policies in the first Reagan term were significantly different than in his second term, and these shifts, amid persistently high deficits, have had significant effects on economic activity and the prices of financial assets.

The widely accepted assertion that actual or expected deficits push up interest rates, which has contributed significantly to the confusion about fiscal policy, is not supported by empirical research.[16] There are four apparent reasons for this lack of evidence of a consistent positive correlation between deficits and interest rates. First, deficits have tended to rise during recessions, when interest rates tend to decline, and to decline during economic expansions, when rates tend to rise—thereby implying a negative correlation. Moreover, the demand for government debt competes with other financial assets, and the changing composition of total debt over business cycles makes it very difficult to find a positive correlation between deficits and interest rates. Second, the correlation may be obscured by Federal Reserve attempts to stabilize interest rates. Also, interest rates embody inflationary expectations, which are not observable, thereby increasing the difficulty of estimating any correlation between deficits and real interest rates.

Third, interest rates and the prices of other financial assets are determined by portfolio adjustments among alternative assets; therefore, it is the stock of federal debt relative to the stock of other assets that affects interest rates, rather than the short-run flow of deficits relative to other financial flows. This suggests a smaller correlation than is implied by financial flow analysis.

Fourth, in an open economy with flexible exchange rates, inter-

---

[16]See Treasury Department, *The Effects of Deficits on Prices of Financial Assets: Theory and Evidence* (Washington, 1984); Congressional Budget Office, *The Economic and Budget Outlook*; James Barth, George Iden, and Frank Russek, "Do Federal Deficits Really Matter?" *Contemporary Policy Issues* (September 1984): 80.

national capital flows may mitigate the interest-rate impact of deficits. Clearly, the high expected risk-adjusted rate of return on U.S. Treasury debt relative to returns on other assets contributed significantly to the rising U.S. dollar in the early 1980s. The rapid increase in real and financial wealth domestically and worldwide, plus the increased efficiency of international capital markets, have served to absorb the rapid increase in federal debt without significantly raising interest rates.

In a sense, efforts to estimate a correlation between deficits and interest rates are misspecified. They assume deficits are exogenous, when in fact they are endogenous and are jointly determined with interest rates. In addition, such efforts are based on consideration of the flows of funds, whereas Keynes and several earlier classical economists established that interest rates are determined by portfolio adjustments that reflect preferences among stocks of assets.

My assessment is that the unanticipated jumps in deficits probably pushed rates higher than they would have been otherwise in the early 1980s, although this one-time occurrence is not revealed in empirical research. In general, however, the impact of deficits on interest rates is substantially smaller than is generally presumed.

Deficits and the Economic Expansion

A widespread concern early in the Reagan administration was that huge deficits would drive up interest rates, which would stifle capital spending and other interest-sensitive output, and choke off an economic recovery. Another concern, shared by President Reagan, was that persistent deficits would be inflationary. Instead, a strong and durable economic expansion unfolded, with strong growth in the interest-sensitive sectors and declining inflation.

This sustained expansion and the significant rise and fall of real rates of interest and exchange—amid persistently high deficits—highlight how earlier assertions about the short-run effects of deficits proved largely incorrect. Clearly, deficits alone (whether or not cyclically adjusted) are wholly inadequate in explaining the shifts in the rate and composition of economic growth and the wide fluctuations in interest and exchange rates. Two key provisions of ERTA—the ITC and the ACRS—lowered the after-tax cost of capital and had a significant impact on economic performance. Combined with the monetary policy-driven rebound in aggregate demand, the

60

tax-policy shift stimulated capital spending. The rapid defense build-up added to government purchases and GNP. Robust real GNP growth, with a rising share of investment, continued through mid-1984. If the rise in the deficit had been due to another source—such as a rise in transfer payments—the economic outcome would have been substantially different.

Through mid-1984, real interest rates rose, but not because of rising deficits. Since interest rates reflect the opportunity cost of current versus future consumption, the pattern of interest rates during the Reagan administration reflects changes in the rate and composition of economic growth, expected rates of return on investment, and changes in inflationary expectations. The rapid rate of economic growth and the rising share of investment generated by ERTA raised the equilibrium rate of real interest by increasing actual and expected real after-tax rates of return on investment. Since the interest elasticity of investment substantially exceeds the interest elasticity of saving, the surge in capital spending, combined with the higher federal borrowing (due to the ITC- and ACRS-generated forgone tax revenues), pushed up credit demands relative to the stock of savings.

In a global context, robust economic growth and the ERTA tax policy raised the equilibrium exchange value of the U.S. dollar. The upward shift in actual and expected real after-tax rates of return on dollar-denominated assets relative to assets denominated in other currencies induced shifts in asset portfolios that raised the demand for dollars. This upward shift was accompanied by declining expectations of U.S. inflation. A sharp slowdown in the flow of U.S. capital to highly indebted developing nations occurred concurrently. The rising demand for dollars generated a net inflow of foreign capital and an upward adjustment of the dollar.

Through mid-1984, the rising real rates of interest and exchange reflected strength in the U.S. economy and the tax-related surge in investment. While federal deficits remained high, interest rates peaked coincident with peak growth rates of economic output and investment, and began receding, while the dollar continued to appreciate through early 1985.[17]

[17]The continued appreciation of the U.S. dollar from mid-1984 through early 1985 remains somewhat of a mystery in light of the shift toward slower economic growth, declining real interest rates, and stimulative monetary policy. The final appreciation

It is important to note that the high real interest rates did not choke off economic expansion, precisely because the stronger economic growth and rising share of investment raised the equilibrium level of rates. In fact, even if deficits were the source of high interest rates (an idea for which there is no empirical support), the higher rates would not necessarily inhibit economic expansion. Insofar as rates serve to allocate resources among different uses, a rise in rates may reduce demand for some categories of output, but that may be more than offset by larger expenditures for other categories of output, such as government defense purchases or consumption of nondurable goods.

Real interest rates declined sharply through 1986 as economic growth slowed sharply and investment spending declined. The debate over and eventual enactment of TRA–86 contributed significantly to the shift in composition of economic output. Treasury I, the precursor to TRA–86, first unveiled in November 1984, proposed elimination of the ITC and lengthening depreciable tax lives of certain assets. Although the Treasury tax initiative was advertised as being revenue-neutral, it was not economically neutral, and it represented a sharp reversal from President Reagan's earlier tax policy. Throughout the tax reform debate in 1985 and 1986, both the House and Senate versions also included provisions that would raise the after-tax cost of capital. In anticipation of enactment, capital spending declined and economic activity shifted sharply away from investment and toward consumption. Consequently, the equilibrium level of interest rates declined, despite a record $220 billion deficit in 1986.

The dollar decline from early 1985 through 1986 was associated with the mounting foreign-debt obligations and some of the same fundamental factors that generated lower real interest rates: weaker economic growth and lower actual and expected real after-tax rates of return on dollar-denominated assets, which reduced the equilibrium rate of exchange, and expansive monetary policy.

The dollar's sharp slide is entirely inconsistent with the widely held but flawed view that high budget deficits drive up the U.S. dollar. Historically, fiscal irresponsibility has not been rewarded by

---

may have been based on market momentum and speculation, or the delayed adjustment of expectations of weaker U.S. corporate profits and lower rates of return on dollar-denominated assets.

an appreciating currency, and the U.S. experience in the 1980s is not an exception. Empirical research fails to find a positive correlation between budget deficits and exchange rates, and at least one recent study has identified a negative correlation.[18] Despite this, the common presumption of a positive linkage dominated the fiscal policy debate in 1984–85. Efforts to cut the deficit were supported as a necessary element to lower the dollar and improve trade. This view posits that in the 1980s, the deficits drove up interest rates, which led to an appreciation of the dollar, which generated the trade deficit, which is mirrored by capital inflows. The uncertain link between deficits and interest rates, and the implausible positive correlation between large budget deficits and exchange rates, challenge this presumed causal linkage. Much of the confusion stems from the positive correlation between the budget deficit and the current account deficit. This is an ex post correlation and does not imply causality.

Exchange rates reflect the capital flows associated with international portfolio adjustments among competing assets. The portfolio shifts in the 1980s, in response to significant changes in differential rates of economic growth, tax on capital, and inflationary expectations among nations, have generated shifts in capital flows. Associated adjustments of exchange rates have affected the demand for imports and exports, and the resulting trade imbalance, along with the budget deficit, is reflected in the current account.

Through early 1985, the rising demand for dollars was fueled by advantageous dollar-investment opportunities relative to foreign investments and expectations of declining U.S. inflation. The subsequent downward adjustment in the dollar has reflected the lower demand for dollars and, through 1986, the rapidly growing money supply as the Federal Reserve pursued stimulative policy. The lower demand has been associated with weaker U.S. economic growth, a declining net investment share, and the perceived need for a downward adjustment in the dollar to generate sufficient improvement in trade to stem the sharp rise in net real external debt obligations.

While the sharp movements in the U.S. dollar have significantly altered the product composition and regional pattern of economic

[18]Paul Evans, "Is the Dollar High Because of Large Budget Deficits?" *Journal of Monetary Economics* 18, no. 3 (November 1986): 227–49.

activity through their impacts on the relative prices of U.S. and foreign products, their effect on the aggregate rate of economic growth has been minor. The earlier appreciation of the dollar generated faster growth of domestic demand than domestic production, by raising consumption of imports and services and lowering demand for domestically produced tradable goods. With a lag, the subsequent downward adjustment in the dollar has generated an improvement in real trade as U.S. products have been substituted for foreign products. Based on the misperception about the role that interest and exchange rates play in allocating (worldwide) resources among alternative uses, earlier fears that the rising dollar would lead to recession turned out to match earlier fears about the economic impact of higher interest rates; that is, they proved to be unwarranted.

Long-Run Effects of Mounting Federal Debt

Recent deficit spending and the mounting federal debt are inimical to long-run economic growth and could possibly lead to increased inflation. Interest costs have risen sharply as a share of the federal outlays and GNP, and the mounting debt implies rising debt obligations in the future. To the extent deficit spending finances consumption activities rather than investment, the nation's long-run productive capacity is not expanded, potential output is constrained, and the mounting debt obligations must be repaid from lower future income. This implies an intertemporal redistribution of wealth and lower standards of living for future generations. The rapid growth in non–means-tested entitlements in the budget suggests that this is the case.

The rising stock of federal debt impinges on credit available for private investment unless offset by increased saving from domestic or foreign sources.[19] The federal debt-to-GNP ratio and private investment are negatively and significantly correlated.[20] In fact, net business fixed investment has shrunk in the 1980s, despite rising

[19]See Benjamin Friedman, "Implications of the Government Deficit for U.S. Capital Formation," in *The Economics of Large Government Deficits* (Boston: Federal Reserve Bank of Boston, 1984), pp. 73–95.

[20]See John Makin and Raymond Sauer, "The Effect of Debt Accumulation on Capital Formation," American Enterprise Institute Occasional Papers no. 1, November 1984.

capital inflows. The long-run effect of lower investment reduces the capital intensity of production, which lowers growth of productivity and potential GNP. As the mounting federal debt replaces other assets, real interest rates rise, reflecting the higher marginal rate of return on scarcer capital and exacerbating the cost of debt service.[21]

The timing and magnitude of the crowding out of capital investment is uncertain, depending in part on how rapidly outstanding federal debt rises. Runaway federal debt accumulation, with the growth of federal debt exceeding the growth of net private wealth, would pose the greatest threat to private capital formation. This worst case now appears unlikely, as recent deficit-cutting initiatives have arrested the sharp rise in the federal debt-to-GNP ratio. Even with a rapidly rising stock of federal debt, several studies indicate that the adverse impact on national income, real wages, and consumption is quite delayed.[22] This suggests that policymakers have sufficient time to slow the debt buildup and limit the long-run consequences. However, the more sensitive economic output is to capital formation, the more pessimistic is the outcome.

In the 1980s, the rapid absorption of foreign saving has provided resources for U.S. consumption, investment, and federal deficit spending, and has mitigated the impact of the rising federal debt on interest rates. However, it has not been costless. Rapid growth of capital inflows increases U.S. indebtedness to foreign creditors. Being a net creditor nation is not necessarily bad—it depends on how the additional resources are used. If the foreign capital inflows finance added investment and the marginal return on the investment exceeds the real cost of interest, U.S. productive capacity expands and national wealth is enhanced, while the debt is repaid. This was the case for a substantial period of U.S. economic development in the 19th century. However, the rising foreign indebt-

[21]A good summary of the issues involved in the long-run effects of persistent federal deficits is given in Congressional Budget Office, *The Economic and Budget Outlook.*

[22]See James Tobin, "Budget Deficits, Federal Debt, and Inflation in Short and Long Runs," in *Toward a Reconstruction of Federal Budgeting,* ed. Albert Sommers, (New York: The Conference Board, 1983), pp. 51–59; Edward Gramlich, "How Bad Are the Larger Deficits?" in *Federal Budget Policy in the 1980s,* ed. Gregory Mills and John Palmer (Washington: The Urban Institute Press, 1984), pp. 43–68.

edness implies that foreign creditors own claim to a rising portion of U.S. productive capacity.

Identifying how foreign capital is used is a very difficult—and generally overlooked—issue. Unfortunately, the recent surge in foreign-capital inflows has not been accompanied by a rise in the net investment. Instead, budget deficits have risen sharply while domestic saving has declined as a percentage of GNP and net investment has languished. In this regard, the rising share of transfer payments in the federal budget and the recent shift in national income from investment to consumption suggest that the foreign-capital inflows have been used in part to finance unsustainably high consumption. Insofar as the rate of return on the foreign capital has been less than its financing cost, the mounting foreign debt obligations and deficit-financed consumption imply that we are using national wealth. Repayment of the sharply rising foreign debt becomes a critical issue, and the burden will fall on future generations as a lower standard of living.

Mounting Federal Debt and Inflation

Concerns about the inflationary impact of deficits and rising federal debt stem largely from potential pressures for the Federal Reserve to monetize a portion of the debt.[23] Certainly, debt monetization is not an objective of Fed policy, and it is not a necessary response to deficits. However, the Fed conducts monetary policy in a complex economic and financial market environment, operating under the close scrutiny of both the administration and Congress, both of which have important and often conflicting goals. The pressures of deficits and the mounting federal debt may induce the Federal Reserve to supply more reserves than it would otherwise. In the short run, the Fed may do so if it perceives that deficits are driving up interest rates and it attempts to mitigate that impact. Several empirical studies have identified a positive and significant correlation between deficits (or rising federal debt) and money supply.[24]

[23]See Thomas Sargent and Neil Wallace, "Some Unpleasant Monetarist Arithmetic," Federal Reserve Bank of Minneapolis *Quarterly Review* (Fall 1981): 1–17; Preston Miller, "Higher Deficit Policies Lead to Higher Inflation," Federal Reserve Bank of Minneapolis *Quarterly Review*, Winter 1983, pp. 8–19.

[24]See Mickey Levy, "Factors Affecting Monetary Policy in an Era of Inflation," *Journal of Monetary Economics* (November 1981): 351–73; Michael Hamburger and Burton Zwick, "Deficits, Money and Inflation," *Journal of Monetary Economics* (Jan-

In the long run, the rising federal debt implies higher interest payments; debt monetization reduces the real value of the debt and associated real interest payments, and thereby lowers the real debt-to-GNP ratio. However, it does so by increasing inflation. With a rising federal debt-to-GNP ratio, a noninflationary monetary policy requires the Fed to absorb a smaller share of the increase in debt. The Fed's flexibility is reduced and the fine line between accommodation and inflationary monetary policy is sharpened.[25] As federal debt rises, the various avenues for financing it become strained and the dangers of inflation persist.

Guidelines for Fiscal Policy

President Reagan's early economic policies were designed to allocate a larger share of budget resources to national security and to shift economic output toward investment, while preventing tax revenues to rise as a percentage of GNP. Misplaced concerns about the short-run adverse impacts of the resulting high deficits have generated misguided recommendations for fiscal policy, particularly the urge to lower deficits by whatever means, including raising taxes.

This misunderstanding has influenced recent fiscal policy, including the Gramm-Rudman-Hollings act in 1985 and TRA–86. Gramm-Rudman-Hollings was designed to impose budget discipline, but it does so through artificial deficit constraints and a process of automatic across-the-board cuts that applies unevenly to different federal programs (it affects most defense spending but only approximately one-third of nondefense outlays). This does not constitute good budget policy; so far, it has elicited short-term quick fixes that are not consistent with needed program reform. TRA–86 raises taxes on capital and lowers taxes on personal income, a policy prescription contrary to President Reagan's long-run priorities of investment and economic growth. It demonstrates the danger of

uary 1981): 141–50; Alan Blinder, "On Monetization of Deficits," National Bureau of Economic Research, Working Paper no. 1052 (December 1982).

[25]See Ronald Hoffman and Mickey Levy, "Economic and Budget Issues for Deficit Policy," *Contemporary Policy Issues* 3 (Fall 1984–85): 96–113.

assuming that a tax-policy change is economically neutral just because it may be revenue neutral.[26]

There are five principles that should guide further efforts to stem the projected rise in federal debt. First, fiscal policy should be conceived and debated, with the primary goal being to create an environment conducive to long-run economic growth. Since monetizing the debt is inflationary and must be avoided, nominal budget deficits must be cut. Given past failures, short-run stabilization goals should not be the focus of fiscal policy.

Second, to preserve production incentives, spending cuts should take the lead in any deficit-cutting efforts. The long-term trend toward higher spending as a pecentage of GNP must be stopped. The reallocation of resources from the private sector to the public sector generated by higher government spending reduces private investment, regardless of how it is financed.

Third, all government spending programs must be considered candidates for budget cuts. In particular, after massive increases in social security and non–means-tested entitlements in the 1970s, real outlays for these programs have been generally maintained in the 1980s. Social security remains exempt from the automatic across-the-board cuts imposed by Gramm-Rudman-Hollings. Consequently, these programs now constitute approximately 47 percent of total federal outlays. Allowing them to remain sacrosanct severely constrains deficit-cutting efforts. Moreover, the rising share of transfer payments is costly economically. It suppresses private investment and contributes to the mounting federal debt without adding to productive capacity.

Fourth, spending cuts should be consistent with long-run program reform. Quick-fix spending cuts to meet deficit goals are not necessarily good public policy if they do not generate long-run savings or if they fail to address structural flaws in government spending programs. Examples abound. Asset sales may be advantageous for economic reasons, but they are inappropriate for achieving deficit targets. Earlier proposed freezes and limitations on cost-

[26]The impact of TRA–86 on economic growth was partially mitigated by the rapid downward adjustment of interest and exchange rates, and by accommodative monetary policy. If the Fed had prevented rates from adjusting downward to their new equilibrium levels determined by TRA–86, economic output and net investment would have been reduced.

of-living adjustments for social security have postponed needed program reform that addresses, among other things, the program's evolving role in retirement planning (relative to savings from private pensions and personal savings plans such as individual retirement accounts and Keogh accounts), and its impact on intragenerational and intertemporal wealth redistribution. Also, it is equally important that defense spending cuts be consistent with long-run national security goals.

Fifth, if political compromise to reduce deficits requires tax increases, they should be assessed on consumption to limit further disincentives to save and invest. Raising taxes on capital reduces productive capacity and the international competitiveness of U.S. producers, and it is counterproductive in the effort to limit the rise in federal debt and foreign debt obligations.

5. Supply-Side Success

Richard Rahn

Is the tax system more or less of an impediment to economic progress than it was before President Reagan took office? The answer is clear. Despite all of the mistakes and indecorous compromises that the administration has made over the years, I suspect that free-market economists are virtually unanimous in their opinion that the tax system is better now than it was in 1980. In fact, it is primarily the changes in the tax system inaugurated by the Reagan administration and the lack of damaging economic policy "initiatives" that have caused the record peacetime economic expansion that we are presently enjoying.

Let us travel back in time to 1980 and recollect some of the finer points of tax policy under the Carter administration. The top marginal tax rate was a modest 70 percent. A two-earner, middle-class family with about $50,000 in annual income paid marginal federal income-tax rates of about 49 percent. More importantly, however, they could eagerly look forward to paying rates of 59 percent within eight years as their nominal income skyrocketed due to the effect of the 13-plus-percent inflation rate we were experiencing at the time. The same inflation that was driving the middle class into tax brackets that were once the exclusive province of the wealthy was also depriving the country of vital investment capital. High inflation and high interest rates made our capital cost recovery allowances increasingly anemic. Finally, the insidious estate and gift tax had become ubiquitous by 1980. In 1980, we should remember, everyone dying with an estate valued at more than $175,000 was liable for estate and gift tax. The specter of middle-class Americans having to retain legal counsel for estate planning purposes no doubt succors the American Bar Association, but most of us logically view that as a waste of society's resources.

The members of the Carter administration seemed to have no comprehension that anything was wrong. They and their many supporters in government, academia, and the media were unable or unwilling to draw any connection between ever-increasing tax burdens and stagnant economic performance. Thus, there was every reason to believe that had Ronald Reagan not been elected president, the situation would have worsened rather than simply stabilizing.

Fortunately, Reagan was elected and was able to secure passage of the Economic Recovery Tax Act of 1981 (ERTA). This landmark piece of tax legislation was the centerpiece of the president's economic recovery program, and it has been an unqualified success. It had three major components. It cut marginal tax rates, including the capital gains tax rate, it enhanced capital cost recovery allowances, and it dramatically reduced estate and gift taxes.

ERTA reduced individual tax rates to a maximum of 50 percent and cut them 25 percent across the board for the middle class. Perhaps most importantly, ERTA indexed tax brackets for inflation. No longer did the welfare state gain new revenues from the middle class by debasing the currency. ERTA cut the individual capital gains rate from 28 to 20 percent. Perhaps a harbinger of compromises to follow, however, was the agreement by the administration to delay the effective dates of the tax cuts and tax indexing. The final 10 percent rate cut did not take place until mid-1983, and tax indexing did not take effect until 1985. Thus, some of the most constructive provisions in ERTA did not take effect until long after it was signed into law. This had the unfortunate effect of delaying the economic recovery.

These rate reductions had a very salutary impact on the economy. Lower rates reduced the relative price of work compared to leisure and thereby promoted work and employment. They reduced the tax bias against savings and toward consumption inherent in the income tax. Finally, they diminished economic distortion by reducing the value of tax shelters.

Counterintuitively, they also dramatically increased the share of the overall tax burden borne by the wealthy. As Table 5.1 illustrates, those earning over $500,000 per year were paying over 151 percent more taxes within three years of their tax rate being cut from 70 to 50 percent. Table 5.2 shows that these taxpayers' share of the overall tax burden grew from 3.1 to 7.2 percent over the same period. Only lower-income taxpayers paid lower taxes.

Table 5.1

TAX REVENUES, BY INCOME CLASS, 1981–84

Adjusted Gross Income ($)	Amount ($)				Percent Change, 1981–84
	1981	1982	1983	1984	
0–9,999	7,945,156	7,089,765	6,273,715	6,282,422	–20.9
10,000–19,999	39,463,703	34,566,629	31,462,510	31,282,852	–20.7
20,000–29,999	55,617,622	51,966,132	46,320,952	44,778,032	–19.5
30,000–49,999	86,453,702	84,994,927	82,628,629	87,280,470	1.0
50,000–74,999	36,131,219	35,892,383	38,352,897	47,355,174	31.1
75,000–99,999	14,544,159	14,594,818	15,392,973	18,759,377	29.0
100,000–199,999	21,142,477	21,868,884	22,014,198	25,762,519	21.9
200,000–499,999	12,380,468	14,032,120	15,613,203	18,775,081	51.7
500,000 and over	8,623,523	12,591,632	16,122,246	21,647,130	151.0
Total	282,302,029	277,597,290	274,181,323	301,923,057	7.0

SOURCE: Internal Revenue Service.

Table 5.2
Percentage of Total Tax Burden, by Income Class, 1981–84

Adjusted Gross Income ($)	Percent				Percent Change, 1981–84
	1981	1982	1983	1984	
0–9,999	2.8	2.6	2.3	2.1	−26.1
10,000–19,999	14.0	12.5	11.5	10.4	−25.9
20,000–29,999	19.7	18.7	16.9	14.8	−24.7
30,000–49,999	30.6	30.6	30.1	28.9	− 5.6
50,000–74,999	12.8	12.9	14.0	15.7	22.5
75,000–99,999	5.2	5.3	5.6	6.2	20.6
100,000–199,999	7.5	7.9	8.0	8.5	13.9
200,000–499,999	4.4	5.1	5.7	6.2	41.8
500,000 and over	3.1	4.5	5.9	7.2	134.7
Total	100.0	100.0	100.0	100.0	

SOURCE: Internal Revenue Service.
Note: Totals may not add up to 100 percent because of rounding.

These results are not difficult to understand if they are analyzed from an incentive (classical microeconomics) perspective and if the analysis is focused on the effect of ERTA on after-tax incomes. The most affluent taxpayers saw the after-tax return for any extra dollar earned increase from 30 cents to 50 cents, or 67 percent. Lower-income taxpayers, in contrast, already paid comparatively lower taxes and saw their after-tax income for any additional dollar earned go from 86 cents to 89 cents, only 3 percent higher. Thus, upper-income taxpayers responded to truly significant increases in the after-tax reward to additional work or savings. The amount of additional income they chose to earn was sufficiently high that it more than compensated the government for the lower tax rates. Thus, ERTA's changes in the taxation of upper-income individuals promoted economic growth, enabled taxpayers to retain more of their own money, increased federal and state revenues, and increased the share of the total tax burden borne by the affluent.

Even social democrats who want to, in effect, exploit capitalism to fund a generous welfare state should support the rate cuts for upper-income taxpayers because they raised federal revenues. Conservatives and libertarians support the rate cuts because they believe in the sanctity of property. Pragmatists of all ideological stripes should be impressed with the positive macroeconomic impact of the rate cuts. Only those who somehow view economic success as sordid or immoral and deserving punitive taxation should rationally remain opposed to ERTA's rate cuts.

Those of us who had so strongly promoted the Kemp-Roth tax cuts were not surprised by these unusual distributional effects of tax cuts for upper-income taxpayers. Precisely the same distributional and revenue effects were experienced when President Kennedy cut tax rates from 94 to 70 percent effective in 1964 and when tax rates were steadily reduced in the 1920s after the confiscatory rates imposed during World War I.[1]

ERTA reduced the tax bias against investment substantially. The new accelerated cost recovery system, combined with the investment tax credit, approximated, in present-value terms, the expensing of capital expenditures. Thus, the cost of capital declined, and

[1]For a more detailed discussion, see Richard Rahn's statement before the House Ways and Means Committee, June 26, 1985.

during the recovery of the next several years, the size of the U.S. capital stock grew at very robust rates. This new investment laid the foundation for sustained economic growth.

ERTA was the most constructive and outstanding economic policy achievement of the Reagan years, bar none. Then the administration's tax policy took a turn for the worse.

Retreat from Tax Reduction

The first serious mistake was making common cause with the Senate Republicans to force the largest tax increase in the history of the republic through Congress only 12 months after ERTA was signed—before many of the rate reductions had even taken effect and before any rate cuts had a chance to have a positive impact on the economy. It increased taxes by $215 billion over five years. The primary thrust of the Tax Equity and Fiscal Responsibility Act (TEFRA) of 1982 was to scale back many of the liberalizations in corporate taxation that had been enacted only months before. Still, the overall capital cost recovery system remained better for most, although not all, plant and equipment. TEFRA needlessly extended the recession that started in mid-1981—a recession caused primarily by the Federal Reserve's very restrictive money policy. About the only good thing that can be said about TEFRA is that it did not raise tax rates.

But in a few more months, the administration was a party to a tax rate increase agreement. The administration agreed to a plan that would bail out the social security system by accelerating previously scheduled payroll-tax rate increases. Unfortunately, the 1983 social security compromise probably marked the last time that changes in social security will be seriously discussed for a decade. And the administration agreed for all intents and purposes to throw good money after bad and to defer the day of reckoning until another presidency. In fairness to the administration, however, we should remember that a cowardly Congress rejected by overwhelming margins each and every reform proposal that the administration sent to Capitol Hill.

The latest installment of those payroll-tax increases went into effect in January 1988 as the combined employer/employee tax rate increased from 14.3 percent to 15.02 percent. Another combined rate increase is scheduled for 1990. These tax rate increases can be expected to have all of the adverse effects on employment and economic growth that other tax rate increases have in the past.

In 1984, the administration once again acquiesced in further dilution of ERTA. Although the 1984 act did not affect tax rates, it did raise taxes by $48 billion over five years. These new taxes came primarily at the expense of business by limiting leasing, imposing new onerous accounting requirements, taxing multinationals more heavily, and calling for further reductions in capital cost recovery allowances.

Tax Reform

During the 1984 presidential campaign, President Reagan requested the Treasury Department under Donald Regan's guidance to study tax reform and to release a proposal by the end of 1984. The department did so, but it was a very poor proposal and was roundly attacked. It had higher tax rates than most other plans, incredibly slow capital cost recovery allowances, and high capital gains rates, and it was administratively very complex. The administration, to its credit, did not accept the plan. By May 1985, the administration released a plan it would call its own. That plan maintained the relatively high top rate of 35 percent but reduced capital gains rates to 17.5 percent, contained adequate capital cost recovery allowances, and eliminated many of the administrative nightmares contained in the Treasury plan. This was the high-water mark of the administration's involvement in tax reform. It soon became clear that the administration wanted a bill more than anything else and that as long as the rates were 35 percent or lower, it would accept the package.

Control over the process then went first to the House Ways and Means Committee and then to the Senate Finance Committee. The final product of the conference committee was accepted by the administration with enthusiasm. On balance, the final product was constructive but it certainly was not the pro-growth dynamo that it could have been. And once again, the full rate cuts were deferred— this time until January 1988. Only in 1988, in my judgment, did tax reform become pro-growth.

In 1988, the maximum individual marginal tax rate is 33 percent (despite the stated rate of 28 percent), and the top corporate rate is 34 percent. These rates represent incredible progress compared to where we stood only seven years ago. Then, the individual rate was over twice as high, at 70 percent, and the corporate rate was one-third higher, at 46 percent. Rates as low as those we enjoy commencing in January 1988 seemed like a pipe dream before Reagan came to Washington. Now they are a reality. These rate reductions represent powerful abatements in the tax disincentive to work, save, and invest, and they will no doubt lead to a healthier, more robust economy than we experienced in the late 1970s. All Americans will benefit from greater opportunities and an improved standard of living because of these dramatically lower tax rates.

Of course, the Tax Reform Act of 1986 is not all good news. The capital cost recovery allowances available to industrial firms that invest in plant and equipment are inadequate. The higher cost of capital implicit in this new regime will reduce our capital stock, productivity, and competitiveness. But lower rates on corporations and their shareholders of the magnitude taking effect in 1988 go far toward mitigating this effect.

Most forms of savings mechanisms that reduced the double taxation of savings income implicit in an income tax were scaled back by the 1986 act. In particular, individual retirement accounts and section 401(k) plans were made unavailable to millions of middle-class taxpayers trying to provide a sound basis for their retirement. It is the height of folly to dramatically cut back these plans when we need domestic savings to promote economic growth and when we know full well that within two decades there will be tremendous, probably unbearable, pressure on the social security system.

Perhaps the most disappointing provision of the 1986 act is the substantial increase in the capital gains tax rate—to 33 percent for individuals and 34 percent for corporations. How quickly members of Congress forgot the damage that high capital gains taxes did during the 1970s. In 1978, the individual capital gains rate was cut from 49 percent to 28 percent and further reduced in 1981 to a top rate of 20 percent. I had hoped that with these victories, the deleterious impact of high capital gains rates would be so widely understood that high rates would not be reimposed. But if the 1980s prove anything, it is that legislative victories are fleeting. Higher capital gains tax rates are economically counterproductive and will clearly cut federal revenues. High rates reduce venture capital formation and hinder the ability of small businesses to raise capital. Perhaps most importantly, high capital gains tax rates reduce market liquidity by providing a powerful disincentive to realize gains. This "lock-in effect" of high capital gains rates actually costs the government revenue. Conversely, the capital gains rate reductions of 1978 and 1981 demonstrably increased federal revenues, and most economists that have analyzed the empirical data have come to the conclusion that a reduction in the present rate would increase revenue. However, there is substantial debate over the magnitude of the gain. Cutting the capital gains rate is just about the only pro-growth tax "increase" available to policymakers.

Conclusion

The Reagan administration presided over a radical reduction in the individual and corporate tax rates. This achievement outweighs the fact that certain savings incentives have been scaled back and that the capital cost recovery allowances (including the investment credit) for certain types of property are not adequate. In many respects, what occurred during the Reagan administration's tenure in office has been multiyear revenue-neutral tax reform. Dramatic tax rate cuts in 1981 and 1986 were followed by substantial base-broadening in 1982, 1984, and 1986, minor base-broadening in 1987, and a series of significant but less important payroll tax rate increases agreed to in 1983.

On balance, this revenue-neutral tax reform is pro-growth and will enhance the standard of living and opportunities available for all Americans to enjoy.

PART II

FOREIGN AND DEFENSE POLICY

6. The Reagan Defense Budget and Program: The Buildup That Collapsed

Lawrence J. Korb

In his campaign for the presidency, Ronald Reagan argued over and over that defense spending had to be increased substantially. However, there was some dispute about the exact size of the increase he was advocating. In a paper that accompanied a speech Reagan made in Chicago on September 9, 1980, the former California governor pledged to increase defense spending by 5 percent per year in real terms. However, several Reagan advisers had committed their candidate to increases of 7 to 9 percent.

There was no doubt that defense spending would rise regardless of who won the 1980 election. Indeed, after coming to office pledging to reduce defense spending by $5 billion a year, President Carter had begun to increase defense spending substantially in real terms in his last two years in office. In fact, the 1981 Department of Defense (DoD) budget was $36 billion, or 25 percent, higher than the 1980 defense figure. Moreover, the five-year defense plan presented to Congress in January 1981 by the outgoing president called for 5 percent growth per year over the 1982–86 period. The Carter program would have increased defense's share of the gross national product (GNP) from 5.3 percent to 6.0 percent and its share of the overall federal budget from 22 percent to 28 percent.

In March 1981, the newly elected Reagan administration proposed a five-year defense program calling for expenditures of about $1.5 trillion in the 1982–86 period. Had this program been completely enacted, the real growth rate of defense between 1980 and 1986 would have been over 10 percent per year, and defense's share of GNP would have risen to about 7 percent and its portion of federal budget outlays to 37 percent. Table 6.1 compares the Carter and Reagan programs of 1981.

The Reagan plan was a truly revolutionary proposal. Real defense

Table 6.1
DEFENSE OUTLAWS AND THE ECONOMY, FY 1982–86

Category	1982	1983	1984	1985	1986
	Outlays as Percent of GNP				
Carter plan (January 1981)	5.6	5.7	5.8	5.9	6.0
Reagan plan (March 1981)	6.0	6.4	6.5	6.8	7.0
Actual	5.8	6.2	6.0	6.2	6.4
	Outlays as Percent of Federal Budget				
Carter plan (January 1981)	24.3	25.0	26.1	27.0	27.8
Reagan plan (March 1981)	30.2	32.4	32.4	35.2	36.8
Actual	24.5	25.4	25.9	25.9	26.8

SOURCE: *Budget of the United States Government*, various years.

spending in peacetime had never increased for more than three consecutive years. Peacetime defense spending between 1950 and 1980 had ranged from $180 to $230 billion and averaged about $200 billion (in 1987 dollars). Reagan's March 1981 plan envisioned at least seven years of double-digit increases and would have averaged well over $300 billion per year (in 1987 dollars). Moreover, in real terms, defense spending would have increased to a level higher than the peak period of the Vietnam War.

The Reagan administration did not achieve all of its objectives in the area of defense spending. However, it did quite well. As indicated in Table 6.2, reductions in the budgetary request or topline of DoD were minimal, and defense spending between 1982 and 1986 totaled $1.3 trillion. Between 1980 and 1985, the size of the defense budget doubled, growing from $142.6 billion to $286.8 billion. When inflation is taken into account, the increase over that time was above 50 percent. Similarly DoD's share of GNP increased to 6.4 percent, and its portion of the federal budget rose to almost 27 percent. Most significantly, by the middle of the decade U.S. military procurement expenditures exceeded those of the Soviet Union for the first time since the late 1960s.

The Reagan administration also revolutionized the distribution of the defense dollar. In 1980, operating costs (personnel and operations and maintenance) consumed 68 percent of the defense bud-

Table 6.2

DoD TOPLINE REDUCTIONS, FY 1982–86 (BUDGET AUTHORITY IN $ BILLIONS)

Category	1982	1983	1984	1985	1986	Total 1982–86
Amendment, March 1981	221.8	254.5	288.9	326.2	367.2	1,458.6
Incremental Adjustments to March 1981 Plan						
Sept. 1981 through FY 1985, enacted	−8.0	−15.0	−30.7	−39.4	−42.4	−135.5
FY 1986 Budget (Jan. 1985)	—	—	—	—	−11.1	−11.1
FY 1987 Budget (Jan. 1986)	—	—	—	—	−24.2	−24.2
P.L. 99–177 (Gramm-Rudman-Hollings Act)	—	—	—	—	−11.0	−11.0
Total Adjustments since March 1981	−8.0	−15.0	−30.7	−39.4	−88.8	−181.9
Current Budget	213.8	239.5	258.2	286.8	278.4	1,276.7
Outlay Adjustments since March 1981	−1.9	−16.1	−29.0	−51.9	−77.6	−176.5

get, while funds for investment accounted for only 32 percent. By the end of his first term, the investment share of the Reagan defense budget had risen to almost 50 percent, its highest level in 25 years. Between 1980 and 1985, real budget authority for investment nearly doubled, while operating funds grew by only 25 percent. In his first six years in office, Reagan purchased nearly 3,000 combat aircraft, 3,700 strategic missiles, 200 ships, and about 10,000 tanks.

During the 1984 campaign, defense spending was again an issue. Once again both candidates called for real increases in the size of the defense budget. Former vice president Walter F. Mondale argued that the real increases should amount to about 3 percent, while Reagan once again called for increases in the neighborhood of 5 percent.

In January 1985, Secretary of Defense Caspar W. Weinberger confidently unveiled a five-year defense program calling for expenditures of about $2 trillion over the 1986–90 period. The defense chief envisioned real increases of about 6 percent per year over the second half of this decade. Had this program been enacted, defense spending would have risen from $287 billion in 1985 to $478 billion in 1990.

For all intents and purposes, it looked as if the Reagan Revolution in defense spending would continue into his second administration. However, this was not to be the case. Indeed, rather than increasing in size, the budget began to go down. Congress slashed the 1986 request by 10 percent, and for the first time since the end of the Vietnam War, the defense budget dropped in nominal terms. In real terms, the 1988 budget will probably be about $25 billion, or 8 percent, below the level of 1985. Moreover, as indicated in Table 6.3, the 1986–90 program has already been reduced by some $450 billion, or 25 percent, and DoD's share of GNP will again drop below 6 percent. Ronald Reagan may have the dubious distinction of presiding over the biggest peacetime defense buildup and the biggest defense decline in the nation's history.

However, more importantly, this sudden and unprecedented shift in the direction of defense spending has created chaos in the Pentagon. Neither the president nor his advisers have shown themselves willing to face this new situation. The current five-year plan still assumes that the budget will grow in real terms by about 7 percent per year. If, as is much more likely, the budget stays at

Table 6.3

TRENDS IN DEPARTMENT OF DEFENSE FIVE-YEAR PLANS, FY 1986–90 (BUDGET AUTHORITY IN $ BILLIONS)

Category	1986	1987	1988	1989	1990	Total, 1986–90	Difference from 1989 Request
Administration request, February 1985	314	354	402	439	478	1,986	—
Administration request, February 1986	278	312	332	354	375	1,651	−335
Administration request, January 1987	281	282	303	323	344	1,534	−452
With freeze plus inflation, 1988–90	281	282	295	305	315	1,477	−509

SOURCE: *Budget of the United States Government,* various years.

about its present level, the shortfall will be between $300 and $400 billion.

Until early 1988, the president and his secretaries of defense have dealt with this changed environment in two self-destructive ways. First, they have slowed down or stretched out the multitude of new production lines opened in the "fat" years of the first administration, thus driving up most unit costs dramatically. For example, in the 1988 budget, a single F–14D fighter will cost nearly $70 million. Second, DoD has slashed infrastructure funding while pursuing the next generation of modernization as if the defense budget were still growing significantly. Over the past two years, service research and development has continued its projected growth while, as Table 6.4 indicates, funding for spare parts, ammunition, and support has dropped about 30 percent below its projected levels each year. In 1988, DoD actually requested fewer active-duty military personnel than were authorized in 1987, in spite of the fact that its force structure is increasing. Moreover, Weinberger requested funding for two new carriers in spite of the fact that sufficient funds

Table 6.4

REDUCTIONS IN READINESS- AND SUSTAINABILITY-RELATED ACCOUNTS IN DEFENSE BUDGET, FY 1987 AND FY 1988 ($ MILLIONS)

Category	Actual FY 1986 Budget	Projection for FY 1987: FY 86 Budget	Request for FY 1987: FY 87 Budget[1]	Congressional Appropriation FY 1987	Projection for FY 1988: FY 87 Budget	Request for FY 1988: FY 88 Budget
Army spare parts	2,329.8	3,238.9	1,994.7 −38.4%[1]	1,798.5 −44.5%	2,364.9	1,823.6 −22.9%
Army ammunition and tactical missiles	4,647.8	5,514.7	4,286.4 −22.3%	4,019.0 −27.1%	4,887.6	4,203.0 −14.0%
Selected army support equipment	2,774.3	3,870.5	2,723.1 −29.6%	2,359.7 −39.0%	3,274.3	2,233.5 −31.8%
Navy spare parts	1,733.7	2,909.3	2,355.4 −19.0%	2,135.5 −26.6%	2,365.7	1,980.1 −16.3%
Navy ammunition and tactical missiles	3,952.8	5,050.4	4,006.0 −20.7%	3,447.6 −31.7%	3,784.2	3,250.1 −14.1%
Selected navy support equipment	4,893.7	5,654.1	4,973.1 −12.0%	4,443.3 −21.4%	5,948.9	3,742.6 −37.1%
Air force spare parts	4,603.5	6,980.1	4,235.4 −39.3%	3,700.6 −47.0%	5,204.3	3,458.8 −33.5%
Air force munitions and tactical missiles	2,204.0	3,686.9	2,815.8 −23.6%	1,956.7 −46.9%	2,313.3	1,654.6 −28.5%
Selected air force support equipment	1,139.5	2,061.9	1,059.8 −48.6%	916.6 −55.5%	1,231.1	780.9 −36.6%

SOURCE: Annual Defense Department reports for FY 1986, FY 1987, and FY 1988.
[1] Percentage refers to the difference between what was projected the year before and what was actually requested in the current fiscal year.

do not exist to fully equip the current fleet of carriers with proper numbers of aircraft.

There is a certain irony in all this. If the defense budget is held to zero real growth in 1988 and 1989, average real growth in the Reagan presidency will be about 5 percent per year, exactly the amount pledged by the president in Chicago some seven years ago. However, if present trends continue, DoD could be in worse shape than when the president took over, despite the expenditure of some $2.1 trillion in the 1982–89 period.

How We Got Here

However, the situation is not hopeless. There are certain steps that can be taken to remedy the situation. To understand how to deal with this current crisis, it is necessary to understand how the mess was created. In my view, there are five reasons for the current state of affairs.

First, the Reagan administration ignored the lessons of history. As noted above, the peacetime defense budget prior to 1980 had never increased in real terms for more than three consecutive years. The administration assumed that the real growth that began in the last two years of the Carter administration would continue throughout the eight years of the Reagan presidency and beyond. Since DoD was already into the third year of real increases when Reagan took office, this would have meant at least 10 straight years of real growth, more than three times greater than any previous period in American history.

This lack of sensitivity to the past was compounded by the failure of the Pentagon leadership to adjust in a timely fashion to the deterioration of public support for the defense buildup. Between 1980 and 1982, popular support for increased levels of defense spending dropped from 58 percent to 16 percent. By early 1983, even the Republican leadership in Congress was telling the secretary of defense and the president that Congress would not keep granting large increases in defense authority. Yet, the Pentagon persisted in treating this as a transient phenomenon. As late as 1986, the secretary of defense and the secretary of the navy were still talking publicly about a return to the climate of the early 1980s. As a result of this attitude, no serious planning was done to deal with the new reality and no hard choices were made. Rather, thousands of programs in the DoD budget were reduced slightly, each with the expectation that large increases would resume in the next year.

Moreover, because the civilian leadership in DoD focused its efforts primarily on trying to push spending levels marginally higher, rather than on how to get the military services to make do with less, Congress was forced to assume that role. This is not a job Congress can or should do if we are to have a coherent military strategy. This point can be illustrated by analyzing the manner in which Congress cut $25 billion in the procurement, operation and maintenance, and R&D accounts from the administration's 1987 request. About $9.2 billion, or 37 percent, of the reduction came from pricing and financing adjustments; an additional $8.2 billion, or 33 percent, came from oversight and stretchouts; readiness-related programs absorbed $5.5 billion, or 23 percent, of the cuts; only $1.9 billion, or 7 percent, accounted for programmatic changes.

Second, the Reagan administration failed to pay sufficient attention to what President Eisenhower called the "Great Equation"—that is, that real national security was the sum of economic as well as military strength. By slashing revenues by 5 percent of GNP at the same time that it launched the massive and unprecedented peacetime defense buildup, which added 1 percent of GNP to the defense budget, the Reagan administration guaranteed that the Great Equation would become unbalanced and that a reaction against the defense budget would set in. In his first term in office, Reagan succeeded both in doubling the defense budget and the size of the national deficit. Moreover, by endorsing the Gramm-Rudman-Hollings budget-reduction law in 1985, while refusing to raise taxes, the president and his advisers ensured that the projected levels of defense authority would be slashed drastically for the remainder of his administration.

Third, the level of defense spending was increased too rapidly, particularly in the procurement area. While the 1985 defense budget was 53 percent higher in real terms than the 1980 one, procurement was more than 100 percent higher. The acquisition system simply was not able to absorb that much money that quickly. The problem was compounded by the fact that the management system was decentralized at the same time. Pouring in that much money while loosening control led to the procurement scandals that undermined the confidence of the American people in DoD's leadership and, along with the deficit problem, contributed to the rapid erosion of the defense consensus.

Moreover, as indicated in Table 6.5, defense did not get its money's worth out of the hardware it procured. This table compares the numbers of weapons systems purchased and dollars spent in the Reagan years (1981–87) with the preceding seven years (1974–80). As noted in the table, between 1974 and 1980 DoD purchased 2,765 combat aircraft for about $65 billion (in 1988 dollars). In the Reagan administration, DoD was able to procure about 8 percent more planes but at an additional cost of about $40 billion, or almost 60 percent. The picture is far worse for most of the other types of weapons systems. In the Reagan years, DoD bought 21 percent fewer missiles but paid twice as much; bought the same number of combatant ships but paid half again as much; and bought twice as many tanks but paid four times as much. Although it is true that the major weapons systems of the Reagan years were somewhat more sophisticated than their predecessors, the increase in capability is not commensurate with the cost.

Fourth, the defense buildup was front-loaded in favor of major weapons systems; that is, major weapons systems were procured in inordinate numbers in the early years of the defense buildup. For example, the 1983 defense budget contained a request for two *Nimitz*-class aircraft carriers. When Congress approved this request, DoD and Congress were committed to spending not only $8 billion for the two carriers but an additional $50 billion for the planes and ships that make up the carrier battle groups and for the people, spare parts, and ammunition necessary to make those battle groups militarily effective. As indicated above, the share of the budget devoted to readiness dropped substantially in the 1980–85 period. The expectation was that as these weapons systems came into the force, manpower and support equipment would then be purchased. However, when it was the turn of the readiness accounts to receive their fair share, fiscal austerity had set in and readiness received a smaller share of declining budgets, even though its needs were greater. The austerity problem has been compounded by the "bow wave" situation; that is, funds for readiness and sustainability were routinely pushed to the outyears of the five-year program, even during the first part of the decade.

Table 6.5

DEFENSE WEAPONS SYSTEMS PROCUREMENTS: NUMBERS PURCHASED AND EXPENDITURES, 1974–80 VERSUS 1981–87

Weapons Systems Type	Numbers Purchased			Total Spending ($ Billions[b])		
	1974–1980*	1981–1987	Percent Increase (+)/ Decrease (−)	1974–1980[a]	1981–1987	Percent Increase
Fixed-Wing Aircraft						
Combat	2,765	2,973	+8	64.8	103.3	+59
Airlift	233	276	+18	1.3	11.2	+762
Rotary Aircraft	975	1,748	+79	4.3	17.4	+305
Missiles						
Strategic/TNF	1,405	3,686	+162	10.6	20.9	+97
Tactical	270,470	214,899	−21	14.6	30.8	+110
Ships						
Combatant	91	91	0	47.0	68.8	+46
Other	21	91	333	4.1	4.7	+15
Tanks and Combat Vehicles						
Heavy	4,898	9,747	+99	6.7	20.0	+198
Light	5,298	2,985	−44	1.1	1.1	0
Other	1,504	3,476	+131	1.2	4.2	+250

SOURCE: Congressional Budget Office.
[a]Excludes transition quarter.
[b]Constant 1988 dollars of budget authority.

Fifth, the Reagan buildup was begun before a coherent national security strategy was developed. Neither during the transition period nor in the first year of the Reagan administration was the Basic National Security Policy Document formulated. Indeed, this document was not promulgated until some time in 1982, a year after the Reagan five-year defense program was submitted to Congress. Rather than letting strategy guide budget choices, the situation was reversed. As recounted by former budget director David A. Stockman in *The Triumph of Politics*, budget totals were agreed upon first. The argument was made that in 1981, the military situation was so bad that it did not matter where the money was spent. Force goals and slogans became a substitute for strategy. Rather than strategy, the air was filled with such slogans as "a 600-ship Navy" and "horizontal escalation." As Les Aspin (D–Wisc.), chairman of the House Armed Services Committee, put it, "When the Reagan administration came in, it had lots of initiatives but no strategy"; or as Sam Nunn (D–Ga.), his Senate counterpart, noted, there is no overall strategy: "You have a Navy strategy, an Army strategy, an Air Force strategy, a Marine strategy." It is significant that Secretary Weinberger's first major speech on strategy was not given until the fall of 1985 and that the administration's first detailed exposition of its defense strategy was made in the 1987 posture statement.

What We Need to Do Now

To extricate ourselves from the present dilemma, we must take several actions, which can be broken down into four categories.

First, the administration must accept the fact that our defense program will exist within a constrained fiscal environment for the foreseeable future, certainly for the rest of this decade. Given the deficit situation, there is simply no room for real growth in the defense budget. To assume that the budget will grow significantly is nothing more than institutional self-deception of the worst kind.

Second, our force-structure goals must be scaled back. However desirable a 15-carrier-battle-group–600-ship navy, an 18-active-division army, or a 40-tactical-air-wing air force may be, this large a force structure is simply not affordable without significant real growth in the defense budget. The army and navy would do well to follow the example of the air force, which will hold its force structure at 35 tactical air wings. By the same token, DoD cannot afford to modernize all three legs of the strategic triad while simultaneously undertaking a large strategic defense program, without sacrificing improvements in conventional forces.

Third, development of the next generation of weapons systems must be delayed. Going ahead with such new systems as the ATF and ATA aircraft and LHX and JVX helicopters at the present time will mean that the current generation of weapons systems will have to be purchased in uneconomical quantities. Paying almost $70 million each for an F–14D fighter or nearly $60 million for each EA–6B electronic warfare plane is absurd. Transferring some of the funds from the next generation of weapons to these ongoing production lines will bring down unit costs substantially.

Fourth, marginal programs must be eliminated. Building new naval bases in Staten Island, the Gulf of Mexico, San Francisco, and Everett, Washington, or fixing up the army bases at Fort Drum, New York, and Fairbanks, Alaska, made little sense in an era of expanding budgets. In the current climate, it makes no sense. That money would be better spent buying ammunition for existing ships and divisions. Moreover, a 550-ship, 13-carrier-battle-group navy, or a 16-division army will not tax our current base structure.

Ronald Reagan did not achieve his goal of placing defense spending on a permanent growth path. However, he accomplished a great deal. The quality of military personnel is at an all-time high, the force is well-equipped and well-trained, and the Soviets are back at the bargaining table. It would be a shame to jeopardize these real achievements by not facing the current fiscal situation.[1]

[1]In early 1988, newly appointed Secretary of Defense Frank C. Carlucci began to face up to this situation by cancelling some programs and reducing force structure.

7. Requiem for the Reagan Doctrine

Christopher Layne

It was predictable that the Reagan Doctrine would lead the administration into a political and moral morass. There was an ironic symmetry in the fact that Reagan's presidency, like Jimmy Carter's, collapsed because of its foreign policy failures (and there was a further irony in that the Ayatollah Khomeini helped bring down two U.S. presidents). After all, Ronald Reagan's 1980 victory rested in large measure on his pledge to arrest America's declining prestige and to conduct a tough-minded foreign policy backed by a restored consensus. Yet, when the Iran-contra scandal broke—severely crippling Reagan's presidency two years before his term expired—friends and adversaries alike regarded the United States not only as weak but as hypocritical as well. It was apparent that in its own way, the administration's grasp of world politics was as flawed as the Carter administration's. Finally, the Iran-contra hearings highlighted the administration's failure to rebuild the postwar foreign policy consensus that the Vietnam War had shattered.

Far more than a set of specific policy prescriptions, the Reagan Doctrine provided the intellectual framework—the Weltanschauung—that shaped the administration's external policies. However, events proved the Reagan Doctrine was an unsuitable basis for a viable post-Vietnam foreign policy because (1) it failed to mobilize sustained support for U.S. engagement abroad, (2) it could not be implemented without circumventing established constitutional and political norms, and (3) it was oblivious to the shifting balance of world forces that marked the end of America's postwar hegemony. Bipolarity was gradually giving way to a more plural world order in which political and economic power was much more widely diffused than it had been in the 1945–65 period.

Truman, Carter, and Reagan

What was the Reagan Doctrine? In what ways was it consistent with, or different from, the policies of other postwar administrations? What went wrong?

The answers to these questions hinge in part on events that transpired before the Reagan administration took office. In 1976, an America disillusioned by Vietnam and Watergate sent Jimmy Carter to the White House. He brought with him a new foreign policy elite. Relatively young, with roots in the Democratic party's McGovern wing, the elite's view of the world was far different from that of the postwar foreign policy establishment that had been broken by Vietnam.

Carterism was the liberals' response to the costs of U.S. intervention abroad and reflected their determination never to pay such a price again. The United States, Carter believed, was a status quo power that needed to get on the right side of change by promoting human rights and supporting progressive movements that would deal with the root cause of Third World revolutions. Because Third World conflicts were said to have indigenous causes and were not part of the East-West struggle, U.S. military power would be ineffective in resolving them. The way to deal with such problems was to act in concert with others to seek diplomatic solutions and provide economic aid.

Carterism was not entirely without some useful insights, but it was neither a viable nor a politically acceptable foreign policy. It overlooked Moscow's imperial ambitions, which were not the sole cause of regional conflicts, to be sure, but certainly a relevant factor. Although vital U.S. interests were seldom at stake in Third World disputes, neither U.S. policymakers (including, ultimately, Carter himself) nor the public were willing to hold to Carterism's laissez-faire approach in the face of the worldwide expansion of Soviet power and influence. The Iranian revolution undermined Carterism's critical assumption that the forces of change could be managed and that change of a non-Marxist character would always be advantageous to the United States. Repeated crises reminded the United States that it indeed had national interests that could not always, or even often, be subordinated to the requirements of multilateral diplomacy and alliance solidarity.

Echoing neoconservative calls for rearmament, revitalization of containment, and renewed vigilance, Reagan's 1980 campaign caught the mood of an "assertive America" fed up with the Vietnam syndrome (which all but ruled out the use of military force to defend U.S. interests abroad) and disillusioned by the string of foreign policy setbacks from Angola to "Desert One" (the abortive 1980 attempt to rescue the U.S. hostages held by Iran). The election gave Reagan a clear mandate to halt the erosion of U.S. military power and self-respect that had occurred during the 1970s. Beyond that, however, it was unclear how far the administration's mandate extended or what the scope of its foreign policy would be.

At the close of the 1970s, Robert W. Tucker observed that Washington would have to choose between "either a policy of a resurgent America intent once again on containing Soviet influence—as well as the expansion of communism generally—or a policy of moderate containment."[1] Both courses entailed risks. Moderate containment might fail to secure important U.S. interests and would require Washington's adjustment to America's declining global influence. Moreover, a more circumscribed approach would break sharply with Washington's postwar commitment to building a stable world order reflecting U.S. liberal democratic values. On the other hand, serious questions arose about America's ability to sustain a more ambitious policy. Global containment in the 1980s—essentially a return to the Truman Doctrine—would be a far different affair from what it had been in the 1947–65 period. In 1981, the late Robert E. Osgood pointed out that the new administration faced "unprecedented constraints on the effective exercise of American power in its economic, diplomatic and military dimensions."[2] The loss of strategic nuclear superiority, the Soviet Union's emergence as a global power, and the relative decline of U.S. economic power had transformed the geopolitical situation to the disadvantage of the United States.

Neoconservatives quickly gained the leading role in shaping and articulating the Reagan administration's foreign policy. Betraying no concern about these adverse international systemic trends—and no post-Vietnam ambivalence about America's world role—neo-

[1]Robert W. Tucker, "The Purpose of American Power," *Foreign Affairs* 59, no. 2 (Winter 1981): 265.

[2]Robert E. Osgood, "The Revitalization of Containment," *Foreign Affairs* 60, no. 3 (1982): 466.

conservatives pushed hard and successfully for a return to global containment, rechristened as the Reagan Doctrine.

The Reagan Doctrine has never been authoritatively defined, but its content can be inferred from various statements made by President Reagan and Secretary of State George Shultz and the writings of such neoconservative foreign policy theorists as Charles Krauthammer, Irving Kristol, and Norman Podhoretz. As commonly understood, the Reagan Doctrine committed the United States to resisting Soviet and Soviet-supported aggression wherever it arose, to building U.S.-style democracies in Third World countries, and to rolling back communism by aiding anticommunist insurgencies. The Reagan Doctrine sought to create an ideologically congenial world and assumed that U.S. security required nothing less. In some quarters, moreover, the doctrine's objectives were framed more expansively to include bringing about the Soviet empire's breakup and, ultimately, the collapse of the Soviet state itself by inflicting a series of what Kristol called "small defeats" on Moscow in the Third World (presumably undermining the Soviet regime's domestic legitimacy), engaging the Kremlin in a high-tech arms race, and pressuring the Soviet Union economically.

In its aspirations, underlying assumptions, and rhetoric, the Reagan Doctrine was strikingly similar to the post–World War II Truman Doctrine. This was unsurprising because the Reagan Doctrine's intellectual architects were the rightful political heirs of the cold war liberalism championed by Democratic presidents Harry S. Truman, John F. Kennedy, and Lyndon B. Johnson and by Sens. Hubert H. Humphrey and Henry M. Jackson. Vietnam transformed cold war liberals into outcasts in their own party and metamorphosed them into what may be termed "neo"-conservatives. Although remaining nominal Democrats (in most instances), they voted for Ronald Reagan in 1980 and 1984, served in his administration, and were vigorous intellectual advocates of its policies.

The Truman Doctrine was based on the Wilsonian premise that the world would be safer and better if it adopted America's political values and structures and on the ostensible geopolitical "lesson" of Munich—that totalitarian states are insatiably aggressive, that peace is indivisible, that aggression must be resisted everywhere, and that failure to do so is foolhardy appeasement. When fused, these assumptions produced a foreign policy that committed the United

States to a messianic global crusade against communism. In a September 1946 memorandum to Truman, presidential adviser Clark Clifford recommended that "the United States should support and assist *all* democratic countries which are in *any way* menaced by the Soviet Union" and underscored that U.S. policies should be "global in scope."[3] Heeding Clifford's advice, the president's March 1947 Truman Doctrine speech declared that "it must be the policy of the United States to support free peoples who are resisting subjugation by armed minorities or by outside pressures" and that "we must assist free peoples to work out their destinies in their own way." Cold war liberalism found perhaps its clearest expression in NSC-68—the critically important national security study prepared by the Truman administration in early 1950. This document depicted the Soviet-U.S. competition as a "basic conflict between the idea of freedom under a government of laws, and the idea of slavery under a grim oligarchy of the Kremlin." In this worldwide ideological struggle, the United States could not afford to be vanquished anywhere because "the assault on free institutions is worldwide and a defeat anywhere *is a defeat everywhere.*"[4]

In its official statements, the Reagan administration simply reprised familiar tunes from the cold war era. Tracking Truman's 1947 remarks, President Reagan stated, in his 1985 State-of-the-Union speech, "We must stand by our democratic allies. And we must not break faith with those who are risking their lives—on every continent, from Afghanistan to Nicaragua—to defy Soviet-supported aggression and secure rights which have been ours from birth." And in his February 1985 speech to San Francisco's Commonwealth Club, Shultz proclaimed the existence of a worldwide "democratic revolution" that American had to support in "word and deed" by standing for "freedom and democracy not only for ourselves but for others."[5] These remarks elaborated upon themes Shultz had enunciated the previous year to the Trilateral Commission. There,

[3]"American Relations with the Soviet Union: A Report to the President by the Special Counsel to the President," in *Containment: Documents on American Policy and Strategy, 1945-1950*, ed. Thomas H. Etzold and John Lewis Gaddis (New York: Columbia University Press, 1978), pp. 67, 70 (emphasis added).

[4]Quoted in Etzold and Gaddis, pp. 387, 389 (emphasis added).

[5]George Shultz, "America and the Struggle for Freedom," address before the Commonwealth Club of California, San Francisco, February 22, 1985.

he had said that the world was a place of great instability and danger and "our security, and our alliances can be affected by threats to security in many parts of the world; and the fate of our fellow human beings will always impinge on our moral consciousness."[6] Although not the world's policeman, the United States was, Shultz said, the free world's strongest power and therefore, "the preservation of our values, our principles, and our hopes for a better world rests in a great measure, inevitably, on our shoulders."

The Truman Doctrine left a doubtful inheritance to the Reagan administration. Both doctrines defined U.S. interests in ideological rather than tangible terms, committing the United States to opposing communism and defending democracy everywhere. This was the logical implication of a foreign policy that held other nations to be threats to U.S. security because of their internal political structures rather than their external policies. Under the two doctrines, by definition, any failure of U.S. resolve, or any curtailment of U.S. commitments, could undermine U.S. security. As Hans Morgenthau wrote in 1951, "The Truman Doctrine transformed a concrete interest of the United States in a geographically defined part of the world [Greece and Turkey] into a moral principle of worldwide validity, to be applied regardless of the limits of American interest and power."[7]

The Reagan Doctrine simply perpetuated this inability to distinguish between vital and peripheral interests. Moreover, both doctrines begged a number of critical questions. For example, were U.S. interests menaced by communist ideology itself or only by the expansion of Soviet political and military power? (After all, Yugoslavia's 1948 break with Moscow and the later Sino-Soviet split showed that nationalism could impel even communist states to follow anti-Soviet foreign policies). Could U.S.-style democracy be successfully transplanted to the Third World, and at what cost? How could an expansive definition of U.S. national interests be reconciled with the imperative of balancing resources and commitments, thereby ensuring that excessive security burdens would not damage the economy? Finally, what effect would a crusading, anti-

[6]George Shultz, "Power and Diplomacy in the 1980s," address before the Trilateral Commission, April 3, 1984.

[7]Hans Morgenthau, *In Defence of the National Interest* (New York: Alfred A. Knopf, 1951), p. 116.

communist foreign policy have on America's domestic political structures and its constitutional processes?

How the Reagan Doctrine Backfired

In 1980, Americans opted for a policy of strength but, in an apparent paradox, they retained their skepticism about U.S. involvement overseas. As public opinion analyst William Schneider observed in 1984, Americans were "suspicious of international involvements of any kind . . . [and] predisposed against U.S. involvement in other countries' affairs unless national interests or national security [was] at stake."[8] For the architects of the Reagan Doctrine its emphasis on the ideological component of the Soviet-U.S. rivalry was a means of overcoming the public's recalcitrance and of mobilizing support for a reinvigorated global containment policy. Because Americans would not make the material or psychological sacrifices required by the Reagan Doctrine merely to preserve the balance of power, it was necessary, Norman Podhoretz wrote, to infuse the superpower rivalry with a "moral and political dimension for which sacrifices could be intelligently demanded by government and willingly made by the people."[9]

It is easy to see why neoconservatives believed that embarking on an ideological crusade would arouse the nation's fervor and persuade it to accept the Reagan Doctrine's domestic political and economic costs. Here again, the doctrine returned to its Truman Doctrine roots. After all, in 1947 Senate Foreign Relations Committee chairman Arthur Vandenberg (R–Mich.) told Under Secretary of State Dean Acheson that the way to gain support for the Truman Doctrine was "to scare the hell out of the American people" about the communist threat.[10] Throughout the cold war—until Vietnam—American leaders won backing for global containment by following Vandenberg's advice. In the 1980s, however, Americans did not answer the Reagan Doctrine's call to battle. Neoconservatives could resurrect the rhetorical framework of global containment, but they could not turn the clock back to 1950 and recreate the cold war

[8]William Schneider, "Public Opinion," in *The Making of America's Soviet Policy*, ed. Joseph S. Nye, Jr. (New Haven: Yale University Press, 1984).

[9]Norman Podhoretz, "The Future Danger," *Commentary*, April 1981.

[10]Quoted in Walter Isaacson and Evan Thomas, *The Wise Men: Six Friends and the World They Made* (New York: Simon and Schuster, 1986), p. 395.

101

mindset. Too much water had passed under the foreign policy bridge for that.

The Reagan Doctrine's strident rhetoric backfired and made Americans less, not more, willing to support an assertive policy abroad. The doctrine raised the twin fears of a possible superpower confrontation and indiscriminate U.S. involvement in foreign conflicts where U.S. vital interests were not at stake. Its overblown rhetoric—its call for a "worldwide democratic revolution"—made Americans skeptical rather than supportive. In terms of Nicaragua, for example, only a handful of naive liberals doubted that the Sandinistas were very bad; but most Americans found it hard to believe the contras were much better—much less that they were the "moral equivalent" of our own Founding Fathers.

Around the world, the Reagan doctrine seemed to require the United States to choose between equally unsavory groups whose brutality was distinguishable only by whether it was used to hold power or seize it. It was hard to see how such choices advanced democratic principles. It also was difficult to accept the Reagan Doctrine's claims. Thus, although Jonas Savimbi's UNITA forces in Angola and Afghanistan's Islamic fundamentalist rebels might have usefully tied down Soviet and Soviet proxy forces, it was clear that they were not fighting for democracy. And there was no credibility in a global democratic revolution whose supporters apologized for Chile, South Africa, and—nearly to the end—the Marcos-ruled Philippines.

Anticommunism had successfully mobilized public support during the cold war years, when the United States was still adjusting to its newly inherited global responsibilities. By the 1980s, however, Americans had a more realistic understanding of the world and saw international politics in shades of gray rather than black and white. Vietnam, Lebanon, Afghanistan, the Persian Gulf conflict, and other upheavals suggested that Third World nationalism had reduced both superpowers' ability to influence the outcome of regional conflicts. Understanding that the United States lacked the psychological and material resources to remake the world in its own image, Americans had rightfully learned to be wary when summoned by their leaders to an ideological crusade to make the world safe for democracy. Unsurprisingly, then, the Reagan Doctrine's militant anticommunism had little resonance with public opinion. Indeed, in 1982—when the mood of assertive America supposedly was at its peak—a Potomac Associates survey found that "anticommunism as a national slogan or marching theme is increasingly on the wane, despite the Reagan Administration's attempts to emphasize it."[11] Perhaps, as the Reagan Doctrine's backers claimed, Americans lacked the stomach for spending the nation's blood and treasure merely to uphold the balance of power. But Vietnam had conclusively demonstrated their unwillingness to make such expenditures for the sake of ideology alone. The Reagan Doctrine had ignored a basic lesson of American history: The domestic consensus needed to sustain an actively engaged foreign policy formed only when Americans believed that ideological aspirations and national security concerns coincided. The Reagan Doctrine failed to give Americans a convincing answer to the crucial question of why the United States should become involved in regional disputes that were, at best, only peripherally connected to its national security.

In the final analysis, the Reagan Doctrine ran counter to Americans' desire for peace, their wise and instinctive aversion to overseas adventures, and—most painfully and paradoxically for the doctrine's architects—to their most cherished democratic values. The Iran-contra debacle made this obvious.

Despite having a meritorious case against a Sandinista regime that even a prudently restrained United States could not allow to become a Soviet military outpost, the administration was unable to rally public support for the contras' cause and was able to gain only sporadic and tenuous congressional backing for its Central American policy. The Iran-contra affair happened because the Reagan Doctrine's backers were not willing to live with the outcome of the democratic process.

The affair raised a basic issue: Could a democracy be a superpower without compromising its domestic political principles? This was not the first time this issue had surfaced during U.S. history. There had always been a sharp split between those who believed the cause of liberty was advanced by the pursuit of world power and those who believed that a foreign policy of restraint was essential to preserving constitutional government at home. Although the

[11]Daniel Yankelovich, "New Rules in American Life: Searching for Self-Fulfillment in a World Turned Upside Down," *Psychology Today*, April 1981, pp. 35–91.

worst fears of the advocates of restraint had not been realized, Vietnam, Watergate, and the Iran-contra affair demonstrated that their concerns were not unfounded.

The Iran-contra affair was not an aberration. It was a scandal waiting to happen because the Reagan Doctrine's underlying ideological ethos led its adherents to believe they had a monopoly on defining the "true" national interest. They viewed world politics as a Manichaean struggle between democracy and communism and thought that the United States was at war in all but name. To prevail, the executive branch needed to be free to conduct diplomacy and covert actions unhampered by congressional or public oversight. A policy of ultimate ends justified the use of any means, and the doctrine's architects believed they were justified in arrogating to themselves the right to ignore political and legal norms in pursuit of what were for them morally transcendent objectives. The crusade against communism was deemed to be too vital to be constrained by such abstract notions as the popular will or constitutional propriety.

No principle has ever existed in American political discourse that permits the governing elite to claim openly that it knows better than the people what is best for the country. But this was precisely what the Reagan Doctrine's advocates believed—although they were foreclosed from saying so. Instead, they resorted to a series of disingenuous arguments to shield the doctrine from attack. Some of these had especially dangerous implications for the U.S. system of government.

When pressed, the Reagan Doctrine's intellectual apologists (and those like Rear Admiral John Poindexter and Lt. Col. Oliver North, who implemented it) did not deny that the administration had ignored legal and constitutional norms and had lied to Congress and the American people in the Iran-contra affair. On the contrary, they tried to justify their actions by invoking the traditional defense of all who purport to be clear-eyed "realists": The end justifies the means. Impatient with constitutional constraints, the Reagan Doctrine's defenders muttered darkly about an alleged conflict between the country's global responsibilities and its democratic system. They embraced Alexis de Tocqueville's indictment that "foreign policies demand scarcely any of those qualities which are peculiar to democracy [and] require, on the contrary, the perfect use of almost all those in which it is deficient."[12]

Tocqueville's observation could not simply be dismissed. The United States does not exist in isolation; it is a great power in an anarchic international system and, like all nations, lives in the shadow of the perennial security dilemma. Potentially, American freedom can be dramatically affected by outside events, and there is a point at which the external environment becomes so threatening that foreign policy must take priority over domestic policy. Thus, in 1940–41 President Franklin D. Roosevelt was justified in acting without congressional or public approval to make the United States a de facto belligerent; a Nazi victory would have posed a clear and present danger to U.S. security. But those who would make foreign policy paramount bear a heavy burden of proof. Only an extraordinarily compelling end justifies a foreign policy whose means require that established political and constitutional processes be circumvented.

The Reagan Doctrine's backers were never able to sustain this burden of proof. In large measure this is because of the fundamental misperception of America's geostrategic relationship to external events. Most great powers in history have had little choice about either the objectives or the means of their foreign policies. The geographical proximity of threatening rivals, a geopolitical reality for Europe's great powers, had necessarily defined security as their overriding purpose and forced them to subordinate domestic objectives to the imperative of safety from external attack. The United States, however, has seldom been compelled to subordinate domestic concerns to its foreign policy goals because of its relative immunity to external danger. The United States has built on its geographical advantage, maintaining invulnerability through nuclear weapons and superior military and economic capabilities.

In today's world, few events abroad affect the core security of the United States. The nation cannot be indifferent to overseas developments, but it can afford to react deliberately to them; this is a luxury denied to less powerful and less fortunate states. Yet, the Reagan Doctrine's obsessive concern with communist ideology

---

[12]Alexis de Tocqueville, *Democracy in America* (New York: Vintage Books, 1964).

(something quite different from Soviet power) led its adherents to consciously choose a foreign policy that undermined America's own political institutions—notwithstanding their recognition that U.S. security was not tangibly threatened.

The Iran-contra scandal was a pointed reminder that Americans should treat with suspicion arguments that "national security" justifies an executive's end run around Congress and the Constitution. In its combination of Bismarck's cynicism and Wilson's self-righteous zeal, the Reagan Doctrine was a prescription for political and moral disaster. The neoconservatives' blend of an asserted hard-edged "realism" with a messianic commitment to defeating communism everywhere with whatever means resulted in a dangerous brew.

Ideologically driven foreign policies such as the Reagan Doctrine have serious effects on domestic institutions. They instill an end-justifies-the-means mentality in policymakers that causes them to place their personal convictions above their constitutional responsibilities. Such policies also disturb the considered allocation of power between branches of the government and encourage an intolerance that coarsens the quality of political discourse. Moralistic, crusading foreign policies foster in decisionmakers a hubris that gives rise to such disasters as Watergate and the Iran-contra scandal. There is a sad and bitter irony in a foreign policy that seeks, as did the Reagan Doctrine, to promote democracy abroad by subverting it at home.

Strategic Overextension

Beyond its adverse effect on democratic values, the Reagan Doctrine contributed to worsening the United States' strategic and economic overextension. It was yet another of the doctrine's paradoxes that a policy premised on restoring U.S. power in fact contributed to accelerating the nation's geopolitical decline.

As the Reagan administration drew to a close, the signs of economic distress stemming from overcommitment were plainly visible. Massive trade and budget deficits threatened to confront the next administration with a Hobson's choice between high taxes or high inflation. In a very short time, the United States had gone from being the world's leading creditor to being its leading debtor. It's share of total world manufacturing output had fallen from 50 percent in 1945 to 31.5 percent in 1980 and was projected to drop to 20 percent by the end of the century. Apart from its quantifiable direct costs (such as the nearly 60 percent of the defense budget being consumed by the U.S. commitment to NATO), the nation's superpower role had hidden serious costs that helped put the United States at a disadvantage in the global economy. While American capital and technology were diverted from the private to the military sector, Western Europe and Japan took advantage of U.S. security guarantees by enhancing their international competitiveness with resources that otherwise would have been spent on defense. Unsurprisingly, there appears to be a significant adverse correlation between high military spending and national productivity gains. In 1983, for example, Japan devoted 1 percent of its GNP to defense; between 1973 and 1983, its national economic productivity improved 2.8 percent. The comparable figures were 3.4 percent and 2.3 percent for West Germany, 4.2 percent and 2.2 percent for France, and 6.9 percent and 0.3 percent for the United States.[13]

Contrary to its supporters' assertions, the Reagan Doctrine was not a cheap means of countering communism. It ruled out devolving security responsibilities to others and indeed increased U.S. commitments (notably in Central America and the Persian Gulf) at a time when a strategically and economically overextended United States ought to have been looking for ways to reduce them. The best illustration of the Reagan Doctrine's likely ultimate costs was the fact that notwithstanding the administration's seven-year buildup, various studies indicated that the gap between U.S. power and U.S. strategic responsibilities had actually grown worse during the Reagan years. Unless this gap was closed, the United States risked possible political embarrassments or military setbacks abroad. By trying to close the power/interests gap through its own efforts, however, the United States risked crippling its increasingly fragile economy—the ultimate foundation of its national power. Unlike real conservatives, the administration's neoconservatives failed to recognize that achieving a harmony between U.S. ambitions and U.S. resources was a moral as well as strategic imperative; states

[13]Rick Atkinson and Fred Hiatt, "The Hidden Costs of the Defense Buildup," *Washington Post National Weekly Edition*, December 16, 1986, p. 10.

that tolerate a persistent imbalance between the ends and means of policy inevitably run the risk of national ruin.

The Reagan Doctrine Balance Sheet

The Reagan years were not without some real foreign policy successes. The Reagan administration did restore the national pride and self-confidence that had been damaged by Vietnam and the 1979–80 Iran hostage crisis, and it also halted the adverse shift in the global balance of forces that occurred during the 1970s. It rightly emphasized that arms control was a largely symbolic issue and not the real centerpiece of Soviet-U.S. relations. At the same time, coupled with the Strategic Defense Initiative, the Reykjavik summit meeting, and the "double zero" arms accord with Moscow (removing from Europe the superpowers' intermediate and short-range nuclear forces) was an implicit acknowledgment that American strategists had finally recognized that extended deterrence could not be credible in an age of nuclear parity. And, whatever its shortcomings, Reagan's Central American policy had the unquestionable merit of reminding Americans that vital U.S. interests would be affected if Nicaragua became a Soviet satellite.

Notwithstanding these pluses, history's overall verdict on the Reagan administration's foreign policy seemed destined to be largely negative. The administration's successes were incomplete and contained the seeds of their own undoing. For example, the short-term benefits of the administration's military buildup had to be set off against the long-term damage that its strategic and budgetary policies inflicted on the economy. And although the administration understood that an obsessive focus on arms control anesthetized Americans (and West Europeans) in terms of the Soviet threat, it failed to offer a politically salable alternative. The administration's attempts to shift the superpower agenda from arms control to regional conflicts and human rights did not work because these issues, while not unimportant, were essentially peripheral to the central aspects of Soviet-U.S. competition.

Furthermore, where an opportunity did exist to change the focus from arms control to more substantive issues, the Reagan administration appeared to miss an important opening to make political and diplomatic progress in Europe. There, generational change in the Kremlin, intriguing hints of new flexibility in Soviet policies, and shifts in European attitudes all suggested the time was ripe for Washington to link superpower military disengagement to a political solution to Europe's division. But the administration's militant ideological bent blinded it to this possibility; instead, it remained wedded to the cold war objectives of "rollback" and "liberation." The unfortunate upshot of this rigidity was to leave with Soviet leader Mikhail Gorbachev the initiative in the political struggle to shape West European public opinion. Similarly, Reykjavik and double zero raised issues that cut to the heart of NATO's strategy, which indeed implicated the alliance's very raison d'être. Yet, the administration made no attempt to initiate the long-overdue restructuring of Atlantic relations that would relieve the United States of the disproportionate share of NATO's strategic risks and economic burdens that it has shouldered for the past four decades.

The failure of the administration's foreign policy was dramatically underscored in Central America. There, it had a compelling geopolitical case to make for its Nicaraguan policy. After all, even the administration's liberal critics acknowledged that vital U.S. security interests required that the Soviets not be permitted to establish military bases in, or provide advanced weapons to, Nicaragua and that the Sandinistas not be allowed to export their revolution abroad.

But this was not the case the administration took to the nation. For the Reagan Doctrine's neoconservative architects—and for Ronald Reagan himself—Nicaragua's Sandinista government was an existential ideological threat. They were more concerned with Nicaragua's domestic political structure than with its foreign policy; they believed Washington could not tolerate a Marxist regime in Managua. For them, the objective of U.S. Central American policy was never in doubt: The Sandinistas had to be removed from power.

Neither Congress nor the American people endorsed these ambitious ideological objectives. In part, this was because of the obvious gap between the administration's professed ends and the chosen instrument of its policy. Simply put, hardly anyone believed the contras could overthrow the Sandinistas; full-scale U.S. military intervention ultimately would be required to achieve that goal. And therein lay the problem. Americans had no enthusiasm for going to war to change Nicaragua's internal political system. Here, the Reagan Doctrine's crusading rhetoric proved self-defeating. Instead of focusing on Nicaragua's special importance because of U.S. geopolitical and historical regional interests, the administration presented its Central American policy as the centerpiece of the global crusade against communism. Americans had not forgotten Vietnam, and the Reagan Doctrine's rationale made Nicaragua look like the first step down the slippery slope to a series of U.S. involvements in Third World quagmires.

The administration's failure to adopt a Nicaragua policy with limited and realistic objectives had baleful consequences. The Central American governments and congressional leadership outmaneuvered the administration and filled the policy vacuum. The resulting Central American peace package did not take account of U.S. security concerns and rested on the dubious premise that the Sandinistas would risk their hard-won political position by democratizing Nicaragua. As the Reagan administration entered its final year, it was unclear whether Washington's Central American policy could be salvaged. The only possibility for doing so was to adopt a policy that would commit the United States to using force, if necessary, both to prevent the Soviets from establishing a military outpost in Central America and to enforce an appropriate regional peace treaty—one exchanging U.S. noninterference in Nicaragua's internal affairs for the Sandinistas' agreement not to subvert their neighbors.

A Foreign Policy for the Future

Ultimately, the transcendent significance of the Reagan administration may simply be that eight more years had passed without the development of a post-Vietnam foreign policy consensus. As it had been for some 15 years, the U.S. foreign policy debate was still dominated by two badly discredited paradigms: the Vietnam syndrome and the Munich analogy. On the eve of the 1988 presidential primary season, political discourse remained polarized between those who believed the United States is omnipotent and obliged to oppose communist aggression everywhere and those who believed the United States should not use force anywhere abroad. At least as far as foreign policy was concerned, the political center that Vietnam had destroyed had yet to be rebuilt.

There was an urgent need for a new foreign policy synthesis. The halcyon days of U.S. hegemony—when it seemed that the United States could pursue all its international objectives without imme-

110

diate sacrifice or adverse long-term economic consequences—were gone forever. The nation was undergoing a difficult transition from the postwar to a posthegemonic world. Yet, the Reagan administration acted as if it could turn the clock back to the 1950s, when America was at the zenith of its power. It did not understand that the end of U.S. hegemony was brought about by complex, objective geopolitical factors; it was not something that could be reversed merely by an assertion of national will or by stirring—but hollow—references to "morning in America." The administration had not come to grips with the fundamental paradox of postwar U.S. foreign policy: America's globalist aspirations had the perverse effect of undercutting the very foundations of national power that had enabled Washington to pursue a globalist foreign policy in the first place. Like previous imperial powers in history, the United States had reached a critical point where its world-order aspirations were no longer compatible with its national interests.

By following a foreign policy that further overstretched U.S. resources, the Reagan administration left a difficult legacy to its successors. The next administration inevitably would have to face the difficult problems involved in beginning an orderly strategic retrenchment. Although formidable, this process would complete America's postwar foreign policy agenda. After World War II, Washington had actively encouraged the diffusion of world economic power in the expectation that it would eventually result in a parallel diffusion of military power, thereby relieving the United States of many of containment's burdens.

It was somewhat surprising that the Reagan administration itself did not begin the process of strategic readjustment. Its failure to do so showed just how far its foreign policy had departed from traditional Republican concepts. After all, traditional conservatives such as President Dwight D. Eisenhower and Sen. Robert A. Taft (R–Ohio) had been deeply concerned about the strains a globalist foreign policy would place on the nation's economy. And President Richard M. Nixon and Secretary of State Henry A. Kissinger had been acutely aware of America's strategic overcommitment. They had moved, somewhat tentatively, to resolve the problem by devolving security responsibilities to U.S. security partners (the "Nixon Doctrine") are erecting a more multipolar world political structure (the "pentagonal balance of power").

For a moment, in November 1984, it appeared that the Reagan administration had finally come to realize the increasing constraints on U.S. foreign policy. In a widely discussed speech, Defense Secretary Caspar W. Weinberger stated that the United States could no longer afford to defend the Western world unilaterally and outlined a rigorous set of guidelines that, if followed, would have sharply curtailed U.S. involvement in the Third World. But the moment passed. Administration policy remained that the United States should contribute more, not less, to its partners' security, and there was no drawing back from Third World commitments. By mid-1987, it was apparent that little remained of the Weinberger Doctrine; it had sunk beneath the waves of the Persian Gulf. There, the United States found itself enmeshed in a violent Third World upheaval—stemming from religious fundamentalism and nationalism—for the primary purpose of defending Western Europe's and Japan's oil.

As the United States prepared to enter the 1990s, it fell to the successor generation—the first group of Americans in this century to have experienced obvious constraints on U.S. power in world politics—to formulate a new foreign policy synthesis. Theirs would be a policy of realism, not isolation; of restraint, not withdrawal. It would reflect an appreciation of both the possibilities and the limits of power and be based on a balance between resources and commitments. It would be a policy that would protect the integrity of America's democratic institutions, preserve national strength, and husband resources and expend them wisely. Such a policy would recognize that the world is not infinitely malleable and that it is beyond America's power to impose order on a recalcitrant world. The attempt to do so can lead only to exhaustion, dangerous overextension, and lasting damage to the fabric of American society.

8. Two Cheers for SDI

Ted Galen Carpenter

Ronald Reagan forever transformed the terms of debate concerning nuclear strategy in his televised address to the American people on March 23, 1983. The president proposed tearing down the old strategic edifice of mutual assured destruction (MAD) and erecting a defensive shield against ballistic missiles. He did nothing less than communicate a vision of liberating the American people—and ultimately, all of humanity—from the specter of nuclear annihilation. Creating a system that could protect civilian populations, Reagan stated subsequently, "would render nuclear weapons obsolete."[1]

Inadequacies of the SDI Debate

The president's speech launched a wide-ranging and frequently emotional debate about the merits and drawbacks of a missile defense system. Often the jargon used by participants reveals their position on the issues even before one has an opportunity to examine substantive arguments. So it was that Reagan and his supporters promptly termed the proposal America's Strategic Defense Initiative (SDI), and since then have often employed the laudatory term "peace shield." Opponents, virtually without exception, refer to the initiative derisively as Star Wars, implying both that it is based on fantasy and that it would mean a dangerous militarization of space.

Thus far, the debate has generated far more heat than light. Moreover, it has largely focused on issues that, while interesting and important, are decidedly secondary.

Critics habitually stress two themes. First, they contend that a system to protect population centers from incoming missiles is not

[1]Inaugural address, January 21, 1985, *Weekly Compilation of Presidential Documents* 21, no. 4, p. 69.

technologically feasible, and that the mere pursuit of such a chimera could waste more than a trillion dollars. Second, they argue that the development and deployment of a missile defense system could dangerously destabilize the existing nuclear balance. An anti-ballistic missile (ABM) system would not only extend the arms race into space, but would impel the Soviet Union to develop counter-measures, most notably an expansion of its offensive missile forces to overwhelm any defensive shield. Consequently, Star Wars would increase, not reduce, the danger of nuclear war.[2]

Proponents of SDI respond, with some justification, that those two criticisms are contradictory. Why, they ask, would the Kremlin expend resources to counter a system that was inherently unwork-able? They also note that the Soviet Union has been vigorously pursuing its own ABM program for years, apparently under the assumption that an effective defense is both technologically and economically feasible. SDI proponents also wonder why critics rarely consider the ambitious Soviet program provocative and destabilizing.

Those are all pertinent points, but the pro-SDI case has its share of ambiguities and inconsistencies. The most serious is a tendency to define SDI at various times as (1) a comprehensive system to protect America's population centers, or (2) a more limited device to protect the nation's land-based intercontinental ballistic missiles (ICBMs). President Reagan has generally stressed the former vision; his subordinates, especially Pentagon spokesmen, typically empha-size the latter one.

That discrepancy highlights a major deficiency in the national debate thus far concerning SDI. The administration has never seemed entirely clear about the fundamental purpose of a missile defense system. Even worse, only superficial consideration is given to how such a dramatic change in the dynamics of nuclear strategy might affect the options available to the makers of U.S. foreign policy. Most critics of SDI have been equally derelict in addressing these crucial issues. That omission is especially unfortunate because how

[2]Examples of that argument can be found in McGeorge Bundy, George F. Kennan, Robert S. McNamara, and Gerard Smith, "The President's Choice: Star Wars or Arms Control," *Foreign Affairs* (Winter 1984–85): 264–78; and Charles Krauthammer, "The Illusion of Star Wars," *New Republic*, May 14, 1984, pp. 13–17.

the larger policy questions are answered greatly determines whether SDI is a benign or malignant concept.

Competing Roles for SDI

President Reagan has stressed from the outset how a missile defense system might protect the American people and free them from nuclear terror. His subsequent offer to share information about SDI technology with the Soviets suggests that he sincerely wishes to liberate all of humanity from the threat of annihilation that has existed now for more than four decades. When the president asked, "Wouldn't it be better to save lives than to avenge them?" he underscored the moral weakness inherent in the current doctrine of MAD. Given that vision, it is difficult to dispute his conclusion that it is "worth every investment necessary" to free the world from the threat of nuclear destruction. Further evidence of a pacific rationale for Reagan's original SDI concept is his admission that defensive systems "raise certain problems and ambiguities. If paired with offensive systems, they can be viewed as fostering an aggressive policy, and no one wants that."[3]

Unfortunately, some of the president's own subordinates seem to regard SDI primarily as a device to enhance the survivability of America's land-based ICBMs, thus clearly pairing it with an offensive system. Prominent Department of Defense officials, as well as SDI supporters outside of the administration, repeatedly emphasize this role and insist that an ABM system will enhance the credibility of America's deterrent. George Keyworth, at the time President Reagan's science adviser, typified this attitude when he asserted that SDI would promote greater stability because it would ensure a fairly large number of our own retaliatory forces surviving an attack.

The defense establishment's view of SDI's role is both more limited and considerably more disquieting than the president's vision. In part, this may be a "fallback" position—a response to critics who contend that Reagan's original proposal is impractical since it would require virtually a "leak-proof" defense system. According to SDI opponents, given the massive number of Soviet strategic warheads, even a failure rate of 5 percent in a system

[3]*Public Papers of the Presidents of the United States: Ronald Reagan 1983* (Washington: Government Printing Office, 1985) book 1, p. 443.

designed to protect population centers would be catastrophic. A perfect "Astrodome" defense, in fact, depends on the development of exotic technologies and the flawless operation of an incomprehensibly complex system. Protecting missiles in hardened silos is a much less demanding operation; even a relatively "leaky" defense would suffice. By ensuring the survivability of at least some of America's land-based strategic forces, SDI would virtually guarantee a devastating retaliation, thereby greatly complicating an aggressor's designs, according to U.S. military strategists.[4]

The Dangerous Lure of Extended Deterrence

Emphasizing a more "feasible" role for SDI may have seemed useful to get a research and development program funded in the wake of intense opposition. But some advocates have another, far less appealing motive to transform SDI into a system to protect offensive missiles. In that incarnation, SDI represents an attempt to turn back the clock nearly three decades to a time when the United States enjoyed undisputed nuclear superiority. There is a faction in the U.S. foreign policy community that wishes to regain such superiority and translate it into tangible political and military gains in Europe, the Persian Gulf, and other portions of the world.

That ambitious objective emerges from statements made by several present and former Reagan administration officials. By enhancing the credibility of America's deterrent forces, they do not mean merely discouraging an unprovoked Soviet attack on the U.S. homeland. The existence of more than 10,000 U.S. strategic nuclear warheads is probably sufficient to accomplish that objective. A massive retaliatory arsenal combined with even a modestly effective SDI designed to protect population centers certainly would be enough.

Advocates of SDI as a component of a strengthened offensive capability have a far more ambitious conception of deterrence. They wish to enhance the waning credibility of extended deterrence— the doctrine of preventing Soviet incursions into regions considered relevant to the United States by linking U.S. nuclear might to the security of allies and clients. Extended deterrence was a concept born in the days of overwhelming U.S. nuclear superiority. As the

---

[4]For a discussion of that point, see Caspar W. Weinberger, "Why Offense Needs Defense," *Foreign Policy* (Fall 1987): 3–18.

116

Soviet Union has gradually attained strategic nuclear parity over the past three decades, the credibility of extended deterrence has correspondingly eroded.

Despite the doctrine's accelerating obsolescence, powerful members of this country's defense and foreign policy establishments continue to embrace extended deterrence. Kenneth Adelman, former director of the Arms Control and Disarmament Agency, candidly expressed the rationale of proponents. According to Adelman:

> [The] credibility of extended U.S. deterrence depends on the Soviet belief that the U.S. would indeed risk nuclear escalation on behalf of foreign commitments. In other words, U.S. strategic forces do not exist solely to deter a Soviet nuclear attack or an attack against the United States itself. Rather they are intended to support a range of U.S. foreign policy goals, including a commitment to preserve Western Europe and even parts of the Persian Gulf against overt aggression.[5]

Adelman added, "U.S. forces should not be fashioned solely for the most remote crisis of all: that of an all-out U.S.-U.S.S.R. nuclear conflict."[6]

In the view of Adelman and some other SDI supporters, such as Keith Payne and Colin Gray, a system protecting U.S. land-based missiles would again make those strategic forces a credible factor in geopolitical confrontations around the globe. Gray has made that connection explicit on several occasions:

> If we can move into an era wherein the American homeland enjoys a growing measure of direct, physical protection, the willingness of U.S. presidents to run risks on behalf of distant allies logically should be strengthened. Far from being an instrument with "decoupling" implications, strategic defense would work to enhance solidarity of behaviour in crisis and war.[7]

Even the president's original speech on SDI blithely assumed that a defense against missiles would be merely one more component in this country's global collective security strategy. At one point he

[5]Kenneth Adelman, "Beyond MAD-ness," *Policy Review*, Summer 1981, pp. 82, 85.
[6]Ibid.
[7]Colin Gray, "Strategic Defenses," *Survival* (March/April 1985): 50–55. See also Keith B. Payne, "Strategic Defense and Stability," *Orbis* (Summer 1984): 215–40.

asked what if Americans "could live secure in the knowledge that their security did not rest upon the threat of instant U.S. retaliation to deter a Soviet attack, that we could intercept and destroy strategic ballistic missiles before they reached our own soil *or that of our allies*? [emphasis added]." A little later in the speech, he stated that by proceeding boldly with new defensive technologies, "we can significantly reduce any incentive that the Soviet Union may have to threaten attack against the United States *or its allies* [emphasis added]." Finally, he affirmed this country's commitment to the doctrines of collective security and extended deterrence in emphatic terms. The vital interests of America and its free world partners "are inextricably linked," Reagan asserted. "Their safety and ours are one. And no change in technology can or will alter that reality."[8]

It was most unfortunate that the president paid homage at the crumbling and increasingly irrelevant shrine of collective security. The greatest deficiency in Reagan's SDI speech was a failure to perceive—or perhaps a refusal to acknowledge—that an effective defense against ICBMs could serve as the basis for a radically different and much safer U.S. foreign policy, one based on strategic independence. As noted below, the European allies immediately recognized SDI's potential in that area.

The president's approach, though, possessed a substantial degree of coherence. He contemplated a comprehensive ABM system that would protect U.S. population centers as well as missile installations. By giving large segments of the population at least some chance to survive a nuclear conflict, such a system might arguably revitalize the credibility of extended deterrence.

But those who believe that a more limited SDI can achieve the same objective are embracing a dangerous illusion. Leaving America's population centers vulnerable while protecting ICBM silos is an attempt to rejuvenate extended deterrence while avoiding the requisite cost. In all likelihood, it would not significantly alter the strategic calculations arising from the reality of nuclear parity. The Kremlin would still question the willingness of U.S. leaders to employ strategic nuclear weapons in defense of an ally as long as U.S. cities remained open to devastation. Only something akin to an impenetrable shield can ever refurbish the credibility of extended

[8]*Public Papers of the Presidents*, p. 443.

deterrence, and even the most passionate SDI advocates concede that a system with that degree of reliability is unlikely.

The danger is that with merely a limited, "missiles-only" shield in place, U.S. leaders might act as though the credibility of extended deterrence has actually been reestablished. There would be a tendency to assume that the United States could compel the Soviets to retreat in every arena of geopolitical confrontation. Employed in that way, SDI would become what its critics contend, a dangerously destabilizing weapons system.

Possible Benefits of SDI

Guided by the proper policy orientation, SDI is not only a benign concept, but may save U.S. civilization from irreparable damage. That is not to say it is possible to create an impenetrable shield capable of protecting population centers from the onslaught of the Soviet Union's entire strategic missile fleet. The critics of SDI are probably correct that a perfect system is not technologically feasible. But a spasmodic, all-out Soviet attack is an exceedingly remote scenario, and a missile defense need not be designed to meet such an unlikely danger.

However, SDI can provide essential protection in other situations. It might represent a crucial difference, for example, in the case of an accidental Soviet launch of a few dozen or several hundred missiles. An ABM system could even minimize the damage caused by a deliberate, but still limited, Soviet attack arising from a confrontation that had escalated out of control. In short, SDI would give the United States options other than surrender or annihilation.

A shield against missiles would also help neutralize potential threats from sources other than the Soviet Union. Nuclear proliferation is a fact of international life, and the situation is likely to get worse in the coming decades. Already nations such as Israel, India, Pakistan, and South Africa either possess small nuclear arsenals or the capability to acquire one rapidly.[9] Within the next quarter-century, at least a dozen other nations may become members of the once-exclusive global nuclear weapons club.

For all their ruthlessness, the political leaders of the Soviet Union

[9]For a discussion of proliferation trends, see Leonard S. Spector, *The New Nuclear Nations* (New York: Vintage Books, 1985).

have acted in a rational and usually prudent fashion. It is impossible to assume that the same will hold true for the leaders of emerging secondary and tertiary nuclear powers. This realization is especially applicable to volatile Third World states. A future Khomeini or Gadhafi in charge of a country possessing even a modest ICBM fleet topped with nuclear warheads would be a frightening prospect indeed. America without any defense against missiles would be at the mercy of such unpredictable foes, because even a hundred warheads could convert the U.S. homeland into a pile of radioactive rubble. Conversely, a reasonably effective shield would protect the vast majority of U.S. population centers and significantly reduce the prospect of nuclear blackmail.

Creation of a workable ABM system may also offer the best hope of at least retarding the pace of nuclear proliferation. U.S. acquisition of such protection would certainly reduce the incentive that aggressive secondary powers might otherwise have to develop nuclear arsenals. Moreover, ABM technology would not remain the exclusive property of the United States for any prolonged period of time. Other Western nations, the Soviet Union, and even some Third World states would soon acquire similar capabilities. The proliferation of defensive measures would further reduce the incentive to develop offensive systems; their great cost could scarcely be justified in a world dotted with sophisticated air defense and ABM installations.

Some scholars have argued that nuclear proliferation is not an unalloyed evil. The "balance of terror" that has prevented the two superpowers from attacking one another, they argue, might well do the same for contentious regional powers.[10] Even if true—and the theory is debatable, to say the least—a similar result could be achieved at a much lower level of risk if such countries acquired comprehensive defensive capabilities. Mutual assured survival would certainly promote stability in the international system as readily as MAD.

Domestic opponents of SDI erroneously assume that because a system cannot protect against an onslaught by the entire fleet of sophisticated Soviet ICBMs, the entire concept is useless. Similarly,

[10]For example, see Kenneth N. Waltz, *The Spread of Nuclear Weapons: More May Be Better* (London: International School for Strategic Studies, 1981).

120

they note that SDI could not significantly impede flat-trajectory, submarine-launched missiles or low-flying cruise missiles, and it would have no relevance to a threat such as small, so-called satchel bombs smuggled into the United States. But it is a fallacy to assume that because SDI cannot accomplish everything, it is worthless. After all, SDI would not be an isolated system. In all likelihood, it would be coupled with expanded conventional air defenses and vigorous antiterrorism measures designed to meet the types of threats for which SDI is not suited. Ideally, an ABM system should be merely one component of an overall strategy to defend the republic from external attack.

Toward Strategic Independence

If SDI is to enhance rather than diminish the security of the United States, however, it must not be linked to a foreign policy based on extended deterrence. Coupling our nation's security to the defense of an assortment of allies and clients around the globe would have constituted a dubious strategy even in the prenuclear era. In an age dominated by thermonuclear weapons, it is the essence of folly. Today, alliances are, in Earl Ravenal's particularly apt phrase, lethal "transmission belts for war"—arrangements that can convert local quarrels and regional conflicts into deadly superpower confrontations.

SDI creates an additional incentive for the United States to extricate itself from the snare of collective security. In reality, the acquisition of nuclear weapons by the United States and the Soviet Union rendered allies largely superfluous, ironically at the point in history when both superpowers rushed to create multilateral security arrangements. The continuing vulnerability of the U.S. homeland to attack tended to obscure that lesson. U.S. leaders clung to alliances and the concept of forward defense to preclude Soviet expansionism that—theoretically—might reach the point where Moscow could isolate the United States and engage in nuclear blackmail. An effective missile defense greatly reduces both the probability and the efficacy of such blackmail. By guaranteeing that the bulk of the U.S. population would survive anything other than an all-out Soviet nuclear offensive, SDI would complete the process of making allies dispensable.

This was a point that the European allies recognized immediately.

The initial reaction to President Reagan's March 1983 speech in most Western European capitals was exceedingly apprehensive for several reasons, including concern that SDI might serve as the basis for a "Fortress America" strategy. "If you have this protection for yourselves," a senior British diplomat observed, "defending Europe becomes harder to justify."[11] The Fortress America epithet aside, such fears are not misplaced. It is no coincidence that the allied governments warmed to the concept of missile defense only after the United States reiterated its commitment to collective security, offered to help Western Europe create its own shield, and took tangible steps to include European firms in the research and development of SDI.

Instead of seeking to reassure allies that SDI will strengthen rather than weaken America's commitment to extended deterrence, U.S. leaders should consider how SDI may expand the republic's foreign policy options. Secure in the knowledge that the U.S. homeland would enjoy a degree of protection previously unavailable, the United States would have the opportunity to forge a new, more flexible and unilateral defense strategy. That is the essence of the concept of strategic independence, and SDI constitutes an important component.

With the crucial caveat that SDI be used to help the nation transcend the doctrines of collective security and extended deterrence, rather than attempt to prolong them, the concept holds considerable promise. If SDI is to fulfill its benign potential, it must be designed to protect population centers, not land-based ICBMs. Ideally, U.S. leaders should couple SDI with a decision to phase out this country's land-based missiles. Reliance on an offensive system that is both inherently provocative (since its principal effectiveness would be in a U.S. first-strike scenario) and also vulnerable to a Soviet first strike has never constituted wise strategy. It also represents questionable wisdom to place a multitude of high-priority military targets in the U.S. homeland when there is no compelling need to do so. America's retaliatory capability would not be degraded by

[11]Peter Osnos, "Europe Finds ABM Ideas Disturbing," *Washington Post*, March 30, 1983, p. 10. See also David S. Yost, "European Anxieties about Ballistic Missile Defense," *Washington Quarterly* (Fall 1984): 112–29; and Manfred Hamm and W. Bruce Weinrod, "The Transatlantic Politics of Strategic Defense," *Orbis* (Winter 1986): 709–34.

relying on a strategic dyad of bombers and submarine-launched missiles, rather than the venerable triad of those two systems and land-based ICBMs.[12] SDI would augment the new strategic dyad by providing a unique, defensive component.

Realistically, SDI will not be able to defend the American people from all nuclear threats. It is even less likely to achieve President Reagan's dream of making nuclear weapons obsolete. But it can minimize a range of serious threats. Indeed, with respect to an accidental Soviet launch or a deliberate attack by a secondary nuclear power, it could represent the crucial difference between suffering severe, but still manageable damage, and the extinction of the United States as an organized society.

The development of SDI would assuredly be an expensive undertaking, as critics of the proposal invariably observe. But that cost must be measured against the potential cost in American lives if we do not go forward. Properly designed, SDI can and should be the foundation of new war-avoidance and damage-limitation strategies for the United States.

[12]For a discussion of that option, see Earl C. Ravenal, "Counterforce and Alliance: The Ultimate Connection," *International Security* (Spring 1982): 26–43.

9. Reagan's Failed Restoration: Superpower Relations in the 1980s

Earl C. Ravenal

The most important foreign policy development of the 1980s has been the change, toward the end of the Reagan administration, in the relationship of the two superpowers, the United States and the Soviet Union, from a sharp and harsh confrontation to a more pragmatic and mutually accommodative structure and tone. At least half of this movement, of course, has been the evolution of the attitude of the Reagan administration. It has gone from accusations of lying and cheating and committing "any crime" to the warm handshakes of three summits and the tangible accomplishments of the double-zero, intermediate-range arms reduction agreement and the foundation of a substantial cut in strategic nuclear arms.

Why has this happened? Should it have been a surprise? Most important for this paper, to what extent does this shift reflect and result from factors other than—both wider than and closer than—changes in the situation and conduct of the Soviet Union itself and U.S. perceptions of these changes? In other words, to what extent does the shift reflect parametric changes in the international system and the status of the United States within that system?

The purpose of this paper is not to consider the major events in the U.S.-Soviet relationship over the past seven years as a narrative of meetings, treaties, and confrontations, but rather to conduct a causal analysis of the factors that occasioned and drove the changed relationship. And the methodology of this paper is not to treat the U.S.-Soviet relationship as such, in its bilateral aspect, as the source of virtually all the factors that have conditioned the change in U.S. behavior, and certainly not to treat a series of presidential speeches as definitive, although they provided striking symbolism of the impending and unfolding changes. Rather, it is to analyze the evolving U.S. stance toward, and within, the international system (of which, of course, the superpower relationship, and the attributes and behavior of the Soviet Union, are very important constituent elements). Further, the paper treats this evolution as a necessary, although grudging, accommodation of the shifting and tightening parameters of the international system (which is virtually composed of the distribution of power and the way power is used and regulated), and also of the U.S. domestic system—political, economic, social, and constitutional.

In these terms, then, Ronald Reagan came to the White House in 1981 committed and dedicated to restoring, not merely the U.S. edge of military superiority over the Soviet Union, but the U.S. hegemony—not quite dominance, but preeminent and practical influence—in the international system, more or less as it had been exercised 25 or 30 years before. Now, in the waning days of the second term of his administration, Reagan is leading the United States into a partial accommodation of the world—although, I would argue, not the final accommodation in a prospective long evolution, or devolution, of U.S. power. It is a story of a failed restoration and an inchoate, partial adjustment.

The U.S. Predicament

The predicament in which the United States finds itself is not unique or unprecedented. It is one of historic resonance and historic proportion: nothing less than the situation of a mature imperial power, beset by multiple challenges around its extensive security perimeter, but unable to generate sufficient resources, of material means and social support, for defense. The term "imperial" is neutral and generic, not pejorative. Empires, throughout history, have performed certain functions; they fulfill them or they falter and fail, or at least are invited to accommodate to their altered situation.

In terms of more concrete policy and strategy objectives, the broad challenge to contemporary U.S. foreign policy is how to perpetuate containment of the Soviet Union in an era of multiple constraints, both international and domestic. Some of these constraints are limits, and thus are more or less unalterable. Others are trade-offs—that is, the price we have to pay to achieve certain objectives of our state and society by containing the Soviet Union. It is doubtful that our society is really committed to pay that price—

not just rhetorically, but objectively; that is not just in the verbalizations of a crust of elites, but in the supportive actions of all of society, taken as a policymaking system. For the question of the perpetuation of containment will not be determined by its abstract desirability, or even by its "necessity," but rather by whether containment is viable strategically and consonant with domestic values. Among those domestic values are economic solvency and the quality of society, including our accustomed freedoms and the unique political system that we undertake to defend in the first place.

Policy—particularly foreign policy—is not a set of items that must be obtained, preserved, or remedied in the world, without reference to situation or contingent cost. It is certainly not the official expression of objectives of state. Rather, policy is an entire system's probable responses to future contingent challenges over a range of issues and geographical areas. Many of the elements that form these responses will not be determined by national authorities. Some policy determinants consist of institutional, military, and resource dispositions that make it more likely that we will respond in a certain way. Other determinants include situations at the time of future decisions or actions, also to varying degrees beyond our control, but not totally beyond our prediction. That is why the description of a proposed foreign policy must begin by tracing the constraints of the international and domestic systems.

Why the Reagan administration has failed to restore clear U.S. predominance in the international system is more interesting than why it tried. The former question has more portents for the United States' future, and is more indicative of the United States' future choices and the constraints on those choices, more suggestive for its alliance policy, for its nuclear strategy, and—to come full circle—for its relations with the Soviet Union.

An Appropriate Methodology

To consider these kinds of matters—namely, the central relationships and situations of a major participant in the international system, one of the shapers and movers of the system—one must have a model, a structured set of propositions that expresses how things work and why they come out the way they do. This paper evaluates contemporary U.S. foreign policy within a quasi-theoretical framework. It describes the main outlines of the foreign policy

127

of the Reagan administration within the relationship of foreign-policymaking and its environment, which consists of the international system and the U.S. domestic political, social, and economic system.

A serious discussion of a nation's foreign policy choices must state, or at least imply, a theory of how policy is made; indeed, it must include a definition of what policy is and is not. This paper cites the domestic elements of the model and also of the international system, especially those parametric changes in the international system that have already been happening and can be further projected. Those changes can be characterized briefly as a diffusion of power, in several senses: nuclear parity and plenty, the rise of significant regional contestants and even hegemones, the fragmentation of political-military alliances, the relative ineffectiveness of military instruments, and the widespread distribution of the capabilities of force in the world. Those changes will further constrict the field for foreign policy choice and, particularly, will frustrate exercises in external intervention, even if that is "justified" and "defensive" or counteroffensive.

Thus, a decision to intervene with military force will not depend on a simple assertion, or even demonstration, of the desirability, or even the "necessity," of achieving or preventing a certain outcome. Rather, such choices will depend on a comparison—a trade-off—between some of the dangerous consequences and the costs of preventing, or substantially diminishing, their emergence (even assuming that any practical degree of effort will succeed in doing this). And, in making these relative calculations for any particular policy or policy object, we are really comparing alternative worlds— that is, kinds of international systems in which our foreign policy would have to operate versus kinds of domestic regimes in which we would have to live. In most general terms, we are trading off the stability of the international system against the propensity of our own system to become involved in conflict (and the character of domestic governance that follows from our propensity to intervene).

To determine the responses of our system, we are thrown back on the analysis of two factors: (1) the strategic orientation that is conditioned by our preparations and built into our institutions and (2) our capabilities and constraints. These factors constitute, respectively, the logic and the logistics of national action. They are both what makes certain responses seem necessary and what causes other responses to be impossible.

First, the evolution of one power's relationship to the world is to a large extent the result of the logic of its national security policy. In these matters, geopolitics and national security are the controlling functions, those that create structures and define relationships. Thus, a nation's defense program is, in many ways, the measure of the significant aspects of its foreign policy; it is surely the price of its foreign policy. Pressures on the defense budget, particularly resource constraints, will have inevitable consequences for the projection of a nation's foreign policy, and soon for the very conception of its foreign policy.

Second, my model of the dynamics of international relations includes, as prominent and often determining elements, the constraints presented by the international system and the constraints posed by a nation's own domestic economic, political, and social processes. In the case of the United States, those constraints have been increasing over the past several decades.

Here, one of the major ironies of contemporary U.S. foreign policy is that those leaders who have most wished to take foreign policy out of the domestic context—to affirm a grand foreign policy plan in the world that would be lifted out of the framework of mere partisan or domestic considerations—have been the ones who have called foreign policies most into question, precisely because of the damaging domestic effects their foreign policies have caused. One who introduced the United States to manipulative balance-of-power Realpolitik, Henry Kissinger, once said; "Foreign policy is essentially a global strategy and . . . domestic considerations should not be allowed to impinge on it."[1]

On another occasion, Kissinger quipped that, if politics really ended at the water's edge, he was in favor of the three-mile limit. In fact, Kissinger's entire tenure as national security adviser and secretary of state was marked by an increasingly desperate attempt to rid foreign policy of the incubus of domestic pressure and constraints—political, social, economic, and, in the end, constitutional

---

[1]Quoted in El-Khawa, *The Kissinger Study of Southern Africa* (Westport, Conn.: Lawrence Hill and Co., 1976), p. 29.

and legal. And in this persuasion, Kissinger is joined by such otherwise strange bedfellows as Richard Nixon and George Kennan.[2]

But events have risen up to mock these kindred theorists and practitioners of Realpolitik. Americans have been getting a vivid lesson in the connection of foreign and domestic policy—how ambitious foreign policies and the high military spending needed to implement them manifest themselves in multiple economic miseries. In several seasons of budgetary strain, it has sometimes seemed that virtually the only significant parameter applying to foreign and military policy is posed by the domestic economy. The connection is integral, although it is indirect. Administrations can pretend for a few seasons to ignore this connection. There was, for instance, Lyndon Johnson's refusal to finance the true costs of the Vietnam War. More recently, there has been Ronald Reagan's invocation of supply-side economics as a cover for spending profligacy. But sooner or later, the constraints of the domestic system will prevail. It is of such domestic stuff, in the last analysis, that foreign policy is made, or unmade. It has been said that foreign policy begins at home; it may also be true that foreign policy ends at home.

To some extent a nation, constrained in the political-military dimension, can "fake it"—that is, continue an ambitious rhetorical, even intentional, pseudo policy without providing the necessary means to implement it in those situations in which it will be seriously tested. But it cannot do this forever, and not to all of its audiences—allies, adversaries, bystanders, its own public. Or, more typically, a nation will grope for "force multipliers"—devices, or alternative strategies, that will invoke intangible elements such as

[2]Note Kennan's curious formulations of this thesis:
> If you say that mistakes of the past were unavoidable because of our domestic predilections and habits of thought, you are saying that what stopped us from being more effective than we were was democracy, as practiced in this country. And, if that is true, let us recognize it and measure the full seriousness of it—and find something to do about it. [*American Diplomacy, 1900–1950* Chicago: University of Chicago Press, 1951, p. 73.]

> The external problems of the country should be given precedence over the internal ones, and foreign policy should not be permitted to become a function of domestic-political convenience. ["Impressions of a Recent Ambassadorial Experience," from a press release issued through the office of Sen. Henry M. Jackson, November 3, 1963.]

130

"resolve" and "will" to get more mileage out of its constrained, and putatively inadequate, forces and major weapons.

The phenomenology of will deserves some comment, if for no other reason because of the saliency of this concept in journalistic and political accounts of the U.S. defensive predicament. It had become a fashion to deplore the supposed absence of presidential leadership, at least until the Reagan restoration of 1981, in which the United States was dealt the semblance of presidential leadership in spades. The absence of this commodity was deplored precisely because it was felt that will was not only the necessary but a sufficient condition for restoring U.S. influence in important international situations. Pundit-journalists, professorial strategists, and even many national security bureaucrats talk almost obsessively about will. Foreign challenges and probes are seen as tests of our resolve; Vietnam was a "trauma" that impaired our capability to respond to threats; we are paralyzed by a "failure of nerve."

But this terminology itself is a tissue of anthropomorphisms and reifications. We are not talking about will in some primal personal sense; the responses referred to are not subjective psychological phenomena. We are talking about the operation of a complex political and social system—not even an organism except in a partially useful but mostly misleading metaphor. "Will" represents a construct—that is, a complex resultant or relationship, which includes as one interactive component the ability of a president to generate and sustain the support of the rest of the political system for some specific purpose. What we are really describing, then, is the structure of a problem, and the structure of the system that deals with the problem.

In the category of force multipliers can be placed even the largest kind of "substitution," relying more on nuclear threats—a lower nuclear threshold, the option of first use of nuclear weapons, in a theater or globally—instead of providing a higher degree of confidence in defense through conventional force actually deployed forward in situations of threat. The problem of creating and sustaining perceptions of power in the absence of sufficient military force is not novel, either for us or for other countries. The Eisenhower-Dulles regime, coming to power in 1953 in the midst of a wasting war and pressures for fiscal stringency, rejected the containment of communism by large U.S. conventional forces and

131

stressed what came to be called, crudely, "massive retaliation" (the reliance on discretionary large-scale nuclear response) and, pejoratively, "pactomania" (the formation of interlocking military alliances). Far from being an aberrant or isolated historical instance, or a play of personalities and pathologies (primarily Secretary of State John Foster Dulles), this stance, in the Eisenhower administration, constitutes a classic syndrome of responses to the problem of projecting power from a straitened domestic base. It illustrates an "economy," in the generic sense of the word, and one that is particularly relevant to America's situation again in the late Reagan administration, although now at much higher levels of defensive output.

In the Eisenhower-Dulles era, or in the Nixon-Kissinger era, when resources of defense money, military manpower, and public support were seen to be pinched, the United States moved to greater reliance on a central strategic reserve, nuclear weapons delivered by the Strategic Air Command, and the introduction of more potent nuclear weapons on the battlefield and in the theater, as well as exemplary uses of force to create an impression of resolve. This kind of response is not unintelligent, but it cannot last forever, since it exposes U.S. society to periodic unacceptable risks, or creates such limited and rigid choices in confrontations that it produces decisional paralysis or invites the calling of the U.S. bluff by an adversary.

Thus, we are brought back to a consideration of our real options: either the expensive generation of more military force or the reduction of demands on our military power. At some point, real forces, and public support for their sharp or sustained use, are necessary to implement, or at least backstop, an active, responsive foreign policy. If those forces and that support are denied, in actuality or even in prospect, an administration must start seeking an adjustment to its situation at a more feasible level of political-military output.

That is roughly what has happened to the Reagan restoration on its way to the forum. And that is roughly why the Reagan administration, in internal doubts and debates (earlier in its career than is commonly realized), began to canvass the possibilities of a pragmatic accommodation with the Soviet Union, in strategic arms and in the regions of the world, that might relieve it (or might provide a pretext for relieving it) of the need to generate expensive physical force over a range of contingencies.

Much popular and partisan opinion, in the United States and abroad, has derided the shallow or even devious intent of these moves. But the question of whether the Reagan administration has been truly serious about arms control is not answered simply in terms of the psychological "sincerity" of President Reagan or the important arms advisers in his administration—say, Richard Perle, formerly assistant secretary of defense—or in terms of whether President Reagan was persuaded that he needed a symbolic response to pressures from the American and European peace movements, or as a ruse to get Pershing IIs and cruise missiles stationed in Europe, or to get arms enhancement legislation through Congress. The answer lies beyond intention, personality, or predilection; it lies in the objective circumstances and tendencies of a decision-making system, such as the U.S. political, economic, and social system.

Thus, even at the apparent nadir of the U.S.-Soviet relationship, against the backdrop of the bellicose Reagan speeches at Westminster, Fontainebleau, Bonn, and Berlin in June 1982, and the lapse into the "evil empire" formulation before the evangelicals in March 1983, the harsh and peremptory judgments in Moscow that the Soviet Union could not do business with the Reagan administration were mistaken. During that time, in mid-June 1982, I had occasion to respond to such judgments by my Soviet hosts at the Institute for the USA and Canada (the "Arbatov Institute"). I said that my hosts were allowing themselves to be swayed by superficial indications, by mere symbolism or even theater (or by rhetoric calculated to pacify the right wing within the Reagan administration and the American public, or to calm America's allies, on the eve of the START talks, which were scheduled to begin on June 30, 1982). I chided my Soviet hosts for being insufficiently Marxist; they should have been keeping their eyes on the "underlying material realities"—in this case, the basis of U.S. military policy in resources and support. Indeed, Georgi Arbatov had originally predicted that Reagan, like Nixon, would move to the political center and that the Soviet Union could cut an arms control deal with him, but then he had shifted abruptly to the opposite assessment. One might have expected Arbatov to know better, in the light of his earlier deciphering of the probable foreign policy of the Nixon administration:

133

As a Marxist, I was never much interested in psychoanalyzing your president. I didn't think the talk about the New Nixon or the Old Nixon was very interesting. What mattered was his response to circumstances—particularly to two changed circumstances in your country. One was the growing complexity of international affairs, which showed, especially in Vietnam, that it was not possible for a single power, however strong, to have everything its way. The other was the change of priorities—the lesson that rulers cannot neglect domestic business.[3]

Something Borrowed, Something New

In any case, it may be useful to trace out the main elements of the Reagan strategy, first to allay the question of whether this administration has a strategy. Critics of the Reagan administration have leveled two kinds of attacks at it that, when taken together, are oddly contradictory. The first is that the administration has no strategy at all—indeed, that it is just throwing money in the general direction of "national security." The second is that the administration has vastly expanded America's international goals, adding some novel strategic elements. That is certainly a case of critical overkill. Both of the criticisms cannot be true. In a sense, neither of them is. For all its increased defense budgetary requests, the Reagan administration has added hardly any manpower or force structure. At most, it has fleshed out some skeleton air wings, added two aircraft carrier battle groups, and created two additional light army divisions. What is striking is that the Reagan administration, far from being able to implement its alleged wish list of expansive military programs and ideological battles with the Soviet Union, has had trouble maintaining a defense program at the level that Jimmy Carter had projected into the 1980s when he left office.

Most of the elements of Reagan's national strategy are borrowed from his predecessor—or, more precisely, from what may be called the second Carter administration. (In two senses, there were two Carter administrations: [1] sequentially, the second beginning in late December 1979 with the Soviet invasion of Afghanistan, and [2] concurrently, with the factional division between the accommodationist and pragmatic Department of State under Cyrus Vance

[3]Quoted in Joseph Kraft, "Letter from Moscow," *New Yorker*, June 24, 1972.

and the confrontational and ideological National Security Council staff under Zbigniew Brzezinski.)

Every administration drags along some of the strategic baggage of its predecessor and also adds a few hallmarks of novelty. Every administration in the last four decades has adhered to the paradigm of national security policy consisting of deterrence (by this I mean extended deterrence) and alliance (designating forward defense), but administrations have oscillated between relative emphasis on one or the other of these elements—one stressing nuclear deterrence, another emphasizing defense by conventional forces deployed forward. And so the Reagan administration has moved, in the classic way but also its own idiosyncratic way, within the overall framework.

Actually, the Reagan administration has incorporated, and perpetuated, virtually all the foreign and military policies of the second Carter administration. If we are willing to screen out much "noise" at intermediate levels of government, we find that the Reagan administration has implemented the programs and strategies of the Carter administration in every consequential area: in the strategic dimension, counterforce; the reinstitution of global defense and direct U.S. involvement in regions, particularly the Persian Gulf and Southwest Asia, featuring the Rapid Deployment Force and the acquisition of stepping-stone bases; the policy of active intrusion into the Middle East; the reinforcement of relations with Communist China and the attenuation of support for Taiwan; and, by the spring of 1982, even the move to arms control, featuring talk of "deep cuts" in nuclear arsenals.

Some of the putative foreign policy departures of the Reagan administration are truly novel; others are extensions of the tendencies of the Carter administration. In Central America, the Reagan administration has seemed to go considerably beyond the Carter limits, although by January 1981, Carter's policy had not yet been tested by an evolving Marxist regime in Nicaragua and a polarized military situation in El Salvador.

That would leave two items of innovation in foreign policy and national strategy: the emphasis on strategic defense and the Reagan Doctrine. (Perhaps one could also cite the leaning toward a "maritime strategy," sometimes equated with a doctrine of "horizontal escalation"—the intention to take a general war to the flanks of the

Soviet landmass in the north of Europe and the Northwest Pacific, mostly through the forward operation of surface naval units.)

With regard to the crucial area of strategic nuclear policy, the charge that the Reagan administration has changed U.S. strategy deserves a more extended examination. Specifically, it has been alleged that the administration moved to a lower nuclear threshold and to a war-fighting, war-winning nuclear strategy. But in what sense might there be grounds for such a charge? Perhaps it is based on the alleged bellicosity of the administration's rhetoric. But I find nothing particularly novel in the utterances of various figures in the Reagan administration to the effect that the United States must design its forces and doctrines so that it will prevail in a nuclear war.

When we concentrate, properly, on the tangible elements of nuclear strategy—our nuclear posture and our doctrine of targeting and precedence of use—we find that the Reagan administration is simply affirming the requisites of extended deterrence—that is, the use of our nuclear weapons to deter all kinds of threats, conventional or nuclear, to our allies as well as ourselves, and to strategic objects and positions of less than truly vital interest to ourselves. This strategy of extended deterrence in turn has necessitated our move to counterforce targeting, which is bound up with our retention of the option of first use of nuclear weapons.

Even the alleged propensity of the Reagan administration to limited nuclear war has its origin and foundation in this logic. It is not something that began suddenly when Ronald Reagan said, in 1981, "I could see where you could have the exchange of tactical weapons against troops in the field without it bringing either one of the major powers to pushing the button."[4] The doubts had been sown long before that, in a series of U.S. strategic initiatives. What, then, are we to make of the preparations for "protracted nuclear war," specified in the famous "Defense Guidance" issued by Secretary of Defense Caspar Weinberger to the military services in 1982?[5] Here, even the proviso that U.S. nuclear forces must "prevail and be able to force the Soviet Union to seek earliest termination of

[4]Bernard Gwertzman, "President Says U.S. Should Not Waver in Backing Saudis," *New York Times*, October 18, 1981.

[5]"Fiscal Year 1984–1988 Defense Guidance," leaked to and summarized by *The New York Times*, in an article by Richard Halloran, May 30, 1982.

hostilities on terms favorable to the United States" has a familiar ring to anyone who has worked and planned in the Pentagon during the past 25 years. But it is particularly redolent of the years of Jimmy Carter and Secretary of Defense Harold Brown, who advanced the concept of prolonged, multiphase nuclear war, with the disabling of Soviet leadership and the sinews of the Soviet state. Also in the development of counterforce weapons, such as the MX, Trident II, and intermediate-range cruise missiles, the Carter administration was the precursor of the Reagan administration. PD–59, Carter's August 1980 presidential directive that codified a nuclear-war-fighting stance, was, in a sense, the first strategic act of the Reagan administration.

Strategic Policy

One can link the discussion of three policy elements: arms control, the Strategic Defense Initiative (SDI), and the attitude toward alliance, particularly NATO, involving extended deterrence. These three elements, which are integrally related, came together in the freewheeling discussions at the Reykjavik summit in October 1986. One of the less noticed aspects of the Reykjavik talks, at the time, was the implication of Reagan's attachment to SDI coupled with the bold—perhaps impulsive—gambits to cut offensive nuclear weapons by 50 percent and perhaps eliminate all offensive nuclear weapons in a foreseeable time frame. This would create essential problems for NATO, which not merely depends on, but consists of, America's one-sided nuclear guarantee.

The combination of deep cuts (and yet the retention of many warheads) in offensive nuclear weapons and the prospect—even the dream—of an impermeable defense of U.S. society would permit the United States either a more aggressive national strategy, most likely in parts of the world other than Europe, or a more passive stance, avoiding (or even quarantining) contextual situations that might lead to the outbreak of wars that could integrally involve the United States. In either case, the United States could remain relatively safe behind its strategic shield. And in either case, its protection of Europe, through extended deterrence, would wither. The coupling that is the basis of the validity of the U.S. defensive guarantee to Europe, and the basis of NATO, would be dissolved. Europe would be left more vulnerable to Soviet conventional attack or pressure. The United States would retreat to a kind of unilateralism and even quasi-isolationism.

This is a vision that will outlast Ronald Reagan's presidency, for it has always appealed strongly to the American right as an escape from the trammels of alliance—the consultation and deference that often degenerate into inhibitions on the actions of the United States. Whether or not fully, explicitly, and consciously intended by Ronald Reagan, the envisaged trade-away of U.S. intermediate-range nuclear forces and the prospective substitution of a space shield for our present forces, nuclear and conventional, on the marches of alliance in Central Europe and East Asia have now been keenly noted by statesmen and strategic observers. Perhaps the most far-reaching portent of Reykjavik is a foreign policy that is not merely unilateral but disengaged, and an America that is not just a Fortress but an Astrodome.

The Reagan Doctrine

Another novel aspect of the Reagan foreign policy is a penchant for rolling back Soviet power, particularly in the Third World. This is a tendency that has not reached the surface of U.S. foreign policy since the early Eisenhower-Dulles era, although rollback was then soon submerged after our failure to intervene in uprisings in Eastern Europe, particularly in Hungary in 1956 to prevent the Soviets from snuffing out Hungary's brief rebellion and independence from the Warsaw Pact. The policy of rollback was implicit in the orientation of the Reagan administration from its inception, though the title "Reagan Doctrine" awaited the columnist Charles Krauthammer's exegesis of a few sentences tucked away in Reagan's January 1985 state-of-the-union address.

Originally devised to characterize our support for "freedom fighters" against Marxist-Leninist governments in Afghanistan, Cambodia, Ethiopia, Angola, and Nicaragua, the Reagan Doctrine, with the cases of the Philippines and Haiti, was broadened to imply U.S. support for any democratic force in the world fighting against any repressive government, whether left or right. In this expanded interpretation, the Reagan administration has turned to a kind of liberal internationalism in the style of Woodrow Wilson, who proclaimed that the mission of the United States was to make the world safe for democracy.

138

What is wrong with the Reagan Doctrine is that its success depends on the fulfillment of three conditions: (1) the people we support must be the "right" people from a strategic standpoint; (2) they must also be the "good guys" from a political standpoint; and (3) U.S. intervention must remain cheap in American money and lives. The classic case was Grenada. However, as critical observers have noted, the easy cases will not be the important ones, and the important cases are not likely to be the successful ones. Therefore, the Reagan Doctrine will end either in disastrous overextension and unbearable risk, or in contemptible hypocrisy and shallow opportunism.

The Soviet Threat

We return to the explicit theme of this paper: U.S.-Soviet relations. Has the Reagan administration added or changed anything with regard to interpreting or quantifying the Soviet threat? Not really. On the subject of "the sources of Soviet conduct" and the question of what the United States should do about Soviet conduct, within the Reagan administration there are the same, identifiable "camps" (in the typology of Alexander Dallin and Gail W. Lapidus[6]): the "essentialists," the "mechanists," and the "interactionists."

The Reagan administration, consequently, is divided on the key aspects of the Soviet challenge:

1. How ideological, and therefore how universal and implacable, are Soviet ambitions in the world?
2. How strong or weak is the Soviet state, and therefore how susceptible is it to U.S. pressures?
3. How conservatively do we interpret Soviet capabilities; indeed, on what basis do we quantify Soviet military efforts? (Further, to what extent do we care about Soviet intentions, as opposed to Soviet capabilities?)
4. Is it useful and productive for the United States to "link" Soviet behavior in different functional areas?
5. Should we oppose any accommodation on the ground that it would confer an absolute benefit upon the Soviets, or should

[6]"Reagan and the Russians: American Policy Toward the Soviet Union," in Kenneth A. Oye, Robert J. Lieber, and Donald Rothchild, eds., *Eagle Resurgent? The Reagan Era in American Foreign Policy* (Boston: Little, Brown, 1987).

we manage the relationship in either a hard-nosed mechanist or a more accommodative interactionist fashion?

What is notable is the shift within the Reagan administration that marks the relative defeat of the hardest-liners, and their grudging acceptance (or their departure) of the move to arms control and collaboration with the Soviets, in a partial condominial arrangement.

Conclusion

It is a significant irony that the Reagan administration, precisely because it has tried so vigorously to do what is (conditionally) necessary to restore U.S. power in the world, and because it has largely failed (and for objective reasons), has illustrated most poignantly the encompassing framework of the United States' problem—what may be called the "imperial dilemma." Further rounds of accommodation will be forced upon succeeding administrations. So far, though, most alternative proposals, including those from the liberal part of the political spectrum, are limited and take the form of advocating selectivity of intervention. Thus, they leave the problem of U.S. adjustment to the world largely unresolved.

In the last analysis, there are only two broad alternatives at this juncture in the United States' international career: (1) a renewed militance, applied virtually universally and sustained by tangible rearmament that would tax this country's economy and burden its society more than the ardent proponents of this course dare to admit; and (2) the contrary policy, which is conformance to the practical limitations of our system and our situation, plus a deliberate, or at least conscious, disengagement from our commitments to protect what we think of as our remaining portion of the world.

Thus, there is a need to consider the diametric opposite of the interventionist paradigm of deterrence and alliance (or forward defense) that has prevailed in U.S. foreign policy for four decades, and to embody that alternative orientation in the institutions and procedures of the national decisionmaking system. That would be a foreign policy of war-avoidance and self-reliance, which translates into geographical distance, strategic autonomy, and political-military restraint. In other words, it is time to consider a broad course of disengagement in the strategic dimension (not the economic or social dimensions) and an accommodation, not to the Soviet Union, but to the overall conditions of the international and domestic environments. Specifically, we should consider the attenuation or transformation of our alliance commitments, with their now-unsustainable costs and inevitable risks.

At the inception of the Reagan administration, I said:

> Viewing the Reagan inauguration—the ceremonies, the festivities—you got the feeling of a kind of Restoration, after a period of usurpation. The trouble is that this administration thinks it has received a mandate to restore the prestige and power, as well as the style, of the 1950s—to "make America great again," in the world as well as among ourselves.
>
> But this invites a cruel dilemma, because no amount of wishing, orating, or posturing will summon the resources for this global task. This dilemma is nothing more or less than the classic situation of the mature empire: it must defend a vast security perimeter that is beset by multiple probes from without, while at home overblown governmental structures, on a rotting base of popular support, run out of fiscal tricks, and thus out of revenues to realize their foreign policy designs.
>
> The beginning of wisdom is to be clear about one's situation. If we are to accommodate ourselves to a world of diffuse challenges and indecipherable signals—most of them indistinguishable from noise—then we have to desensitize ourselves, to blunt our responses rather than sharpen our attitudes. We have to cultivate, at the official national level—though not necessarily at the private personal level—a studious neutrality, almost an indifference, in the literal sense, to opportunities of foreign intervention—even if that intervention promises to set things right.
>
> In the continuing glow of the Reagan Restoration, that might seem strange, even forbidding advice. But it is the basis for a constructive adjustment of America's posture to a confused and antagonistic world.[7]

Now, in the Reagan administration's nostalgic twilight (fortunately not a climactic Götterdämmerung), that critical commentary is the Reagan administration's unwilling legacy.

[7]"The Reagan Restoration," *Libertarian Review*, April 1981.

10. Making Friends in the Third World

Doug Bandow

If it is U.S.-Soviet relations that dominates the headlines, it is U.S. policy toward the Third World that may have the greatest impact on future U.S. influence around the globe. That is because the economic development and political orientation of more than 100 developing states are directly affected by U.S. actions. Whether the United States is viewed as friend or foe tomorrow by a large bloc of nations whose power will grow over time depends in large part on how this country treats its less-developed neighbors today.

For years, U.S. policy toward the Third World has been simultaneously patronizing, mercantilist, and accommodationist. First, billions of dollars in foreign aid was channeled overseas annually to buy influence for U.S. diplomats; some of the money was honestly labeled security assistance, but many of the de facto bribes were presented as economic or development aid. That the recipients of U.S. assistance were often disreputable tyrants—Anastasio Somoza in Nicaragua and Mobuto Sese Seko in Zaire, for instance—did not deter one U.S. administration after another from continuing to support rulers who were believed to generally reflect Western interests.

Second, U.S. programs to promote international development did more to advance the cause of domestic manufacturers and interest groups than to encouraage self-sustaining economic growth abroad. Foreign aid was bluntly sold on Capitol Hill by representatives of private industry, philanthropic groups, and bureaucratic functionaries who benefited from the outlays. Moreover, the funds were uniformly channeled to foreign governments, which subsidized disastrous state-led development programs and enriched ruling elites.

Third, the focus of U.S. bilateral relations with underdeveloped states was to avoid political confrontation through continuing aid flows, irrespective of the recipient's behavior toward the United

States and its attitude toward Western values. Aside from the time when Daniel P. Moynihan served as U.S. ambassador to the United Nations, this accommodationist philosophy also dominated U.S. participation in the many international organizations. Smooth relations and the promotion of international "order" were deemed higher goals than the protection of U.S. interests or principles.

How has the coming to power of conservative Ronald Reagan affected U.S. relations with the Third World? Aside from its more combative stance toward selected UN agencies, the Reagan Revolution has been more rhetorical than practical. In fact, the Reagan administration has been more vociferous than its predecessors about the importance of buying influence abroad. And although Reagan has grandly articulated a market-led development strategy abroad, his aid policies differ little from those of past administrations.

Buying Influence

Much, if not most, of U.S. foreign assistance—nearly $14 billion worth in 1987—is intended to bribe foreign officials to support administration policy goals. Of course, it would be impolitic for U.S. officials to describe their goals so crudely, but no one doubts this objective. Observed the Commission on Security and Economic Assistance, headed by Frank Carlucci, now Reagan's secretary of defense: "The United States seeks international political relationships that promote U.S. national interests."[1] The official report goes on to pay its respects to democracy, open political systems, and economic development; the fundamental basis of U.S. policy, however, is clearly to advance U.S. diplomatic interests abroad.

In the past, conservative Republicans have been most vocal in their opposition to foreign aid. It might have been expected, therefore, that the Reagan administration would have moved to scale back international outlays. Despite persistent efforts by budget director David Stockman, however, foreign aid has been one of the major growth areas under President Reagan. In 1980, Jimmy Carter's last full year as president, foreign-assistance outlays totaled $13.8 billion; spending dipped the following year after passage of the Reagan budget program, but then steadily rose to $19.8 billion

---

[1]Commission on Security and Economic Assistance, *A Report to the Secretary of State*, November 1983, p. 9.

in 1985, a 43.5 percent increase over 1980. Aid levels fell sharply in 1986, but only because of the deficit and the Gramm-Rudman-Hollings bill, which forced Congress to trim some outlays. The administration, led by Secretary of State George Shultz, bitterly protested the cutbacks.

Nevertheless, in one respect the administration has significantly changed the direction of foreign assistance. In the same way that Reagan has changed overall federal budget priorities, he has shifted funds between different categories of foreign aid. Assistance officially labeled as developmental fell from 55.5 percent of total aid expenditures in 1980 to 35.5 percent in 1986; security programs accounted for 34.5 percent of spending in 1986, compared to just 22 percent in 1980. And Economic Support Fund outlays—cash transfers that most closely approximate out-and-out international bribes—have increased from 22.5 percent of total expenditures to 30 percent.

This increased emphasis on direct military and political aid flows complements the administration's more activist stance abroad. Reagan has reinforced military forces prepared for foreign intervention, such as the Rapid Deployment Force, inserted U.S. combat forces in such flashpoints as the Persian Gulf and Lebanon, and pioneered the Reagan Doctrine by actively supporting insurgencies in Nicaragua, Afghanistan, and Angola.

What the United States has succeeded in purchasing with the $112.6 billion in foreign-assistance expenditures since Reagan took office is not clear. Even the Carlucci Commission—which lavished praise on U.S. foreign-assistance programs—conceded that success was difficult to assess, since it "is largely measured by what does not happen—the attack or insurrection that did not occur, or did not succeed."[2]

Even when large amounts of U.S. aid have bought a measure of influence abroad, it has often been subsequently wasted when the U.S.-supported dictatorships, such as those in Iran and Nicaragua, were overthrown. During the Reagan years, past assistance did not prevent the Sudan, long a client state, from moving away from the United States after its pro-Western leader was overthrown. Morocco, the recipient of some $500 million in security aid since 1962, stunned

[2]Ibid., pp. 32-33.

the Reagan administration by making (but later breaking) the Treaty of Arab-African Unity with Libya, perhaps the U.S. government's international enemy number one. The administration felt it necessary to repudiate its long-time ally, Ferdinand Marcos in the Philippines, after generously underwriting him for years. Nevertheless, it does not appear that the administration, for all its rhetoric about strict scrutiny of federal spending, has seriously reconsidered the use of foreign assistance to buy influence overseas.

Promoting International Development

Bilateral economic assistance became a major tool of U.S. foreign policy after World War II. Although initially focused on Europe through the Marshall Plan, the program has since distributed more than $150 billion in financial assistance to every continent and almost every country.

The "major objective" of these large financial transfers, stated the Agency for International Development (AID) shortly after its creation in 1961, was "to assist other countries that seek to maintain their independence and develop into self-supporting nations."[3] In 1973, however, Congress passed the Foreign Assistance Act, which redirected U.S. goals from encouraging economic growth to underwriting so-called basic human needs, essentially turning AID into an international welfare agency that promoted dependence, not development. That economic assistance had failed in its purported goal to promote economic growth was clear from the fact that many aid recipients, especially in Africa, were moving backward rather than forward; aside from South Korea and Taiwan, there were no obvious success stories in which U.S. clients had graduated from the international dole.

In this area of U.S.-Third World relations, at least, Ronald Reagan appeared ready to make dramatic changes. At the 1981 Cancun summit, for instance, Reagan told the Third World nations in attendance that they should not look for more aid transfers as a panacea: "We are mutually interdependent, but above all, we are individually responsible."[4] And that, he told another audience, meant that

[3]Agency for International Development, *Principles of Foreign Economic Assistance* (Washington, 1963), p. 1.

[4]Ronald Reagan, Statement at the opening of the International Meeting on Cooperation and Development, October 22, 1981, p. 2.

146

developing countries had to choose an economic strategy that worked—one based on "market-oriented policies," which would "create rising agricultural productivity, self-sustaining capacity for research and innovation, and stimulation of job-creating entrepreneurship."[5]

In practice, though, there has been little change in U.S. policy. Overall development assistance grew from $2.6 billion in 1980 to $3 billion in 1985, before falling under congressional pressure. Food aid—the famous Food for Peace program, which is more an attempt to dump U.S. crop surpluses than to promote international development—rose from $2 billion to $2.3 billion over the same period. Contributions to the multilateral development banks, such as the World Bank and the International Monetary Fund, fell from $2.1 billion to $1.6 billion, but it was Congress, not the administration, that forced the reduction.

Moreover, those agencies most responsible for formulating and implementing U.S. assistance policies—AID and the Department of State—have largely maintained the failed policies of the past. Virtually all foreign assistance goes to governments, for instance. According to an official AID study, barely 4.4 percent of outlays— under the most optimistic of assumptions—directly benefited the foreign private sector. In some nations, AID support for state enterprises is even higher; in Grenada, for instance, less than 1 percent of AID outlays has gone to the private sector.

The Reagan administration created the Private Enterprise Bureau within AID, but the new entity has had virtually no money and has devoted much of its resources to such tasks as buying Xerox machines for local chambers of commerce. Admitted one senior AID official in 1985, it will take "ten years for AID to become comfortable with the private sector."[6]

It may be impossible to channel assistance to foreign private sectors without corrupting local businesses, but current programs, which directly underwrite governments that inhibit development through their statist domestic policies, are clearly counterproductive. Indeed, under Reagan, U.S. foreign assistance has directly

[5]Ronald Reagan, Speech to the World Affairs Council of Philadelphia, October 15, 1981, p. 7.

[6]Peter Schaefer, "Seven Steps to Improve U.S. Bilateral Foreign Aid," Heritage Foundation Backgrounder no. 599, August 19, 1987, p. 6.

147

subsidized a socialistic land-reform program in El Salvador, as well as the creation of government marketing boards, which have hampered crop production the world over. U.S. aid flows have even underwritten avowedly Marxist states such as Mozambique.

In the latter case, of course, the Reagan administration is using "economic" aid in an attempt to buy influence. But Mozambique provides an obvious illustration of why such bribes are almost certainly doomed to fail. Mozambique did not turn toward the West until it had been desolated by a combination of civil war and collectivist economic policies. For the Maputo regime's modest change in rhetoric, the United States is paying tens of millions of dollars a year; the gains are not permanent, since Mozambique would probably drop its pretense of reform if the aid stopped flowing. In the meantime, U.S. dollars have helped insulate a brutal regime from the natural consequences of its own collectivist policies, prolonging the agony of its subject people.

Finally, while AID has engaged in "policy dialogue" with the recipients of U.S. assistance, the agency has had little effect because it is often unable and usually unwilling to withhold funding if policy reforms are not made. Numerous Third World nations have begun moving in a more market-oriented direction, although their progress has been tediously slow. But they have done so largely because the failure of statism has been so disastrous, not because of U.S. advice. Indeed, not all U.S. officials understand which policies would most promote development abroad: AID has urged several African states to raise already prohibitive tax rates and tighten their enforcement practices.

Reagan's policy toward the multilateral banks, too, originally looked like it might mark a dramatic change from the past consensus in favor of ever-increasing international loans. The Treasury Department under Donald Regan officially questioned the lending policies of the World Bank and the regional multilaterals; the first replenishment of the International Development Association (IDA), a World Bank affiliate, under the Reagan administration resulted in a lower capital infusion than previously, a result that would have been considered inconceivable under other administrations.

By late 1982, however, Reagan was backing a multi-billion-dollar infusion for the International Monetary Fund. And when James Baker replaced Regan as treasury secretary, U.S. policy toward the multilateral financial institutions changed dramatically. In October 1985, for instance, Baker proposed his much-heralded, but never implemented, Program for Sustained Growth, which envisioned a three-year, $9 billion increase in official lending, as well as a hike in private loans.

In 1986, the Reagan administration agreed to $11.5 billion—which went to $12.4 billion through supplemental contributions from Japan and other nations—in new money for IDA. In 1987, the Treasury Department, which handles U.S. dealings with the multilateral financial institutions, agreed to treble the capital of the African Development Bank to $20.8 billion; negotiations over new funding for the Inter-American Bank broke down only because that institution was unwilling to increase U.S. leverage over loans.

And at the 1987 Venice summit, President Reagan announced his support for a general capital increase for the World Bank. In 1988 the administration backed a bank proposal to hike the existing capital by $75 billion; the bank wants to double its lending by the 1990s.

It is true that the Reagan administration has urged the multilaterals to promote free-market reforms in borrowing nations. But there is no evidence that the banks themselves share such a commitment. In 1983, Stanley Please reflected on his two decades at the bank, the last three years as senior adviser to the institution's senior vice president:

> "As a committed socialist . . . I was surprised and shocked by the emphasis which the bank at the time gave to the public sector in general and to the government in particular. Here was an institution which had the reputation of being ultra free enterprise and market-oriented, yet had more confidence in the rationality, morality and competence of governments then I ever had."[7]

Throughout the 1970s, the bank committed roughly 80 percent of its funds to government enterprises, or parastatals; indeed, it regularly financed the bloated state sectors that are now pulling scores of Third World debtors under. Even worse, the bank underwrote all manner of social engineering schemes, providing $10 million to the Tanzanian government, for instance, to, in the bank's

[7]Stanley Please, "A Candid Look at Yesterday," *The Bank's World*, September 1983, p. 7.

words, assist "the half million inhabitants of the Kigoma Region to resettle in *ujamaa* villages"—Julius Nyerere's forced collectivization program that brutalized peasants and destroyed the nation's agricultural economy.[8]

Under the last two bank presidents, both Reagan appointees, the rhetoric has changed, but not the policy. The bulk of bank lending still flows to public enterprises, and the institution still funds coercive attempts by governments to remake their societies. In 1985, for instance, the bank supported, albeit indirectly, the Ethiopian resettlement program that two different humanitarian groups have estimated has killed as many as 100,000 people. The Ethiopian government borrowed $30 million for "relief and rehabilitation services," including the purchase of trucks, which were the primary means used by the government to forcibly move people from the rebel-held north to the government-controlled south.

Even if the administration had had greater success in reforming its own bilateral aid programs, its efforts to transform the international lending agencies were probably doomed to failure. The United States lacks a veto and has never successfully blocked a loan by the World Bank, for instance. As long as the administration agrees to increase U.S. funding of the multilaterals, they have no reason to take seriously U.S. concerns about policy reform and private-sector support.

While the United States has promoted additional foreign aid outlays, it has choked off much of the private financial flows necessary for the growth of developing states. In early 1981, for instance, the administration agreed to revive sugar import quotas as part of a deal to win votes on budget cuts. The quotas have grown increasingly stringent, disrupting sugar production throughout the Caribbean.

Similarly, Reagan has imposed "voluntary" steel quotas, which have damaged the newly industrializing Third World nations, such as Brazil and South Korea. Moreover, the administration's tightened controls over textile imports—admittedly initiated partly in response to congressional pressure—have harmed developing states across the globe. The administration's protectionist policies have harmed indigenous private firms, further enhancing the power of

[8]World Bank, *Annual Report 1975*, p. 23.

150

Third World regimes and reinforcing the dependence of those countries on aid transfers. Only a vibrant world economy will encourage the sort of private-sector development and economic expansion necessary to liberate poverty-stricken nations around the globe.

Accommodating the United States' Foes

Reagan chose Jeane Kirkpatrick as his first ambassador to the UN, thereby immediately changing the tone of U.S. relations with the international organization. Kirkpatrick spoke of the United States taking off its "kick me" sign; she sharply attacked critics of the United States and showed obvious contempt toward what the UN had become. Overall, Kirkpatrick's combative stance provided a dramatic contrast with the actions of her predecessors, Donald McHenry and Andrew Young.

Kirkpatrick's attitude toward the General Assembly was matched by U.S. policy toward other UN bodies. Throughout the 1970s, virtually every UN agency had become a tool in the Third World's campaign for a New International Economic Order (NIEO). Although the NIEO amounted to a call for global socialism, prior U.S. administrations apparently feared antagonizing Third World governments by forthrightly opposing the NIEO. Instead, U.S. officials often joined with those of other nations in promoting vast new regulatory schemes that would enhance the UN's power and stifle international commerce. Even when the United States was critical of UN proposals, it devoted most of its efforts to damage control, moderating inflammatory resolutions and trying to delay adoption of any mandatory programs.

But the administration quickly moved in the opposite direction. In February 1981, barely one month after Reagan's inauguration, the Third United Nations Conference on the Law of the Sea was preparing to conclude the Law of the Sea Treaty (LOST). The treaty—which would have established a massive international bureaucracy to control deep seabed mining—had been under negotiation since 1973 and had been supported by the Nixon, Ford, and Carter administrations. However, Reagan attempted to renegotiate key sections of the treaty. After failing in that effort, the administration opposed the treaty when it came before the conference for a vote in 1982 and led several Western nations in refusing to sign. Today,

151

even as the official preparatory commission meets year after year to haggle over treaty rules and regulations, the LOST is a dead letter.

The Reagan administration also resisted proposals for increased international economic regulation in such bodies as the UN Industrial and Development Organization, Food and Agricultural Organization, UN Conference on Trade and Development, International Telecommunications Union, Center on Transnational Corporations, and World International Property Organization. Where reform seemed impossible, the administration proved willing to take even more dramatic action. The UN Educational, Scientific and Cultural Organization (UNESCO), for instance, was pressing for a New International Information Order to subordinate the media to member governments; the Soviet bloc joined many Third World nations in advocating licensure of the press, standards for "responsible" reporting, and requirements that the media promote state policies. The administration attempted to reform UNESCO, but the organization's leadership was corrupt, its budget was controlled by an irresponsible majority, and its original, nonpolitical focus had been permanently lost. In 1984, therefore, the administration withdrew from the organization, crippling UNESCO financially.

Since then, however, Shultz has adopted a more accommodationist stance toward the UN. While Congress has reduced the U.S. contribution in an attempt to meet the Gramm-Rudman-Hollings deficit targets, Shultz has lobbied not only for bilateral aid programs but also for increased support for the various UN bodies. Some Department of State officials are urging that the United States reenter the LOST process; others have advocated returning to UNESCO.

The Reagan administration's approach to bilateral relations with Third World nations has varied less from that of its predecessors than has its participation in the multilateral agencies. Aside from a few celebrated instances—as, for instance, when the administration cut off aid to Zimbabwe after the Mugabe regime criticized U.S. policy—the Reagan Department of State has attempted to use aid transfers to mollify Third World governments in the same way as did the Carter administration.

Indeed, since most cases of bilateral relations between the United States and small foreign states do not warrant presidential attention, this continuity in policy largely reflects the fact that the same Foreign Service officers have implemented policy under succeeding administrations. The time-honored Department of State approach, even under Reagan appointees Alexander Haig and George Shultz, is to use foreign aid to buy influence, avoid controversial issues if possible, and smooth over relations with more money if bilateral irritations should arise.

This desire to get along at almost any cost has undermined the administration's half-hearted attempt to promote free-market policy reform abroad. For the administration has made no effort to cut off funds to nations whose domestic policies make international development impossible; instead, AID has urged that tens of millions of dollars in additional funds be provided to encourage Third World governments to change their economic policies. Under Reagan, no less than under Carter, officials have recognized that handing out money is far more popular with foreign regimes than is cutting back assistance.

Conclusion

As in other areas, the Reagan administration originally promised dramatic reforms in U.S. policy toward the Third World but failed to deliver. In practice, its approach to developing states remains patronizing and mercantilist. The administration has been more confrontational in dealing with international agencies controlled by developing states, but its attitude toward bilateral relations remains relatively accommodationist: Use aid money to keep foreign officials happy.

Unfortunately, the failure of the administration to dramatically break with past policy does not reduce the need for a new policy approach to the Third World. The widespread attempt to buy influence with foreign aid, for instance, should be abandoned for the futile, counterproductive exercise that it has proved to be. In the long term, peaceful economic and cultural relations, including private investment flows—untainted by support for local autocrats—will operate most effectively to promote U.S.–Third World cooperation.

Government-to-government aid for the purpose of promoting international development, too, should be deemphasized; such transfers assist governments rather than people. Instead, the United

153

States should promote freer international markets, encouraging private-sector development abroad.

Finally, U.S. officials should further reduce U.S. participation in and financing of international organizations that are committed to objectives fundamentally inimical to U.S. interests. This policy should apply to bilateral relations as well. Instead of trying to buy friendships, the United States should try to depoliticize bilateral relations, allowing economic and cultural contacts to dominate political relations.

Despite the fact that the Reagan record has proved to be an overall disappointment, the administration has laid the foundation for some important changes in the future. Reagan's willingness to withdraw from a UN agency and kill a global treaty, for instance, set enormously important precedents; the administration's emphasis on free-market reforms in Third World states has helped advance the international economic debate. But more fundamental reforms will have to await the inauguration of a new administration.

PART III

MONEY AND BANKING

11. Monetary Policy: Monetarism to Fine-Tuning

William Poole

On February 18, 1981, shortly after entering office, the Reagan administration released a document entitled *America's New Beginning: A Program for Economic Recovery*.[1] The first item in this comprehensive plan for reforming economic policy was a Reagan speech to a joint session of Congress. Reagan put the fourth plank of the plan this way: "The final aspect of our plan requires a national monetary policy which does not allow money growth to increase consistently faster than the growth of goods and services. In order to curb inflation, we need to slow the growth in our money supply."[2] The body of this document contained a section on monetary policy with the administration's policy assumption "that the growth rates of money and credit [will be] steadily reduced from the 1980 levels to one-half those levels by 1986."[3]

The main theme of this chapter is that the Reagan administration did pursue these monetary policy principles at the beginning but gradually backed away from them. A policy that started out emphasizing control over money growth ended up as an effort in fine-tuning. At the time of this writing the policy emphasized control over the exchange rate, but this focus could easily change.

In *America's New Beginning* and in other documents, such as the annual reports of the Council of Economic Advisers, the Reagan administration presented far more detailed analyses of monetary

The author is indebted to Richard Nisenson for research assistance and to Data Resources, Inc., for the data in Figures 11.1 and 11.2. However, the views expressed here, and any errors, are solely the author's.

[1]This document was published by the White House, February 18, 1981 (U.S. Government Printing Office: 1981 0-339-055).

[2]*America's New Beginning*, Part I, p. 8.

[3]*America's New Beginning*, Part II, p. 23.

policy than any previous administration. But these statements should not automatically be accepted as defining administration monetary policy. Analysis of any administration's monetary policy is complicated by the fact that legal authority in this area rests primarily with the Federal Reserve System, an agency with independent statutory authority. Also, of course, political statements often obscure the true direction of policy.

In one sense, the political reality of presidential control over monetary policy differs little from the reality of control over other types of policy. For example, policy with regard to the welfare system must be negotiated with Congress. What makes monetary policy different is that it is perfectly acceptable for a president to propose changes in the welfare system, but proposals to change monetary policy bump up against the generally accepted view that monetary decisions ought to be nonpolitical and that the Federal Reserve System ought not to be subject to political pressure. The reality, of course, is that monetary policy is highly political, as it should be, and subject to substantial presidential control.

There is another problem. Especially during the first Reagan term, there were so many disparate views on monetary policy within the administration—views argued internally and publicly—that it was sometimes difficult to discern *the* Reagan monetary policy. During the second term, the problem was different: Reagan and his top officials said relatively little about monetary policy and what they did say was vague. The way to understand the Reagan administration's monetary policy is to concentrate on what the president himself said and on what a few key officials said. The conflicting statements of supply-siders, monetarists, traditional conservatives, Wall Street types, and others in minor administration positions should be largely ignored.

The Macroeconomy, 1980–87

President Reagan took office at a time of high inflation, high interest rates, and considerable uncertainty about monetary policy and the future course of the economy. Inflation and interest rates had been rising for several years. In 1980 the economy suffered a short recession, which bottomed out in July. Then economic activity recovered and unemployment fell. However, interest rates and money growth both rose sharply.

The Federal Reserve had changed monetary policy in October 1979 to emphasize control of money growth. After this policy change, money growth and interest rates both became considerably more volatile. However, the average rate of money growth did not fall very much until 1981.[4]

It is convenient to divide the Reagan administration's time in power into three phases. Phase A extended from January 1981 to August 1982. During this period the Federal Reserve continued to pursue the policy introduced in October 1979; money growth and interest rates were both extremely volatile from October 1979 through the end of Phase A. Phase B, which ran from August 1982 to September 1985, was a transitional period during which the Federal Reserve and the administration gradually abandoned efforts to control money growth. During Phase C, which began in September 1985 and continues to this writing, the administration targeted the exchange rate. Initially the focus was on depreciating the dollar, but in early 1987 policy turned to supporting the dollar. Figures 11.1 and 11.2 show major macroeconomic variables over these three phases.[5]

The economy reached a cyclical peak in July 1981, and interest rates reached peaks at about the same time. Thereafter, interest rates fell as business activity weakened. As interest rates fell, the Federal Reserve permitted money growth to fall also. Despite the deepening recession, the Fed worked vigorously to restrain money growth to convince the markets that the monetary authorities would not cave in once again. Money growth was cut in half in one year instead of over five years as envisioned by the administration.

In August 1982, interest rates fell dramatically and stock prices soared. At the October meeting of the Federal Open Market Committee, the Fed formally adopted a new policy, which it labeled a "borrowed reserves target." This policy was de facto a reversion to the policy followed before October 1979.

The period from August 1982 to September 1985 was a transitional one in terms of the Fed's efforts to keep money growth within announced target ranges. In the early part of this period, the Fed

[4]The M-1 definition of money is used in this analysis because that is the definition preferred by the Federal Reserve and by most economists in the early 1980s.

[5]Given the controversy over exchange rate measures, it is worth noting that the exchange rate in Figure 2 is the Federal Reserve index.

159

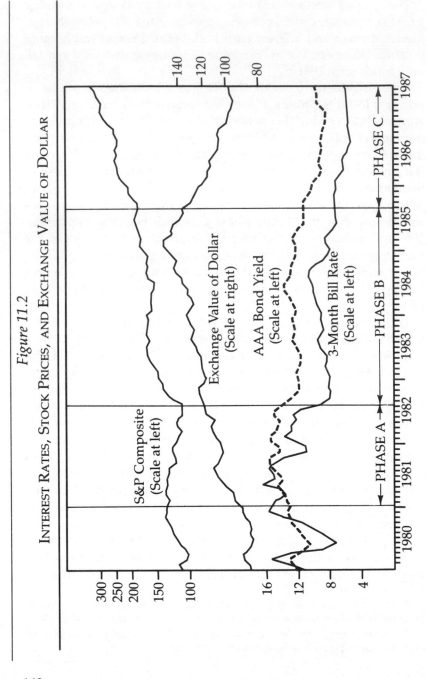

Figure 11.2

INTEREST RATES, STOCK PRICES, AND EXCHANGE VALUE OF DOLLAR

S&P Composite
(Scale at left)

Exchange Value of Dollar
(Scale at right)

AAA Bond Yield
(Scale at left)

3-Month Bill Rate
(Scale at left)

PHASE A   PHASE B   PHASE C

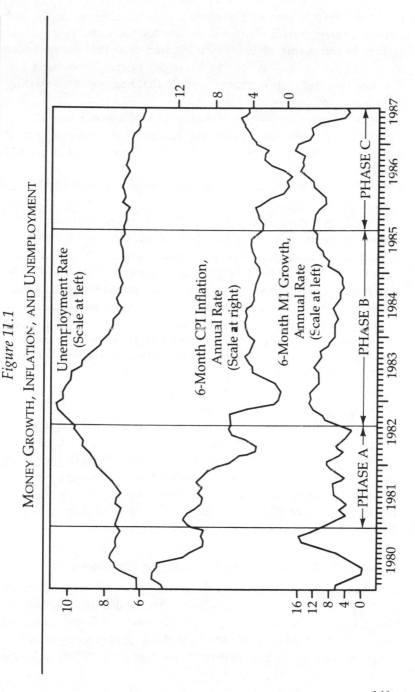

Figure 11.1

MONEY GROWTH, INFLATION, AND UNEMPLOYMENT

paid considerable attention to money growth, although it did not pursue money-growth targets with anything like the vigor it had earlier. In the spring of 1983, as it became clear that the business recovery was under way, the Fed nudged interest rates higher to slow the very high rate of money growth that had prevailed starting in August 1982.

The business recovery proceeded at a vigorous pace in 1983 and 1984. Interest rates rose somewhat, following the normal cyclical pattern. In 1985, the pace of the recovery slowed and remained sluggish through mid-1987. In early 1985, the Fed permitted M1 growth to rise substantially, and money growth remained high through early 1987.

Phase B ended in September 1985 with the negotiation of the Plaza Agreement by the Group of Five finance ministers. After this agreement, U.S. monetary policy was constrained by administration efforts to control the foreign-exchange value of the dollar. The importance of this policy shift should not be underestimated. Before September 1985, monetary policy paid considerable but diminishing attention to controlling money growth and reducing inflation. After September 1985, policy was driven by the protectionist politics of the trade deficit, which is what led the administration to focus on the dollar exchange rate.

The dollar, which had started to fall in March 1985, fell almost continuously after September 1985 and into early 1987. Then monetary policy turned from encouraging depreciation of the dollar to preventing further depreciation. Interest rates rose substantially and money growth slowed. It is clear that the effects of the policy shift in September 1985 have not played themselves out. The U.S. current-account deficit is still very large. And experience suggests that a policy oriented to controlling the foreign-exchange rate usually causes substantial problems sooner or later.

Monetary Policy Views of Reagan and His Appointees

Reagan stated his views on monetary policy with considerably greater precision early in his first term than he did later. During the 1980 campaign and during 1981–82, there were several consistent themes. Reagan often mentioned the damage caused by inflation. Of course, politicians always express concern about inflation. In his

162

speeches, however, Reagan did not talk of the need to balance the goal of reducing inflation against other goals.

An important theme that appears often and cuts across many different policy areas is that of stability and predictability of government policy. Reagan's commitment to stable policies was deep enough that during the 1982 midterm campaign he even used the unlikely political slogan, "Stay the course." There were more policy adjustments than the slogan indicated, but it is still true that policy had a longer-run cast to it than was generally true in prior years.

Early on, Reagan attributed inflation to both deficit spending and money creation. It is not surprising that the deficit theme disappeared as deficits became chronic. But Reagan typically emphasized that excessive money growth causes inflation, and he pointed out that the blame for inflation does not rest with those who raise prices.

Reagan did not view interest rates as a measure of monetary policy but as a result of inflation expectations. Inflation rather than irresponsible private behavior was the cause of high rates. On occasion, however, Reagan seemed to hint that the market was holding rates too high.

Another important policy during the first term, especially in retrospect, was that the administration withdrew from active intervention in the foreign-exchange markets, except in the case of disorderly markets. The Federal Reserve opposed the policy of nonintervention, but Secretary of the Treasury Donald Regan and Under Secretary of the Treasury Beryl Sprinkel defended it vigorously.

Finally, the Reagan policy theme of encouraging economic growth should be mentioned. Reagan did not link growth to monetary policy, except that he viewed low inflation and low interest rates—apparently nominal rates—as being conducive to growth. He did not suggest that monetary policy could influence growth directly. I mention this point because some Reagan supporters have argued that the Federal Reserve was responsible for slowing the economy's growth and thereby offsetting the effects of other policies—especially tax reduction—designed to increase growth. Reagan's view on this matter is less clear during the second term.

These, then, are the core first-term Reagan themes on monetary policy, and they reflect vintage Chicago school monetarism. Money creation causes inflation, and inflation causes high interest rates.

Monetary policy should maintain a stable, predictable course; there should be no fine-tuning—no effort to employ "quick fixes," as Reagan often put it.

Reagan Appointments to the Federal Reserve Board

By far the most important position on the Board of Governors of the Federal Reserve System is that of chairman. The law provides that the president name the chairman from among the sitting members of the board. The chairman's term runs four years from the date he assumes office. President Carter appointed Paul Volcker chairman in August 1979, and so Volcker's term as chairman ran to August 1983.

In 1983, Reagan faced the issue of whether to replace or reappoint Volcker as chairman. Volcker was a dedicated inflation fighter and he had handled the debt crisis of the less-developed countries in 1982 with great skill. However, a number of administration officials distrusted Volcker. He had a substantial independent political base, and his critics believed that he could not be trusted to further the Reagan administration's interests. Moreover, many were infuriated by Volcker's frequent public references to budget deficits, a continuing political problem throughout the Reagan years. Reagan did reappoint Volcker in 1983, but at the end of Volcker's second term in 1987 the president appointed Alan Greenspan to chair the Fed. Volcker resigned from the board at that time, leaving the entire membership of the board consisting of Reagan appointees.

Neither Volcker nor Greenspan is a monetarist, and in that sense neither seems to exactly fit Reagan's views on monetary policy. However, both place great weight on price stability, and neither dismisses money growth as irrelevant to monetary policy, as some Keynesians and some supply-siders tend to do. Unlike Carter's first appointment to the Fed chairmanship, G. William Miller, Volcker and Greenspan are both highly respected in the financial community (as they were at the time of their original appointments), and both have had substantial political experience.

Reagan did not appoint Greenspan in 1983 because many Reagan conservatives opposed him for many of the same reasons they opposed Volcker. Greenspan was viewed as an establishment conservative who was less committed to radical reforms than some of the Reagan conservatives would have liked. Reagan reappointed

Volcker in 1983 because there was no obviously superior candidate and not because Reagan's advisers inside and outside the administration were unanimously enthusiastic about him. Edwin Meese III and Regan were opposed, while James Baker, Sen. Paul Laxalt, George Shultz, and David Stockman, supported Volcker's reappointment.[6]

Reagan's first appointment to the board, in late 1981, was Preston Martin, who was named vice chairman.[7] Martin had substantial Washington experience as chairman of the Federal Home Loan Bank Board during the Nixon administration. He was from California, which is typically represented on the Federal Reserve Board.

Reagan's second appointment to the board was Martha Seger. Seger filled the seat held by Nancy Teeters, whose term expired in February 1984. Seger did not have expertise in monetary policy but was a political conservative with experience as a bank regulator in Michigan.[8]

In October 1985, Reagan made two more appointments to the board. One was Manual Johnson, assistant secretary of the Treasury for economic policy, who had been heavily involved in shaping the administration's economic forecasts and in Treasury debates over tax reform. Wayne D. Angell, the other appointee, had ties to the agricultural community and was also known as a monetarist who placed special emphasis on commodity prices as a guide to monetary policy.[9]

In March 1986, Vice Chairman Preston Martin resigned, apparently because Reagan would not provide assurance that he would be named to the chairmanship when Volcker's term expired in August 1987.[10] Reagan named Johnson as vice chairman and

[6]Steven R. Weisman, "Volcker Renamed by Reagan to Run Federal Reserve," *New York Times*, June 19, 1983, p. 1; and Jonathan Fuerbringer, "Final Choice of Volcker Is Attributed to His Experience and Solid Support," *New York Times*, June 19, 1983, p. 26.

[7]Robert D. Hershey, Jr., "California Businessman Is in Line for Fed Post," *New York Times*, December 23, 1981, p. D1.

[8]"Finance Professor Nominated to Fed," *New York Times*, June 1, 1984, p. D2.

[9]Peter T. Kilborn and Steven Greenhouse, "New Fed Nominees," *New York Times*, October 15, 1985, p. D1.

[10]"Internal Battle Changes Tone of Federal Reserve," *New York Times*, March 24, 1986, p. A1.

appointed H. Robert Heller to fill Martin's seat. Heller was said to have a reputation as a "nondogmatic monetarist."[11]

As of this writing, Reagan's last appointment to the board was Edward W. Kelley, Jr., a Texas businessman. Kelley was a friend of Treasury Secretary Baker, but had neither political nor banking experience. This appointment was announced in January 1987.[12]

During Reagan's first term, by the end of which only two members of the board (Martin and Seger) were Reagan appointees, the Reagan administration influenced but certainly did not control monetary policy. Things were different during the second term. By mid-1985 Reagan appointees filled four of the seven seats, and by August 1987 six seats, with the seventh one vacant. It is reasonable to conclude that monetary policy during the second Reagan term closely approximates the policy that would have prevailed if the Federal Reserve were an executive branch department instead of an independent agency.[13]

Excluding the board chairman, who should always be discussed separately from the other board members, Reagan's appointments to the board are quite typical of those appointed in the past. Board members have relatively little power, and few seek the position; instead, the administration in power seeks suitable candidates. The appointees quite naturally have political beliefs—in this case conservative—that fit those of the administration. Some of the Reagan appointees were politically active and some were not. Some were economists and some were not. Some had reasonably well-developed views on monetary policy and some did not. Reagan's appointments to the board were not substandard, but neither did they set a new standard of excellence.

Reagan Appointments to Administration Positions

With regard to economic policy, the key position in the Reagan administration has been that of secretary of the Treasury. In the

[11]Robert D. Hershey, Jr., "Martin's Post at Fed Filled," *New York Times*, May 13, 1986, p. D1.

[12]"Texas Businessman Nominated for Fed," *New York Times*, January 22, 1987, p. D2.

[13]This comment may seem to give too little weight to the Fed's independence. However, it should be noted that executive departments often have substantial independence due to the power of their constituencies. In fact, during his second term Reagan probably had more control over monetary policy than, say, over agricultural policy.

first term that position was held by Donald Regan, who was chairman of Merrill Lynch at the time of his appointment. Regan did not have settled views on monetary policy when he joined the administration, except that he believed that inflation was a serious problem. During his first several years in office, he seems to have been influenced substantially by Beryl Sprinkel, who was under secretary of the Treasury for monetary affairs from 1981 to 1985 and then chairman of the Council of Economic Advisers. Sprinkel had long experience as a Fed watcher and was a well-known monetarist. Over time his influence within the administration dwindled.

James A. Baker III became secretary of the Treasury at the beginning of the second Reagan term, after serving as chief of staff in the White House during the first term. Baker is a policy generalist, skilled in administration and political problem-solving. His monetary-policy instincts typically favored low interest rates. His close adviser, Richard Darman, seems to have been suspicious of monetarism. Baker accumulated power over time, and by the time of this writing his role in administration economic policy is clearly far greater than that of any other Reagan appointee.

With this changing cast of characters, and with the changing economic conditions over the Reagan years, it is not surprising that Reagan monetary policy in 1987 differs from that of 1981.

The Evolution of Reagan Monetary Policy

Early in Reagan's first term, administration officials—especially Regan and Sprinkel—pressed the Federal Reserve both publicly and privately to maintain stable and gradually declining rates of money growth. However, the administration was unsuccessful in getting its views across to the public. One journalist commented, "Outsiders confused about the Administration's policies toward the Federal Reserve Board might be interested to know that there is some internal confusion as well. In the last year and a half, Mr. Regan and Treasury officials have criticized the Fed for being too loose, too tight and too erratic with the money supply."[14]

Nevertheless, in 1981–82 the administration was basically supportive of the Fed's efforts to bring inflation down. In keeping with

[14]Steven R. Weisman, "Mixed Signals Fray Nerves as Dog Days Set In," *New York Times*, June 25, 1982, p. A14.

his standard approach to such matters, Reagan talked of staying the course and avoiding quick fixes. If the administration had complained about high interest rates and unemployment instead of about volatile money growth and inflation, the Fed might not have had enough political support to maintain its restrictive policy.[15]

As the recession deepened in 1982, continuing monetary restraint became less and less palatable. In addition, the near default of Mexico on its international obligations raised a pressing new issue in August. I do not know the precise sequence of events, but my guess is that senior administration officials, including Regan and Baker, reached an agreement with Volcker that a loosening of monetary policy was necessary. The Fed pushed interest rates down dramatically and, through the remainder of the year, used a series of lame excuses to explain away the rapidly rising money growth. Administration support for the Fed's new policy is indicated by the fact that, for a time, administration officials altogether ceased making public complaints about volatile money growth.

Interest rates rose in 1983 and into the beginning of 1984. With the approach of the presidential election, some members of the administration became nervous about the Federal Reserve's policy. Regan in particular began to criticize the Fed publicly for permitting interest rates to rise. With the near bankruptcy of the Continental Illinois Bank in May 1984, the markets became extremely unsettled. There was concern that the Federal Reserve might be forced to flood the economy with liquidity to prop up Continental Illinois and to hold interest rates down. President Reagan settled the matter in a press conference. In response to a question concerning his advisers' fears about rising interest rates, he said the Fed is "back up on target [for money growth] and where they should be with a normal rate of increase tied to the increase in the economy."[16] By emphasizing that the Fed should control money growth, Reagan eased the market's fears that excessive money growth might cause inflation and interest rates to get out of hand once again.

Interest rates fell quite conveniently during the weeks leading up

[15]Regan and others did complain about high interest rates from time to time, but their message was ineffective because it was mixed in with complaints about money growth and volatility.

[16]"President's News Conference on Foreign and Domestic Issues," *New York Times*, May 23, 1984, p. A22.

to the election in November 1984. Money growth remained at a relatively modest pace of about a 5 percent annual rate. Monetary policy was not a contentious issue at this time.

Economic conditions facing the second Reagan administration were quite different from those facing the first. At the end of 1984 growth in real gross national product (GNP) slowed markedly and unemployment stopped falling. Inflation remained low in 1985. As the year continued, however, there was growing concern over the sluggish performance of the real economy. Protectionist pressures arose for the usual political reasons, and the case for protection seemed to mount as the dollar remained high and the trade deficit widened.

In September 1985 (as already noted) the administration changed policy toward the exchange rate. The new policy of deliberate depreciation of the dollar was pursued by holding down interest rates in the United States and pushing up or holding up interest rates in other countries. The avowed purpose of the policy was to reduce the U.S. trade deficit.

The most immediate purpose of the Plaza Agreement was to provide evidence of administration action to reduce the trade deficit to head off protectionist legislation in Congress. The agreement also had an important side benefit for the administration. Money growth was high in 1985, but the economy remained sluggish. Some analysts felt that the Federal Reserve ought to raise interest rates to control excessive money growth. The Plaza Agreement made interest-rate increases very difficult politically for the Federal Reserve, and thereby prevented adoption of a more restrictive monetary policy. The Fed could not raise interest rates at this juncture because to do so would have been in direct opposition to the policy of the president—a policy that was widely supported because of national concern over the trade deficit.

Moreover, by 1985 (if not before), the monetarist case for money-growth targets had become highly questionable. The decline in velocity that had begun in 1982 had continued. Indeed, in 1985 money growth rose and GNP growth fell, and so velocity declined very sharply. There was no sign of inflationary pressure in the economy. Monetarists did not offer a satisfactory explanation of the decline in velocity and did not provide a new formula for basing monetary policy on money-growth targets. By default, monetary

169

policy went back to total reliance on controlling short-term interest rates; the Fed adjusted rates as seemed appropriate, given the state of the economy and the political situation.

Reagan made the policy change very clear in his State of the Union message in February 1986:

> The constant expansion of our economy and exports requires a sound and stable dollar at home and reliable exchange rates around the world. We must never again permit wild currency swings to cripple our farmers and other exporters. . . . We've begun coordinating economic and monetary policy among our major trading partners. But there's more to do, and tonight I am directing Treasury Secretary Jim Baker to determine if the nations of the world should convene to discuss the role and relationship of our currencies.[17]

Oil prices broke sharply downward at the beginning of 1986, and the effect was large enough to lead to an outright decline in the consumer price index in the early months of the year. Inflation remained very low in 1986, and the real economy grew only slowly. Interest rates continued to fall; short-term rates bottomed out in the fall of 1986 and long-term rates at the beginning of 1987.

During 1986 Volcker expressed increasing concern that dollar depreciation might go too far, and in early 1987 foreign governments, the markets, and the administration joined him in worrying that dollar depreciation was becoming excessive. Inflation and inflation concerns rose. Both the U.S. and foreign governments began to support the dollar rather than encourage further depreciation. The Fed permitted interest rates to rise rapidly enough that money growth fell sharply.

In late September 1987, James Baker raised the prospect of a new role for gold in monetary policy. The idea seemed to be that policy might become tighter if gold prices are rising and easier if gold prices are falling. When pressed for details Baker replied, "The statement speaks for itself."[18]

That was surely correct. Baker's policy involved a deliberate

---

[17]"State of the Union: Reagan Reports to the Nation," *New York Times*, February 5, 1986, p. A20.

[18]Peter T. Kilborn, "Baker Hints at Gold As Guide on Policy," *New York Times*, October 1, 1987, p. D1.

170

vagueness and obfuscation about what the monetary authorities were doing and should be doing. Some supporters of the gold standard embraced Baker's initiative, but they should not have. The proposed policy rested on principles exactly opposite to those of the gold standard. The classical gold standard involved a commitment that the government buy and sell gold at a fixed price, and that commitment carried the force of a constitutional provision. Such a rules-based approach is inconsistent with unbridled Federal Reserve discretion to look at all relevant information in attempting to reach wise decisions on monetary policy.

But the analysis should be pushed further. "Looking at" gold, commodity prices, foreign exchange rates, stock prices, and other possible indicators of the state of the economy suffers from a fatal internal contradiction. The idea on the surface seems sensible enough. If the economy is developing inflationary pressures, then rising demand will push up commodity prices. Similarly, speculators fearing inflation may bid up gold prices and bid down bond prices. But here is the problem. Suppose current monetary policy is exactly right but speculators fear that next year's policy will become inflationary. For example, when François Mitterrand was first elected president of France, the franc plunged on the basis of expectations about *future* French monetary policy. In this example, the message from the market was that the government should retain its current policy and not introduce the expected inflationary policy. In this circumstance it would have been a mistake to tighten current policy.

Suppose the monetary policy of "looking at" a particular economic indicator were pursued to the extreme of pegging the price of gold (or the exchange rate, or whatever). In this case, clearly, the price of gold could not provide any evidence whatsoever on what the Fed *should* do. The price of gold would instead measure what the Fed *is* doing. Watching the price would provide as much guidance on what the Fed should do as watching the Fed's discount rate.

In principle, prices in speculative markets could provide useful information on the economy if there were independent information on investor expectations about monetary policy. Then, price movements could be partitioned into parts due to expectations and due to underlying economic conditions. In practice, reliable information on expectations is not available. Thus, "looking at" speculative

171

prices will not provide useful guidance to policymakers on how they should adjust policy. In fact, raising the prospect of looking at gold will increase uncertainty because investors will not know whether the Federal Reserve will or will not respond to changes in the price of gold.

In fact, the Federal Reserve could find itself in the box of having to respond unwisely to a gold price or exchange-rate change to "prove" to the market that the monetary authorities meant what they said. At the time of this writing, the weak dollar and somewhat higher gold prices would seem to preclude any Fed steps to raise money growth, which has been very low in 1987, by lowering interest rates.

By October 1987, the market did not believe that there was much to the discussion involving gold, but policy toward the foreign-exchange rate was a different matter. The policy of targeting the exchange rate will eventually collapse in one of two possible ways. In one scenario, a weakening domestic economy will require lower interest rates at the same time a weak dollar requires higher interest rates. The outcome is likely to be a period of uncertainty during which either the present administration or the next one will try to retain the policy of targeting the exchange rate by holding interest rates up. Clear evidence of a weakening economy will force a change in policy, and as that policy change becomes more likely, the dollar will fall as the market concludes that the Fed will abandon the dollar to bring interest rates down to stimulate the domestic economy. However, given that monetary policy affects the economy with a lag, an expansionary monetary policy will not arrive in time to prevent a recession.

In the second scenario, rising U.S. inflation pushes up interest rates, but monetary policy resists the upward pressure. Higher inflation eventually leads to a loss of confidence at home and abroad, and the dollar sinks rapidly. This is the pattern of the late 1970s, and it also ends with recession.

If an exchange-rate target is retained, one of these two scenarios is bound to arise sooner or later because it is impossible to achieve two goals—domestic economic stability and a particular exchange rate—with the single instrument of monetary policy. Pursuing the exchange-rate goal is ultimately self-defeating because instability of the domestic economy will cause instability of exchange rates. These are exactly the kinds of problems that the policy of nonintervention in the foreign exchange market was designed to avoid. Unfortunately, it is unlikely that the administration will drop foreign exchange targeting before serious problems appear, in that this policy is being used in the effort to head off protectionist legislation. Protectionism will not disappear soon, and so exchange-rate targeting will not either.

Reagan's Monetary Policy Legacy

Reagan will leave office with both pluses and minuses in the monetary-policy area. Volcker will retain credit for taming inflation, and it may well be that the importance of Reagan's support of this policy will remain underappreciated. In any event, the success of the policy will be remembered for some time and should serve to increase the probability that the Fed will pursue a restrictive policy again when inflation next becomes a problem.

On the minus side, the adoption of exchange-rate targeting will create problems for the next president, if not for Reagan himself before he leaves office. This policy is sure to fail. The industrialized nations are unwilling to sacrifice their monetary independence to the extent necessary to make relatively fixed exchange rates work. Currency values will not settle down, and so policies that try to stabilize exchange rates will in time be abandoned. But the United States will cling to the policy longer than makes sense on economic grounds because success in maintaining an exchange-rate target will count as a political victory and letting the exchange rate go will count as a political defeat. However, in the process of holding onto the exchange rate, the United States will damage its own economic stability and that of the international financial system.

Reagan will leave office with a monetary policy based on fine-tuning the economy in response to the latest economic data. There is a heavy focus on symptoms rather than on fundamentals. The trade deficit is not itself an economic problem; the low saving rate in the United States is. Manipulation of the exchange rate cannot affect the saving rate, and neither can monetary policy. In short, subordination of monetary policy to the politics of protectionism will not earn Ronald Reagan favorable mention in the history books.

173

12. Weakening the Dollar: The Tax No One Has to Vote For

Jerry L. Jordan

The economic policies of the Reagan administration in its second term are so different from those in the first term that it is as though a new administration took office in January 1985. The change in the administration's policies toward intervention in the foreign-exchange markets reflects the more general shift away from a laissez-faire philosophy in the first term to an activist, discretionary involvement in the economy in the second term.

Upon taking office in 1981, the administration held the view that our essentially capitalist economy is inherently stable. According to this view, actions by the government are more frequently destabilizing, rather than stabilizing, factors in the economy. Thus, many fluctuations resulting from private-sector actions are actually caused by attempts to second-guess government policies.

Administration rhetoric during the long and deep recession of 1981–82 reflected this view, with such expressions as "stay the course," "no quick fixes," and "magic of the marketplace" all being designed to communicate enormous confidence in the natural workings of our economy. Yet, clearly that view was held only by a minority of economists; very few politicians and business leaders accepted it. By the end of Reagan's first term, such rhetoric had vanished, and early in the second term we saw numerous examples of a return to activist, discretionary, "demand management" approaches to economic problems. Exchange-rate policies in the second term are just one example of this reversal. This reversal reflects the ongoing debate in the economics profession regarding the necessity and desirability of various types of stabilization policies on the part of the federal government.

In 1969, Professor Axel Leijonhufvud argued that, "In my opinion, the central issue in macroeconomic theory is . . . the extent to which the economy, or at least its market sectors, may properly be regarded as a self-regulating system. In what respect does it, or does it not, behave in such fashion? How well, or badly, do its 'automatic' mechanisms perform?"[1]

Much earlier, F. A. Hayek and W. H. Hutt had argued that a private, market-oriented economy is inherently resilient and naturally gravitates toward full utilization of its productive resources following any kind of shock that has temporarily depressed economic activity. These shocks include wars, droughts, price changes in energy or other commodities, perverse government policies, and substantial exchange-rate movements.

This view of the natural tendencies of the economy is diametrically opposite to the "stagnation thesis" of the 1930s that raised concerns about the adequacy of "aggregate demand" in the absence of government actions ensure a sufficient amount of total spending. The idea of a "demand failure" persists to the present time. Several generations of economists in the private sector, as well as in government and academia, argue that even an economy that relies primarily on private property and a market mechanism could stagnate at less than full utilization of its productive resources unless the central government pursues an activist policy to ensure sufficient demand.

Doing something to deal with this perceived problem consists of actions that result in increasing government spending, including so-called jobs programs, cutting personal taxes to raise personal disposable income, increasing credit availability, and attempting to reduce market interest rates. During the second term of the Reagan administration, the return to demand management has included pressure on the economic policymakers of Japan and West Germany to engage in "pump-priming" stimulus to their domestic demand and become part of the U.S. "locomotive" for faster world growth.

Historical Review of U.S. Exchange-Rate Policies

The Bretton Woods fixed-exchange-rate system broke down because, during the 1960s, the United States chose inflation rather than explicit taxes as the method of financing the Great Society and

---

[1]Axel Leijonhufvud, "Effective Demand Failure," in *Information and Coordination: Essays in Macroeconomic Theory* (New York: Oxford University Press, 1981), p. 104.

the Vietnam War. The monetization of the deficits arising from an unbalanced fiscal policy produced inflation.

When Bretton Woods worked, it was because the United States pursued policies resulting in low inflation, and because the United States and its major trading partners were willing to live with the periodic devaluations of the currencies of the higher inflation countries. The move toward floating exchange rates in the early 1970s was intended to give every country greater flexibility in pursuing appropriate domestic economic policies while eliminating some of the constraint from international considerations.

However, the experience of the late 1970s and now the mid-1980s suggests that the system is asymmetrical. The reason is that the U.S. dollar is the "numeraire" for international transactions and is the "N−1 currency." When the United States has highly inflationary policies and other countries try to maintain a lower rate of inflation, the resulting appreciation of their currencies causes political pressures on their central banks to be more expansionary, usually through nonsterilized intervention, so they experience "imported inflation."

A fixed exchange rate between the United States and Hong Kong can work because Hong Kong is quite small and is willing to let the Federal Reserve make monetary policy. But, a fixed exchange rate between the United States and Japan is not possible because neither country is willing to give up sovereignty over its monetary policy. That being the case, and since the United States is now experiencing, and will continue to experience, higher inflation than Japan, an interest-rate differential must exist to reflect the difference in expected inflation rates. Furthermore, in view of the large and rapidly growing national debt of the United States and the continued increases of its already huge external debt, foreign investors are rationally skeptical of U.S. determination to resist the temptation to reinflate.

More stable exchange rates would be desirable. That, however, does not mean it would be desirable for central banks to attempt to intervene to try to stabilize exchange rates. One of the greatest uncertainties faced by traders in the financial markets continues to be possible actions of the central banks.

During the past two years, there has been much talk about "policy coordination," but it is leading nowhere—and for good reason.

There is no coordination of economic policies between Congress, the White House, and the Federal Reserve. Getting the United States to coordinate its economic policies with another country is impossible. What policy coordination means to U.S. officials is that other countries should give up sovereignty over their economic policies and allow U.S. economic policies to dictate how much inflation they will experience. To economic policymakers in many other countries, policy coordination means the United States should reduce its budget deficit and achieve a more stable monetary policy. The policies now being urged on the United States by foreign officials are the same as those policies the Reagan administration announced for itself in its first term. Until the United States adopts stable and consistent policies over time, there is no possibility that the world will have stable exchange rates.

The Reagan First Term: Nonintervention Policy

The first annual report of the Council of Economic Advisers issued by the Reagan administration set forth a decidedly non-interventionist policy:

> There is no conclusive evidence that official intervention in the past has achieved its purpose. The large purchases of dollar denominated assets by foreign central banks in 1977–78 did not prevent the dollar from depreciating, and their large sales of dollar assets in 1980–81 did not prevent the dollar from appreciating.
>
> Moreover, intervention may have been counterproductive. Market participants did not know whether it signaled a change in monetary policy, thereby leading to increased uncertainty on their part.
>
> When the previous Administration left office, intervention by the United States was being conducted at a relatively high volume virtually on a day-to-day basis with the objective of using the periods of dollar strength first to cover outstanding foreign currency liabilities, and later to build foreign currency reserves. This was the first time, at least in recent history, that the United States had embarked on a deliberate policy of acquiring substantial foreign currency reserves. Early in 1981 the new Administration scaled back U.S. intervention in foreign exchange markets.
>
> In conjunction with the strong emphasis on economic fundamentals, this Administration has returned to the policy of intervening only when necessary to counter conditions of severe disorder in the market.

As in the past, no attempt has been made to define disorderly market conditions in advance. When making the decision on whether exchange market conditions justify intervention, the U.S. government will consult closely with governments of other major industrial countries. Also as in the past, the Department of the Treasury and the Federal Reserve will keep the public informed regarding the U.S. exchange market intervention policy. Although the Administration does not expect intervention in the exchange markets to occur on a regular basis, it will continue to monitor closely developments in those markets.[2]

The subsequent two annual reports, issued in early 1983 and early 1984, were similarly negative toward intervention on foreign-exchange markets. In the February 1983 report, the view was put forth as follows:

Since March, 1981 the United States has abstained as much as possible from direct intervention in the foreign exchange market. This unwillingness to intervene is based on doubts about whether exchange market intervention is effective or desirable. As long as the Federal Reserve continues to pursue a policy of targeting monetary aggregates, any U.S. intervention on the foreign exchange market must be *sterilized*—that is, offset by other transactions on domestic financial markets. These transactions are likely to wipe out most of the effect of the initial exchange-market intervention.[3]

In the February 1984 report, we find an excellent discussion of foreign-exchange intervention:

It is nearly impossible to imagine the world economy going through the past ten years in a straight jacket at fixed exchange rates. Given the events of this period, notably the large changes in oil prices and the divergent macroeconomics policies among the industrialized countries, floating exchange rates have performed well. . .[4]

[2]"The United States in the International Economic System," *Economic Report of the President and the Annual Report of the Council of Economic Advisers*, February 1982, p. 172.

[3]"The United States in the World Economy: Strains on the System," *Economic Report of the President and the Annual Report of the Council of Economic Advisers*, February 1983, p. 68.

[4]"The United States in the World Economy: Challenges of Recovery," *Economic Report of the President and the Annual Report of the Council of Economic Advisers*, February 1984, p. 50.

179

A second measure that has been proposed to improve the trade balance is intervention in the foreign exchange market by the monetary authorities to force down the value of the dollar and thus to restore price competitiveness to American industry. At the beginning of August, 1983, and later in the year, U.S. authorities did intervene on a small scale, buying marks and yen in exchange for dollars, in cooperation with monetary authorities in other countries. The intervention did not noticeably depress the value of the dollar, nor was it intended to. It is U.S. policy to intervene only to calm disorderly markets.

There are two kinds of foreign exchange intervention, known as *sterilized* and *unsterilized*. Sterilized foreign exchange intervention occurs when the central bank, at the same time that it is buying foreign currencies with domestic currency, sells Treasury securities in the market in order to take the domestic currency back out of circulation. The point of sterilizing the foreign exchange intervention is to keep the domestic money stock unchanged. This is the type of intervention the U.S. monetary authorities undertake when they do intervene.

Unsterilized intervention has the effect of increasing the domestic money supply. This would have a strong downward effect on the value of the domestic currency. But like any other increase in the money supply, it can be inflationary.

The effect of sterilized intervention is much less clear than the effect of unsterilized intervention. The 1983 summer intervention amounted to $254 million on the part of U.S. authorities. This was only 1 percent of the flow through the U.S. interbank foreign exchange market on a typical day in 1983. It was even less significant relative to the trillions of dollars in funds that investors around the world can commit to the foreign exchange market if they think that the exchange value of the dollar has been temporarily pushed below the true market level. Investors will move in quickly to exploit the potential profit opportunity, buying dollars, and thereby returning the price of the dollar to its previous level. This process ensures that, unless monetary authorities are prepared to intervene, on a massive scale, any effects on the exchange rate will be transitory. After the Versailles Summit of 1982, a working group with representatives of the seven Summit countries was set up to study exchange market intervention. Its report, released in April 1983, concluded in part, that there was "broad agreement that sterilized intervention did not generally have a lasting effect."

If monetary authorities were prepared to intervene on a sufficiently massive scale, there could conceivably be some permanent effect on the exchange rate, even if the intervention were sterilized so as to leave the money supply unchanged. But to the extent that sterilized purchases of foreign currency were successful in reducing the value of the dollar, they would also be successful in raising the U.S. interest rate. The reason is that sterilized intervention does not leave market participants holding any more dollar currency than before; it leaves them holding more dollar Treasury securities than before. The interest rate would have to rise to induce the market to hold a greater quantity of Treasury securities, just as it does whenever the government sells large enough quantities of Treasury securities. The exporting and import-competing industries would be happy with the lower value of the dollar. But the capital goods, construction, and other interest-sensitive industries would be unhappy with the higher interest rate.[5]

The Reagan Second Term: Deliberate Pursuit of a Weak Currency

The final report of the Council of Economic Advisers for the first Reagan term, issued in February 1985, did not contain any discussion of foreign-exchange markets and did not set forth a policy regarding intervention on foreign-exchange markets. It did include an excellent chapter on trade policies, but the implicit policy reflected by the omission of a discussion of foreign-exchange intervention is that the market would simply be allowed to operate with regard to financial flows.

At the beginning of the second Reagan term, the inventory of economic problems commanding the attention of a new team of policymakers in the administration was very lengthy, but it did not include achieving price stability. Achieving a higher pace of economic growth had begun to take precedence over inflation. Among the problems the administration concluded to be worthy of serious attention were savings and loan association failures in Ohio and Maryland, federal Farm Credit banks in trouble because of the financial problems of the agriculture sector, growing problems in the energy sector, stagnation of employment in the manufacturing sector, a large and growing trade deficit with the rest of the world, and continuing concerns about the possibility of an international debt crisis.

In view of this growing list of problems that were thought to be deserving of attention, there emerged a perception that if the

[5]Ibid., pp. 60–61.

administration did not appear to be part of the solution, the voters might get the idea that the administration was part of the problem and retaliate at the next election. Consequently, the first year of the second term saw increasingly frequent calls for a return to demand management, especially on the part of certain other industrialized countries.

However, there were a couple of major problems with simply leaning on other countries to open their monetary spigots and help spend the world back to prosperity. The strength of the U.S. dollar—or the weakness of other currencies—meant that if central banks in other major countries such as West Germany and Japan were to ease monetary policy overtly, their currencies would fall further relative to the dollar. The increased strength of the dollar would then precipitate even greater pressures for protectionist trade legislation by the U.S. Congress.

The reaction of foreign economic officials to the Reagan administration's initial overtures for demand stimulus persuaded the administration that the United States had to become the "lead locomotive" to give the other countries room to become more expansive. That conclusion led to another problem—how to package a "weak currency" policy without it appearing to be a return to the policies of the Carter administration. During the first term, the president had taken considerable pride in the strength of the U.S. currency as a symbol of world confidence in his policies. As the dollar had risen in value from 1981 through 1984, it was taken as a sign that deregulation, tax reduction, lower inflation, and an effort to "get the government off the backs of the people" had created a highly desirable environment for capital formation in the United States, and Americans were repatriating their capital while foreigners were seeking a safe haven for their savings.

How, then, could the administration in its second term adopt a weak-currency policy? The answer was that in form it did not, even though in substance it did. By the time of the Plaza Agreement among the five major industrial countries on September 22, 1985, it was anticipated that a policy of raising the value of foreign currencies would not be seen by the U.S. public as the same thing as the policies of reducing the value of the dollar of the Carter administration. Accordingly, the United States entered into the Plaza Agreement, which stated:

The Ministers and governors agreed that exchange rates should play a role in adjusting external imbalances. In order to do this, exchange rates should better reflect fundamental economic conditions than has been the case. They believe that agreed policy actions must be implemented and reinforced to improve the fundamentals further, and that in view of the present and prospective changes in fundamentals, some *further orderly appreciation of the main nondollar currencies against the dollar* is desirable. They stand ready to cooperate more closely to encourage this when to do so would be helpful.[6]

The subsequent annual report of the Council of Economic Advisers, issued in February 1986, did not contain any discussion about foreign-exchange markets and was silent on the administration's attitudes toward intervention in the exchange markets.

However, the annual report issued in January 1987 stated:

Since the first quarter of 1985, the real value of trade weighted dollars has fallen by 20 percent back to its late 1981 level. Although the causes of this steep depreciation of the dollar are difficult to isolate with precision, the decline in real GNP growth in the United States since mid-1984 likely contributed to the dollar's fall. In addition, the announced intentions of the Group of Five to seek a lower dollar in the Plaza Agreement and subsequent actions to back up these intentions, especially the continuation of the easing of U.S. monetary policy that began in late 1984, probably contributed to further dollar depreciation after September 1985.

There is general agreement among economists that better convergence of economic performance and better coordination of economic policies among the leading industrial countries is both desirable and essential for achieving greater stability of exchange rates. At the Tokyo Economic Summit, the leaders of the seven largest industrial countries agreed to a flexible approach to improving the international monetary system by providing more effective procedures for the coordination of economic policies. The approach adopted in Tokyo represents an important step down the path to greater convergence of economic performance and better coordination of economic policies—a path that was charted at earlier Economic Summits and Ministerial Meetings, including especially the Versailles Economic Summit and the Group

---

[6]"Statement Excerpts on Economic Problems," *New York Times*, September 23, 1985 (emphasis added).

183

of Five meeting of September 1985. Three features of the approach outlined at the Tokyo Summit deserve particular emphasis.

First, efforts at policy coordination will not focus narrowly on achieving specific values or ranges for exchange rates. Policy makers are to consider a broad class of indicators of economic performance and economic policy: . . . The Tokyo Summit Leaders explicitly stated that the objectives of policy coordination are much broader than limiting exchange-rate movements.

This agreement does not preclude official intervention in foreign exchange markets, when such intervention would be useful. However, it does place the emphasis for policy coordination where it belongs—on the economic policies that ultimately influence important developments in the world economy.[7]

Intervention Is Speculation

In effect, when the United States buys dollars, it is selling a foreign currency, and vice versa. In 1985 and 1986, intervention by the Federal Reserve to reduce the foreign-exchange value of the dollar meant the United States was accumulating foreign currencies, which are referred to as international reserves. In 1987, intervention by the Federal Reserve to "support the dollar" has meant selling parts of the inventory of foreign currencies. After the inventory is depleted, further intervention is made possible by way of so-called swap agreements, wherein the Federal Reserve borrows foreign currencies from foreign central banks. The subsequent sales of these borrowed currencies is, in effect, the same as selling short in any financial market.

If the dollar continues to fall against the shorted currency, the swap agreement can be unwound (repaid) only by the purchase of the higher valued currency in the foreign-exchange market, which means that the United States incurs a loss on the transaction. In fact, generally accepted accounting practices require that the local currency value of exposure (liability) be computed and reported at regular intervals, so the paper losses are recorded even while the swap liability is outstanding.

In essence, then, politicians tend to think of intervention to stabilize the currency as being virtuous, but the actual transaction

[7]"Growth, Competitiveness, and the Trade Deficit," *Economic Report of the President and the Annual Report of the Council of Economic Advisers,* January 1987, pp. 116, 119.

184

amounts to speculative short-selling in foreign-exchange markets. Once the public and members of Congress understand that intervention by the Federal Reserve means foreign-exchange losses that add to the budget deficit, their support for such actions is likely to be diminished.

Conclusion

My interpretation of the thinking that led to the return to demand management and the increased policy activism in the second Reagan term is as follows. In the first term, tax rates and tax revenue were reduced, but there was no reduction in real tax burdens since government spending was not reduced. At the beginning of the second term, there was an increasing disparity in the economic performance of various sectors and regions of the country and a feeling that the disinflation/deflation process had gone on too long and was too painful to too many Americans (voters). Fiscal activism of the usual variety was not possible because of the budget deficits. There could be no new jobs programs, public works initiatives, or tax-relief measures as long as the huge deficits persisted. Since spending reduction to decrease the deficits proved to be unattainable, the drumbeat for higher taxes was building. However, the 1984 presidential election campaign demonstrated that the public accepted the president's view that explicit tax hikes would merely result in greater spending—not lower deficits.

Since fiscal policy tools were not available, monetary policy was, in effect, the only game in town. Reducing the purchasing power of a nation's currency is simply another way to impose a tax, but it need not originate in the House Ways and Means Committee, and it cannot be vetoed. It is the tax no one has to vote for. A policy of reducing the value of a country's currency on foreign-exchange markets is identical to raising the prices of foreign-produced goods paid by the nation's consumers. It reduces their real disposable income, similar to any explicit tax. Also, higher prices of foreign goods are intended to increase the competitiveness of domestic producers who compete with imports on foreign, as well as domestic, markets. A weak-currency policy is a form of monetary protectionism—an alternative to legislated protectionism.

In other words, a lower value of the dollar makes it possible for domestic producers to improve their profit margins, which is another

185

way of saying they can raise prices. There is no way to interpret the policies other than as a method of reducing household incomes for the benefit of domestic producers. It is not possible, nor was it intended, to reduce the foreign-exchange value of the dollar without reducing the real disposable income of American consumers.

The analysis undertaken by the first Reagan administration was that sterilized intervention had no effect, so no intervention should occur. The conclusion reached early in the second term was that intervention should not be sterilized, with the intended result of a very sharp acceleration of monetary growth in 1985 and 1986. The policy of trying to get the country moving again through expansionary monetary policies is achieving the intended results, albeit at the cost of higher inflation. The objectives of the second term will be judged to be equally as successful as the policies of the first term—but in the opposite direction.

13. Financial Services Regulation: Driven by Events

Catherine England

Several thoughts come immediately to mind about the Reagan administration's record in finanical services regulation. First, in terms of how much the financial markets have changed since 1981, the Reagan administration seems to have been in office a long time. Second, as in many other areas of regulation, this administration has had less substantive impact than a casual observer might deduce from either its rhetoric or the common perceptions about what has been happening in the financial markets. Third, Congress plays an important, even dominant, role in this area, and it has been a major source of the bottlenecks constraining the adjustments by financial services firms to a changing environment. Finally, the story of the Reagan administration's impact on financial services is not yet fully written, and it may not be completed until long after President Reagan steps down in January 1989.

To explore these observations, let us examine three broad categories—events, appointments, and policies—before considering Reagan's likely legacy in the financial services area.

Events

When Ronald Reagan took office in 1981, interest rates were high, but they had not yet reached their peak. A few academics and regulators were concerned about the financial health of the thrift industry, but there was no widespread sense of crisis. There was no general dismay over the amount of lending that banks were doing in Third World countries. Relatively few people had heard of Penn Square in Oklahoma. Continental Illinois was considered a model of good bank management. Texas was still booming. Banks

The author would like to thank Joe Belew, John Doherty, Chris Edwards, William Haraf, Bonnie Ohri, and Fran Smith for helpful comments.

in the Midwest were healthy. Money market mutual funds were beginning to grow rapidly as most rates payable on bank deposits were legally constrained to below-market levels. Nonbank banks were not an issue. There were, as yet, few doubts about the desirability of federal deposit insurance as it had been operated since 1933. Indeed, coverage had just been increased from $40,000 to $100,000, and no one had expressed concern about the role of money brokers in moving deposits around the country. No regional interstate banking compacts had been established. And depositors in many Maryland and Ohio thrifts simply assumed they had federal (or at least state-backed) deposit insurance.

With the benefit of hindsight, we can see that there was considerable weakness in the system, and several problems were waiting to happen. As these problems (the seeds of which were planted in the economically volatile 1970s) began to capture the attention of regulators, Congress, and the public, it became politically more difficult to advocate substantive deregulation.

For example, most members of the Depository Institutions Deregulation Committee were sympathetic with the need to remove limits on rates payable on deposits.[1] But how quickly could they move when mortgage rates were already so high that real estate brokers, thrift managers, and homeowners were sending house keys to congressmen in protest? Similarly, while the 1982 Garn–St Germain Depository Institution Act of 1982 granted new powers to thrift institutions, how could one strongly advocate new powers for banks when large money center banks were looking for direct and indirect aid in handling a growing Third World debt problem and the extent of the Penn Square fiasco was becoming known? If bankers could do such damage with traditional banking powers, imagine what harm could be done if they were allowed to engage in a broader range of activities.

Then, as inflation was brought under control, oil and agricultural

[1]The Depository Institutions Deregulation Committee was formed by the Depository Institutions Deregulation and Monetary Control Act of 1980 and was charged with phasing out deposit interest-rate ceilings. It was composed of the secretary of the treasury, the chairman of the Federal Reserve Board of Governors, and the heads of the Federal Deposit Insurance Corporation, the Federal Home Loan Bank Board, and the National Credit Union Administration. The comptroller of the currency was a nonvoting member.

prices fell and problems developed with "farm" and "energy" banks. And rather than abating as expected, the thrift industry problem continued to get worse, eventually creating headlines throughout the country as the Ohio and Maryland thrift insurance funds collapsed. Of course, there was also the Continental Illinois episode, which (we are told) threatened the stability of the entire U.S. banking system. As if there were not enough problems among depository institutions, the insurance industry faced a funding crisis that was attributed to adverse liability rulings, and the securities industry was rocked by insider trading scandals. These events led to further questions about the desirability of allowing insurance and securities firms into banking or banks into these industries.

Finally, on October 19, 1987, the financial services industry, along with the rest of the nation, was stunned when the Dow-Jones average for the New York Stock Exchange fell more than 500 points in a single day of trading. Although there appeared to be little or no direct spillover from the stock market's plunge to banks and most other financial institutions, opponents of deregulation seized the opportunity to urge even more caution in the crawl toward a more competitive environment. The Reagan administration responded by appointing a commission to investigate the causes of the dramatic fall in stock prices and to suggest policy responses.[2]

By most standards, the past six to seven years have been a tumultuous period for the financial services industry, and many observers have blamed deregulation for the problems confronting the nation's depositories and other financial services firms. The Council of Economic Advisers must have felt like a lone voice crying in the wilderness when it wrote in early 1986, "A more persuasive case can be made for the opposite conclusion—that inappropriate and excessive regulation, combined with inflation and then disinflation, contributed to an environment in which many depository institutions could not have continued to operate without deregulation."[3]

[2]The Brady Commission was composed of Nicholas Brady, chairman of Dillon Read and Company; James Cotting, chairman and chief executive officer of Novistar International Corporation; Robert Kirby, chairman of Capital Group; John Opal, former chief executive officer of International Business Machines Corporation; Howard Stein, chairman of Dreyfus Corporation; and Robert Glauber, a Harvard Business School professor.

[3]Council of Economic Advisers, *Economic Report of the President* (Washington: Government Printing Office, 1986), p. 210.

Appointments

Meanwhile, the appointments of the Reagan administration to the agencies that oversee financial services were, for the most part, good ones—especially in the early years. Appointees generally advocated a market-oriented approach to regulation, reflecting, perhaps, the administration's broad rhetorical interest in regulatory reform and deregulation.

Donald Regan as secretary of the treasury appeared particularly interested in reforming the banking laws (surprisingly so, some might suggest, for a man who came from Wall Street). Todd Conover as comptroller of the currency not only advocated change, he took a lead by approving nonbank bank applications in significant numbers. William Isaac at the Federal Deposit Insurance Corporation (FDIC) was one of the first policymakers to talk openly about the incentive problems created by a federal deposit insurance system that not only does not price for risk but that also frequently extends its de facto protection far beyond legal requirements. Richard Pratt at the Federal Home Loan Bank Board announced early on that he was uninterested in overseeing the death of the thrift industry, and consequently he pushed for new powers and an expanded economic role for thrift institutions. And John Shad at the Securities and Exchange Commission promoted the idea of financial services holding companies that would be allowed to offer a wide range of services—from banking to securities to insurance—regulated by function. In fact, one political observer has commented that the early appointees were too aggressive in urging deregulation of the financial services industry, that they attempted to move further and faster than most Washington policymakers—particularly those in the House of Representatives and at the Federal Reserve Board—were ready to go.

Although more recent appointments have been somewhat less noteworthy, there are those of them who do continue to strongly advocate change. Among them, the Federal Reserve Board governors appointed by this administration have frequently challenged the status quo. Martha Seger and Robert Heller, in particular, have been outspoken advocates of allowing banks into other lines of business, and of allowing those who own and operate other financial services and commercial firms into banking. And Alan Greenspan, the new Federal Reserve Board chairman, has long called for

190

the substantive deregulation of the banking and financial services industry. In addition, George Gould, under secretary of finance at Treasury, has been a strong proponent of change, arguing for the need to revise the existing regulatory structure with more emphasis on market discipline and competition. William Seidman, who followed William Isaac at the FDIC, initially appeared less vocal than his predecessor in promoting deregulation. Recently, however, Seidman has renewed the call for a broad-based revision of the banking laws—because, some observers suggest, of support for such proposals from the Greenspan-led Federal Reserve. Notably, the FDIC recently issued a study concluding that adequate safeguards could be established in a bank holding company structure to protect the federal insurance fund and, thus, allow for significant deregulation.[4]

On a slightly less positive note, some have observed that Secretary of the Treasury James Baker seems to be less interested in questions of financial institution regulation than was his predecessor, Donald Regan. Robert Clarke, the current comptroller, has also appeared less vocal in supporting change than did his predecessor, Todd Conover. But the harshest criticism has been directed at former Federal Home Loan Bank Board chairman Edwin Gray.

Gray's attitude toward regulating S&Ls seems to have been diametrically opposed to that of his predecessor, Richard Pratt. Where Pratt had urged greater diversification of the industry, Gray encouraged a return to the traditional activities of the thrift industry— specifically, mortgage lending. Citing the difficulties associated with the growing liabilities of the Federal Savings and Loan Insurance Corporation, Gray also sought to limit the growth rate of some of the more aggressive thrifts.

While there is much to criticize in Gray's approach to regulating the thrift industry, the difficulty of the situation with which he was faced should also be acknowledged. Throughout Gray's tenure, Congress dallied, refusing to provide the FSLIC with the resources necessary to close a growing number of insolvent S&Ls. Thus, the bank board was required to regulate an industry with both solvent firms attempting to position themselves to compete effectively in a

---

[4]Federal Deposit Insurance Corporation, *Mandate for Change: Restructuring the Banking Industry* (Washington: Government Printing Office, 1987).

rapidly changing financial services market and insolvent firms willing to take admitted long shots in an effort to recapitalize their institutions. This congressionally supported situation presented a virtual "Mission Impossible" in its challenge to balance, on the one hand, the need to constrain insolvent firms with, on the other, the case for allowing healthy institutions more flexibility.

Gray was followed at the bank board by Danny Wall, but it is still too early to assess Wall's policies. Although Congress did make provisions for some additional funding for the FSLIC in the Competitive Equality Banking Act of 1987, the additional funds, by most accounts, are inadequate, and Wall must face the further difficulty of congressionally mandated "forbearance" in deciding which thrifts to close.[5]

Policies

It is helpful to review what has—and has not—occurred in the area of financial services regulation.[6] We can view regulatory restrictions as falling into five broad categories: (1) entry restrictions, (2) balance sheet restrictions (for example, capitalization requirements), (3) activity limits, (4) pricing rules, and (5) consumer-protection rules.

At the federal level, there has been no easing of entry restrictions. In fact, the Competitive Equality Banking Act increased entry barriers by prohibiting the further expansion of limited-service (or nonbank) banks. Capital requirements for banks have been tightened recently, although they have obviously been eased in practice, if not in law, for the thrift industry. Activity restrictions for S&Ls were eased in 1980 and 1982, and the Fed has taken steps toward easing activity restrictions for bank holding companies. But the 1987 banking legislation temporarily ended state and federal regulators' authority to allow banks more freedom. Officials appointed by the Reagan administration did remove interest-rate ceilings on most

[5]The 1987 banking legislation requires that the Bank Board "forbear" in closing S&Ls with below-minimum capital as a result of prevailing economic conditions (for example, reduced energy or agricultural prices) until the thrifts have had an adequate opportunity to overcome their problems.

[6]The following discussion borrows from Thomas Durkin, "The Slow Pace of Federal Financial Deregulation," a paper presented to the International Conference on Research in the Consumer Interest, Racine, Wisconsin, August 15, 1986.

deposits in compliance with the legislation enacted in 1980.[7] Finally, consumer-protection laws are still in place and were added to by the 1987 legislation. In short, there has been little progress in changing federal banking laws in a way that would lead to more competition or improved market discipline.

This is not entirely the fault of the Reagan administration. Particularly during the first term, the Treasury Department and regulatory agencies supported Sen. Jake Garn's efforts to produce comprehensive banking legislation. Although a Garn-sponsored bill passed the Senate by an overwhelming majority in 1984, nothing like it came out of the House Banking Committee.

On a more positive note, the administration was supportive of efforts to privatize the federal housing finance agencies. Although that goal was not accomplished, there was more success in limiting the growth of these agencies, allowing more room for private alternatives to the Federal National Mortgage Association ("Fannie Mae") and the Federal Home Loan Mortgage Association ("Freddie Mac"). In addition, the Treasury Department has been termed "instrumental" in passing legislation that helped equalize the treatment of different firms acting as government securities dealers, thus increasing the degree of competition in that market.

In December 1982, the Task Group on Regulation of Financial Services was formed with Vice President George Bush at its head. Among other things, the task group recommended introducing risk-related deposit insurance premiums, and it reiterated the administration's support for the financial services holding company concept. It is perhaps best remembered for recommending a major reorganization of the federal bank regulatory agencies in a manner that would have added considerably to the Federal Reserve Board's power. But little has resulted from the task group's recommendations.

For many, the most disappointing policy to emerge from this administration was the decision in May 1984 to bail out Continental Illinois in Chicago. Prior to that, the FDIC had taken a number of praiseworthy steps in its handling of bank failures. In July 1982, Penn Square was allowed to fail, and uninsured depositors were told they would have to await, with other creditors, the sale or liquidation of the bank's assets. The FDIC's William Issac also began

7There are still interest-rate restrictions on demand deposits.

193

experimenting with a "modified-payout" plan under which, although a failing bank was merged with a healthy institution, large depositors were not fully protected. Rather, funds exceeding $100,000 were made available on the basis of the FDIC's conservative estimate of what it would recover from questionable loans and other assets.

And then, along came Continental Illinois. It was, in part, because the FDIC's new policies were working so well that the Continental Illinois crisis appeared to develop so quickly. Large foreign and domestic depositors, faced with growing evidence that Continental Illinois's loan portfolio was worth substantially less than its book value and uncertain about how the FDIC would handle their claims if the bank failed, began to transfer their funds to other, more stable institutions—exactly what advocates of market discipline would hope to see. But the bank regulators panicked when it became clear how well their new policies were working, and they issued a blanket guarantee to all creditors of the bank holding company.

The nation's smaller banks vigorously protested, and with good reason. Why should depositors with accounts exceeding $100,000 at the nation's largest banks be granted blanket guarantees when similar depositors at smaller institutions were subject to loss in the event of failure? Such a policy clearly would serve to further concentrate large deposits in large banks. Consequently, the experiment with modified payouts and increased market discipline was abandoned.[8]

Another disappointment was the decision by the president to sign the Competitive Equality Banking Act of 1987 into law. In essence, this legislation was an attempt to freeze the U.S. financial services industry into a long-outdated mold that ignores changing competitive and technological conditions, both domestically and internationally. But the bill also provided some, albeit inadequate, additional funding for the FSLIC. Apparently, Secretary Baker felt that additional funding for the FSLIC was needed immediately, and he engineered a compromise. In exchange for additional funds for the thrifts' deposit guarantor, the administration would accept the temporary moratorium on new bank powers. Baker did receive assurances from Rep. Fernand St Germain and Sen. William Prox-

[8]For a detailed account (and defense) of the Continental Illinois bailout decisions, see Irvine H. Sprague, *Bailout: An Insider's Account of Bank Failures and Rescues* (New York: Basic Books, 1986), particularly chapters 8–12.

mire that the moratorium would not be extended beyond March 1, 1988.

The Brady Commission report was also something of a disappointment.[9] Although the commission members should be praised for resisting the temptation to blame computerized trading and arbitrageurs for the October stock market plunge, they did make some unwelcome proposals. Most alarming was their suggestion that the Federal Reserve Board become a superagency overseeing the regulatory actions of the Securities and Exchange Commission and the Commodity Futures Trading Commission. In the first place, there was no evidence of any particular regulatory ineptitude by either agency leading up to the October 19 crash. So what would the Federal Reserve have done differently? Second, there is already a strong argument that the ability of the Fed to pursue an optimal monetary policy is undermined by conflicts of interest inherent in its roles as both a bank regulator and the central bank. Those problems would certainly be compounded by any attempt to take on the additional task of regulating the securities markets. Fortunately, the current board of governors appears little interested in pressing for these additional powers.

The Brady Commission also recommended that daily limits on price swings, total volume, or some other measure be imposed on the securities markets. This may, in fact, be desirable. But these are limits best set and enforced by those directly involved in the securities markets—specifically, their individual governing boards. Certainly, these groups have a much more direct stake than does any government agency in maintaining customer confidence in the markets. We would therefore expect these private regulatory groups to be in a much better position to balance the trade-off between maintaining liquidity (and thus avoiding closing the markets) and ensuring that the trading remains orderly. To the credit of the administration, there has been no rush to enact the commission's proposals through regulation or legislation.

This review of administration policies and proposals raises several "what if" questions. Although the Treasury Department was interested, early on, in promoting reform of financial services reg-

[9]*Report of the Presidential Task Force on Market Mechanisms* (Washington: Government Printing Office, 1988).

195

ulation, there was never any evidence that these issues were of great interest at the White House. Consequently, there was never any apparent desire on the part of the administration to expend significant political capital pursuing change. Would it have made a difference if these regulatory questions had, at some time, topped the president's policy agenda?

In some cases, it appeared that the administration, or its appointees, lacked the courage of their convictions. What would have happened, for example, if the comptroller's office, the Federal Reserve, and the FDIC had fashioned a response to the Continental Illinois crisis that protected the liquidity of correspondent banks while imposing losses on depositors and other Continental Illinois creditors?

Finally, could the administration have sustained a veto of the 1987 banking legislation if it had offered as a substitute a "clean" FSLIC bill that dealt just with the problems facing that agency?

The Reagan Legacy

The final chapter has yet to be written concerning the Reagan administration's impact on the financial services industry. This is primarily a result of the importance of the Federal Reserve Board in establishing bank regulatory policies. As the central bank, the lender of last resort, and the dominant bank regulatory agency, the Fed has a great deal to say about the way the system will respond to unexpected shocks, as well as about the future of bank regulation. Its board of governors can go a long way toward setting the terms of the debate regardless of who is president. In pursuing further deregulation, it would be useful, for example, if the Federal Reserve Board took the lead in articulating a new policy for dealing with large bank failures. Such a policy should (1) protect the liquidity of the banking system while (2) imposing losses on uninsured depositors and creditors of the bank holding company, and/or the financial services holding company. Thus, the Federal Reserve Board, led by Alan Greenspan, might accomplish in the future what the Reagan administration has failed to achieve in the way of regulatory reform for the financial services industry.[10]

[10]In fall 1987, the Federal Reserve Board requested comments on proposed regulations that would allow bank holding companies to acquire healthy (rather than only troubled) thrifts. Presumably, this demonstrates some desire on the part of the

In addition to naming Federal Reserve Board members whose terms will extend long after Reagan has left office, this adminstration will also leave behind a legacy in terms of its willingness to reassess the existing financial regulatory structure. It has been instrumental in putting new ideas on the policymakers' menu. The financial services holding company, an idea that some believe to be the most politically feasible route for moving toward a more deregulated, competitive environment, was introduced into the public policy debate by this administration. The modified-payout proposal, risk-based deposit insurance premiums, and risk-based capital requirements became part of the policy debate when they were advocated by Reagan appointees. Although the particulars of some of these proposals can be criticized, their introduction represented a readiness to recognize the shortcomings of the existing regulatory structure and to search for constructive solutions.

These actions reflect a healthy change in the Reagan administration's attitude toward regulation generally. Although this more skeptical attitude was inconsistently applied and the record is often one of missed opportunities, at least the broad rhetoric was on target. We may expect gains to result from the stance that government is not always the solution and is often the problem.

Conclusion

In sum, not much in the way of substantive change has been accomplished by the Reagan administration. Reform of the financial services regulatory structure was never a top priority at the White House. And many have argued that the administration's posture toward financial institutions was determined by exogenous events rather than its own agenda. Still, the appointments of the administration were, as a rule, good ones, and many of these individuals brought to their posts a fresh eye and an inclination to challenge the status quo. This has certainly affected the environment in which the debate is taking place and has helped put on the defensive those who seek continued government protection through perpetuating

---

current Federal Reserve Board to move forward with deregulatory initiatives as soon as allowed by law.

the existing regulatory structure. The rest of the story is now largely in the hands of the Federal Reserve Board governors, and its outcome will depend on how effective a role they are able to play in future debates.

PART IV

TRANSFER PAYMENTS

14. Social Security: Look at Your Pay Stub

Peter J. Ferrara

To evaluate the performance of the Reagan administration on social security, one need only look at one's paycheck. In 1980, the total combined payroll-tax rate on employers and employees was 12.26 percent. It is 15.02 percent for 1988 and scheduled to increase to 15.3 percent in 1990. In 1980, the maximum annual payroll tax for a worker, including both the employer and employee shares, was $3,175. This year, the maximum tax is $6,750, an increase of 112 percent.

Total payroll-tax revenues have climbed from $140.6 billion in 1980 to a projected $309 billion in 1988, an increase of 121 percent. Total spending for the entire payroll-tax-financed, trust-fund-based system, including Medicare and disability benefits, has climbed from $149.1 billion in 1980 to a projected $282.6 billion in 1988, an increase of 90 percent.

Clearly, on social security, the Reagan administration never even showed up. The lack of any impact in this area, moreover, is no minor omission. The social security system accounts for about 30 percent of federal spending and over 50 percent of federal domestic spending. Social security, national defense, and interest on the national debt together account for about 70 percent of total federal spending. The unbroken increase in social security expenditures, along with increased costs for national defense and interest on the debt, explains why the Reagan administration has had no apparent impact in reducing federal spending.

The Reagan administration did make one major early effort to reduce social security expenditures.[1] Reagan came into office facing

---

[1]For further discussion about the proposed Reagan social security reforms in 1981 and the later Greenspan Commision, see Peter J. Ferrara, ed., *Social Security: Prospects for Real Reform* (Washington: Cato Institute, 1985), pp. 33–67.

a severe social security financing crisis. By the spring of 1981, the latest official government projections showed that even under intermediate assumptions, the program would run short of funds to pay promised benefits in less than two years, with a widening financial gap in the future.

To address this crisis, the administration proposed a package of reforms in May 1981 centered around three major items:

- a one-time permanent three-month delay in the program's annual cost-of-living adjustment (COLA) increases;
- a reduction in benefits for workers who chose early retirement in the future, although full benefits would still be available to those who waited until age 65 to retire; and
- a temporary change in the formula used to calculate increases in future benefits for today's workers, which would result in an eventual 10 percent cut in expected benefits for those retiring in the next century, although benefits would still have been higher in real terms than today.

The president had pledged in the 1980 campaign that he would not cut social security benefits for present retirees. This package fundamentally kept that pledge, with only the delay in COLA increases affecting present retirees, and even that arguably did not reduce current benefits.

Nevertheless, the proposals met with a firestorm of criticism. The Republican-controlled Senate handed the newly elected Republican president the harshest blow of all on the issue by voting 96–0 in favor of a resolution warning him not even to send the proposals to Congress.

The Greenspan Commission

After that, the Reagan administration was never really heard from again on social security. The president withdrew his proposals and established a commission to resolve the crisis. The commission included five members appointed by Reagan; five appointed by the Senate majority leader, Howard Baker; and five appointed by the House speaker, Tip O'Neill. The commission chairman was Alan Greenspan, now chairman of the Federal Reserve Board.

The commission included mostly representatives of political lobby groups and intellectually timid politicians who were anxious to minimize controversy. The purpose of this group was clearly to forge a political compromise, not to develop meaningful reforms.

The commission ultimately offered a package of recommendations at the end of 1982 that included the following major elements:

- Accelerate the payroll tax increases already scheduled through 1990;
- Increase payroll taxes on self-employed workers, from 75 percent of the total combined employer and employee tax rates to 100 percent;
- Permanently delay annual COLA increases for six months, moving the increase back from the middle of each year to the start of the next;
- For married retirees with annual family income over $32,000 and single retirees with annual family income over $25,000, subject half of social security benefits, at that time completely tax-exempt, to the federal income tax, with the revenues going into social security. The income thresholds would be deliberately not indexed for inflation, so that eventually almost all workers would have half their social security benefits taxed.
- Eliminate the right of employees of state and local governments and nonprofit organizations to withdraw from social security, as they were choosing to do in increasing numbers.
- Reduce windfall social security benefits for government employees who qualify for the program's benefits based on short periods of private employment.
- Adopt an automatic trigger that would reduce annual COLA increases to the lesser of wages or prices whenever the program's trust funds fall to less than 20 percent of one year's benefit expenditures.

Because of widespread fear that attempts to alter any single element in this package would cause the grand compromise to unravel, Congress adopted the commission's proposals almost without change. The taxation of benefits was modified so that half of all benefits would not be immediately subject to the tax upon reaching the income thresholds. Rather, benefits were taxed only up to 50 percent of the amount by which income exceeded the threshold. More importantly, Sen. William Armstrong (R–Colo.), who had served on the commission and dissented from its recommendations, successfully led a fight to add a provision that phases in a delay in the normal social security retirement age, until it reaches 67 in 2022.

The final legislation as passed managed to hurt just about everyone. The elderly saw their benefits cut, workers saw their taxes raised substantially, young people saw their future returns promised under the social security program cut to almost nothing, and virtually every last worker in the economy was corralled into the insatiable program against his will. In Washington, this is known as public interest legislation—whereby everyone gets burned.

Two of the best intentioned of Reaganites, Jack Svahn and Dorcas Hardy, served as social security commissioners during Reagan's tenure. But the measure of their success within the administration seems to have been nothing more than keeping the program out of the newspapers. When the administration ultimately did propose another change in the program, the proposal was to expand benefits. Under prior law, retirees received a COLA only when inflation in one or more years exceeded 3 percent. Under the Reagan proposal, which was adopted, a COLA is granted for the amount of inflation every year, even if it is less than 3 percent.

The administration did one thing right tangentially related to social security. It included in the 1981 tax bill a provision extending individual retirement accounts (IRAs) to all workers. The IRAs were broadly popular, with about 40 million Americans contributing to them at least once. This participation helped Americans to see in concrete how they could take more direct responsibility for providing for their own retirement through the private sector. The administration proposed in its tax-reform bill to expand IRAs further, by increasing contribution limits. But in the tax-reform give and take, the administration not only traded away its proposal but also accepted the elimination of the IRA contribution deduction for most workers.

What Could Have Been Done

What should the administration have done? Of all government programs, social security has the most broadly utilized and widely recognized private-sector alternatives. Pensions, IRAs, Keogh plans, 401 plans, and other savings vehicles perform the same basic function as social security retirement benefits. Private life insurance

204

performs the same function as social security survivors benefits for workers. Private disability insurance performs the same basic function as social security disability insurance. Private medical insurance performs the same basic function as Medicare.

Social security nationalizes a huge proportion of the private financial industry, replacing a competitive, decentralized, and flexible private market with a rigid, centralized, and coercive government monopoly. It eliminates the freedom of workers to choose among the private alternatives to the extent of their forced social security contributions each year. This may have been of little concern when the maximum annual social security tax was $60 per year, as in 1949, or $189, as in 1958, or even $348, as in 1965. But not when it is $6,750, as in 1988, and heading for close to $8,000 in 1990. One can imagine no good reason why today's workers must be forced to invest so heavily for their retirement and insurance needs only through social security.

This heavy mandated participation in the program means that virtually all Americans are required to be dependent on the government for the bulk of their income for what is now a major portion of their lives—their retirement. This dependency naturally adds up to a high burden of fundamentally unneccessary government spending. Such dependency and unnecessary spending, and the program's socialization of a major portion of the nation's financial industry, amount to a radical departure from a general economic system of free markets, private property, and free exchange.

For those favoring free markets and the private sector, the policy goal in regard to social security should be clear. The role of the private sector should be expanded to take over the functions of the program to the extent practicable. The case for this policy goal does not depend on any particular financial difficulties facing the program in either the short or long term.

Social security does face, however, a number of further problems that make the heavy mandated investment in the program for today's workers even less sensible. The biggest problem is that payroll taxes have now climbed so high that even if social security pays all benefits currently offered to today's young workers, they will still be receiving low, below-market returns (or effective interest rates) on taxes paid into the system over the years, close to zero or even below zero in real terms for many workers.[2] Moreover, whether social security can pay even the inadequate returns and benefits promised to these young workers remains questionable. Under the latest "intermediate" projections of the Social Security Administration, paying all such benefits to those entering the work force today would require a 50 percent increase in the total social sercurity payroll-tax rate, to 23 percent.[3] Under the more prudent "pessimistic" assumptions, the total tax rate would have to be increased over 100 percent, to 35 percent.[4]

The program's payroll taxes are already far too high, seriously hampering economic growth and limiting job opportunities for today's young workers. The payroll tax is simply a tax on employment, and here as elsewhere the result of taxing something is that there is less of it. In a society deeply concerned about employment opportunities, the payroll-tax burden on employment is already ludicrous.

The social security benefit system is also riddled with inequities. Workers are not paid equal returns on past taxes paid into the program. In particular, the program pays discriminately lower returns to two-earner couples, workers without children, and single workers. Blacks and other minorities with below-average life expectancies also tend to receive discriminatorily lower returns as they tend to live fewer years in retirement to collect benefits. A recent study calculates that for a median-income black worker entering the work force today, the real rate of return or effective interest rate he will receive on tax payments into the system over his career will be below zero.[5]

One approach for addressing these problems is to cut social security benefits. But this approach is unlikely to be fruitful. Social security naturally involves unusually intense political sensitivity. In a democracy, proposing sharp cuts in a program that pays benefits to everyone's grandmother hardly seems a politically promis-

---

[2]See Peter J. Ferrara, *Social Security Rates of Return for Today's Young Workers* (Washington: National Chamber Foundation, 1986).

[3]See *1987 Annual Report of the Board of Trustees of the Federal Old-Age and Survivors Insurance and Disability Insurance Trust Funds* (Washington, 1987).

[4]Ibid.

[5]National Center for Policy Analysis, *Social Security and Race* (Dallas, 1987).

ing strategy. Moreover, focusing the reduction on future retirees means that all workers currently bearing the huge payroll-tax burden are to be told that they will get an even worse deal under the program in return for their tax payments.

The problem is not just a matter of the current political climate. From any angle, the benefit-cut approach just has no populist rhyme or meter, no sex appeal. One cannot imagine it being popular or practical in any political climate. The experience of the Reagan administration with its early 1981 benefit-cut proposals only further confirms this view. Such a benefit-cut approach will at best result in relatively small reductions, purchased at enormous political cost.

A more politically sensitive approach would be to reject benefit cuts and instead allow workers the freedom to choose the private alternatives in place of at least some of their social security coverage. This alternative presents a purely positive approach to voters. Instead of taking benefits away, the proposal is simply and directly expanding freedom, opportunities, and prospects for workers.

The old chestnut used to be that if a private option for social security was allowed, the program would collapse. This is because at least some workers would no longer be paying into the system, and since the program relies not on savings but on current receipts to pay current benefits, there would be insufficient funds to pay benefits to the current elderly.

But recent proposals avoid that problem.[6] Workers who choose the private alternatives can be allowed income-tax credits to offset their continued payment of social security taxes into the system. To the extent that workers receive such tax credits for private contributions over the years, they would receive less in social security benefits under a proportional formula, with the benefits from the private alternative likely more than making up for such forgone social security benefits. Allowing a private option to social security is that simple.

The option could start for a relatively small part of social security to keep down the revenue loss from the income-tax credits. Such revenue loss would eventually be offset completely by reduced

[6]See Ferrara, *Social Security: Prospects for Real Reform,* chapter 11; Peter J. Ferrara, "Social Security Reform: The Super IRA," in *Beyond the Status Quo: Policy Proposals for America,* ed. David Boaz and Edward H. Crane (Washington: Cato Institute, 1985), chapter 4.

social security expenditures as workers relied on the private benefits instead. During the interim, even if the government simply borrowed to offset the revenue loss, the private alternatives would hold increased savings to offset such borrowing. Such government borrowing would in fact involve nothing more than the explicit recognition of debt that already exists implicitly in the unfunded liabilities of social security. Ideally, however, the revenue loss would be offset by reduced government spending, the sale of unused government assets (such as excess commercial-use lands), and increased economic growth resulting from the reform. This would result in an immediate, substantial increase in savings on net and more rapid development of the full benefits of the reform.

In Great Britain, an analogous private option for half of that country's social security retirement system was adopted in 1978, but permitted only for workers in heavily unionized industries. About 90 percent of eligible workers have exercised the private option. The Thatcher administration has recently enacted reforms that will extend that option to all workers. The concept of private alternatives to social security systems seems to be gaining growing popularity across Europe.

Partial Reforms

Such a reform is what the Reagan administration should have adopted. But it is probably far more than could be expected from what has developed into an increasingly issueless, unimaginative administration. Barring the ideal, however, the administration could have at least taken several helpful steps.

First, the administration could have consistently expanded IRAs instead of restricting them in the Tax Reform Act of 1986. This would have helped to enhance public recognition and support for private-sector means of providing for retirement. It would have provided additional private resources to meet retirement needs, reducing the pressure for further government aid. IRAs also represent the proper tax policy toward investment. They offset the current triple taxation of capital investment through corporate income taxes, individual income taxes, and capital gains. IRA tax treatment merely removes the still powerful bias in our tax code toward consumption and against investment.

Second, the administration could have focused on providing workers with an option for just one small piece of social security that might be much less controversial. For example, workers could have been given an option just to substitute private life insurance for social security survivors insurance. Social security pays $10–25 billion in benefits each year to the survivors of young workers, performing nothing more than the function of private life insurance. There is no conceivable policy reason for the government to be preempting such a large portion of the private life insurance market in this way.

Or workers could have been given an option to substitute private disability insurance for social security disability insurance. The disability program has shown a tendency to allow too many workers on the rolls who are not actually disabled or to continue benefits even after beneficiaries could go back to work. The government bureaucracy lacks real incentives to enforce the program's standards. Periodic attempts to clean up the problem fail in any event because of the heavy politicization surrounding the program, which can preclude rational, objective consideration of disability cases. Disability insurance could be provided in a superior manner through the private sector. Private insurers would have concrete incentives to prevent nondisabled claimants from receiving benefits, for if they failed to do so, their costs would be too high and they would be unable to compete. The far less politicized private environment would also allow more objective consideration of disability claims.

Rep. French Slaughter (R–Va.) has introduced legislation, with bipartisan cosponsorship, to provide workers with an option to contribute to private savings and insurance accounts over the years in place of some of their Medicare coverage. This bill was specifically designed to reduce or eliminate the long-term Medicare financing crisis by developing a bigger role for the private sector and thereby reducing the burden on Medicare. It addresses the problems of catastrophic insurance and long-term care in nursing homes. Medicare is in such disarray that the administration might have been able to rally substantial public support for such fundamental reform. But instead, the administration proposed a politically unstable Medicare expansion initiative aimed at catastrophic-health care, which has turned into a tax-increasing, expenditure-increasing fiasco on Capitol Hill, as predicted.

Until supporters of the free market learn how to address the social security issue, no meaningful change in total government spending or the size and scope of the welfare state is likely.

15. Social Welfare Policy: A Failure of Vision

Kevin R. Hopkins

Two of the most important benchmarks of a democratic government's commitment to freedom and individual action are the way in which it treats those who "have" and the way it treats those who "have not." The government's policy toward the haves of society—ranging from the reasonably well-off working class to the wealthy—is perhaps best reflected in the nation's tax policy. Here, despite a few egregious stumbles—the Tax Equity and Fiscal Responsibility Act (TEFRA) of 1982 comes most notably to mind—the Reagan administration has succeeded beyond most realistic expectations in redirecting U.S. tax policy. The original rate reductions, the indexing of individual income-tax brackets, and the Tax Reform Act of 1986 all were bold, fundamental changes enacted against substantial opposition from the Washington establishment. For these achievements—and for his recent steadfastness against further tax increases—the president deserves much credit and commendation.

Unfortunately, one cannot be so laudatory in assessing the administration's policies toward society's poor. Here, the enhancements of freedom—for both those who pay for the benefits and those who receive them—have been minuscule. By almost any significant measure, the Reagan "revolution" in social welfare policy has been little more than a few fizzled musket shots. As Stuart Butler of the Heritage Foundation observed earlier this year, after more than six years of the Reagan presidency,

> the basic structure of the Great Society is still firmly intact. Despite the Stockman axe, virtually no program has been eliminated, and most are still enjoying steady growth. To be sure, many reforms instituted during the Reagan Administration have improved the targeting of federal efforts, enabling more money to reach those genuinely in need. And both responsibilities and discretion for

implementing a number of programs have been shifted in some degree to the states. But the system has not changed significantly.[1]

It would be easy to spend the remainder of this brief presentation cataloging the nature and extent of the administration's failures in this area. But scholars at the Cato Institute, the Heritage Foundation, and elsewhere have repeatedly carried out this important exercise, and, besides, anyone interested in doing so himself could pick up the latest copy of the federal budget and read the details of that rather dismal story there. What I would like to do instead is to suggest from the perspective of one who was in the White House in those critical years 1981 to 1985 what went wrong: Why, given his demonstrable successes in reformulating tax policy, was President Reagan so decidedly unable to bring about a more freedom-oriented welfare policy?

No Challenge to the Great Society

As in any political postmortem, there are a number of possible explanations. But in reviewing the last seven years, one explanation stands out: the administration simply did not try to bring about a freedom-oriented welfare policy. I'll explain shortly what I think pursuing this kind of policy implies, but for now let me suggest that the administration's welfare problem goes beyond the assertion common among disillusioned conservatives, as Stuart Butler has put it, that conservative leaders "have not painted a clear picture of what we would put in the place of today's welfare state."[2] On the contrary, the Reagan administration did paint such a picture— but it was the wrong picture.

There seem to me to be three specific failings here. First, the administration accepted, virtually in its entirety, the Great Society premise that the government has a responsibility to provide cash and cashlike aid to otherwise able-bodied people who have fallen on hard times. As a result, the administration could not contest the principle underlying most social welfare programs, and instead locked itself into advocating second-best cost-saving measures that, while many were desirable in their own right, necessarily came

[1]Stuart M. Butler, "Power to the People: A Conservative Vision for Welfare," *Policy Review*, Spring 1987, p. 3.

[2]Ibid.

212

across as punitive. Under the various Reagan proposals, for example, welfare programs were to be transferred to the states at less than their current funding levels, the financially better-off poor were to be categorically removed from the rolls, and, for those allowed to remain, recipients were to be forced to "work off" their benefits. Combined with the green-eyeshade explanations provided by the White House, policies such as these helped critics erect a powerful "fairness" argument against Reagan's budget changes from which the administration never was able to recover.

Second, in the few cases in which the administration did attempt to reform welfare in more fundamental ways, these proposals generally were limited to means of improving the functioning rather than the nature of the social welfare system. Thus, with the exception of workfare—itself only a half-step—and of housing vouchers, none of the Reagan welfare initiatives were intended to alter the direct-aid concept that animates the Great Society's arsenal of programs. Instead, these initiatives ratified the concept, and entrenched it further by seeking primarily to increase the efficiency of delivering the aid, thus reducing one of the main political liabilities of the programs.

Finally, for both of these reasons, the administration proved unable to state a persuasive rhetorical case for its welfare policies. It could appeal to the economic common sense of voters and their representatives, but it could not appeal to their emotions. The importance of this failure should not be understated. Even conservatives hardened by past welfare abuse often were troubled by the notion of cutting off benefits to unskilled, unmarried mothers, or else forcing them to work as punishment for their having to rely on welfare. Yet, this largely negative message—wrapped up with the sometimes fickle promise of economic growth—was the thrust of what the administration had to offer. Compared to the Democrats' professions of compassion, however expensive, the most conservatives could hope for in the public debate on welfare was an uneasy stalemate.

To be sure, these three failings—and the uninspiring welfare policy picture they gave birth to—stemmed in some measure from problems of implementation, including the dominance of the Office of Management and Budget over the policy development office in the White House policy process, the accommodationist sentiment

213

that often governed top White House decisions, and the insufficiently ideological communications operation. But the administration's failures in welfare policy resulted in greater part from a deficiency that must be traced to the president himself—the lack of a compelling, positive, and manifestly compassionate vision of how society should treat its poor. For all his obvious commitment to freedom in other areas, the president never publicly thought through the implications or demands—or the public appeal—of assuring freedom for the nation's poorest.

Indeed, the administration's original welfare objectives read more like a bureaucratic battle plan than a declaration for changing minds and freeing souls. As summarized in 1983 by Martin Anderson, the first and most libertarian of President Reagan's domestic policy chiefs, the major objectives of Reagan's welfare policy were as follows:

- The achievement of economic growth and the kind of a healthy economy that provides direct, immediate benefits to the poor.
- The restoration of fair, sensible eligibility levels in all federal social welfare programs.
- The reduction of fraud, waste, and extravagance in social welfare programs.
- The improvement of the operation of certain social welfare programs by returning authority and responsibility for them to the states and localities, along with the tax resources necessary to pay for them.
- The avoidance of any attempts to establish a guaranteed income.[3]

The important point to emphasize is that these were not his own personal views that Anderson was stating, but the president's. And the clear signal from these objectives is that except for the proposed realignment of responsibilities among levels of government, the president explicitly wanted to preserve the Great Society pretty much as it was—he just hoped to make it work better. This presumption is reinforced by two specific statements made by Anderson, who, despite the enormous positive influence he brought to

[3]Martin Anderson, "The Objectives of the Reagan Administration's Social Welfare Policies," in D. Lee Bawden, ed., *The Social Contract Revisited* (Washington: Urban Institute, 1984), p. 19.

214

bear on Reagan's policies in his 15 months in the White House, apparently felt constrained to adopt the defensive approach that all too often has characterized White House advocacy of its own positions.

In reporting on the president's views, Anderson proclaimed, among other things, that "the Reagan administration . . . is far, far more concerned about ensuring that people who cannot help themselves receive help, than it is about resolving the . . . dilemma that the very fact of receiving help, by definition, makes the person dependent."[4] Later, he added that "it is misleading to state that elimination of ineffective programs is a major objective when, in fact, the major objective was to reform and improve ineffective programs, while reserving the elimination option for those few programs that had demonstrated clearly that they were either inappropriate or redundant."[5]

Thus, while hoping, as we all do, that vigorous economic growth would offer new job opportunities to many of the poor who wanted to work their way off welfare, the administration founded its early welfare reform efforts on objectives that were only tangentially related to that end. The conclusion one must draw from this is that there never was even an incipient Reagan revolution in welfare policy, only a proposed changing of the guards.

Unfortunately, the latest administration welfare policy does nothing to improve this situation. The new Reagan solution to the welfare problem—state experimentation—comes about six years late. And like federalism, experimentation inherently suffers from three major flaws as a vehicle for dramatic improvements in the nation's welfare system. First, both federalism and experimentation are administrative, not substantive, reforms, and therefore do not guarantee a change in the direct-aid concept that underlies welfare. Second, these initiatives almost completely abdicate responsibility for welfare policy formulation to the states—that is, they explicitly reject the notion that a conservative federal government should try to establish some new notion of the purpose of welfare. And if Michael Dukakis's Massachusetts is to be considered the shining star of state welfare experimentation, as it is among much of the popular press, then libertarians and conservatives should not take

[4]Ibid., p. 17.
[5]Ibid., p. 18.

215

much heart in devolution as an end in itself. Finally, and perhaps most importantly in terms of actually getting something done, neither federalism nor state experimentation will ever do much to excite an electorate and motivate Congress to support a more freedom-oriented welfare policy.

The Problems with Welfare

These, then, appear to me to be the main reasons why little has changed in the social welfare area during the Reagan administration. Of course, all of this discussion assumes that such change was warranted—that there are some serious and intrinsic flaws in the current welfare system that make it less than desirable from the point of view of promoting freedom.

To most of us, I suspect, the existence of such flaws is self-evident, but they are worth spelling out. The first, and most obvious, problem is that the direct-aid concept involves an enormous redistribution of income from those who work to those who theoretically could work but do not. This transfer principle arose largely from the belief that society should assist its less-fortunate members. Now, helping the needy is certainly a good idea in itself, and in many ways is a distinction of a civilized culture. But as practiced through welfare, this notion has been subverted into one in which the poor are held almost totally blameless for their condition. They receive assistance regardless of the causes of their poverty, regardless of the length of their poverty, and essentially regardless of what they do toward becoming self-sufficient. In other words, welfare as currently structured absolves the poor of responsibility for the conduct of their lives.

Saying this is nothing new; conservative commentators, most prominently Lawrence Mead and Stuart Butler, have made this point repeatedly in recent years. But a more subtle and less often recognized fault of welfare as now structured is that it also deprives the poor of real opportunity for bettering themselves. Here I am speaking of relative, not absolute, opportunities, because the poor have just as much chance to compete in the job market as does anyone else. But to understand why fewer than 10 percent of welfare recipients are working at any given time, it is necessary to assess self-improvement opportunities from their point of view— and here the picture changes markedly.

216

Because of categorical eligibility standards in the Aid to Families with Dependent Children (AFDC) program, almost all welfare recipients are unmarried mothers with children. Compared to other subpopulations, these women tend to be less educated and less skilled, and so the wages they could obtain in the job market, assuming they could find a job, are likely to be low. Similarly, because of the low levels of work effort among the men of lower socioeconomic status that these women are most likely to marry, these women probably tend to perceive the economic advantages of marriage to be low as well. By contrast, they often see AFDC benefits, even if relatively meager themselves, as the preferred option, at least for the short term. This is especially likely to be the case when the guaranteed availability of AFDC and the freed-up leisure time are taken into account, and it is especially likely to be so among those who have grown up in a social environment where welfare receipt is the norm.

Reliance on welfare, therefore, becomes not only a rational choice but often the only sensible option for a woman concerned with caring for her family on a day-to-day basis in the best way she can. Even offers of job training, skill enhancement, and minimum-wage jobs often hold little appeal when their immediate effect is to deprive the woman of time at home while adding little to her income. And the promise of future wage gains is too often seen as a luxury that cannot be indulged in when the woman must first worry about how to feed her children next week.

In this context, welfare becomes a genuine trap, not only because of the economic calculations it invokes but also because it strips so many other opportunities of their attractiveness. Thus, welfare destroys these opportunities, as they are perceived by many of the poor, just as surely as it would if there were no jobs or job training available at all. It should be of little surprise, then, that even the best work experience and job-training programs tend to succeed only among those people already determined to work their way out of poverty.

The consequences of the combined operation of these two factors are somewhat sobering. More than three-fourths of all unmarried women who first join the welfare system below age 25 spend at least five years on the rolls. The average total welfare stay for these women is more than nine years, and many women remain on the rolls almost continuously until their last eligible child leaves home. If these same figures were calculated separately for never-married mothers who first joined AFDC as teenagers, the average length of welfare stays would be even greater.

All of this suggests that the overriding problem with the current welfare system is that for far too many poor people, it either permits or positively encourages long-term dependency on public support payments. And, contrary to the suppositions of analysts from both sides of the political spectrum, this result does not appear to derive as much from the level of AFDC benefits, benefit tax rates, or outside job opportunities as it does from the very presence of the AFDC program itself. On this point, the finding of a comprehensive review of the evidence on welfare dependency, which I just completed at the Hudson Institute, is instructive. The study concludes that

> as long as AFDC exists and provides at least marginally adequate benefits, it will continue to serve as an alternative means of support for women who otherwise would have no choice but to seek to meet their needs themselves through either marriage or work, and will continue to serve as a means by which young lower class women can bear a child outside of marriage without great fear of financial risk.[6]

A Freedom-Oriented Welfare Policy

By contrast, a more freedom-oriented welfare policy would have as its explicit and primary objective the promotion of individual self-sufficiency and the elimination of dependency. This objective would serve the interests of freedom both for the taxpayers, who would be relieved of the burden of paying money to support those who could work but did not, as well as for the poor, who could acquire the material and spiritual freedoms that greater self-sufficiency affords. And from a political standpoint, this objective would create a much stronger basis for persuasively appealing to both liberals and conservatives alike.

Stating such a principle is the easiest part of the job, however. Far more difficult is the design of a responsible program that would

---

[6]Kevin R. Hopkins, *Welfare Dependency: Behavior, Culture and Public Policy* (Alexandria, Va.: Hudson Institute, 1987), pp. 10-91–10-92.

incorporate the objective, be likely to work in practice, and have a reasonable chance for congressional passage. While there is neither the time nor the mandate to outline the details of such a program here, it should be apparent that the first order of business must be the repudiation of the direct-aid concept of caring for the able-bodied poor. There are two ways to achieve this. One, as has become conventional wisdom among conservatives, is to impose work requirements on all welfare recipients. That is certainly a step in the right direction, and it is an idea that has won a good deal of public support. But in practice, workfare just doesn't work. As the mounting evidence clearly demonstrates, workfare plans are invariably watered down by exemptions and options that leave only a minority of recipients actually obligated to work.

Yet, even a perfectly implemented workfare scheme does not appear to be the answer to the welfare dependency problem. There are, in fact, two problems. First, workfare explicitly retains the direct-aid concept of welfare. That is, work requirements compel work only after aid has been offered. The notion that society owes the able-bodied poor cash assistance would remain, and with it the ever present likelihood that Congress would attempt once again to "destigmatize" welfare receipt by eliminating the punitive and "dehumanizing" work requirements. A second problem, of course, is what government should do about those recipients who claim to be unable to find a job. The typically glib answer by workfare proponents is that these people should be made to perform useful public service work. However, not only does this possibility increase the punitive impression surrounding workfare, but those who offer this response typically oppose the kind of public jobs program that would make such public service work possible.

Rather than trying to doctor the welfare system in this fashion, the preferred step would be to completely eliminate the AFDC program, food stamps, and similar programs, thereby compelling the poor to confront the same income equation that mainstream Americans face: If you need money, get a job. Although he has since backed away from this proposal, Charles Murray originally advocated just this approach in *Losing Ground*.[7] But as Joan Kennedy

[7]Charles Murray, *Losing Ground: American Social Policy, 1950–1980* (New York: Basic Books, 1984).

Taylor, although speaking favorably of the early Murray approach, has conceded, while "disbanding the present system would clearly help many people immediately, . . . it would also leave some in distress."[8]

To be specific, not only might some people need counseling, child care, and other services on entering the job market, perhaps for the first time, but some unskilled people might not be able to find jobs. If private charity proved insufficient—and that, too, is certainly a possibility—poor mothers and their children might be left to starvation and sickness. Although these numbers might be small, even a handfull of cases would be writ large on the evening news. Obviously, Congress would not let this happen, even if an administration were willing to tolerate it. Demands would spring up immediately for a transitional aid system, and welfare would be reborn.

The point is, although eliminating welfare is probably the only thorough way of scaling back the twin abridgements of freedom inherent in the contemporary welfare system, such a step is likely to be politically impossible unless something is put in its place. And that something has to be work. Certainly, all people should be encouraged to find jobs on their own, preferably in the private sector. But in cases where those jobs cannot be found—and, in fact, to politically ensure that they always will be found—an administration that eliminates welfare must also guarantee jobs. To be specific, it must ensure that all able-bodied people needing income to support their families will be able to work and be able to do so as many hours per week as they desire. As a former Delaware governor Pete du Pont has described this approach, "For able-bodied people in America, welfare would be replaced with work; welfare checks would stop; paychecks would start; [and] the policy of the nation would become: if you don't work, you don't get paid."[9]

In the best of all worlds, to be sure, government would not have to provide either income support or jobs. But if we want to achieve our larger goals—in this case, the elimination of the direct-aid

[8]Joan Kennedy Taylor, "Deregulating the Poor," in David Boaz and Edward H. Crane, eds., *Beyond the Status Quo: Policy Proposals for America* (Washington: Cato Institute, 1985), p. 244.

[9]Pete du Pont, "Replacing Welfare with Work," speech delivered at Daniel Webster College, Nashua, N.H., March 12, 1987.

220

concept of income support and hence the elimination of welfare—we have to be practical, which requires us to explicitly address the issue of a backup public provision of jobs. After all, paying people to work, even if it's for the government, is certainly better than paying them not to work. As du Pont has said, "It is plain common sense that giving a job to able-bodied Americans is better than just giving them a check."[10] Not only that, but turning the country's welfare class into a working class gives everyone—even the poorest citizens—a much greater stake in a freer America. And in the long run, that may do the most good of all for the libertarian cause. In any case, it would be a revolution in social policy truly worth fighting for in the years and decades ahead.

[10]Ibid.

16. Health Care: The Tyranny of the Budget

Roger D. Feldman

President Reagan took office in 1981 against a background of both high stakes and high hopes for health care policy. The high stakes were due to the growth of health care spending—which was manifestly out of control—and the failure of the previous three presidents to fashion an effective health care policy. The Nixon and Ford administrations had relied on a price freeze and exhortation in their unsuccessful efforts to control health care spending. President Carter had proposed a regulatory approach to hospital cost containment. The twice-defeated Carter proposal showed that the strategy of direct government control of health care prices, capacity, and use was dead politically, as well as economically.

The high hopes were due to a unique conjunction of health-policy analysts and policymakers in support of a set of four principles. Those principles were that (1) each consumer have a choice of competing health care plans, (2) employers (or the government) contribute a fixed-dollar subsidy toward the purchase of health plan membership, (3) all competing plans play by the same rules and (4) providers be organized into competing economic units. These proposals, know as the "competition strategy," were supported by a group of health-policy analysts who wished to see the principles of competitive markets applied to health care.[1] The same proposals also claimed an extraordinary amount of support among health policymakers: no fewer than five pro-competition bills had been introduced in the 96th Congress, and three of the sponsors of that

---

[1] For a discussion of the competition strategy and an optimistic assessment of its early prospects, see Alain C. Enthoven, "The Competition Strategy: Status and Prospects," *New England Journal of Medicine* 304, no. 2 (January 8, 1981): 109–12.

legislation would soon assume high positions in the Reagan administration or in the 97th Congress.[2]

In addition, the philosophy of competition appealed to the new president and his supporters. An informal health-policy advisory committee had recommended giving first priority to a pro-competition bill.[3]

This does not mean that all the competition advocates supported identical approaches. Some, notably Alain C. Enthoven, favored a more structured approach in which health plans would be encouraged or coerced to provide comprehensive benefits and to practice community rating (charging the same premium to all consumers enrolled for the same benefits in the same market area, regardless of observable risk differences among consumers).[4] Others favored a more wide-open approach to competition under which health plans would have few restrictions. Nevertheless, it appeared to Enthoven that "these issues can be resolved by a compromise within the context of a fair, competitive market system."[5]

Seven years later, the competitive health care strategy is still unrealized. The only thing remotely resembling it is a provision in the Tax Equity and Fiscal Responsibility Act of 1982 (TEFRA) that encourages prepaid health care organizations to enroll Medicare beneficiaries on a risk-taking basis. This legislation has expanded the options available to beneficiaries who prefer an alternative to standard fee-for-service Medicare. Otherwise, the major health-policy accomplishment of the Reagan administration has been a price-control system, known as the DRG (diagnosis-related group) method, for Medicare hospital admissions. It is also likely that a catastrophic-illness health insurance bill will be enacted before President Reagan leaves office.

[2]Sen. Richard Schweiker (R–Pa.) would become secretary of health and human services; Sen. David Durenberger (R–Minn.) would become chairman of the Health Subcommittee of the Finance Committee; and Rep. David Stockman (R–Mich.) would become director of the Office of Management and Budget.

[3]William B. Walsh, "Report of the Chairman of the Health Policy Advisory Group to President-elect Ronald Reagan" (Millwood, Va., November 14, 1980).

[4]Alain C. Enthoven, "Consumer-Choice Health Plan (Second of Two Parts)," *New England Journal of Medicine* 298, no. 13 (March 30, 1978): 709–20.

[5]Enthoven, "The Competition Strategy," p. 111.

What Happened to the Competition Strategy?

The competition strategy almost immediately ran into heavy opposition from major business organizations, organized labor, the insurance industry, and medical groups.[6] The most contentious issue was a proposal to place a limit on the amount of health benefits paid by private employers that could escape personal income and social security taxes. The present tax law provides an unlimited exemption for employer-paid health insurance benefits. This proposal was favored by competition advocates who believed that employers would be more likely to curtail their policy of subsidizing the marginal purchase of health insurance if such contributions were no longer tax-exempt.

Instead of the tax cap, the administration began to lean toward a more modest approach in which employees who chose cheaper health plans could receive a tax-free rebate. This approach was offered as a compromise by Donald W. Moran, executive associate director for budget in the Office of Management and Budget (OMB). The *New York Times* quoted Robert J. Rubin, assistant secretary for planning and evaluation in the Department of Health and Human Services (HHS) and a leading administration architect of the competition strategy, as saying that the new approach was a recognition of political "reality."[7]

Despite the opposition, the administration's policy was far from dead in 1981 and 1982. It still enjoyed wide support within the administration and among key members of Congress. On February 28, 1983, President Reagan transmitted to Congress proposed legislation for a health-incentives reform program.[8] Key features of this program included:

- Expanded Medicare coverage for catastrophic illness involving lengthy hospital stays; at the same time, coinsurance would be imposed for a maximum of 60 days annually to encourage beneficiary cost-consciousness during short hospital stays.

[6]See John K. Iglehart, "Washington Report," *Journal of Health Politics, Policy and Law* 6, no. 2 (Summer 1981): 361–64.

[7]Robert Reinhold, "Reagan Changing Health Cost Plan," *New York Times*, March 14, 1982, p. 1.

[8]White House press release, February 28, 1983.

- Medicare hospital payment would be determined on a prospective basis for each of 467 DRGs.
- The bill would limit tax-free health benefits paid by an employer to $175 per month for a family plan and $70 per month for individual coverage. These limits would be indexed to increase yearly in proportion to the consumer price index.
- Medicare beneficiaries would be given the opportunity to enroll in private health plans, with a cash rebate if the health plan's premium were less than Medicare's contribution.
- Medicare customary and prevailing fees for physician services would be frozen at 1983 levels for one year beginning in July 1984.
- The premium for physicians' services under Medicare would be increased gradually until it reached 35 percent of program costs for the elderly (in contrast to the present 25 percent). The deductible on physicians' services would be indexed so as to maintain a constant dollar value.

Testifying on the health-incentives reform program before the Senate Committee on Labor and Human Resources, Martin Feldstein, chairman of the Council of Economic Advisers, cited "first-dollar" hospital insurance as a factor that severely distorts the appropriate level of health care expenditures.[9] He blamed the widespread presence of comprehensive first-dollar insurance on the special tax advantage that health insurance receives, and he defended the proposal to place a cap on the amount of tax-free payment that employers can make in this form. He also argued that the administration's proposal to reform Medicare was guided by the same principle of concentrating insurance on large expenses. The conservative Heritage Foundation also praised the administration's proposals, including its initiative in the area of catastrophic-illness health insurance.[10]

Not everyone was happy with these proposals, however. Apart from the temporary freeze on physicians' fees, the only significant part of the 1983 health-incentives reform program that passed was

[9]Martin Feldstein, "Mechanisms to Solve Health Care Cost Inflation," testimony before the Senate Committee on Labor and Human Resources, May 25, 1983.

[10]Peter G. Germanis, "Mobilizing Competition to Cut Health Costs," Heritage Foundation Backgrounder, no. 266 (Washington, May 10, 1983).

the Medicare hospital prospective-payment system (PPS). After a bruising two-year fight, the tax-cap proposal was finally withdrawn in 1985.

The failure of President Reagan's major health-policy initiative can be explained by the "political-economic" approach to policy analysis. As developed by George Stigler[11] and applied to health policy by Alain C. Enthoven[12] and Theodore Marmor,[13] the political-economic approach predicts that "the outcomes of political or regulatory processes in medical care are likely to depend primarily on the number of gainers and losers associated with a given policy proposal, the relative magnitude of the gains and losses, and the ability of the affected groups to organize and participate in the political process."[14] In the case of health-policy reforms, the political market is decidedly unbalanced: doctors, hospital administrators, union officials, and insurance companies all oppose potentially successful measures to restrain inflation, since the costs of such policies are concentrated on them. These groups, moreover, have easy access to the political process through lobbyists and campaign-contribution committees.[15] On the other hand, the benefits of controlling health care cost inflation are diffused among many consumers, each of whom can expect only a small gain (in a probabilistic sense).

Adding to the problem of diffused benefits is the fact that the competition strategy may not produce immediately visible gains. Competition involves long-run structural changes in the economy that promote efficient allocation of resources. Although the benefits

[11]George J. Stigler, "The Theory of Economic Regulation," *Bell Journal of Economics and Management Science* 2, no. 1 (Spring 1972): 3–21.

[12]Alain C. Enthoven, "How Interested Groups Have Responded to a Proposal for Economic Competition in Health Services," *American Economic Review* 70, no. 2 (May 1980): 142–48.

[13]Theodore R. Marmor, Donald A. Whittman, and Thomas C. Heagy, "The Politics of Medical Care Inflation," in *Health Care Policy: A Political Economy Approach*, ed. Theodore R. Marmor and Jon B. Christianson (Beverly Hills, Calif.: Sage Publications, 1982), pp. 16–81.

[14]Theodore R. Marmor and Jon B. Christianson, "Future Policy Directions: The Political Economy of Competition," in *Health Care Policy: A Political Economy Approach*, p. 218.

[15]See "AMA Budgets $500,000 to Defeat Stark, Jacobs," *Washington Report on Medicine and Health* 40, no. 30 (July 28, 1986).

of such actions are sometimes quickly translated into lower prices—as in the case of airline deregulation—the competition strategy does not promise immediate payoffs. Even its optimistic supporters have argued that 5 or 10 years might be required to change the course of the health care system.[16] Such pronouncements have limited appeal to elected officials, whose time horizon is decidedly shorter than 10 years.

Not surprisingly, labor, the insurance industry, and consumer-advocacy groups opposed the Reagan proposals. Labor's opposition was based on its longstanding commitment to universal health insurance, which may be viewed as a way of shifting the costs of health insurance to taxpayers at large, only 20 percent of whom are union members. The insurance industry's opposition was also quite predictable, given that the objective of the proposed tax cap was to remove the marginal subsidy for health insurance from the federal tax code.

More surprising was the unfavorable reception given to Reagan's proposals by big business. One might think that business would support a plan to control health care costs, since about two-thirds of all nonelderly Americans obtain health insurance through their jobs and health insurance costs have risen rapidly (and according to some, uncontrollably) in recent years. Nevertheless, the U.S. Chamber of Commerce and the Washington Business Group on Health both opposed the health-incentives reform program. Willis Goldbeck, head of the Washington Business Group on Health, said, "We are not buying into a survival of the fittest system."[17] He added that health care services could not be treated like other commodities and that business favored a gradual shift toward competition.

This ambivalent attitude would not have surprised some health-policy analysts, who recognize that employers see health benefits as a way of attracting qualified employees to their company or as a way of discouraging unionism.[18] Others have emphasized that health benefits are extremely popular among workers and that employers

[16]See Walter McClure, "Implementing a Competitive Medical Care System Through Public Policy," *Journal of Health Politics, Policy and Law* 7, no. 1 (Spring 1982): 2–44.

[17]Quoted in "Reagan Changing Health Cost Plan."

[18]See Alain C. Enthoven, "Consumer-Centered vs. Job-Centered Health Insurance," *Harvard Business Review* 57, no. 1 (January/February 1979): 141–52.

are reluctant to jeopardize them, especially when fringe-benefit costs are not burdensome and vigorous cost-control action might alienate workers, unions, or important forces in a firm's local community.[19] Finally, some employers may have feared that the administration's push against health benefits would set a precedent for altering the tax treatment of other noncash benefits offered to workers.

Organized health care provider groups found themselves caught in an uncomfortable position by Reagan's proposals. On the one hand, such providers can be expected to oppose health care cost control because it adversely affects their incomes. On the other hand, they fear that if nothing were done to control health care costs, the roof would fall in and something worse than the health-incentives reform proposals would be passed by Congress and signed by the president. Ultimately, only the American Medical Association actively opposed Reagan's proposal. The American Hospital Association (speaking for the nation's nonprofit hospitals) was ambivalent, and the Federation of American Hospitals, the national lobby of the proprietary hospital management companies, aggressively supported the competitive health care model.[20] The disarray and ambivalence of provider groups may explain why the only items on the president's agenda to be enacted—a price-control system for Medicare hospital admissions and a freeze on Medicare physician fees—concerned provider reimbursement.[21]

Although the political-economic model is interesting and persuasive, it does not provide a complete explanation for the evolution of President Reagan's health policy. A complete explanation must also rely on what Andrew B. Dunham and James A. Marone have

[19]See Harvey M. Sapolsky, Drew Altman, Richard Greene, and Judith D. Moore, "Corporate Attitudes Toward Health Care Costs,"*Milbank Memorial Fund Quarterly* 59, no. 4 (Fall 1981): 561–85; and Roger Feldman, Gail Jensen, and Bryan Dowd, "What Are Employers Doing to Create a Competitive Market for Health Care in the Twin Cities?" *Contemporary Policy Issues* 3, no. 2 (Winter 1984–85): 69–88.

[20]See Iglehart, "Washington Report"; and Marmor and Christianson, "Future Policy Directions."

[21]It is interesting to note that the final version of the PPS contains a large subsidy for teaching hospitals. This subsidy, which substantially increases the profits of teaching hospitals relative to nonteaching hospitals, effectively bought off the influential lobbying groups for the Association of American Medical Colleges and the Council of Teaching Hospitals.

called the preferences of the "autonomous" state.[22] The specific case study that Dunham and Marone analyze is the adoption of a DRG-based price-control system by the state of New Jersey in 1978. They show how a centralized policy process, with a strong governor and weak legislature, made it difficult for interest groups to affect public policy in New Jersey, a state with a political culture that tolerates government regulation. Moreover, a committed group of professionals within state government—a group hired outside of civil service channels, supported by the courts, and lured by the prospect of federal grants—pushed for the new regulations. All of these forces contributed to the adoption of DRGs in New Jersey.

Dunham and Marone's model points to the relevance of the preferences and needs of government agencies in any explanation of the regulatory process. Unfortunately, however, it does not suggest what those preferences and needs might be in any given situation. To apply their model to health policymaking in the Reagan administration, therefore, one must uncover the preferences and needs of the agencies and individuals whose interactions determined that policy. In other words, it helps to view the policymaking process from the inside.

Fortunately, I was able to participate in that process during 1984–85 as a senior staff economist on the president's Council of Economic Advisers (CEA). I took part in Cabinet Council working groups, authored a chapter in the 1985 *Economics Report of the President*, and represented the CEA on the White House Working Group on Health Policy and Economics. This working group, created in 1984 as part of the long-range planning process in the White House, was chaired by William Roper (then special assistant to the president for health policy and now administrator of the Health Care Financing Administration). The primary objective of this working group was to examine long-term structural reforms in federal programs that would ensure quality and availability of health care services at a minimum cost to the taxpayer. These experiences form the basis of my observations on the agencies and personalities that made Reagan's health policy.

Health policymaking during the first two years of President Rea-

[22]Andrew B. Dunham and James A. Marone, *The Politics of Regulation: The Evolution of DRG Rate Regulation in New Jersey* (Princeton, N.J.: Health Research and Educational Trust of New Jersey, 1983), p. xxvi.

gan's administration was characterized by a triangle with three points: the White House Office of Domestic Policy, HHS, and OMB. Each of these agencies played a role in policy formulation; the White House was represented by domestic policy adviser Jack Svahn, HHS by Secretary Richard Schweiker, and OMB by Director David Stockman. In Congress, Schweiker and Stockman had been leading advocates of the competition strategy.

Beginning in 1983 and accelerating rapidly during the next two years, the health policy triangle became unbalanced, with influence slipping away from HHS and toward OMB. The reasons for decreased HHS influence are, in part, quite personal. Margaret Heckler, the new secretary of HHS, was a poor administrator who could not successfully fill the top positions in her department or carry through with the policy initiatives of the previous secretary.[23] She was no match for David Stockman and John Cogan, the associate director of OMB for health.

But behind the personalities, there lurked what I call the "tyranny ot the budget." Beginning in FY 1982, the federal budget deficit began to increase rapidly. The total deficit for 1982–84 ballooned to $521 billion, compared with $193.9 billion during the preceding three fiscal years.[24] Given these background conditions, it is easy to predict that programmatic decisions would be made solely on the basis of their effects on the deficit. Many conservatives realized this fact, and even welcomed it, because they viewed the budget as a noose by which to hang needless federal programs. But this was a mistake. A budget-driven policy has only one criterion— whether or not the policy will save money for the federal government. The competition strategy, on the other hand, is concerned with long-run structural changes that promote efficient allocation of resources. Budgetary considerations are important, ot course, since federal taxing and spending decisions affect the allocation of resources, but they are of secondary consideration. As William Niskanen said in the 1985 *Economic Report of the President*:

[23]The best analysis I have seen of this shift in influence is "Reagan Health Policy in Transition," *Washington Report on Medicine and Health* 39, no. 35 (September 9, 1985).

[24]See *Economic Report of the President* (Washington: Government Printing Office, February 1985), Table B–72.

Changes in the budget also affect the economy, in ways that depend critically on the type of expenditure and the detailed characteristics of the tax code. For any meaningful evaluation of the effects of the Federal budget on the economy, fiscal policy should be defined in terms of the levels of government services, the eligibility conditions and payment rates for transfer programs, and the statutory tax rates on private activity.[25]

Niskanen's statement emphasizes that it is not the budget totals that should be given primary scrutiny, but how the money is raised, how it is spent, and the integration of programmatic changes into the existing level and mix of federal services. All of this is lost on the budget cutter, however, whose primary goal is to find the "quick fix" of a better bottom line. In the Reagan administration, the ultimate watchdog over the bottom line was OMB.

To illustrate the difference between the competition strategy and the tyranny of the budget, consider the following meeting that took place on December 18, 1984. Crowded into a meeting room on the second floor of the Old Executive Office Building, the director of OMB and his top aides were reviewing the HHS budget. When he got to the Medicare hospital PPS (the price-control system for Medicare hospital admissions), there were three items on Stockman's agenda: how to update the payment rates, how to pay for medical-education costs in hospitals, and how to pay for capital costs.

On the first item, the budget working group had recommended indexing hospital payment rates to the price of a market basket of hospital inputs, minus 2 percent. Stockman, however, opted to freeze payment rates for 1986 and then to let them increase at the market-basket rate. Relative to baseline projections, Stockman's strategy would have cost almost $2 billion more than the budget working group's recommendation by the end of 1990. He chose the freeze simply because it would have a bigger short-term effect on the deficit.

The second item was payment for medical-education costs in hospitals. The present payment system includes a special subsidy for teaching hospitals that greatly increases their profits relative to nonteaching hospitals. The budget working group had recom-

[25]*Economic Report of the President*, pp.65–66.

232

mended a substantial reduction in this subsidy; Stockman agreed with this sensible proposal.

The last item on the agenda was payment for hospital costs, which are presently covered on a pass-through basis. Health-policy analysts believe that this open-ended payment system distorts hospital input use, leading to excessive capital intensity and unnecessarily high hospital costs. Incredibly, Stockman opted for a continuation of the capital pass-through. He said that the budget cuts decided on up to that point (which totaled $3.112 billion in 1986) were the most that could be gotten from Congress without creating unbearable industry complaints.

Here we have an example of budget-cutting logic at its best: when the agreed-upon cuts reach a certain number, all items on the agenda past that point are safe. This is what an economist would call "lexicographic"decision making. It means that the ordering of an issue can affect the decision made on that issue, regardless of the merits of the case. I fired off an angry memo to my boss, Bill Niskanen, but nothing much could be done about it. The tyranny of the budget had prevailed.[26]

Thus, my impression was that the Reagan administration had reached a sort ot mid-life crisis in 1984–85. The health policy triangle had become unbalanced, with HHS no longer exerting leadership that could offset the influence of the budget cutters at OMB. This was precisely the time when strong leadership might have spelled the difference between success and failure for the competition strategy. That leadership was not forthcoming, however, and the competition strategy was not enacted.

What Did We Get Instead of the Competition Strategy?

Even though the competition strategy was not enacted, the Reagan administration has seen several major changes in health policy. The first of these is the Medicare prospective payment system for hospitals. Under PPS, which was created by the Social Security Amendments of 1983 and implemented in 1984, about 80 percent

[26]This is not the only example of a budget-driven policy process that I could mention. The administration's tax-cap proposal, despite strong support within the White House and HHS, never received David Stockman's wholehearted endorsement. At the meeting described here, the director decided, almost without discussion, to table the tax-cap proposal.

of hospitals are being paid a prospectively determined rate for each discharge. The amount of the payment is determined by the DRG in which the discharge is classified. Certain types of expenses, such as capital and medical education, are still paid on a cost basis.

As I wrote in the 1985 *Economic Report of the President*, "The virtue of the prospective payment is that it uncouples prices from the costs of individual hospitals. This idea, which lies at the heart of the prospective payment system, is that hospitals will strive to reduce their costs below the level of these fixed prices."[27] These predictions are being borne out by the experience of hospitals under PPS. On the whole, the American hospital industry has reported sharp increases in profits at a time when admissions and occupancy rates are falling.[28] Evidence indicates that increased profitability is due to sharply reduced length of stay under PPS.

However, PPS creates strong incentives for hospitals to shift costs to other parts of the Medicare system. For example, discharging a patient quickly contributes to higher outpatient costs since the quickly discharged patient uses more outpatient services covered by Part B of Medicare. Medicare Part B payments for the first 10 months of the current fiscal year, through July 1987, cost 22 percent more than in the corresponding period of the prior year.[29] This increase has prompted the Health Care Financing Administration to request a 38.5 percent increase in the monthly Part B premium, from $17.90 to $24.80. This would be the largest premium increase in the 22-year history of the program.

The major problem with PPS is that the system of prices it established has no relation to the prices that would cause hospitals to produce the amount of services that consumers desire to buy at the right quality and the minimum cost. PPS is essentially a price-control system. A disadvantage of any price-control system is that it tends to become the target of groups who seek concessions for their special circumstances. I have already noted the adjustment made for medical-education costs in the PPS rates. Similar adjust-

[27] *Economic Report of the President*, p. 149.

[28] See Stuart Guterman and Allen Dobson, "Impact of the Medicare Prospective Payment System for Hospitals," *Health Care Financing Review* 7, no. 3 (Spring 1986): 97–114.

[29] Robert Pear, "38.5% Rise Asked in 1988 Premiums of Medicare Users," *New York Times*, September 15, 1987, p. 1.

234

ments are made for area wage differences, urban and rural location, and "outlier" cases. Certain types of hospitals are accorded special treatment under PPS, including sole community providers, regional referral centers, cancer treatment and research centers, and Christian Science sanatoria. Other hospitals and units that treat specialized cases are excluded from PPS altogether.

Despite the fact that an inordinate amount of time and talent are being poured into purported refinements of this already illogical system, and that the White House working group regarded it as a transition from cost reimbursement to a more comprehensive payment system based on competitive principles, PPS seems to be here to stay. The present policymaking logjam over PPS is due to several causes. First, although PPS is flawed, it is manifestly so much better than the system of cost reimbursement that it replaced that few Reagan administration officials would recommend scrapping it, at least not without something better in sight. Second, the hospital industry, although uncomfortable over some aspects of PPS, is willing to live with a system that rewards it for reducing costs. In addition, the industry has successfully co-opted the advisory board that was set up to advise the secretary of HHS on updating the hospital payment rates. Third, the PPS has found a friend in OMB, which views it as a convenient method for controlling Medicare hospital spending. The OMB position illustrates once more the tyranny of the budget over health policymaking in the Reagan administration.

The second major health-policy act of the Reagan administration was a provision of TEFRA that permitted prepaid health care plans to enroll Medicare beneficiaries on a risk-taking basis. The original 1965 Medicare legislation had authorized capitation payments to physicians. However, these arrangements covered only Part B services, and capitation payments were adjusted according to the physicians' costs, thereby reducing the incentives for the physicians to be efficient. Further amendments to the Social Security Act in 1972 and 1976 were not successful in attracting prepaid plans into the Medicare business. TEFRA expanded the types of provider groups that were eligible to receive capitation payments and (subject to some technical provisions) permitted them to retain any savings. Final regulations to implement the TEFRA legislation were published in January 1985.

Enrollment in risk-taking capitated Medicare plans has increased rapidly since January 1985. Through April 1987, HCFA's Office of Prepaid Health Care had negotiated contracts with 152 health plans in 34 states.[30] Another 34 contract applications were pending on May 1, 1987. At that point, almost one million beneficiaries had voluntarily enrolled in those plans, representing about 10 percent of the elderly who live in areas served by Medicare-approved health-maintenance organizations (HMOs).

TEFRA health plans must offer the standard Medicare benefit package at no charge (beyond the Part B premium) to beneficiaries. They may also sell additional benefits and appear to do so as loss leaders to their basic coverage. (That is, HMOs are overpaid for the basic package of Medicare services, but HCFA cannot prevent them from competing over the price and quality of marginal services. They appear to sell additional services at a loss, in order to compete for customers. This is a common form of "rent-seeking" behavior in regulated industries.) Clearly, TEFRA health plans are an attractive addition to standard fee-for-service Medicare.

Nevertheless, this new policy option is not completely successful, if it is judged according to the competitive-market strategy. There are two major problems. First, the method used to pay TEFRA health plans is a price-control system based on 95 percent of the estimated costs of serving enrollees if they had remained in the fee-for-service sector. This payment system violates the principles of a competitive market, in which competition would bid prices down until they were equal to the marginal costs of the TEFRA plans and lower than the cost of the old fee-for-service technology.

The second major problem with TEFRA health plans is that consumers have no financial incentive to choose one plan over another, apart from differences in the premium for marginal services. Some consumers may prefer to purchase the basic bundle of services and receive a rebate in cash. This option would have been permitted by the health-incentives reform proposal of 1983, which called for an optional Medicare voucher. The voucher proposal would have built on TEFRA by allowing beneficiaries to enroll in a wider variety of private health plans and to receive a cash rebate for choosing a plan

[30]John K. Iglehart, "Second Thoughts about HMOs for Medicare Patients," *New England Journal of Medicine* 316, no. 23 (June 4, 1987): 1487–92.

with a premium lower than Medicare's contribution. This proposal was not enacted.

Most of the proposals described thus far—including both the successful and unsuccessful ones—were crafted by groups of strong advisers at the cabinet and subcabinet levels. President Reagan himself takes little interest in health policy except in one instance: he supports legislation to provide coverage for catastrophic medical expenses. A catastrophic-illness proposal was included in the 1983 health-incentives reform package, and it appears likely that some version of a catastrophic-illness bill will be enacted before the president leaves office.

A revamped catastrophic-illness proposal was presented by Secretary Otis R. Bowen to the Domestic Policy Council, where it received a cool reception on December 3, 1986. Conservative advisers on the council were concerned that a new federal insurance benefit would interfere with private Medigap insurers. Ironically, catastrophic-illness health insurance legislation enjoys more support in the Democratic Congress than in the Domestic Policy Council of a Republican White House. Both branches of Congress enacted sweeping catastrophic-illness bills in 1987 and on May 25, 1988, a House-Senate conference committee reached agreement on a compromise bill. Although President Reagan had threatened a veto if the final bill too closely resembled the more generous House version, Bowen has recommended that the president sign the compromise legislation.

Certain aspects of the final catastrophic-illness insurance bill are indeed ludicrous. In place of Bowen's original plan, which called for personal spending limits of $2,000 for beneficiaries who voluntarily pay $4.92 per month, the final bill adds numerous expensive benefits to the Medicare program. To pay for these benefits, it will levy a premium that will start at about $4 per month in 1989 and rise to $10.20 per month in 1993, plus an income tax surcharge on upper-income beneficiaries that will add $42 on each $150 of tax liability by 1993. Needless to say, the price of this coverage is so unreasonable that few upper-income beneficiaries would voluntarily purchase it and, therefore, the final bill calls for mandatory catastrophic-illness coverage.

However, I am unconvinced by the conservative claim that such a program is objectionable per se because it interferes with the private sector. The private health insurance industry is notoriously hostile to competition.[31] A government-sponsored plan with a fair-market premium might inject some competition into this sector. On the other hand, Bowen's position on government-sponsored insurance could be turned around to become a more radical criticism of the present Medicare program: Why should this program be the exclusive monopoly of government? In other words, the catastrophic-illness insurance debate could have presented free-market critics with another opportunity to propose Medicare vouchers that would allow private health plans to compete for basic Medicare coverage. Of all the presidential advisers, only CEA chairman Beryl Sprinkel grasped the fact that Medicare vouchers were a reasonable alternative to government-sponsored catastrophic-illness health insurance. His proposal did not succeed in the Domestic Policy Council, however.

The three initiatives discussed above—the Medicare PPS system, TEFRA health plans, and catastrophic-illness health insurance—have occupied much of the health-policy limelight during President Reagan's two terms. At the same time, and much less noticed, many health-policy skirmishes were being fought and won by the administration. Speaking collectively and generally, the point of these actions was to reduce or eliminate some very outdated federal health programs. President Reagan's successes in this area will leave a legacy of a more efficient health care system for future administrations. I will mention only two instances, although others could be discussed.

First, President Reagan successfully eliminated the federal health-planning program, which was enacted in 1974 to oversee hospitals' plans to build or expand and to purchase new capital equipment. Numerous studies have shown that this regulatory approach contributed to higher hospital costs than in the absence of such regulations.[32] Elimination of this program was part of the president's 1981 policy agenda. However, congressional opposition caused health

---

[31]Witness the industry's opposition to the tax-cap proposal. See also Roger Feldman, "Health Insurance in the United States: Is Market Failure Avoidable?" *Journal of Risk and Insurance* 54, no. 2 (June 1987): 298–313.

[32]See, for example, David S. Salkever and Thomas W. Bice, *Hospital Certificate of Need Controls: Impact on Investment, Cost, and Use* (Washington: American Enterprise Institute, 1979).

planning to be continued until October 6, 1986, when it was finally phased out.

By eliminating the federal mandate for health planning, President Reagan turned the process over to the states, where it belongs. Free to experiment according to their own needs, 10 states had repealed their "certificate of need" (CON), or hospital capital control, laws as of June 1, 1987. During this same period, the 40 states that kept CON were raising thresholds, narrowing the scope of review, and streamlining the review process.[33]

Second, President Reagan drastically cut back or eliminated many federal health manpower programs. An example is the National Health Service Corps of the U.S. Public Health Service, which, for 15 years, has handed out scholarships to medical and dental students in return for their promises to accept assignments in remote rural areas and inner-city neighborhoods. Despite very loose definitions of shortage areas, only about one-third to one-half of all scholarship recipients settled permanently in the communities where they were assigned.[34] In addition, more than 10 percent of the participants have defaulted on their scholarship obligations. President Reagan cut back this program to the point where only 35 scholarships were awarded in 1986, compared with more than 2,000 annually during the late 1970s.

Although he has been hostile to federal subsidies for health education, President Reagan has resisted more extreme calls for mandatory reductions in the size of medical school classes. This attitude points to a more deep-seated bias within the Reagan administration—that of definitely being hostile to the interests of organized provider groups. This is reflected, for example, in the fact that the administration's freeze on Medicare physicians' fees was roundly opposed by the American Medical Association. This bias might surprise those who believe that a Republican administration will naturally support the interests of "the rich" and "big business." But we must not forget that the Reagan administration is, first and foremost, an ideological administration. Its free-market ideology has led it on numerous occasions to oppose the lobbying efforts of

[33]"Most Local Health Planning Agencies Close," *Washington Report on Medicine and Health* 41, no. 27 (July 6, 1987): 2.

[34]Frank E. James "Despite Federal Aid, Doctors Are Still in Short Supply in Rural Areas," *Wall Street Journal*, June 23, 1987, p. 1.

providers, the health insurance industry, and other interest groups. Liberal critics, who can find much to criticize in Reagan's health policy, might give the administration some credit on this score.

Summary

President Reagan and his advisers have proposed a bold new strategy to control health care costs and to make health care markets more efficient. In this sense, the Reagan administration has had an activist health policy, more so than the Carter and Ford administrations. Its activism in this area can best be compared to that of the Nixon administration, although the Nixon strategy was based largely on regulation, an approach opposite to that of the Reagan administration.

Under Reagan, however, little of the competitive health care strategy has been put into place, and those features that have been enacted (PPS and the TEFRA health plans) rely on price-control methods rather than market forces. The failure of the competition strategy had two causes: first, the competition strategy failed because its supporters lacked a natural constituency whereas its opponents could mobilize effectively to block it. The hardest political battles were fought over the proposed tax cap on deductibility of employer-paid health insurance premiums. One wonders whether the competition strategy might have succeeded if it had been separated from this highly controversial tax proposal.

Second, the competition strategy failed because it faced powerful opposition within the administration itself. Much of the policy-making process became driven by the tyranny of the budget, as interpreted and enforced by OMB.

This does not mean that the Reagan administration has a poor health policy record, however. Some of its best initiatives have occurred in the area of cutting back or eliminating outmoded federal programs and regulations. The effects of these initiatives, some of which have gone virtually unnoticed, will be felt in coming years and will have a beneficial impact on the U.S. health care system.

Finally, the larger lesson from the Reagan administration's health policy experience is this: conservatives should not confuse budget cutting with the competitive market agenda. These two goals are at best unrelated and may even be in conflict. Budget cutting goes for the quick fix whereas competition is concerned with long-run structural changes that will increase economic efficiency. Its inability to make this distinction is the Reagan administration's greatest health policy failure.

17. Agriculture: Growing Government Control

Robert L. Thompson

American farmers have been addicted to government price and income supports and acreage-reduction policies for 50 years. In 1981 the Reagan administration talked about the need to cut the cost of the farm program and move toward a free market in agriculture, but consider the developments we've seen since then: We've seen the cost of the farm program go from $3 billion in 1980 to $26 billion in 1986. We've seen a return to explicit agricultural export subsidies. We've seen stricter import quotas on sugar. We've seen tighter controls over the acreage that may be cultivated, which have induced growers to carve up large farms into smaller, less efficient units. To the sources of uncertainty that farmers normally face, such as weather and market conditions, we've added an unpredictable agricultural policy. And we've seen the U.S. Department of Agriculture become an issuer of currency.

The Farm Situation in 1981

Now consider the conditions that prevailed in 1981. Perhaps the most important one was the aftermath of a land-price boom that can only be characterized as a speculative bubble in the land market. During the 1970s, on the strength of inflationary expectations and unrealistic export-growth expectations, land prices had been driven up to more than twice the level that could be sustained on a cash-flow basis.

In addition, agricultural exports had taken on a more important role in the U.S. economy. In 1981 the produce of one out of every three acres of American farmland was sold overseas. There had also been a substantial overcapitalization in American agriculture; by the end of the 1970s the farm sector's per capita investment in machinery, equipment, and buildings was more than twice as large as that of the manufacturing sector. Finally, farm debt had jumped from $70 billion at the beginning of the 1970s to over $210 billion at the beginning of the 1980s. The Farmers Home Administration had pumped out between $6 billion and $7 billion worth of so-called economic emergency credit in the late 1970s, thus sharply increasing the debt load of a number of farmers.

So in 1981 we had high land prices, burgeoning exports, an overcapitalized farm sector, and a high farm debt as well as a high rate of inflation and a fairly cheap dollar. At the end of that year Congress passed a farm bill. Many viewed it as a do-nothing bill because it didn't give the administration much in the way of market liberalization. The bill's worst aspect was that it established minimum price supports up to four years in advance, without regard to the exchange rates, the domestic supply/demand balance, or the global supply/demand balance. Up to four years in advance it telegraphed to the rest of the world the minimum nominal-dollar price below which we would not sell each of our commodities during a given year.

What did the 1981 farm bill, which was in effect from 1982 to 1986, accomplish? Well, farm exports fell from $44 billion in 1981 to $26 billion in 1986. That downturn in farm exports, which occurred as exchange rates rose and the global economy went into a recession, reduced the nominal-dollar prices of U.S. commodities. But as soon as the prices reached our loan rates, the Commodity Credit Corporation stepped in with an infinitely elastic demand, guaranteeing to buy any quantity of a product it was offered and to pay a fixed price.

Thus, the 1981 bill converted the United States into a residual supplier to the world market—or, as I like to put it, into the Saudi Arabia of the international grain cartel. Saudi Arabia, of course, made all the supply adjustments necessary to keep the world price of petroleum at the level established by the oil cartel. We ended up making all the production cutbacks necessary to support the world price of grain at our loan rates.

As government stocks accumulated, we paid our farmers to take more and more land out of production. That policy culminated in the infamous payment-in-kind program of 1983, a year in which we paid our farmers to take almost 80 million acres out of production—more land than Western Europe *planted*. It was the largest year-to-year reduction in food production in history.

The effect of the cutback lasted for two years. Today our stocks are as high as they were in 1982 because we kept following the policy of establishing rigid minimum loan rates, or price supports. That was a guaranteed formula for the demise of the United States as a large exporter, and not surprisingly in a shrinking world market, all of our competitors increased their exports. So we took up the slack not only for the shrinkage of the market but also for the increase in our competitors' exports; we invited them to underprice us by a few pennies a bushel and export everything they grew while we made all the production cutbacks necessary for the whole world.

A second important event of the early 1980s was what can only be described as a land-price bust. It was inevitable that the speculative bubble in the land market would burst at some point. The reduction in U.S. exports, combined with an increase in interest rates and a decrease in the rate of inflation, eroded investors' confidence in the land market and set the land-price downturn in motion.

The burst was bound to occur sometime, and it occurred with a vengeance in the early 1980s; the total value of American farmland declined by more than $300 billion between 1981 and 1985. The land-price bust, which led to a sharply increased farm failure rate as well as a rate of rural bank failures that set a record for the post-Depression period, was probably the most important factor that influenced the debate over the 1985 farm bill.

As a result of the 1981 farm bill, particularly the provisions that established rigid minimum price supports and committed the government to making large deficiency payments, the cost of the agriculture program ratcheted from $3 billion in 1980 to $19 billion in 1985. In fact, during that period the Reagan administration spent more money on farm policy than any previous administration had. Unfortunately, the administration chose to brag about that fact in the 1984 presidential election campaign.

The 1985 Farm Bill

As we wrote the 1985 farm bill, several other important factors affected the debate. One was a consensus that the cost of the agriculture program had to be reduced; we were in the same environment that gave us Gramm-Rudman. Another was a widespread misconception that farm-family income was low. It's hard to find evidence of that. Government payments have skyrocketed, more than compensating for the decline in export revenues. In every year of the 1980s there has been a new record high in net cash farm income.

Although the payment program has kept farmers with little debt in very good shape during the 1980s, it hasn't even come close to saving the one out of seven farmers with a heavy debt load. If the $210 billion farm debt that we inherited at the beginning of the 1980s had been uniformly distributed among all U.S. growers, there probably wouldn't have been a serious problem. But the distribution has been heavily skewed; the debt is in the hands of about 15 percent of the growers in the United States, and no amount of government payments that are proportionate to production could possibly save that group. There's been lots of rhetoric to the effect that large government payments are needed to help farmers in financial distress. But in practice, very little of the money has been going to the people with a debt problem, because there has been a weak correlation between the degree of farm debt and the volume of total sales.

Other factors that influenced the 1985 farm bill debate include the 40 percent decline in U.S. exports that occurred in the early 1980s and the perception that the government's agriculture policy itself was becoming an important source of uncertainty.

What did the 1985 farm bill accomplish? The Reagan administration came in with a very strong argument that we needed to get the government out of agriculture—to free up markets—but it was totally defeated in that objective. However, one provision of the 1985 farm bill is at least moving us in the right direction: our loan rates, or price supports, were reduced by 25 percent in the first year of the bill and will be reduced by 5 percent a year thereafter until they reach 75 percent of the market price (calculated on a moving-average basis).

That is probably the greatest accomplishment of the 1985 farm bill, because it is an acknowledgment that we're pricing ourselves out of the world market; we cannot remain a large farm exporter if we insist on trying to unilaterally support the world market price. By dropping our loan rates, we are increasing our trading partners' price uncertainty and getting the United States back into a more competitive position in the world market.

But the cost of getting that provision into the farm bill was that the administration had to accept a freeze on target prices, which are the determinants of the income transfers to American farmers, and that's what ratcheted the total cost of the agriculture program from $19 billion in 1985 to $26 billion in 1986. The objective of reducing the cost of the program fell by the wayside. Believe it or not, the movies *Country, The River,* and *Places in the Heart* did a great deal to convince Congress that all American farmers are in trouble and that only larger government payments will keep them whole. The commodity organizations used that argument to great advantage as they lobbied for larger payments.

One of the worst features of the farm bill is the maintenance of the acreage-reduction programs. In order to qualify for government payments, a farmer has to retire, say, 25 percent, 27½ percent, or 35 percent of his land—the percentage depends on the commodity produced. Every producer of a given commodity, no matter how efficient or inefficient, has to cut back by the same amount. That requirement raises the average cost of production because it forces each grower to spread his fixed costs over less than the full capacity of his operation. Moreover, it greatly reduces the competitiveness of our most efficient producers—and hence the nation's competitiveness as an exporter. The farm bill also tightened our import quotas on sugar, further restricting our most regulated agriculture market.

Our daily price supports are another perennial problem that has not been eliminated by the 1985 farm bill, thanks to the dairy lobby. The administration wanted to reduce the price supports significantly, but in exchange for getting some reductions during the last three years of the five-year farm bill, it had to accept a whole-herd buyout in the first year; farmers were compensated for slaughtering their herds. Unfortunately, in the face of frozen price supports and a 25 percent reduction in the cost of feed, which represents about 50 percent of a dairy farmer's production cost, the rest of the farmers have had a strong incentive to continue producing milk.

There have also been regional market tightnesses. The government has an open-ended commitment to pay guaranteed prices for any quantities of butter, cheese, and powdered milk that are offered to it. So even efficient milk processors have had incentives to bid up the prices they pay farmers—by doing so, they can stimulate

247

milk production, maintain throughput in their plants, and sell more dairy products to Uncle Sam. It's a great system.

Finally, there are 17 passages in the 1985 bill that authorize payments in kind—giving farmers government-owned commodities such as grain and cotton in lieu of cash. In the Office of Management and Budget's accounting system, if an asset of the federal government is given away, it is not booked as a current outlay, so the incentive to make payments in kind was very strong. But the device created to implement those giveaways was the so-called generic payment-in-kind certificate. It's dollar-denominated, fully negotiable, payable to the bearer, and better than cash because it's backed by real goods—commodities. Thus, the 1985 farm bill put the Department of Agriculture in the position of being an issuer of U.S. currency by giving it the right to issue those certificates. Moreover, it greatly increased the Department of Agriculture's control over the volume of commodities, and hence the liquidity, in the market in the short run.

The fraction of the government's payments that are in kind versus in cash and the timing of the delivery of the certificates to farmers (and therefore the timing of the delivery of commodities to the market) are the two most important determinants, in the short run, of the supply of commodities in the market. Because the government is the biggest holder of inventories, the amount of a commodity that it feeds back into the market through the certificates is the most important determinant, in the short run, of the liquidity in the market. So the 1985 farm bill put the Department of Agriculture in the incredibly powerful position of influencing short-run market price movements. An administration that wanted to get the government out of the marketplace has gotten the government far more deeply involved in the marketplace than it's been in recent decades.

Conclusion

I've stressed the negative consequences of the 1985 farm bill, but at least it has helped to restore our export competitiveness by reducing our domestic price supports. Our export recovery is a result of that reform and the decline of the dollar.

We have come to recognize that being a large exporter imposes certain limitations on our freedom of action in domestic policymaking. Moreover, getting world market prices down by refraining from supporting them is hastening the day when the GATT's Uruguay round gives serious consideration to agricultural policy reform. During the first five years of the 1980s we reduced the cost of our competitors' farm policy by holding world market prices up at no cost to their taxpayers. But our new policy is costing our competitors so much that they are coming to the negotiating table.

In addition, I suppose that by maintaining a large cash flow to the farm sector, we prevented a few farmers from being pushed over the brink into financial distress. But that's the limit of the positive results of the 1985 farm bill.

If we've got to continue making income transfers to American farmers for political reasons, it's essential that we decouple those payments from production so that no one will have to plant crops that are in surplus in order to qualify for them. That is the most important step that we need to take. We also need to get the Department of Agriculture out of the business of issuing currency through generic payment-in-kind certificates and thus reduce its control over the liquidity in the international commodity market.

PART V

DOMESTIC POLICIES

18. International Trade: Better than Congress

Murray L. Weidenbaum

My former colleague on the Council of Economic Advisers (CEA), William Niskanen, frequently described the council's main role as being to operate a damage-limitation mechanism. You certainly would not expect a council of free-market economists to generate proposals for brave new government programs. In any event, it has been the council's destiny to be a gal—or rather, guy—who can say "no." Or, in the words of the opposition, the council was just a den of ivory-tower, knee-jerk, pristine[1] free-trade theorists who cared more about vague burdens on the general consumer than about real benefits to specific companies.

The continuing battle for free trade is a cogent example of the damage-limitation mechanism working at full capacity. To be sure, the Reagan administration started off with a very good "Statement on U.S. Trade Policy," issued in July 1981. That policy document stressed the commitment to achieve open trade. One of the central components of the administration's trade policy was "reducing government barriers to the flow of trade and investment among nations."[2]

On occasion, we did roll back the tide of protectionism a bit. A good case in point is the quotas on shoes (also known by the euphemism "orderly marketing agreements") imposed by the Carter administration. President Reagan let those quotas expire. But it was not just the brilliance of the CEA's economic analysis that made the difference.

---

[1]One of the dictionary definitions of pristine is "uncorrupted." See, for example, *Webster's Collegiate Dictionary*, 5th ed. (Springfield, Mass.: G. & C. Merriam Co., 1946), p. 789.

[2]*Economic Report of the President, February 1982* (Washington: Government Printing Office, 1982), pp. 176–77.

Somewhat surprisingly, the free-trade position was supported by members of the cabinet who veered toward protectionism in many other instances. Sparing the details, I will just note that some old-fashioned politicking on the part of the CEA chairman was involved. Dumb luck also helped. Unlike other demanders for protectionism, the shoe delegation to the White House was not led by a powerful Republican member of the Congress, but by the senior senator from Massachusetts. So much for theoretical college professors and practical businessmen. In 1985, by the way, the president rejected the shoe industry's renewed petition for "import relief."

However, our luck ran out on other trade matters. In most cases, President Reagan and senior members of his administration found themselves torn between two conflicting value systems. One side of the conflict involved their philosophical support for competition in the marketplace; free trade is clearly a logical extension of free markets at home. The second side involved their concern for promoting business interests. Thus, when the loss-ridden automobile industry complained of "unfair" competition, the administration was very sympathetic to its plea. (It seems, by the way, that competition is only fair if it occurs among your suppliers.) The obvious answer offered by those most committed to this second concern was to limit imports of the most popular foreign cars, those made in Japan. The argument was made, of course, that such action would be temporary, so that a return to the free market could be speedily envisioned.

Automobile Import Quotas

In retrospect, the 1981 action on automobile imports was typical of how the debate on free trade versus protectionism has proceeded during the 1980s. In response to pressure from the automobile manufacturing industry and the United Automobile Workers union, members of Congress introduced legislation to impose firm statutory limits on the number of Japanese cars that could be imported.

The three major economic policy agencies—the Treasury, the Office of Management and Budget, and the CEA—were instinctively opposed. The other participants in the internal debate within the administration agreed that statutory quotas were undesirable restrictions on the discretion of the president. Yet they wanted to do something for the industry and its unemployed workers. They characterized free trade pejoratively as a "do nothing" policy. Of course, my position was described quite accurately by the wise-crack, "Don't just stand there, undo something."

Under the circumstances, the majority of Reagan administration decisionmakers favored informal and temporary restraints, which the Japanese themselves would voluntarily adopt and administer. Anyone participating in the discussions with representatives of the Japanese government quickly saw how "voluntary" the action was. In any event, that was the position adopted by the president. It is fascinating to note that when the extended quotas expired four years later, the Japanese auto industry and the Ministry of International Trade and Industry (MITI) saw the benefits to themselves very clearly. They volunteered to continue the trade restraints on a unilateral basis.

Looking back, we may ask ourselves whether there was any politically realistic alternative to the nonstatutory, limited-duration quotas. Of course, we can only guess. It is helpful, however, to recall the state of the U.S. automobile industry back in 1981. Imports represented 27 percent of U.S. auto sales, up from 18 percent in 1977. Sales of domestically made cars stood at a 20-year low—6.2 million units, down 6 percent from 1980. Between 1977 and 1981, production of domestic cars had fallen 32 percent, and 1981 was the fourth straight year of decline in the industry's output.

The four domestic auto manufacturers had incurred losses totaling $4.2 billion the year before and were running in the red once again. (Net losses in 1981 turned out to be $1.3 billion.) Over 1,600 domestic car dealers—more than 6 percent of the total—had gone out of business in 1980; that was three times the number of failures in 1975. About 300,000 members of the United Automobile Workers were reported to have been laid off, most of them on indefinite layoff.[3]

Given the importance of the industry to the economies of several key states, I believe that—in the absence of action by the president—the odds were in favor of Congress passing legislation imposing firm quotas on Japanese auto imports. I do not believe that the

[3]Murray L. Weidenbaum, *Business, Government, and the Public*, 3d ed. (Englewood Cliffs, N.J.: Prentice-Hall, 1986), pp. 279–83.

support for protection was sufficient to override a veto, but that was a fight the administration preferred to avoid.

Other Restraints on Imports

Free traders in the Reagan administration have won a number of victories, such as the veto of a tough textile import restriction bill in 1985 and the president's refusal to curb copper imports. The successful opposition to local content legislation—the fair practice in automotive products bill—was another example. The bill itself illustrates the need to extend the truth-in-labeling law to the products of government.

Yet the damage-limitation operation did not always work.[4] The automobile case was a bad precedent, encouraging the push for trade restrictions. All sorts of special interests were able to cite it subsequently as an example of what would likely happen when the administration got down to the wire. The free-trade rhetoric of economists would be pushed aside in favor of the more activist policies supported by many of the former business executives in the cabinet.

Since 1980, the United States has become much more protectionist than it had been. Ironically, this change has occurred at the same time that the U.S. government has been pressuring the Japanese— with modest success—to roll back some of their many obstacles to imports.

The U.S. trade barriers that have been imposed or increased during the Reagan administration constitute an impressive array. In 1981, the federal government agreed to an extension of the Multi-Fiber Arrangement controlling imports and exports of textiles and textile products on a multinational basis. In 1982, the administration successfully pressured Western European governments to agree to quotas to keep their steel exports to about 5 percent of the U.S. markets (predictably, Asian producers expanded their sales to U.S. customers). The president imposed quotas on sugar imports in an effort to prop up the domestic price-support programs.

Important protectionist steps were taken in 1983. The president ordered a sharp increase in import duties on large motorcycles

---

[4]Vinod K. Aggarwal, Robert O. Keohane, and David B. Yoffie, "The Dynamics of Negotiated Protectionism," *American Political Science Review* (June 1987): 345–66.

(mainly from Japan). Also, quotas were imposed on imports of stainless and specialty steel and on 30 textile imports from China.

The move against China occurred even though the United States at the time enjoyed a large trade surplus with that nation. So much for the sophistry of modern-day reciprocity. The Chinese promptly curbed their imports of U.S. farm and chemical products. We no longer enjoy a trade surplus with China. The protectionists love to talk about the unfairness of one-way free trade, so it is only fair to needle them on the unfairness—and the results—of one-way reciprocity.

To continue the chronology of the march away from free trade, in 1984, the federal government tightened "rules of origin" to increase protection for domestic clothing producers. In 1986, five-year quotas on machine tool imports were negotiated with West Germany, Switzerland, Japan, and Taiwan. In the case of Japan and Taiwan, imports of machine tools were rolled back to their 1981 shares of the U.S. market. Swiss imports were pushed back only to the 1985 levels. Some West German import levels were based on 1981 and others on 1985. I do not recall any justification for the differences, but after all, a foolish consistency is the hobgoblin of little minds. Perhaps that is not a reversible proposition.

The administration warned seven other countries not to expand their shares of the U.S. machine tool market at the expense of the four countries that agreed to cut theirs back. Such competition supposedly would not be viewed as fair.

In 1986, the Multi-Fiber Arrangement was renewed. Also, the wood-chip war with Canada, although it did not last long, was a cogent reminder of the great damage to the basic foreign relations of the United States that results from thoughtless efforts to assist a domestic industry.

In the summer of 1986, the United States developed a "spectacular" innovation in the trade-policy area—that contribution to open trade known as the Semiconductor Trade Agreement. In plain English, we formed a cartel comprising the major producers of memory chips and in the process guaranteed a minimum price to U.S. chip manufacturers. Early in 1987, the U.S. government enforced cartel pricing by imposing duties on Japanese goods; this action was taken in an attempt to punish Japan for selling chips at below-market prices in third countries. Subsequently, MITI pressured Japanese chip producers to reduce production of the most widely used device in this field: dynamic random access memories (DRAMs).

Big surprise: the resulting DRAM shortage is now hurting our domestic computer manufacturers. After pushing so hard for the accord with Japan, our companies apparently now want the enforcement reduced. I am reluctant to label this a belated conversion to a free-trade viewpoint, especially in view of the industry's advocacy of increased federal subsidy of research in this field. Apparently, the more than $500 million that federal agencies are spending for semiconductor research in 1987 has only whetted the industry's appetite.[5] To avoid running afoul of our strange anti-dumping regulations, the Japanese were forced to fix the prices of their chips to cover all costs plus a generous 8 percent profit.

It is most unlikely, by the way, that the ruler of the Soviet Union would have been treated as roughly on any issue as the prime minister of Japan, Yasuhiro Nakasone, was during that trade dispute. In any event, after imposing tariffs of 100 percent on about $300 million of Japanese imports, the United States did relent a bit during the Venice economic summit.

All in all, the proportion of imports entering the United States duty-free declined from 54 percent in 1950 to 32 percent in 1984.[6] That percentage is likely to be even lower today. In addition, the numerous ongoing investigations of allegedly unfair trade practices constitute an invisible trade barrier because they create uncertainty as to the prices that foreign firms ultimately will receive.

Restraints on Exports

We should not forget the self-inflicted wounds on our international trade in the form of U.S. government restraints on U.S. exports. The administration's regulatory relief effort has not extended to asking Congress to eliminate such silly and anachronistic statutory restrictions as bans on exports of timber from federal lands in the West and oil from the North Slope of Alaska.[7] Both barriers

[5]Congressional Budget Office, *The Benefits and Risks of Federal Funding for Sematech* (Washington: Government Printing Office, 1987), pp. 5–6.

[6]Stephen L. Lande and Craig Van Grasstek, *The Trade and Tariff Act of 1984* (New York: Lexington Books, 1986), p. 4.

[7]The Trans-Alaska Pipeline Authorization Act effectively prohibits the export of oil from North Slope fields. A rider to an appropriation act for the Department of the Interior bans timber exports from federal lands west of the 100th meridian.

were erected in the form of riders to broader legislation. They were defended within the administration on the grounds that it is not in this nation's interest to sell the Japanese raw materials while we buy large quantities of highly processed (and hence more labor-intensive) goods from them. But why, oh why, don't they buy more rice from our farmers?

Meanwhile, other parts of the administration—led by the Department of Defense—have been determined to use the Export Administration Act to bar the shipment of virtually all high-tech products to the Soviet bloc. It has not made any difference to the holders of this position whether the same or similar items are readily available elsewhere in world markets. Fortunately, the Department of Commerce has led a counterattack and the results have varied from case to case.

The incident involving U.S. suppliers to the construction of the natural gas pipeline between the Soviet Union and Western Europe was a low point in terms of the United States attempt to impose trade restrictions unilaterally on its friends and allies. The embargo was lifted when it became apparent that the main impacts were negative to our own foreign policy interests. The damage to U.S. relations with the NATO allies exceeded any harm to the Soviets. Also, the entire episode exacerbated the overseas concern about U.S. firms being unreliable suppliers.

On average, about 10 percent of U.S. exports are now subject to barriers imposed by our own government.[8]

Some Conclusions

Protectionist actions are far more counterproductive than the public realizes. Two recent studies underscore that point. An economist at the Federal Reserve Bank of Boston has shown that almost 40 percent of U.S. foreign trade consists of transactions between U.S. firms and their foreign affiliates or parents.[9] Thus, American companies bear a large portion of the burden that protectionists are trying to impose on foreigners.

Moreover, my colleague Arthur Denzau at the Center for the

[8]Department of State, Bureau of Public Affairs, *U.S. Export Controls* (Washington, 1985), p. 1.

[9]Jane S. Little, "Intra-Firm Trade," *New England Economic Review* (May/June 1987): 46–51.

Study of American Business has shown that the net effect of trade restrictions is to reduce domestic employment. He examined the 1984 "voluntary" restraints on steel exports to the United States, showing that they did save approximately 14,000 jobs in our domestic steel industry. However, the higher costs for our steel-using industries resulted in eliminating over 50,000 jobs, for a net loss of 36,000 jobs.[10]

There is one positive by-product of the protectionist battle. It puts the lie to the canard that economists are always in disarray. Keynesians, monetarists, supply-siders, and eclectic conservative economists compose a solid free-trade phalanx.

On balance, it is clear that the United States has become more protectionist since Ronald Reagan moved into the Oval Office. By 1985, the Reagan administration had openly adopted the "fair trade" term that traditionally has been the protectionists' euphemism for trade restrictions.[11] The 1981 statement on open trade turned out to be a temporary victory.

But fairness does require us to acknowledge that the administration's move toward protectionism has been much less rapid than would have been the case if the administration had merely followed the lead of Congress. In comparison to your favorite senator, every member of the Reagan cabinet is a paragon of free trade.

[10]Arthur T. Denzau, *How Import Restraints Reduce Employment* (St. Louis: Washington University, Center for the Study of American Business, 1987), p. 5.

[11]See, for example, *Economic Report of the President, February 1986* (Washington: Government Printing Office, 1986), pp. 123–25.

19. Antitrust: An Incomplete Revolution

James L. Gattuso

Throughout most of this century, the scope of the antitrust laws was being almost continually expanded. "Big is bad" was the reigning philosophy of the merger laws, regardless of any economic benefits that a merger might bring to consumers. A wide range of other business practices had been ruled to be per se illegal, thus prohibiting such activities regardless of possible gains to consumers. As recently as the Carter administration, the Federal Trade Commission was trying to push the bounds of antitrust law even further—bringing well-publicized cases involving everything from oil companies to cereal manufacturers.

Over the last decade, however, there has been a revolution in antitrust law. Today, the merger laws are applied with an eye toward potential economic efficiencies, making possible restructuring in many industries that would have been undreamed of 10 years ago. The number of business practices judged to be per se illegal has been substantially reduced, as courts now, more than ever before, are willing to look at the benefits to consumers of such practices.

This revolution in antitrust policy, however, was not a Reagan Revolution. While the Reagan administration can take the credit for helping these changes along, perhaps speeding their implementation by years, the sea change in antitrust policy was not solely the result of a favorably disposed administration. Rather, it was the consequence of sustained academic critiques of the antitrust laws throughout the 1960s and 1970s. Even without Ronald Reagan, changes in antitrust policy would have proceeded, although perhaps at a slower pace. Moreover, they will not disappear when Ronald Reagan leaves office in 1989. Things will never again be as they were.

This does not mean there is no need for further change. The antitrust revolution is still an incomplete one. Despite favorable court rulings and improved enforcement practices by federal authorities, the basic antitrust statutes have remained virtually unchanged throughout the Reagan years. Although a reversion to the old days of antitrust is unlikely, the lack of statutory change does leave the door open.

Furthermore, the antitrust revolution is incomplete because antitrust itself was never really challenged. Complete antitrust deregulation was never a goal of the Reagan administration. Its policies were consistently aimed at simply reforming antitrust law to make it more efficient, while defending the need for such laws in a competitive economy. This view is strongly at odds with a growing school of thought that maintains that the antitrust laws are themselves inherently anticompetitive and should be more severely scaled back or abolished altogether. It is too soon to say whether these critics will succeed in accomplishing a second antitrust revolution. The debate, however, promises to be interesting.

Developments in Antitrust under Reagan

Antitrust law is not determined by a single forum or institution; instead it is shaped by three separate, though overlapping, forces: court decisions, legislation, and executive-branch enforcement policies.

The Courts

The state of antitrust law, as interpreted by the courts, improved tremendously during the Reagan years. Throughout this period, the courts increasingly applied principles of market economics in their decisions, resulting in a significant narrowing of the scope of the antitrust laws.

This trend in the courts actually began in the late 1970s. In the landmark 1977 case *Continental T.V. Inc.* v. *G.T.E. Sylvania, Inc.*, for instance, the Supreme Court reversed a decade-old precedent and ruled that a manufacturer's restriction on where its distributors could operate would not be considered per se illegal. Rather, the "rule of reason" would be applied, meaning that the economic justifications for the manufacturer's restriction could be considered. In reaching its conclusion, the Court relied heavily upon the "new economic learning" advanced by adherents to the Chicago school of economics—citing Robert Bork, Richard Posner, and others who maintained that such restrictions, by increasing the efficiency of distribution systems, could considerably benefit consumers.

During the Reagan years, the Court increasingly applied the insights of the Chicago-school economists in its antitrust decisions, significantly loosening the grip of antitrust regulation on the economy. Consider the following four cases, for example.

First, in *Copperweld* v. *Independent Tube Corp.*, decided in 1984, the Supreme Court found that an agreement between a corporation and its own subsidiary cannot be an illegal "conspiracy" in restraint of trade. Liability should turn upon the economic realities of a situation, the Court stressed, rather than upon the "garb in which a corporate subunit [is] clothed."

Second, in *Monsanto Co.* v. *Spray-Rite Corp.*, also decided in 1984, and in the *Business Electronics Corp.* v. *Sharp Electronics Corp.*, decided in 1988, the Court made it significantly more difficult to find a firm liable for restricting the prices charged by its distributors, known as "resale price maintenance." Bork and other analysts had long maintained that such restrictions should not be per se illegal, because, like nonprice restraints, restrictions on what a distributor can charge often can lead to efficiencies, to the benefit of consumers. The Court's decision stopped short of ending the per se illegal treatment of resale price maintenance, but it did require plaintiffs to put forth clear evidence of an actual agreement between the manufacturer and a distributor to maintain a particular price level.

Third, in the 1986 case of *Matsushita Electric Industrial Co.* v. *Zenith Radio Corp.*, the Court upheld a summary judgment, or dismissal without trial, of a "predatory pricing" charge against Matsushita. In so doing, the Court dealt a severe blow to the legal theory of predatory pricing, or pricing a product below its actual cost to drive out competitors. Citing Bork and other analysts on this issue, the Court found "a consensus among commentors that predatory pricing schemes are rarely tried, and even more rarely successful." Further, because a finding of predatory pricing punishes a firm for lowering its prices, the Court found that it "chill[s] the very conduct the antitrust laws are designed to prevent."

Fourth, in *Cargill* v. *Monfort of Colorado, Inc.*, decided in 1987, the Supreme Court made it more difficult for competitors to block mergers among their rivals. In the past, firms had consistently tried to protect themselves from increased competition by filing antitrust suits to block mergers that promised to make their rivals stronger. In *Cargill*, the plaintiff claimed that the merger in question would injure it by making it possible for the merged firm to lower its prices. Fifteen years ago, the Court might have accepted such a claim. In this case, it ruled that to protect a competitor from such injury would be "perverse," and it ruled against the plaintiff.

Given the appointments to the federal bench made by President Reagan, it is likely that the Court will continue to increase its use of economic analysis and continue to circumscribe the scope of the antitrust laws. Reagan appointed many of the leading advocates of antitrust reform to federal circuit courts, including Robert Bork, Richard Posner, Frank Easterbrook, and Ralph Winter. In addition, Antonin Scalia, another leading advocate of an economic approach to law, has been appointed to the Supreme Court. These men will exert a major influence on antitrust law long after Reagan has left the White House.

Legislation

There has been far less progress in changing antitrust statutes. For the most part, the U.S. antitrust statutes today are essentially the same as they were before Ronald Reagan took office. However, antitrust reform has been enacted in some limited areas. Among these are the following:

- The Export Trading Company Act of 1982 loosened antitrust restrictions on export trading companies to allow American goods to be marketed abroad. Under the provisions of this act, export trading companies can receive certification from the Department of Commerce, with the approval of the attorney general, that provides them with limited freedom from antitrust regulation.
- The National Cooperative Research Act of 1984 loosened antitrust restrictions on joint research and development ventures. After reporting their ventures to antitrust officials, participants are protected from treble-damages liability and, in case of a lawsuit, are entitled to have the venture judged under a "rule of reason" rather than per se standard.
- The Shipping Act of 1984 broadened the protection from antitrust regulation for joint U.S. shipping conferences, thereby

permitting U.S. companies to compete more effectively with foreign vessels.

In addition, the Local Government Antitrust Act of 1984 protected local governments from monetary damages in antitrust suits. However, by protecting local government regulations from such damages, the net effect of the act may have been an increase, rather than a decrease, in government intervention in the economy.

Between 1981 and 1987, the Reagan administration did make several attempts to make more sweeping changes in the antitrust laws. Its most ambitious reform effort began in late 1985, when it proposed to Congress a broad antitrust reform package. Among the elements of this package were the following:

- A modification of the Clayton Act, to ensure that courts give weight to certain economic factors in reviewing mergers, rather than reverting to a "big is bad" approach.
- Revision of the trade laws to allow the president to give temporary relief from the antitrust laws to industries particularly hard hit by foreign competition.
- Elimination of treble damages in private antitrust suits, except for such offenses as price-fixing.
- A requirement that the losing side in an antitrust lawsuit pay the attorney's fees of the prevailing party.

If enacted, these reforms would have been a substantial step forward in loosening the burden of antitrust regulation. Unfortunately, they received a less-than-warm reception from Congress. In fact, rather than look seriously at proposals such as these, Congress appears more inclined to strengthen the antitrust laws. For instance, in 1988 a bill to overturn the Supreme Court's *Monsanto* and *Sharp* decisions and put the bar on resale price maintenance into statutory form was easily approved by the House of Representatives and nearly approved by the Senate. Thus, despite enactment of some favorable measures, it appears that the antitrust revolution that has so changed the academic world and the courts has yet to have had a real effect on Capitol Hill.

Enforcement Practices

Although the revolution in antitrust was already beginning in the courts before Reagan took office (but had little influence in Con-

265

gress), the Reagan administration has had a clear effect on the policies pursued by the U.S. antitrust enforcement agencies—the Antitrust Division of the Department of Justice and the Federal Trade Commission. During the 1970s, the federal antitrust authorities were aggressively attempting to extend the frontiers of antitrust law. These policies abruptly changed in 1981. With the new administration came a new antitrust philosophy and a new way of looking at antitrust cases. Symbolic of the new view of antitrust was the appointment of James C. Miller III to chair the FTC. Miller, an economist, was the first nonlawyer to hold that position, sending a strong signal that the Reagan administration would stress economic analysis in applying the antitrust laws.

The new approach has had an unmistakable impact on the federal government's antitrust policy. In 1982, for instance, the Antitrust Division dropped its 13-year-old case against IBM. If the case ever did have any merit, rapidly increasing competition in the computer industry had made the case untenable from an economic point of view. In the same year, the long-standing monopolization case against AT&T was settled. While the settlement called for the divestiture of AT&T's local operating companies, it allowed the firm to keep its long-distance operations virtually intact, although their divestiture was one of the original goals of the suit.

The FTC and the Antitrust Division virtually stopped bringing cases against "vertical," or manufacturer-distributor, restraints altogether. These restraints, which were receiving increasingly favorable treatment in the courts, were viewed by Reagan antitrust officials as almost never harmful to consumers. In fact, the Antitrust Division had even planned to argue to the Supreme Court in the *Monsanto* case that per se illegal treatment of resale price maintenance should be ended—but then Congress, through an appropriations rider, prevented the division from doing so.

Moreover, the administration significantly altered the analysis employed in merger cases. Since the 1960s, the Antitrust Division had used a very structural approach to merger analysis. The basic operating assumption was that competition in an industry was inversely related to concentration—a principle known as the "market-concentration doctrine." Studies, in fact, had shown that firms in more concentrated industries did have higher average profits. Thus, as stated in the division's 1968 merger guidelines, mergers that increased concentration in an industry would be routinely challenged.

By the 1970s, however, the basis of the market-concentration doctrine began to crumble. An increasing body of research showed that concentrated industries actually had higher productivity gains and smaller price increases than less concentrated markets. While the bigger firms in markets did have higher profits, this was attributable to the fact that the more efficient firms were naturally more profitable and more likely to grow in size.[1] Concentration alone was thus not a reason to bar a merger.

With this evidence in hand, the Reagan administration in 1982 scrapped the old 1968 merger guidelines and promulgated new ones. Under the new guidelines, as slightly revised in 1984, few mergers would be challenged simply on the basis of a firm's market share.[2] Instead, the Antitrust Division would review the ease with which new competitors could enter the industry, the financial condition of the firms involved, and any ongoing changes in the industry. Thus, the division would rely on the facts of each individual case to determine whether a merger would be harmful to consumers.

The division, however, did not totally reject the use of concentration figures in its merger analysis. Firms in highly concentrated industries still would receive much closer scrutiny. If a merger in a highly concentrated industry would increase concentration beyond a certain amount, the merger would be challenged, except in extraordinary cases. On the other hand, except in extraordinary circumstances, the division would not challenge a merger in unconcentrated industries, thereby providing them with a safe harbor, free from uncertainty.

The result of the new merger policy was a marked decrease in the number of cases brought by the federal government. For instance, the Carter administration had sought to block 9 of the 868 mergers for which companies sought approval in 1979, but the Reagan administration objected to only 4 of 1,949 mergers in 1986.[3]

[1]See Thomas W. Hazlett, "Is Antitrust Anticompetitive?" *Harvard Journal of Law and Public Policy* 9 (1986): 277.

[2]Although the FTC did not issue any guidelines, its merger policies have been generally consistent with those of the Antitrust Division.

[3]Ruth Marcus, "Rule Defends Antitrust Enforcement," *Washington Post*, September 4, 1987.

Because of these changes in antitrust enforcement policy, many people have the impression that the Reagan administration has abandoned antitrust enforcement. As put by the recent commentators, some "believe that the antitrust agencies have defected to the enemy; it's as if Custer had joined forces with Crazy Horse and Sitting Bull to wipe out the wagon trains on the Oregon Trail."[4] However, contrary to the fears of some and the hopes of others, the Reagan administration never did abandon its enforcement of, or its basic faith in, the antitrust laws.

For instance:

- While the number of civil suits is down, the Reagan administration has pursued criminal suits for price-fixing and bid-rigging more vigorously than have other administrations. During the Reagan years, the Antitrust Division has brought an average of 77 criminal cases per year, compared to 37 per year during the Carter administration.
- The Antitrust Division and the FTC have not hesitated to strike down mergers, even though the total number of rejected mergers is down. In 1984, for example, the division initially rejected the merger of the LTV and Republic Steel companies, a decision labeled by Secretary of Commerce Malcolm Baldrige as "a world class mistake."[5] In 1986, the FTC blocked the mergers of Pepsi and Seven-Up, and of Coca-Cola and Dr. Pepper. The high market shares of the companies were primarily responsible for the decision, although they accounted for only a small percentage of the total beverage market.[6] Moreover, although the approval of the major airline mergers in 1986 is often cited as evidence of the administration's "laxity" in antitrust, the Department of Justice actually opposed several of the largest of those mergers, including those between Northwest and Republic, TWA and Ozark, and, initially, Texas Air and Eastern. Putting less weight on simple market concentration statis-

[4]Joe Sims and Robert Lande, "New Forces Chip Away at Agencies' Policy of Antitrust Abandonment," Legal Times, April 20, 1987, p. 14.

[5]Quoted in Thomas J. Campbell, "The Antitrust Record of the First Reagan Administration," Texas Law Review 64 (1985): 353, 367.

[6]See Craig C. Carter, "Yes, Antitrust Can Still Say No," Fortune, September 1, 1986, p. 63.

tics, and more on the ease of entry into the airline industry, the Department of Transportation eventually allowed each of those mergers to go forward.

• The antitrust enforcement agencies have had a much higher impact on the economy than indicated by the number of mergers formally challenged. Unlike prior administrations, the Reagan antitrust enforcers have made a practice of working with firms that have proposed to merge and proposing particular divestitures or changes in business practices to allow the mergers to satisfy the antitrust laws. From the point of view of a businessman, this is quite valuable: problems can be worked out before the matter ends up in court. The process, however, increases the ability of the antitrust authorities to intervene in the market without filing a formal complaint. It has even been described as "a kind of hidden industrial policy by which the shape of entire industries can be molded by Government."[7]

Despite the claims of some critics, the Reagan administration has not stopped enforcing the antitrust laws, nor do its officials believe that antitrust regulation is undesirable. This should not be surprising in that the antitrust economics of the Chicago school, which the Reagan administration has broadly followed, is not synonymous with free-market economics. The administration's goal has not been to abolish antitrust law, but to enforce it in an economically efficient manner, distinguishing good economic behavior from bad. Thus, Custer has not joined the Indians. He is no longer shooting at them indiscriminately but is still firing, in the hope that he can distinguish the "friendly" Indians from the "hostile" Indians. Whether the Antitrust Division can meet with more success than the original Custer is open to question.

Prospects for the Future

There remains much to be done to complete and protect the improvements in antitrust policy seen over the last seven years. Since the antitrust statutes have been virtually unchanged over the last decade, there would be little to stop a new administration from trying to resurrect the activist policies of prior years. Moreover,

---

[7]Nathaniel C. Nash, "U.S.'s 'Fix-It' Antitrust Policy," *New York Times*, September 16, 1986.

private antitrust lawsuits, spurred by the prospect of trebled damages, can still present a problem to businesses in terms of litigation costs and uncertainty. For this reason, it is necessary to seek changes in antitrust statutes.

Nevertheless, it should be remembered that it will not be easy for opponents of antitrust reform to turn back the clock on antitrust policy. The improvements in antitrust policy achieved over the last seven years will not simply disappear when Ronald Reagan leaves office. The changes made were not just the result of one man or one election, but were the culmination of over a decade of new learning in law and economics. Antitrust was beginning to change before the 1980 election and will continue to do so after the 1988 election.

In fact, the antitrust debate over the next decade may not be so much over whether to return to the policies of the past as whether to take the antitrust revolution even further. The basis of antitrust itself has not yet been seriously challenged. Administration antitrust officials, as well as most economists of the Chicago school, have never given up the belief that antitrust regulation is beneficial to a market economy, if only it is enforced properly. In the last few years, however, this belief has been disputed by an increasing number of analysts who question the very basis of antitrust regulation—ranging from D. T. Armentano, who has claimed that antitrust has lost "all of its claim to legitimacy," to Thomas Hazlett, who has suggested that federal enforcement of antitrust should itself be considered a *"per se* restraint of trade."[8] It is this debate that may be the most interesting in the coming years.

[8]Hazlett, p. 336; D. T. Armentano, *Antitrust Policy: The Case for Repeal* (Cato Institute, 1986), p. 74. Other works suggesting repeal include: Fred S. McChesney, "Law's Honour Lost: The Plight of Antitrust," *The Antitrust Bulletin* (1986), p. 359; and Fred L. Smith, Jr., "Why Not Abolish Antitrust?" *Regulation* (January-February 1983), p. 7.

20. What Ever Happened to Deregulation?

Robert W. Crandall

Students of regulation might have been excused for expecting an acceleration of the deregulation movement when President Reagan assumed office in 1981. After all, if liberal Democrats in Congress and the Carter administration could lead the charge in dismantling airline and trucking regulation, surely a conservative Republican regime with a Republican Senate could do even better. With open talk of an economic Dunkirk facing the country, the new economic policymakers appeared ready to accelerate the Ford and Carter administrations' assaults on the enormous regulatory apparatus that had been growing since the 1930s.

Now, seven years later, the regulatory landscape surprisingly looks much as it did on January 20, 1981. There have been few new deregulatory statutes passed.[1] Regulatory review seems little more potent than in the Carter years. Environmental groups are still able on occasion to obtain a massive new program from Congress. On the surface at least, it appears that the Reagan appointees have only prevented a return of regulation where deregulation was under way, slowed the pace of new rulemaking, and repulsed most emotional calls for new regulation.

In this paper, I begin with a survey of federal regulation from the perspective of an economist. Given the breadth of federal regulation, I cannot cover all types of economic or social regulation, but I can attempt to examine the regulatory areas with the most important impacts on the economy. This survey enables me to then construct a report card on the Reagan efforts at taming the fourth branch of government—the regulatory agencies.

---

[1]The Bus Regulatory Reform Act of 1982 is perhaps the only important deregulatory legislation of the Reagan era.

Economic Regulation

For about 50 years, the federal government has had a major responsibility in regulating transportation, communications, finance, and energy. It has only been in the past 15 years, however, that momentum has built for reducing the degree and extent of such regulation. There has been substantial progress made toward deregulation in transportation and communications, but somewhat less in relieving the energy and financial sectors of government's heavy hand.

Transportation

Between 1978 and 1980, Congress passed four major pieces of legislation that deregulated airlines and air cargo and liberalized the regulation of trucking and railroads.[2] Since 1980, only the Bus Regulatory Reform Act has been added to this impressive legislative assault on the regulation of transportation. The Reagan administration was required to carry out the administration of regulatory reform (in trucking and railroads) or to preside over the dismantling of regulation (in airlines), but it can claim little credit for returning most of these sectors to the discipline of market forces.

Trucking. The most significant aspect of the 1980 trucking legislation was the increase in flexibility granted to the Interstate Commerce Commission to allow new route authority to existing carriers or entrants. At first, the new Reagan ICC threatened to slow the pace of new route awards, but it found such dilatory tactics impractical and soon abandoned them under pressure from many existing carriers who sought to expand their networks.

Since 1980, trucking rates appear to have fallen substantially. Cash flows of a number of existing carriers have declined because of the increased competition, and a number of firms that operated private trucking fleets to avoid high common-carrier rates have begun to dismantle these fleets. In an early article, Thomas Gale Moore found that rates began to fall even in advance of the passage of the 1980 act and that employment actually increased in the truck-

[2]Amendment (H. R. 6010) to the Federal Aviation Act of 1958, passed in 1977; the Airline Deregulation Act of 1978; the Motor Carrier Act of 1980; the Staggers Rail Act of 1980.

ing industry.[3] The increased competition among existing carriers and from new entrants has depressed unionized wage rates in the industry. Since 1980, hourly compensation in trucking has lagged behind the overall economy by a substantial margin.[4]

Some observers claim that the increase in competition and closer links between railroads and trucking firms have reduced transit time and thereby have reduced the required costs of inventories. These savings have not been fully documented, however, nor have there been any comprehensive studies of the 1980–87 increase in economic welfare due to lower freight costs and more efficient trucking-rail networks. Nevertheless, it appears quite likely that trucking deregulation has resulted in substantial gains in economic welfare.

Railroads. In 1980, Congress passed the Staggers Act, which deregulated certain commodities but required continued ICC regulation of rates for those commodities and routes on which there is a "dominant" carrier. The ICC is required to limit rates on these monopoly routes to between 170 and 190 percent of variable costs. In practice, such regulation affects only bulk commodities—such as coal or low-valued chemicals—along routes on which there is little competition from barges or trucks.

The ICC retains authority over rail mergers, and its authority has been exercised by the Reagan ICC in blocking several mergers, including the largest ever proposed—the Santa Fe–Southern Pacific combination. The ICC's antimerger actions represent the most aggressive antimerger activity anywhere in the Reagan administration and is the subject of considerable debate.

Airlines. Airline deregulation has been the most controversial, yet most clearly successful, of all of the recent exercises of deregulation. Under the 1978 Airline Deregulation Act, entry was liberalized gradually and carriers were afforded an initial period of fare flexibility. In 1984, however, the Civil Aeronautics Board quietly disappeared as the industry was effectively totally deregulated. The

[3]Thomas G. Moore, "Rail and Truck Reform—The Record So Far," *Regulation* (November/December 1983), pp. 33–41.

[4]Robert W. Crandall, "Economic Rents as a Barrier to Deregulation," *Cato Journal* 6, no. 1 (Spring/Summer 1986): 283, Table 1.

Department of Transportation (DOT) retains some regulatory authority over a few minor aspects of domestic airline service, the negotiation of international routes, and all airline mergers.

The results of deregulation thus far are quite clear. Revenues per passenger mile have fallen, and the frequency of service has improved as airlines have used their expanded route authority to develop hub-and-spoke route configurations. Even though load factors have increased and travel times have risen with the increase in travel generated by lower fares, Steven Morrison and Clifford Winston estimate that deregulation had contributed as much as $8 billion per year (in 1977 dollars) to economic welfare by 1983.[5]

The Reagan DOT's administration of its authority over airline mergers has generated considerable controversy. In the past three years, a series of acquisitions by large carriers such as Continental, Delta, and Northwest has created a far more concentrated market on most major routes than early advocates of deregulation had anticipated. DOT has allowed all of these mergers after only minor procedural delays and in spite of Justice Department objections in many cases. Many of the new entrants permitted by deregulation have disappeared.

The strength of competition among the large national carriers depends to a great extent upon the contestability of airline markets. Many hubs are now dominated by one or two carriers, and new entrants or other carriers may have difficulty entering markets served by these hubs. Indeed, Morrison and Winston have shown that some barriers to entry apparently still exist, for departures from the optimal service-fare configurations in each market depend importantly upon the number of carriers on each route.[6] Thus, it is possible that a liberal merger policy combined with restrictive entry practices at certain airports may be keeping deregulation from achieving its full promise.

Financial Markets

Deregulation of financial markets has not proceeded as rapidly as deregulation of transportation. Insurance companies continue to

[5]Steven Morrison and Clifford Winston, *The Economic Effects of Airline Deregulation* (Washington: Brookings Institution, 1986). p. 51.

[6]Morrison and Winston, pp. 64–66.

be regulated by state authorities and exempt from the federal anti-trust laws as a result of the McCarran-Ferguson Act. Banks continue to be regulated by three separate authorities—the Federal Reserve Board, the comptroller of the currency, and the Federal Deposit Insurance Corporation—despite administration proposals for restructuring this regulatory maze. Thrift institutions, or savings-and-loans (S&Ls), are regulated by the Federal Home Loan Bank Board.

In the late 1970s, rising interest rates created strong pressures for disintermediation. During this period, brokerage concerns began to offer new types of investment vehicles, including money-market funds. At the same time, banks in some jurisdictions began to offer NOW (negotiable order of withdrawal) accounts, allowing depositors to earn interest on accounts that were essentially demand deposits. As interest rates rose, the pressure on banks and thrift institutions from money-market funds increased substantially. Congress was forced to act in 1980 and then again in 1982, first to raise the ceilings on regulated interest rates and eventually to permit full-fledged competition for deposits among money-market funds, banks, and thrift institutions on the basis of unregulated interest rates.[7]

Despite the deregulation of banks and thrift institutions on the liability side of their balance sheets, the regulation of the asset side remained in place. S&Ls were permitted to expand their activities somewhat, but this authority has been limited by the Federal Home Loan Bank Board. National banks and bank holding companies continue to be barred by law from a variety of financial markets such as real estate, insurance, and securities brokerage. The separation of investment banking from commercial banking continues to be prohibited by the Glass-Steagall Act of 1933.

These various prohibitions on banks' activities and state regulation of banking have encouraged the development of "nonbank banks" that offer a variety of services, including commercial lending, or accept deposits, but not both. On several occasions, the Reagan administration has tried to accelerate the pace of the deregulation of financial markets, proposing a relaxation of the restric-

[7]For a discussion of recent regulatory and legislative events in this sector, see Robert Litan, *What Should Banks Do?* (Washington: Brookings Institution, 1987), chapter 2.

tions on commercial banks, but it has not succeeded. Most recently, in 1987, the administration conceded defeat on liberalization of restrictions on banks and nonbank banks to gain an increase in funding for the Federal Deposit Insurance Corporation.

Communications

The most controversial new economic regulatory policies during the Reagan era have been in the telecommunications sector. Since 1934, the Federal Communications Commission has been responsible for the regulation of interstate telephone services and broadcasting. In the past 10 years, however, these markets have changed dramatically, in part because of deregulation.

Telephones. For more than 40 years, the supply of telephone services had been assumed to be a "natural monopoly" by most policymakers. In the 1960s, prodded by the courts, the FCC began to admit some competition into the telephone industry, which had been controlled by AT&T and a handful of independents since competition had been ended by congressional and regulatory actions in the early part of the century. This selective-entry policy backfired on the FCC when, unable to justify continued restrictions on entry elsewhere, it suddenly found itself responding to simultaneous demands for entry and for protection of the new entrants from AT&T's potential market responses.

At the outset of the Reagan administration, these conflicting pressures had already resulted in a change of venue—from the regulatory arena to the antitrust courts. In late 1974, the Ford administration had brought a case—based on Section 2 of the Sherman Antitrust Act—against AT&T, which the Carter administration prosecuted through early 1981. During this period, the FCC continued to struggle with the problem of regulating AT&T while allowing AT&T's rivals to chip away at the equipment and long-distance markets without the hindrance of formal regulation of rates or prices.

In 1982, the Reagan Antitrust Division reached an agreement with AT&T to settle the antitrust charges with a modification of an earlier consent decree that would allow AT&T to enter noncommunications markets but would require AT&T to divest itself of its local operating companies. The decree also required that the divested operating companies not participate in interstate long-distance service, equipment manufacture, or downstream "information services." The purpose of the settlement was to divorce the local "bottleneck" facilities from all other communications markets so as to prevent the franchised local monopolies from using these bottlenecks to snuff out competition in adjacent markets.

The AT&T decree can hardly be considered to be the result of deliberate policy choices in the Reagan administration. With the attorney general recused because of earlier conflicts, the assistant attorney general, William Baxter, was able to overcome the strong opposition of both the defense and commerce departments to continuing the case, much less settling it in such dramatic fashion. Later, the administration gave its support to a bill submitted by Sen. Robert J. Dole (R–Kans.) that would relieve the courts from the regulation of AT&T under the open-ended 1982 decree and return all authority to the FCC. Failing in this proposal, the Reagan Department of Justice delivered the first of the required triennial reports on the status of competition in the telephone industry to the court administering the decree. This report advocated a lessening of the restrictions on the divested operating companies.[8] The court recently ruled on the extension of these restrictions, refusing to allow such a dramatic change in the terms of the 1982 decree less than four years after the effective date (1984) of divestiture.

Meanwhile, the Reagan FCC is trying to find a mechanism for continuing to regulate interstate communications without drawing such rigid boundaries around the various markets. By requiring equal access or "comparably efficient interconnection" of all suppliers of services requiring local telephone company connections to their customers, the commission hopes to address one concern: the denial of access. But since the FCC cannot hope to regulate the rates for all services without risking the cartelization of competitive suppliers, it also needs some regulatory control mechanism other than rate-of-return regulation, which potentially allows for cross-subsidization from regulated to unregulated services.

In 1987, the FCC proposed to substitute a system of rate ceilings for rate-of-return regulation, but the prospects for such a proposal are uncertain at best. Unless Congress totally deregulates all inter-

<hr />

[8]Department of Justice, *The Geodesic Network: 1987 Report on Competition in the Telephone Industry* (Washington: January 1987).

state communications, however, the FCC will have to struggle with the difficult task of continuing to police the regulated-unregulated market boundary or trying to arbitrate disputes among sellers of different sizes and relative efficiency.

Perhaps the most important accomplishment of the Reagan FCC has been its decision to press ahead with the repricing of telephone services despite enormous popular (populist) opposition. Under the pre-divestiture regulatory regime, state and federal regulators increasingly transferred the fixed costs of local subscriber lines to the long-distance services so as to keep the local monthly access/usage charges low. This distortion in rates went largely unnoticed as long as long-distance and local services were offered by the same monopolist, AT&T. Now, these services are offered by different companies, and the cost of the local loops is defrayed in large part by an access fee paid by long-distance companies that is far above the avoidable costs of providing access.

The FCC has begun to change the method of pricing access by requiring a monthly "subscriber line charge" to defray more of the fixed costs of the local subscriber loops. This pricing is more efficient because it does not require that the price per minute of long-distance service be elevated to cover the fixed costs of local connections. This repricing also is likely to stunt the growth of "bypass" investments by long-distance companies or their customers seeking to avoid these uneconomic charges. But it has been extremely unpopular since it has raised local telephone charges while allowing long-distance charges to fall in line with costs. A very large share of long-distance charges are paid by businesses; hence, populists see the issue as a "consumerist" issue when, in reality, it is one of economic efficiency.

Broadcasting. The most important recent liberalization of restrictive broadcast regulation came during the Carter administration when the carryover Ford FCC was rebuffed by the courts in its pay-television rulemaking. The Carter FCC decided not to revisit this issue, and unfettered competition between pay cable and off-the-air broadcasting was born. In 1979, the FCC also removed most of the restrictions on cable television's use of broadcast signals. These rules, like the pay-television rules, had been designed to protect broadcasters' monopoly rents.

The Reagan FCC has done very little to increase competition among broadcasters who continue to enjoy monopoly rents from a highly restrictive spectrum-allocation plan devised in the 1950s. It has, however, reduced the procedural burdens on broadcast licensees and reduced the ability of third-party "public interest" groups to derive gains by threatening to harass broadcasters at renewal time.

Recently, the FCC also abandoned the "fairness doctrine" that required broadcasters to air all views on significant issues. Congress has proved unable to force this doctrine upon the FCC through legislation, but the final arbitration of the matter in the courts has not occurred.

Energy

The Reagan administration's singular achievement in deregulating energy markets has been its 1981 decision to accelerate the process of abolishing oil-price regulation already begun in the Carter administration. It has failed to enact deregulation of natural gas despite the overwhelming case for the removal of government controls. The current battle is over the regulation of pipelines by the Federal Energy Regulatory Commission. The wellhead price of natural gas has fallen by more than one-third since 1984. Pipelines are caught with billions of dollars in take-or-pay contracts at higher prices and need continued regulation to prevent users from obtaining gas at lower prices. Unfortunately, FERC has not found a way to break this impasse, and the administration has not offered legislation that would allow the lower prices of gas to be passed through to the final consumers.

Social Regulation

The Reagan record on economic regulation is one of preserving the progress made during the Ford-Carter years. In virtually all of the major regulated sectors, the hand of government is less heavy today than in the mid-1970s. The Reagan administration can claim only a small share of the credit, but it has at least continued a policy of increasing reliance upon market forces.

In the area of social regulation, however, the Reagan administration faced the task of trying to reverse previous policies, not simply to ride the momentum of deregulation. Regulation of environmen-

279

tal quality, occupational health and safety, and product safety had been increasing throughout the 1970s, but the wave had begun to crest by 1980. The business community had complained bitterly about excessive, costly regulation throughout the 1970s, particularly during the Carter administration with its activist agency appointees. One might have expected a pro-business, conservative administration to begin tackling the excesses of these social regulatory programs in 1981.

Environment

Perhaps no single area of regulation should have invited the attention of Reagan's reformers more than environmental policy. Major federal environmental programs began in the late 1960s with standards for automobile emissions and accelerated in the early 1970s with the passage of numerous statutes and the establishment of the Environmental Protection Agency (EPA). Enormous expenditures on pollution controls in the 1970s had not achieved the expected results in terms of environmental improvements. A program of reform might be attractive to both environmentalists and antiregulation forces if it could actually improve environmental quality at a lower cost.

Throughout the 1970s, the costs of pollution controls rose steadily. Real (inflation-adjusted) business spending on pollution controls increased at an annual rate of more than 5 percent between 1972 and 1976 (Tables 20.1 and 20.2). Surprisingly, despite a spate of legislation in 1976–77, the activist Carter years saw business spending on pollution controls rise more slowly—at an annual rate of 3.3 percent. In fact, business spending reached a temporary peak in 1979 at $38.35 billion (in 1982 dollars).

When the Reagan administration assumed office, it was expected to tackle the environmental issues with a vengeance. At the very least, it would slow the pace of new regulations and offer new clean-air legislation for congressional consideration. Unfortunately, a concerted assault on environmental issues never occurred, in part because of distractions created by numerous minor controversies within EPA. The first Reagan EPA leadership team lasted less than three years, resigning virtually en masse in 1983 after a variety of petty scandals enveloped it.

Table 20.1
BUSINESS SPENDING ON POLLUTION CONTROLS, 1972 TO 1985 ($ BILLIONS*)

Year	Air	Water	Total
1972	11.07	12.19	26.77
1973	13.29	13.39	30.62
1974	13.22	12.60	30.05
1975	14.52	12.93	31.50
1976	14.79	14.22	33.23
1977	14.32	15.03	35.18
1978	15.98	15.68	36.63
1979	16.88	15.89	38.35
1980	17.01	15.03	37.89
1981	17.08	14.53	37.54
1982	16.05	14.44	35.61
1983	16.08	15.23	36.53
1984	17.45	16.07	39.44
1985	17.72	16.71	40.77

SOURCE: Kit D. Farber and Gary L. Rutledge, "Pollution Abatement and Control Expenditures," *Survey of Current Business*, July 1986, pp. 94–105; May 1987, pp. 21–25.
*In 1982 dollars.

Table 20.2
AVERAGE ANNUAL GROWTH OF BUSINESS SPENDING ON POLLUTION CONTROLS, 1972 TO 1985 (PERCENT)

Period	Air	Water	Total
1972–76	5.4	7.2	3.9
1976–80	3.3	3.5	1.4
1980–85	1.5	0.8	2.1

SOURCE: Kit D. Farber and Gary L. Rutledge, "Pollution Abatement and Control Expenditures," *Survey of Current Business*, July 1986, pp. 94–105; May 1987, pp. 21–25.

Surprisingly, the Reagan administration never offered new versions of either the Clean Air Act or the Clean Water Act. An intensive study by the Business Roundtable might have been expected to result in definitive suggestions for such reform proposals.[9] Unfortunately, no such consensus ever developed. Nor did the administration succeed in derailing the drive for an ever-larger Superfund pork barrel.

There are six possible explanations for the Reagan administration's inaction on environmental policy. First, it may simply have decided that there were more pressing issues on which to spend its political capital, such as tax incentives for investment, a reduction in direct nondefense government expenditures, and a rebuilding of the military.

Second, the pressure for reforming environmental programs may not have been sufficient to spur the administration to action. As we have seen, real business spending on pollution controls was actually falling in the 1979–82 period, and business people may have thought that the worst was over.

Third, the disproportionate effects of environmental policy across industries and between areas of the country made it difficult to assemble a coalition for reform. Perhaps no issue better demonstrated these differences than the "dirty coal" issue in which legislators from Appalachia and Midwestern coal-mining states pressed for increasingly bizarre new-source policies requiring stack-gas scrubbers simply to promote the mining of sulfur-laden coal and to decrease the demand for low-sulfur coal from the West.

Fourth, the environmental lobby was a potent force to be reckoned with, appealing more to emotion than to results. Any suggestion of reform would be met with grass-roots campaigns charging that Republicans were conspiring with evil business forces to endanger the health of current and future generations.

Fifth, most sensible suggestions for reform involved either a sacrifice of the fine tuning of environmental control required in the ambitious 1970–77 acts or a substitution of economic incentives for mandated controls. There was little support for either.

Finally, environmental activists discovered that by transforming environmental policy into a pork barrel they could be as successful as defense contractors and army generals at keeping wasteful government activity alive. Nowhere was this more apparent than in

9The Business Roundtable, *Air Quality Project*, 1980 (New York: National Economic Research Associates, Inc.).

the lavish funding of municipal sewage-treatment facilities. The pork barrel would later appear in dramatic form when the excessive concern over hazardous waste became the latest environmental scare.

To change environmental policy in a fundamental sense, it is necessary not only to have a decision rule for selecting the pollutants to regulate, but to find a mechanism for rationing these discharges. The historical answer to these two problems is (1) to regulate each pollutant for which there is new evidence on potential environmental damage with little regard for its relative risk to humans or the environment, and (2) to establish a set of detailed standards that vary across industries or individual sources.

The choice of priorities is a problem that continues to bedevil politicians and regulators responding to various new sources of emotional concerns. Smog gives way to acid rain as a priority; acid rain gives way to hazardous waste. In each case, regulation ensues to the maximum degree that is politically feasible, rather than what is economically or ecologically rational. The Reagan administration seems to have dealt relatively well with the recent surge in concern over acid rain, buying time until we understand much more about how to deal with it and how big a problem it may be.

The standard-setting process has been perhaps the most important target of opportunity for the Reagan EPA team. As long as EPA and the states try to set thousands of different discharge standards, politics will hopelessly distort, and enforcement complexity will defeat, the control effort. In 1976, EPA began to move away from detailed point-source standards by allowing "offsets," or trades of pollution reductions, by firms building new sources that emitted air pollutants in areas that failed to meet national air-quality standards. This program has been extended into a rather confusing set of tradable instruments now known as bubbles, offsets, and banks.[10]

The progress toward trading air-pollution rights was slowed by the tumult within EPA in 1981–83, but it now appears to be substantial. Unfortunately, legislation is undoubtedly required to eliminate some of the worst mandated new-source standards. Nor has

[10]For an analysis of this program, see Thomas Tietenberg, *Emissions Trading: An Exercise in Reforming Pollution Policy* (Washington: Resources for the Future, 1985).

this approach to pollution control spread to other media, such as water.

Perhaps the most disconcerting aspect of environmental policy in the past six years has been the steady shift from pollution control to political pork barrel. Throughout the early Reagan years, the Office of Management and Budget (OMB) had considerable success in cutting EPA's operational budget, but not its wasteful multi-billion-dollars-per-year sewage-treatment grant program. More recently, political debate on hazardous wastes has raged not so much over the degree or technique of control or cleanup as over the size of the fund to be amassed to pay for digging up thousands of old sites. The 1986 Superfund legislation created a new, broad-based business-tax program of $1.8 billion per year that is more a pork barrel than a serious environmental program. Without convincing evidence that hazardous waste constitutes a serious threat to public health and, perhaps more importantly, that disturbing these hazardous-waste sites reduces any purported threat, we are now distributing this $1.8 billion around the country much as we distribute highway projects and wastewater treatment funds. That the Reagan administration could not slow this assault on the taxpayer is evidence of its impotence in the environmental arena.

Occupational Safety and Health

While not as controversial as the EPA machinations in 1981–83, the first Reagan appointee to head the Occupational Health and Safety Administration, Thorne Auchter, created his own waves by changing OSHA's enforcement philosophy. Records checks were substituted for on-site inspections in many cases, and penalties were reduced for certain violations. In retrospect, much of the controversy was unjustified, given the magnitude of the potential effects of OSHA on safety anyway. Viscusi has suggested that the shift of OSHA inspections to riskier employment sites was justified but implemented rather poorly.[11] He has suggested more rigorous enforcement in firms that are clearly above their industry's average injury rate.

The most recent evidence suggests that OSHA continues to have very minor effects on occupational safety because of the intimate

[11]W. Kip Viscusi, "The Structure and Enforcement of Job Safety Regulation," *Law and Contemporary Problems* 49 (Autumn 1986):127–50.

relationship between worker perception of risk and actual workplace conditions.[12] Workers cannot be easily protected from risks that they are willing to bear. Nor do they need federal government instructions to negotiate with employers over safety in the workplace. In fact, the movements in both the lost-workday and worker-fatality rates have been predictably cyclical and related to the experience of the labor force.

It was most unlikely that the Reagan administration could have sought to reduce or even eliminate federal occupational-safety standards. If there was a case for reform at OSHA, it would have been to place more emphasis on health standards and less on safety standards on the grounds that workers often cannot adequately know the former risks but are clearly knowledgeable about the latter.[13] This is not the policy of the Reagan OSHA, which has placed more emphasis on safety standards.

Highway Safety

There has been little substantive change in the regulation of highway safety by the National Highway Traffic Safety Administration. An early decision by Reagan's first NHTSA administrator, Raymond Peck, to rescind the passive restraint standard was reversed by the court of appeals. Subsequently, NHTSA reimposed the standard by requiring that passive restraints be phased in over a period of years if the coverage of state seat-belt laws did not exceed two-thirds of the national population. In addition, the bumper standard (not a safety standard per se) was weakened. Otherwise, there has been little change in highway-safety regulation during the past seven years.

Toting up the Costs

The three major health, safety, and environment programs reviewed above continue to impose substantial costs on the U.S.

[12]Anne Bartel and Lacy Thomas, "Direct and Indirect Effects of Regulation: A New Look at OSHA's Impact," *The Journal of Law and Economics* 28, no. 1 (April 1985):1–26; W. Kip Viscusi, "The Impact of Occupational Safety and Health Regulation, 1973–1983," *Rand Journal of Economics* 17, no. 4 (Winter 1986):567–80.

[13]In a recent article, Morrall has shown that regulators of health and safety are likely to place a higher implicit value on lives protected from health risks, such as carcinogens, than lives protected from physical safety risks, such as occupational accidents or airplane accidents. See John F. Morrall III, "A Review of the Record," *Regulation* (November/December 1986), pp. 25–34.

economy. Surprisingly, the available data suggest that, despite the public image of some of the administrators of EPA, OSHA, and NHTSA, the Reagan administration has allowed social regulatory costs to rise more rapidly than the Carter administration permitted with its pro-regulation appointees (see Table 20.3). Between 1976 and 1980, the real total costs for these programs rose by 5.3 percent, but between 1980 and 1985, they rose 9.9 percent. Perhaps President Reagan would have been better advised to keep the Carter appointees inside his tent!

Table 20.3

ENVIRONMENTAL AND SAFETY EXPENDITURES FOR THREE MAJOR PROGRAMS, 1972 TO 1985 ($ BILLIONS*)

Year	Environment	Occupational Safety and Health	Highway Safety	Total
1972	26.8	6.4	3.8	37.0
1973	30.6	6.5	6.7	43.8
1974	30.0	7.8	7.2	45.0
1975	31.5	5.8	5.7	43.0
1976	33.2	5.0	6.8	45.0
1977	35.2	5.8	7.1	48.1
1978	36.6	8.5	6.7	51.8
1979	38.4	5.4	6.1	49.9
1980	37.9	4.8	4.7	47.4
1981	37.5	5.6	4.4	47.5
1982	35.6	4.6	3.4	43.6
1983	36.5	5.0	4.1	45.6
1984	39.4	6.3	4.4	50.1
1985	40.8	6.9	4.4	52.1

SOURCES: For environment, Kit D. Farber and Gary L. Rutledge, "Pollution Abatement and Control Expenditures," *Survey of Current Business*, July 1986, pp. 94–105; May 1987, pp. 21–25; for occupational safety and health, Data Resources, Inc., "Real Capital Expenditures on Occupational Safety and Health"—figures given include only capital expenditures; and for highway safety, Robert W. Crandall et al., *Regulating the Automobile* (Washington: Brookings Institution, 1986), pp. 36–38—figures given represent total costs of safety and regulation, including fuel penalties, deflated by the consumer price index.
*In 1982 dollars.

Regulatory Review

Among the major disappointments of the Reagan regulatory program is the regulatory review process, which was launched with enormous fanfare in January 1981. Executive Order 12291, requiring OMB clearance of all major new rulemakings, was issued immediately and given great prominence by James C. Miller III, the new director of information and regulatory affairs at OMB. One of his first objects of scorn was the nine-digit zip code, which OMB assayed with zeal but with little practical effect. Today, we have the nine-digit code. This was an omen of things to come.

The regulatory review process had been launched by the Ford administration in the Council of Wage and Price Stability as a public process. COWPS would file openly in regulatory proceedings, but would not generally attempt to influence politically responsive agency administrators nor meet with affected parties. This activity continued during the Carter years in much the same fashion. The OMB process, begun in 1981, represented the first use of political appointees in the Executive Office of the President attempting to delay, block, or alter proposed rules. As a result, the new process was much more controversial from the beginning.

There is little doubt that the new process under Executive Order 12291 initially caused a reduction in the rate of new rules and had an influence upon some of the pending rulemakings. In 1983, the Reagan administration issued a report on the accomplishments of its regulatory review process. It claimed savings in one-time investment costs of $11 billion and annual savings of $10.255 billion.[14] Unfortunately, most of the components of these purported savings appear to have been overstated. Some decisions, such as DOT's automobile passive-restraint standard, were eventually overturned in court. Others, such as supposedly OMB-stimulated changes in EPA's emissions-trading program were simply wild guesses of changes that may have had little to do with regulatory review. It is unlikely that the entire emissions-trading program, begun in 1976, has had the effects suggested by OMB for just those changes made in 1981–83.

In the past two years, OMB's review process has been stalled by

[14]Presidential Task Force on Regulatory Relief, *Reagan Administration Regulatory Achievements,* August 11, 1983.

intense congressional opposition, particularly from Rep. Jack Brooks (D–Tex.) and Rep. John Dingell (D–Mich.). With the Democrats controlling both houses, there is a strong possibility of legislative termination of the entire program by eliminating it from the OMB budget. In 1986, congressional reauthorization of the Office of Information and Regulatory Affairs, the OMB office that conducts the review program, required that OIRA focus its attention upon paperwork-reduction activities. However, the appropriations act for OMB contains no such instructions. At this point, it is clear that OMB is on notice from Congress not to continue its intervention in regulatory proceedings.

Too much has been made of the entire regulatory review process. Some central control of agency administrators by the White House may be necessary and useful, but such control is inevitably limited. Regulatory statutes require detailed decisions over numerous complex matters that no regulatory review process can cope with adequately. "Major" rules can be subdivided endlessly. If various constituent groups are given access to the regulatory reviewers as well as the agency process, there is little reason to believe that there will be a fundamental change in the results.

The administrators of EPA, OSHA, and NHTSA are appointed by the president, as are the director and associate directors of OMB. If anything, the debate over the "openness" of the review process at OMB is a sham. Agency administrators routinely use the delay required by the Administrative Procedures Act to sound out the political repercussions of each decision. It would be ludicrous to suppose, for example, that Raymond Peck and Joan Claybrook— NHTSA directors in the Reagan and Carter administrations, respectively—reached different decisions on passive restraints on automobiles through simply reading the written record and consulting with various technicians at NHTSA.

The Reagan regulatory review officials point proudly to a reduction in new rules and in pages of the *Federal Register* as dispositive evidence of its success.[15] Since the cost of paper is a small part of the total cost of regulation, these successes can be considered only Pyrrhic victories. As we have seen, the real cost of the most expen-

[15]Office of Management and Budget, *Regulatory Program of the United States, April 1, 1986–March 31, 1987* (Washington: Government Printing Office, 1987).

sive regulatory problems has risen more rapidly under Reagan than under Carter. This may or may not be good for the country—it depends upon the benefits achieved by these costly regulatory programs. But the result is surely not what Reagan intended.

At this juncture, the promise of regulatory review as a means of restraining overzealous regulators has faded. It would be difficult to imagine that President Michael Dukakis would place a young Jim Miller or Murray Weidenbaum in OMB to restrain the various Naderite appointments he makes to the regulatory agencies. Nor is it likely that President George Bush would have to use OMB to restrain his appointees to these agencies. The review process is useful as an educational one that can bring out the follies in some regulatory policies. It can signal where legislative reform is needed, but it cannot make sense of poorly designed programs enacted by popularly elected legislators.

21. Educational Schizophrenia

David Boaz

The 1983 report of the National Commission on Excellence in Education, *A Nation at Risk*, had a stunning impact on public debate. Its declaration that "a rising tide of mediocrity" threatened America's public schools was the subject of repeated presidential speeches, cover stories in *Time* and *Newsweek*, and wailing and gnashing of teeth by all the Democratic presidential candidates.

It's hardly surprising that education was the subject of so much attention. Nothing is more important to the future of any country than the quality of education. Education—which, of course, is far broader than mere schooling—is the process by which young people learn the skills they will need to make a living, the knowledge they will need to make intelligent decisions as citizens, and the values they will live by.

But there is something strange about the reception given to the commission's report. Washington reacted as if some devastating new information had come to light. But had there really been a lack of information about the woeful state of public education in the United States?

Nationally, SAT scores had been falling for 20 years, from an average of 978 in 1963 to 890 in 1980. The National Institute of Education reported in 1978 that in a given month some 2.4 million secondary school students were robbed and 282,000 were attacked.[1] The National Assessment of Educational Progress reported in 1980 that the achievement of American 17-year-olds in science, writing, social studies, and mathematics had dropped regularly during the 1970s.[2]

Washington got a dramatic illustration of the state of American education in 1976, when the valedictorian of the District of Colum-

---

[1]Quoted in Ed Clark, *A New Beginning* (Ottawa, Ill.: Caroline House, 1980), p. 60.
[2]Quoted in "Help! Teacher Can't Teach," *Time*, June 16, 1980, p. 54.

bia's Western High School was refused admission to George Washington University because he had a combined score of only 600 on the SAT. One could hardly disagree with Joseph Ruth, the university's admissions dean, who said, "My feeling is that a kid like this has been conned. . . . He's been deluded into thinking he's gotten an education."[3]

The horror stories, of course, continue today. Most recently, the National Endowment for the Humanities has reported that more than two-thirds of America's 17-year-olds are unable to locate the Civil War in the correct half-century and that two-thirds of them cannot identify the Reformation or Magna Carta.[4]

While this widely documented decline in the quality of U.S. education has occurred, spending on education has risen dramatically. Total U.S. spending on education has risen from $24.7 billion in 1959–60 to $165.6 billion in 1979–80 to an estimated $308 billion in 1987–88. In real terms, spending has risen 218 percent in 28 years and 20 percent in just 8 years. The federal share has risen even more sharply, up from $1.8 billion in 1960 to $15.1 billion in 1984. These figures, it should be noted, do not reflect increasing enrollments. Elementary and secondary school enrollments peaked in 1972, while per-pupil expenditures (in constant 1987 dollars) have soared from $2,392 in 1970–71 to $4,538 in 1987–88. As SAT scores declined steadily, per-pupil expenditures rose by 139 percent from 1960 to 1981.

Increasingly, our education spending has gone to pay for activities other than classroom teaching. The average teaching salary fell about 12 percent in real terms between 1973 and 1983, although it has risen since then.[5] The percentage of education dollars spent on teachers' salaries fell steadily during the 1970s, from 49.2 percent in 1970–71 to 38.7 percent in 1980–81.[6] One reason for this is clear:

[3]Quoted in Paul Copperman, *The Literacy Hoax* (New York: William Morrow, 1978), p. 105.

[4]Lynne V. Cheney, "American Memory: A Report on the Humanities in the Public Schools" (Washington: National Endowment for the Humanities, 1987), p. 6.

[5]Lawrence Feinberg, "Teacher Share of School Dollar Drops," *Washington Post*, August 24, 1983, p. A1.

[6]National Center for Education Statistics, quoted in E. G. West, "Are American Schools Working?: Disturbing Cost and Quality Trends," Cato Institute Policy Analysis no. 26, August 9, 1983.

between 1960 and 1984, the number of teachers grew by 57 percent, the number of principals and supervisors grew by 79 percent, and the number of other staffers grew by 500 percent.[7]

The Reagan Administration's Goals

In response to all of this, the Reagan administration came into office with some fairly clear goals. The 1980 Reagan campaign's official statement on education called for abolishing the Department of Education, reducing federal regulatory control of local school districts, transferring federal funding programs back to the states, and giving parents more choice in where to educate their children through education tax credits or vouchers. Although it wasn't in the official statement, it was generally known that Ronald Reagan was also an enthusiastic supporter of "returning traditional values to the classroom," the most specific example of which was a constitutional amendment to permit prayers in public school classrooms.

As Lawrence A. Uzzell and Chester E. Finn, Jr., have noted, there is a certain schizophrenia in these positions.[8] Some of President Reagan's original goals—abolition of the Department of Education, deregulation, and parent-choice measures—tend toward decentralization and a reduction in federal control of education. His support for a federal school prayer amendment (and later for measures that move us toward a national curriculum), however, reflects a willingness to use federal legislation to bring about certain kinds of educational results.

What have been the results of administration policy in the area of education? Shortly after he left the administration, former secretary Terrel H. Bell wrote:

> When President Reagan appointed me to his Cabinet as Secretary of Education, a great many people were surprised, and right-wing conservatives were downright angry. To this day, I'm not sure why I was selected by the President, especially in view of the fact

[7]Cheney, p. 25.

[8]See Lawrence A. Uzzell, "Contradictions of Centralized Education," Cato Institute Policy Analysis no. 53, May 30, 1985, p. 11, and Chester E. Finn, Jr., "Our Schizophrenic Educational System," *Wall Street Journal*, October 23, 1984.

that I had once testified favorably on the bill that created the Department of Education.[9]

Such indifference to whether key staffers were committed to the administration's policies has been a hallmark of Ronald Reagan's career. He once appointed as lieutenant governor of California a man he had met only once, at a reception, and who, like Bell, professed to be mystified as to why he had been chosen. Similar examples have occurred throughout his two terms as president.

The goal of abolishing the Department of Education didn't last long. It is not much of an overstatement to say that it was never heard again after January 20, 1981. Bell did submit to Congress a proposal to replace the department with a Foundation for Education Assistance modeled on the National Science Foundation. This would have kept virtually all federal educational programs intact and in one place, and it would still have given the federal education chief direct access to the president. Bell says that this idea was first suggested by Edwin Meese III. But this proposal was of little interest to the critics of the department, so it never received any great support. Senate Republican leader Howard Baker and Senate Labor and Human Resources Committee chairman Orrin G. Hatch had no interest in taking on the department, and the proposal was ignored by Congress. The abolition idea died more formally in 1985, during the confirmation hearings on Secretary William J. Bennett, when the White House sent a letter assuring Sen. Lowell Weicker that it would not propose to abolish the department.

Indeed, although the administration did submit smaller budget requests for the department, the education budget has grown from $14.8 billion in 1981 to $19.6 billion in 1987. Secretary Bennett has recently urged Republican candidates not to "look at education through the green eye-shades of the accountant,"[10] and in 1988 the administration for the first time requested a significant budget increase for education.

Somewhat more progress was made on deregulation and decentralization of federal funding. The administration proposed to com-

[9]Terrel H. Bell, "Education Policy Development in the Reagan Administration," *Phi Delta Kappan*, March 1986, p. 487.

[10]William J. Bennett, "Education Reform and the 1988 Election," address to the National Press Club, Washington, September 8, 1987.

bine many categorical grant programs into block grants for education. The idea was that this would lessen federal control of education and give state and local authorities more freedom to spend their federal dollars as they thought best. Like revenue sharing, of course, such a program raises the question of why a bankrupt federal government should be handing out checks to other governments. At least with the categorical grants, the argument was that the federal government wanted certain programs undertaken, so it provided funds for them. One might also argue that a basic principle of democratic government is that any government that spends money ought to have to assess taxes to raise that money. These basic considerations aside, however, the block grant program probably did reduce federal control to some degree. Unfortunately, the administration was unable to get folded into the block grant either the largest categorical grants—aid to disadvantaged children, aid to the handicapped, and vocational education—or two programs that had raised the most objections among Reagan supporters—bilingual education and the Women's Educational Equity Act Program. As it happened, only about 5 percent of the Department of Education budget ended up in the block grant.

Little progress on deregulation has been made since 1981. Aside from those combined in the block grant, no federal education programs have been abolished during the Reagan years. And new education and training programs, costing very little money at present, have been included in many different laws passed by Congress, just waiting for an infusion of funds under a new education secretary.

Whatever Happened to Choice?

Many of the severest critics of our educational system believe that only one policy change is necessary to achieve dramatic improvements: giving parents the freedom to choose the schools their children will attend. Education vouchers or tax credits would instantly transform the schools from monopoly to competition, with all the beneficial results that normally flow from competition. Parental choice is a program that could have united the Reagan constituency. It is important to the religious right, but it has great appeal to more libertarian young voters as well. And played properly, it should have placed the administration on the side of inner-city minorities, who get the worst education in America, against the reactionary education establishment. Unfortunately, none of this has happened.

One major problem is that tax credits have come to be seen as part of the "social agenda," along with school prayer and anti-abortion measures, and the administration has done little to dispel this notion. Tax credits need some prominent secular humanist spokespeople to get across the point that there is nothing uniquely religious or conservative about wanting your children—and other people's children—to get the best possible education.

Education tax credits passed the House of Representatives during the Carter administration. However, under Reagan administration leadership, in a more Republican House, they failed in 1982. Secretary Bennett proposed a partial choice plan in 1985, the TEACH proposal, which would have turned Chapter I education funding for low-income students into a voucher. Once again, however, the administration didn't get very far with it. Perhaps if it had been introduced with press conferences in the inner city, if there had been more discussion with the Congressional Black Caucus and with black church groups, if it had simply been given more priority by administration planners, TEACH would have been a success. It certainly should have been; no one can argue that educationally disadvantaged students have done well under the present system. Surely a change that would give their families more power would have been appealing to everyone except the education establishment and reactionary defenders of statism across the board.

Today, parental choice is regularly mentioned in Secretary Bennett's speeches, but it has ceased to be a matter for emphasis. A dramatic illustration of the administration's declining interest in educational choice—and perhaps of our national tendency to embrace fads and drop them with blinding speed—can be found in the annual records of President Reagan's speeches. According to the indexes to the Public Papers of the Presidents of the United States, President Reagan referred to tuition tax credits 21 times during 1983, 12 times during 1984, 3 times during 1985, and once during 1986.

The National Minister of Education

Today we have a very vigorous and visible education secretary, perhaps the most popular member of the cabinet among conser-

296

vatives—and probably the most controversial outside the Reagan constituency. He has made the secretary's job a bully pulpit from which to expound his views on education policy, not to mention his views on sex, drugs, AIDS, and other topics. If not parental choice, what is his main concern?

In his first major speech as secretary of education, Bennett said his agenda would be the "three C's—Content, Character, and Choice."[11] Since then, his choice has been to concentrate on content and character. He has stressed the need for schools to improve students' understanding of history, science, and the humanities. His concern that students are not learning enough of such basic subjects has been echoed recently in the National Endowment for the Humanities *report* and in books by E. D. Hirsch, Jr., and by Chester E. Finn, Jr., and Diane Ravitch.[12]

In addition to content, Bennett has stressed the role of the schools in developing character, by which he means helping students "develop a reliable standard of right and wrong."[13] He goes on in later speeches to define character as "specific traits such as thoughtfulness, fidelity, kindness, diligence, honesty, fairness, self-discipline, respect for law, and taking one's guidance by accepted and tested standards of right and wrong, rather than by, for example, one's personal preferences."[14] These traits are hard to disagree with, although one might wish for some mention of self-reliance and independent thought. Bennett objects specifically to the term "values" because, he says, "the term seems to suggest that judgments of what is right and wrong, noble and base, just and unjust, are mere personal preferences, that things are worthwhile if and insofar as individuals happen to 'value' them."[15] But if not because they are of value to individuals, by what standard do we judge things to be worthwhile?

[11]William J. Bennett, address to the National Press Club, Washington, March 27, 1985.

[12]E. D. Hirsch, Jr., *Cultural Literacy* (Boston: Houghton Mifflin, 1987), and Chester E. Finn, Jr., and Diane Ravitch, *What Do Our 17-Year-Olds Know?* (New York: Harper & Row, 1987).

[13]Bennett, March 27, 1985.

[14]William J. Bennett, address to the 29th annual convention of the California Association of Teachers of English, San Diego, February 13, 1987.

[15]Ibid.

As one "auxiliary to character," Bennett recommends that "voluntary prayer in school [not] be prohibited."[16] But the prayer the Reagan administration has in mind is voluntary only for the school district, the principal, or the teacher, not for the student. Voluntary prayer by individual students—which would presumably be silent—is not prohibited by the Supreme Court; how could it be? Personal, silent prayer, rather than public, government-sponsored prayer, would seem to be appropriate in the public institutions of a democracy; it is also the kind that has been recommended by such experts as Jesus.

Both content and character are reflected in Bennett's emphasis on teaching students to "study, nurture and, yes, defend Western civilization."[17] By studying Western history, literature, and philosophy, students will know their own society's history and will know, if not the difference between right and wrong, at least what our society's greatest thinkers have had to say on the subject.

Although I have expressed some reservations about Bennett's specific ideas on content and character, in the main they are unobjectionable. Of course we want our children to come out of school knowing when the Civil War occurred, what the Declaration of Independence means, what the Milky Way is, and how to write a decent paragraph. Bennett cites a 1984 Gallup poll that, he says, "found that Americans in overwhelming numbers want schools to do two things: to teach students how to read, speak, and write correctly, and to help them develop a reliable standard of right and wrong."[18]

But to say that we want the schools to do something is not necessarily to say that we want the federal government to bring it about. Those who opposed the creation of the Department of Education worried that it would further centralize American education. Rep. John Erlenborn said that if such a department was created,

> There would be interference in textbook choices, curricula, staffing, salaries, the make-up of student bodies, building designs, and all other irritants that the government has invented to harass

[16]Bennett, March 27, 1985.

[17]William J. Bennett, "Why Western Civilization?" address at Smith College, Northampton, Massachusetts, April 16, 1987.

[18]Bennett, March 27, 1985.

the population. These decisions which are now made in the local school or local district will slowly but surely be transferred to Washington.[19]

In his dissenting views on the committee report that recommended establishing the department, in which he was joined by seven other Republican congressmen, both moderate and conservative, Erlenborn wrote, "The Department of Education will end up being the Nation's super schoolboard. That is something we can all do without."[20]

Such concerns were not limited to conservatives. David W. Breneman and Noel Epstein wrote in the *Washington Post*, "Establishing a cabinet-level department is a back-door way of *creating* a national education policy."[21] And Richard W. Lyman, president of Stanford University, testified before Congress that "the two hundred year old absence of a Department of Education is not the result of simple failure during all that time. On the contrary, it derives from the conviction that we do not want the kinds of educational systems that such arrangements produce."[22]

In short, there was a concern, particularly among conservatives, that a secretary of education would turn into a national minister of education. It seems arguable that Secretary Bennett is becoming just that. We don't yet have a centralized educational system on the model of such countries as France. Congress's reservations about federal control of education were strong enough that the bill creating the Department of Education prohibits the department from interfering in school curriculums, and Bennett has not sought to do so directly. But he is using his position vigorously to propound his ideas on what a curriculum ought to be.

Bennett wants to expand the National Assessment of Educational Progress to include state-by-state comparisons of educational achievement. This is an understandable goal, but it seems inconsistent with the goal of decentralization.

[19]John Erlenborn, "Education Department," *Human Events*, July 22, 1978, p. 19.

[20]Reprinted in *Congressional Digest*, November 1978, p. 275.

[21]Quoted in "New Education Department: 'Big Brother' for Your Kids," *Human Events*, August 19, 1978, p. 4.

[22]Quoted in "Cabinet Department of Education Proposal Stirs Congress," Heritage Foundation Education Debate, April 1979, p. 3.

There are two major approaches to educational reform, which have been designated "neocentralist" and "neopluralist." As Lawrence Uzzell has written, "The nation's most famous education reformer, Ronald Reagan, has a foot in both camps."[23] Bennett no doubt reflects the president's preferences in education policy, and the contradictions in the administration's early goals are still apparent. Bennett's push for content, character, and school prayer, as well as his enthusiastic support for centralized state education reform packages, must be seen as part of the centralist agenda. Yet he continues to back the most important part of the pluralist agenda—parent-choice measures. (He has, as noted, given up another important element of the pluralist agenda, abolition of the Department of Education.)

The current enthusiasm for education reform is merely the latest of what Richard Mitchell calls Great Lurches Forward. Every time outsiders—such as parents or legislators—discover a problem with the schools, the education establishment responds, Oh, so *that's* what you want us to do; well, we can do that, but it's gonna cost you.

The schools were called on to be part of the national defense in the 1950s; in fact, the first major piece of federal legislation in the education area was the National Defense Education Act of 1958. In the 1960s, the schools were summoned to enlist in the civil rights movement and the war on poverty. In the 1970s, nonsexist education was all the rage. Now, in the 1980s, we have discovered that somehow education got lost in the shuffle, and we demand a return to minimum standards of competence, as well as the teaching of society's values. (A side issue in the 1980s is computer literacy and technological education, intended to improve our international competitiveness. This fits well with the other demands because it, too, costs a lot of money.)

Toward Quality Education

What, then, should be our assessment of the Reagan administration's education policy as we prepare for a new president? Unfortunately, Terrel Bell was probably correct when he wrote, "My four years in the Reagan Cabinet taught me the importance of insuring

[23]Uzzell, p. 10.

that education is represented by a seat at the Cabinet table. In my view, the continued existence of that seat is now assured."[24] Bennett also takes credit for subverting Reagan's original policy goal: "It's much less likely you'll see abolition of the Department of Education in the future, largely because of me," he recently told the Senate Appropriations Subcommittee on Education.[25] Whoever gets the credit—or blame—the Department of Education is here to stay, and after two Reagan terms, parents still have little choice about where to educate their children.

But President Reagan, Secretary Bennett, and the National Commission on Excellence in Education have created a useful national debate on the quality of education. We now recognize that there are serious problems with our public schools, although there is little understanding of the fundamental reasons for those problems. The administration has also kept the issue of parental choice more or less in the public eye. Choice among public schools has been endorsed by the National Governors Association and implemented in several places, notably Harlem, whose schools have moved from dead last to near the middle among New York City's 32 school districts. Education voucher and tax-credit initiatives are under way in several states, and even *Phi Delta Kappan*, the professional educators' journal, recently (June 1987) devoted an issue to articles on choice.

Meaningful educational reform will never emerge from a stagnant monopoly. The last 20 years have demonstrated that more money is not the answer to the schools' problems. Only competition and parent empowerment will make a real difference. In every other sector of the economy, we recognize the benefits of competition in providing better goods and services at a lower price to consumers. It's time we applied those insights to education. People tend to take a static view of the education market: in our city there are public schools, Catholic schools, a fundamentalist school, and an elite private academy. But if all parents could afford to choose the schools they wanted for their children, more options would spring up. Word would get around—through advertising, the news media, and most importantly, through networks of friends and neigh-

[24]Bell, p. 493.

[25]Jill Lawrence, "Hearing Turns into Hot Debate on Secretary Bennett's Record," *Washington Times*, May 11, 1988, p. A4.

bors—that certain schools provided the discipline and the solid education that most parents want. Good schools would attract more customers, and other schools would be forced to improve their product or suffer the consequences. Secretary Bennett wants more accountability in the schools; *this* is how you make schools accountable.

We should encourage states to come through with the public school choice plans that they have promised, but we should insist that choice among bureaucratic institutions is not enough. Bureaucracies don't compete very well; it isn't in their bones. Government-run schools will still be governed by layers of administration and subject to all the political pressures that have squeezed education out of the schools. And unless public schools that cannot attract enough students are allowed to go out of business, with the principals and teachers thrown out of work, they won't have the incentive system that makes competition work. Vouchers or tax credits must be extended so that middle- and low-income parents have the same access to independent schools that wealthy parents do.

Educational choice is an important part of equal opportunity. Those who are condemned to inner-city schools where they are more likely to be knifed than educated are denied the opportunity to get out of the ghetto and into the mainstream of American society. As Phil Keisling has written, they are "consigned to lives of failure because their high school diplomas are the educational equivalent of worthless notes from the Weimar Republic."[26] There is a patronizing attitude among the education establishment and other elite groups toward poor and black parents, an attitude that poor people aren't really qualified to choose their children's schools. A flippant response is that a dart board would give inner-city black children better school choices than the current system does. More seriously, there is simply no evidence that most poor black parents cannot do an adequate job of finding good schools—if they have the wherewithal to do so. And if even 20 percent of the parents in an inner-city neighborhood left the local public schools, the pressure on the public schools to shape up would be severe.

The battle over vouchers and tax credits is a battle for power. Who will have the power to choose the education that students will

[26]Quoted in Lucy P. Patterson, "Department of Education," in *Agenda '83*, ed. Richard N. Holwill (Washington: Heritage Foundation, 1983), p. 115.

receive—parents or the education establishment? Choice plans empower families to control their own destinies.

Choice must not be seen as a tool of Catholics and the religious right. Those families are already sending their children to private schools. Many of their schools would have to improve once they were faced with more competition than from the public schools. But the real beneficiaries of vouchers or tax credits would be those students currently unable to escape government schools. Advocates of educational choice need to seek new allies, among yuppie parents concerned with quality and diversity and among inner-city families well aware of the catastrophic condition of their neighborhood government schools. Only then will we have the schools that a free people deserve.

22. Energy Policies: A Few Bright Spots

Robert L. Bradley, Jr.

Surveying the ruins of President Carter's energy policy, candidate Ronald Reagan called government intervention the problem rather than the solution. Pervasive price and allocation regulation, he said, was the cause of the 1979 energy crisis, as had been the case with oil and gas shortages earlier in the decade. The Department of Energy (DOE), with a budget greater than the combined profits of the industry it regulated, was a textbook bureaucracy. The windfall profits tax dimmed supply incentives vital to the nation's energy security and represented an unfair, unaffordable industry burden. Reagan's criticisms were hailed by the industry as the dawn of a new era; the electorate, victimized by regulation, was also supportive of a new approach to energy policy.

The Republican platform of 1980 rebelled at the resource pessimism and supply-and-demand regulation permeating the Democratic approach to energy.[1] It criticized the Carter administration for 20,000 pages of regulations, a $10 billion bureaucracy, hundreds of legislative and executive initiatives, and the rhetoric of "the moral equivalent of war." Ten specific policies were proposed as an alternative:

1. oil price and allocation decontrol,
2. natural gas wellhead decontrol,
3. repeal of the Crude Oil Windfall Profits Tax (with certain exceptions),
4. elimination of natural gas marketing restrictions,
5. "limited" subsidization of synthetic-fuel demonstration projects,
6. government research to "speed up" renewable energy technology development,

---

[1]"1980 Republican National Convention Platform," *Congressional Record*, 96th Cong., 2d sess., July 31, 1980, pp. 24–27.

7. resumption of filling the Strategic Petroleum Reserve toward its 500-million-barrel short-term and billion-barrel long-term goals,
8. encouragement of the domestic gasohol industry,
9. accelerated petroleum leasing on federal land, and
10. reduced money-supply growth to reduce world oil prices (denominated in U.S. dollars).

Increased energy supply, new energy technologies, more efficient energy use, enlarged energy choices, and "a steady and orderly path toward energy self-sufficiency" were the results envisioned by the Republican party and its standard-bearer, Ronald Reagan. In addition, another energy initiative was promised by Reagan on the campaign trail: abolition of the DOE.

Reagan's Market-Oriented Policies

Some free-market policies received strong support from the Reagan administration. Other market-oriented policies got less Reagan emphasis but were still signed into law.

Oil Price and Allocation Deregulation

Executive Order 12287, issued just eight days after Reagan's inauguration, ended a decade-long experience with pervasive energy regulation, born of President Nixon's wage-and-price control program and continued under the Emergency Petroleum Allocation Act in the Ford and Carter administrations. This order deregulated the price of crude oil and remaining covered products, including gasoline, while ending complementary regulations such as the monthly refinery entitlements transfer.[2] Transition "safeguards," desired by some industry sectors concerned about their fate in the postcontrol era, were resisted, to Reagan's credit. But the free-market initiative was not all Reagan and had some inconsistencies. Decontrol was initially Carter's program, with the 27-month phase-out 8 months shy of completion. Certain industry segments were jawboned by Reagan and his first energy secretary, James Edwards, to act moderately with their newfound freedoms. Another motivation for accelerated decontrol was tax revenue; between $4 and

[2]*Federal Register* 46 (January 30, 1981): 9909. Several important remaining regulations were terminated soon after; see *Federal Register* 46 (February 19, 1981): 12945.

$6 billion in windfall profits tax proceeds were anticipated to aid another Reagan campaign promise—a balanced budget.

The decontrol order issued one week into Reagan's term was a forceful beginning. It was responsible for a decline in DOE's regulation budget from $155 million in 1981 to $52 million a year later (which would subsequently decline to $22 million in FY 1988). But an even stronger repudiation of price and allocation regulation was yet to come.

In the decontrol era, strong support for standby regulation remained among independent refiners, resellers, and marketers, as well as major oil companies, in the event of another embargo or energy emergency. The emergency energy policy bill authorizing standby price and allocation controls, sponsored by Sen. James McClure (R–Idaho), breezed through Congress with bipartisan support, but Reagan vetoed the bill on March 24, 1982, and lobbied forcefully to prevent an override. If accelerated decontrol was somewhat redundant and overly cautious, Reagan's veto of standby regulation was principled action. The president correctly recognized that pricing and allocation flexibility was as essential in emergencies as it was in tranquil times.

Rejection of Higher Oil Tariffs

A second example of Reagan's principled support for the free market was his refusal to increase oil tariffs as a budget-balancing aid in 1985 and as a "national security" measure in 1986. The latter decision was particularly noteworthy given the pressure from the American Petroleum Institute, the Independent Petroleum Association of America, and other leading industry groups for a floor beneath crude prices, even from a major tariff. The Reagan administration and the current secretary of energy, John Herrington, have given lip service to the "national security" concerns of industry but have avoided protectionism because of Reagan's aversion to new taxes and because of staunch opposition outside of the petroleum sector.[3]

[3]See the Department of Energy, *Energy Security* (March 1987) for a blueprint of the current energy picture and policy alternatives from an administration viewpoint. One industry benefit from the 1986 depression was Reagan's decision to retain remaining portions of the depletion allowance and intangible drilling costs in the Tax Reform Act of 1986 (P.L. 99–514, 100 Stat. 2085). In the 1984 "Treasury I" proposal, Secretary Donald Regan targeted these two historic oil-industry deductions for repeal.

On a negative note, while Reagan has rejected major tariff hikes on crude oil and oil products, a number of small fees discriminating against oil imports have been enacted with administration support. These include Customs Service and harbor "user fees" of 0.04 percent and 0.22 percent respectively, an oil-spill fee of $0.013 per barrel, and a $0.117-per-barrel Superfund fee on oil imports. The Superfund import fee, containing a $0.035-per-barrel differential above a domestic oil production Superfund tax and labeled a "backdoor tariff" by the *National Petroleum News*,[4] has caused consternation among our trading partners. These levies, in addition to long-standing nominal tariffs under the Revenue Act of 1932, ranging from $0.0525 per barrel for heavy crude to $0.525 per barrel for gasoline and jet fuel, amount to limited protectionism. In addition, subtle foreign policy gestures toward Persian Gulf powers for price "stability" have worked against open trade petroleum.

Relaxation of Mandatory Conservation

A third area of market-oriented action has been to repeal or liberalize Carter-era "demand management" conservation regulations. One of Reagan's first energy actions was to rescind Carter's thermostat regulations, extended only a month before by the lame-duck president, which set a 65-degree winter temperature maximum and a 78-degree summer minimum for commercial buildings.

Another Reagan administration move toward market decision-making has involved gasoline. Corporate average fuel efficiency standards for automobiles, enacted in the Energy Policy and Conservation Act of 1975, have been relaxed in recent years by the National Highway Traffic Safety Adminstration. Legislation allowing states to increase the maximum speed limit from 55 miles per hour to 65 miles per hour has been enacted, although pork-barrel amendments to the bill forced Reagan to veto the measure despite his support for the speed-limit change. Congress overrode the veto.

Within the DOE, conservation appropriations were sharply reduced in Reagan's first year from over $700 million to $145 million. This 80-percent reduction was followed by a large increase to $429 million

[4]"Reagan Signs Superfund; 'Backdoor' Import Fees," *National Petroleum News*, December 1986, p. 52.

in 1983, however, before subsequent reductions to its 1988 level of $86 million.

Most recently, Reagan signed into law the Fuel Use Act Amendments of 1987, which rescinded remaining restrictions on natural gas and oil use in industrial and power-plant boilers that gave coal an artificial advantage over the other fossil fuels.[5] This will maximize interfuel competition to the advantage of consumers and help the natural gas industry's marketing efforts to reduce surplus deliverability. Another initiative on natural gas conservation, however, did not go Reagan's way. He pocket vetoed a bill setting national standards for appliances in 1986, but the next year, Congress overwhelmingly approved a similar bill, which Reagan, facing an override, reluctantly signed into law.[6]

Natural Gas Import Policy

Natural gas imports served as a lifeline to domestic supply during shortages in the 1970s and came to be resented by Carter-era regulators forced to accept their high prices. Border price ceilings were set by U.S. regulators, and import licenses were denied, particularly for liquefied natural gas. This policy was changed by DOE's Economic Regulatory Administration in early 1984 to sanctify private contracts as long as the resulting terms were "competitive" and in the "national interest."[7] To date, the ERA has consistently followed this open-trade policy by approving Canadian gas-import applications despite protests from a number of independent domestic producer groups. However, export regulation on the Canadian side and a recent ruling by the Federal Energy Regulatory Commission (FERC) blocking the automatic pass-through of fixed costs in the demand charge of U.S. pipelines have worked against ERA policy to discourage open natural gas trade between the two countries.[8]

[5]P.L. 100–42, 101 Stat. 310 (1987). A companion measure repealed incremental pricing, a rate-design policy discriminating against industrial gas users

[6]National Appliance Energy Conservation Act, P.L. 100–12, 101 Stat. 103 (1987).

[7]*Federal Register* 49 (February 22, 1984): 6684. The DOE has also rejected the coal industry's arguments to restrict electricity imports from Canada. See "DOE Secretary: Canadian Power Subsidies Do Not Violate Trade Laws," *Electric Utility Week*, November 3, 1986, p. 9.

[8]Opinion 256, 37 FERL 61535 (December 8, 1986). This ruling, characterized by Canadian exporters as backdoor protectionism, has prompted protest from leading Canadian officials to the Reagan administration.

Reduced Paperwork

The deregulation of oil prices and allocation in early 1981 opened the door for the DOE to reduce paperwork for the industry. By 1982, an estimated two million hours had been saved annually by eliminating federal forms for oil producers, refiners, resellers, and marketers as well as gas distributors and electric utilities.[9] Since 1982, another 330,000 hours have been trimmed to reduce the paperwork burden from a Carter high of over three million hours in 1979 to 670,000 hours in 1986. This reduction would have been greater if a lawsuit had not blocked the proposed termination of the financial reporting system applicable to 26 (now 22) major oil companies, which at one time required over 100,000 man-hours a year to complete.

Partially Market-Oriented Policies

Several Reagan initiatives contained elements of both government planning and the free market. In two cases, the final decision has been market-oriented, but previous decisions promoted government intervention in energy affairs. Another "mixed" policy, without a market outcome, was expanded access to government land by private industry for oil and gas exploration and production.

The Synthetic Fuels Corporation

The Energy Security Act of 1980 established the Synthetic Fuels Corporation (SFC), hailed by Carter as "the cornerstone of U.S. energy policy," to expand the DOE's previous commitments toward private-sector synfuel development with an $88 billion budget. Despite quick staffing and an early solicitation for grants in the final weeks of the Carter administration, the infant program was an easy target for budget cutting if not de facto immobilization. This quickly became an issue within the Reagan administration, but true to a platform commitment of "limited" subsidies for synfuel development, Reagan decided to fill vacancies and make project commitments (including a $1.5 billion loan guarantee to the Great Plains Coal Gasification Project) to give to the SFC.

This decision came to be regretted. As the energy market turned toward a surplus, the administration began to push for reduced

[9] "Paperwork for Industry Cut by Two Million Hours," *Energy Insider*, August 1982, p. 1.

SFC budget allocations, which Congress, witnessing mismanagement and conflicts of interest at the agency, eventually came to support. With continuing problems culminating with the Great Plains default, the SFC was abolished on December 19, 1985, with Congress, no longer viewing synfuels as America's energy salvation but as corporate welfare, leading the way.[10]

Oil and Gas Equipment Exports

In mid-1987, President Reagan by executive order revoked the ban on exports of wellhead and pipeline equipment to the Soviet Union first imposed by President Carter in 1978.[11] This end to an ineffectual sanction was too late to help the devastated U.S. oil-field supply sector. Once the supplier of 25 percent of the Soviet Union's oil-field equipment, U.S. firms had under 1 percent of this premier export market, with Japanese and European firms becoming entrenched in the void.

The high costs of the sanction on the domestic oil industry, estimated at $1.8 billion and 46,000 jobs by the Petroleum Equipment Suppliers Association, is not only Carter's legacy but Reagan's as well. In late 1981, after martial law was declared in Poland, Reagan expanded the equipment and technology ban to cover transmission and refining. Reagan tightened the export prohibition again in June 1982 by including foreign subsidiaries of U.S. firms.[12] Subsequent changes incrementally relaxed the export regulations before decontrol in 1987.[13]

Oil and Gas Leasing on Federal Lands

Replacing oil tankers laden with foreign crude with production from the outer continental shelf (OCS) and public domain (onshore) was a major plank in the Reagan energy platform. Interior secretary James Watt answered the Reagan call by announcing the most ambitious program of OCS drilling in history, but the "billion

[10]P.L. 99–190, 100 Stat. 1185 (1985), p. 1249.

[11]*Federal Register* 43 (August 1, 1987): 22699. In another policy reversal, sanctions against Syria were removed in 1987.

[12]See *Federal Register* 47 (January 5, 1982): 141; and *Federal Register* 47 (June 24, 1982): 27250.

[13]In another, less consequential policy change, a November 1986 Reagan administration request for U.S. oil firms to cease operations in Libya because of the latter's link to terrorist activities was rescinded 10 months later.

acre reserve" plan was scaled back after encountering stiff opposition in Congress and from environmental lobby lawsuits. Nonetheless, on-shore and off-shore leasing has expanded significantly in
the Reagan years compared to the Carter era. Outside of a 20-
percent increase in OCS oil production, however, production of oil
and gas in the federal domain in Reagan's first six years has been
comparable to that in Carter's term.

The Reagan administration kept its promise for expanded leasing
and production on the federal domain, although outside constraints
still have kept vast expanses of promising acreage off-limits. From
a free-market perspective, however, the result is decidedly mixed.
"Pro-development" is not privatization, and the only such initiative
to date by the Reagan administration has been a half-hearted proposal in 1986 to sell the Elk Hills (California) and Teapot Dome
(Wyoming) naval petroleum reserves to private buyers. This deficit-
reduction trial balloon, like another privatization proposal to sell
the five federal power marketing administrations, received a chilly
reception in Congress.

Interventionist Policies

Several major Reagan policies have been inconsistent with a free-
market approach to energy. They represent either deviations from
campaign promises or fulfillment of platform planks advocating a
role for federal energy involvement.

Survival of the DOE

An oft-cited campaign promise by Reagan was to abolish the
DOE, which embodied the wrong-headed approach of the Carter
administration. Reagan's first energy secretary, James Edwards,
echoed the president's sentiments by stating his desire to "close
down the DOE, bury it once and for all, and salt the earth over so
that it won't spring up again."[14] This resolve within the Reagan
administration proved to be lacking in substance, however. The
energy reorganization bill of 1982, designed in Reagan's words to
"preserve and, in important ways, strengthen essential govern-
ment-related energy activities," was long on transfer and short on

[14]*Oversight of the Department of Energy and Its Enforcement Program*, Hearings before
the Committee on Energy and Commerce, U.S. Congress, 97th Cong., 2d Sess.
(Washington: Government Printing Office, 1982), p. 4.

abolition.[15] The bill's savings were questioned by Congress, which saw the reorganization as "disorganization," and the bill was not supported.[16]

Reagan can be credited with reducing DOE expenditures in specific areas (such as in the aforementioned regulation and conservation budgets), but the DOE remained intact and aggregate expenditures failed to register significant reductions. The agency's budget authorizations increased from $11.4 billion in 1982 to $14.3 billion in 1988. Subtracting out atomic energy defense activities and related overhead to focus on nondefense energy allocations, it is evident that DOE spending decreased only 6 percent, from $6.5 billion to $6.1 billion, in the same period. (The major culprit, discussed in more detail below, was Strategic Petroleum Reserve spending, which has accounted for over $12 billion in Reagan's tenure to date.) The inability to abolish or significantly cut DOE spending has been a low point for the administration.

Survival of the Windfall Profits Tax

Tax reform in the Reagan years did not include repeal of the Crude Oil Windfall Profits Tax of 1980, despite Reagan's themes of reducing taxes in his first term and simplifying and removing uneven tax provisions from the Internal Revenue Code in his second term.[17]

Reagan's fiscal policy was "hooked" on WPT revenues from the start, and when push came to shove, he needed the money. The push occurred in 1982, when a lower federal court invalidated the crude excise tax on the grounds that it violated the Constitution's uniformity clause because it did not apply equally to all states. At stake were not only future collections but a refund of over $50 billion in past collections, and the Reagan Department of Justice

[15] "White House Letter Outlines Role of Federal Government in Energy," *Energy Insider*, June 1982, p. 1.

[16] For a look at the multifarious political complications surrounding abolition of DOE, see Milton Copulos, "Why Reagan Should Keep His Word and Shut Down D.O.E.," Heritage Foundation Backgrounder (Washington, March 30, 1983).

[17] Although the Tax Reduction Act of 1981 reduced the windfall profit tax for royalty owners (P.L. 97–34), the Deficit Reduction Act of 1984 (P.L. 98–369) delayed scheduled reductions. Another indication of the importance of oil taxation for government revenues was Reagan's push for a $0.05-per-gallon increase in the federal gasoline tax that became law in the Surface Transportation Assistance Act of 1982 (P.L. 97–424, 96 Stat. 2097 [1983]).

quickly headed off the fiscal threat. The decision was appealed to the Supreme Court, which reversed in the *Ptasynski* decision.[18]

With the windfall profits tax producing only burdensome paperwork instead of revenue since early 1986, the administration has come full circle and now supports abolition of the tax. With Congress warming up to repeal, the administration may belatedly be able to keep its promise.

Survival of Wellhead Natural Gas Controls

Reagan's "honeymoon" period in early 1981, which was centered on tax reduction but included an executive action to deregulate oil, was devoid of wellhead natural gas decontrol. Administration inaction continued in 1982, an election year, despite several deregulation bills introduced in Congress. Early the next year, the natural gas consumer regulatory reform amendments of 1983, authored by Energy secretary Donald P. Hodel, became the centerpiece for Reagan's natural gas policy. The bill was as regulatory as it was deregulatory, however, substituting regulation here for regulation there. Trying to "guarantee" consumer gains under the bill, FERC gas-cost prudency powers (regulation by indirection) were expanded, and a careful phaseout of price ceilings was stipulated. In all, its roundaboutness was reminiscent of the DOE reorganization proposal, achieving through the back door what was banned at the front of the house.

Legislative gas deregulation was not to be. Administrative deregulation has come to pass with FERC Order 451 of June 1986, which set a ceiling of $2.57 per million British thermal units plus inflation, currently above market levels, for remaining regulated (pre-1978) gas vintages.[19] This palliative has conditions blocking its universal application, however, and can be reversed either administratively or by the courts. It is inferior to legislative decontrol and to this extent has been one of the disappointments of Reagan energy policy.[20]

---

[18]*United States* v. *Ptasynski,* 103 S.Ct. 2239 (1983).

[19]*Federal Register* 51 (June 18, 1986): 22168.

[20]Several other FERC decisions, creating turmoil in the natural gas market, should be mentioned. The Order 380 series voided the variable-cost portion of minimum-bill contracts between interstate pipelines and their customers that opened up the market to nontraditional suppliers and spot gas. This action also exposed pipelines

Federal Energy Subsidies

The Republican platform contained three areas of government intervention: synfuel subsidies, federally sponsored energy research and development (R&D), and expansion of the Strategic Petroleum Reserve. All of these planks have been honored, and the taxpayer has paid dearly.

Between 1982 and 1988, energy R&D appropriations administered by the DOE have totaled approximately $14 billion, with fossil fuel R&D and alternative fuel production adding $3.2 billion more. While the price tag for synfuels was far less than what was appropriated, the Great Plains Coal Gasification Plant default hit Treasury for $1.54 billion, and more costs are being incurred daily as the DOE seeks a buyer for the ill-fated project. The SFC could have been much worse for taxpayers—only 6 out of over 150 projects were approved for aid, which totaled under $3 billion in taxpayer commitments out of a once-planned $88 billion program.

A general theme of Reagan's candidacy and his party's platform was fiscal restraint and resource optimism. The Strategic Petroleum Reserve was another matter. As a substitute for standby price and allocation controls in Reagan's emergency contigency energy pro gram, the federal oil stockpile was exempt from fiscal constraints.

Between its beginning in 1977 and the end of Carter's term, the average fill rate for the reserve was 56,500 barrels per day. In Reagan's first term, the fill rate averaged 230,000 barrels per day, in part from the Omnibus Reconciliation Act, signed into law by Reagan in August 1981, which mandated a target fill rate of 300,000 barrels per day.[21] As Reagan stated in mid-1982, "We continue a firm policy of filling the reserve as fast as permanent storage can be made available."[22]

Acquisition prices in Reagan's crash program were far above Carter's. While Carter purchased crude oil at under $20 per barrel

---

to take-or-pay liabilities under producer contracts that depended on minimum-bill–take levels. This problem has been exacerbated by Order 436 (now Order 500) that strong-arms pipelines to substitute transportation services for system sales. These problems can be associated with Reagan appointees but more generally with the sacrosanct Natural Gas Act of 1938.

[21]P.L. 97–35, 95 Stat. 357 (1981).

[22]Quoted in "Bill Sets Minimum SPR Fill Rate at 220,000 B/D," *Oil and Gas Journal*, August 9, 1982, p. 72.

and suspended purchases in November 1979 because of rising crude prices, Reagan purchased a record 292,000 barrels per day at over $30 per barrel in 1981.

Market realities and fiscal pressures would lead Reagan in his second term to ask Congress for lower fill rates and even an expenditure moratorium, which Congress overruled. But the fiscal damage had been done. Today's 525-million-barrel reserve, at a cost of nearly $20 billion, or $38 per barrel, not only represents Carter's overreaction and misunderstanding of the energy crisis but also fiscal imprudence in the Reagan years, particularly in the first term.

The Remaining Free-Market Agenda

Ronald Reagan's energy program cannot be characterized as laissez-faire. As seen above, his platform advocated a government role in energy areas, and he has failed to remove government involvement as promised in other areas. Taken together, these areas constitute an unfinished free-market agenda. Potential free-market reforms for the post-Reagan era include:

- termination of energy R&D subsidies,
- privatization of government energy assets such as federal oil lands, the naval petroleum reserves, oil-bearing Indian lands, the Strategic Petroleum Reserve, and the federal power marketing administrations,
- repeal of the Natural Gas Act of 1938 to deregulate natural gas wellhead prices and interstate transmission,
- abolition of the DOE and the fossil fuel functions of the Department of Interior,
- repeal of the Petroleum Marketing Practices Act of 1978, which regulates service station contracts,
- repeal of the Hepburn Amendment to the Interstate Commerce Act, which regulates interstate oil pipelines,
- legalization of Alaskan and Californian crude oil exports,
- repeal of oil and gas import fees,
- withdrawal from the International Energy Agency,
- repeal of the Connally Hot-Oil Act, which prohibits interstate transportation of illegally produced oil (under state proration laws),

- repeal of the Federal Power Act of 1920, which subjects inter-state sales of electric power to public utility regulation,
- repeal of the Public Utilities Holding Company Act of 1935, which regulates integration between the gas and electric firms,
- repeal of the National Appliance Energy Conservation Act, which sets minimum energy efficiency levels for appliances, and
- repeal of the Public Utilities Regulatory Policy Act of 1978, which requires utilities to purchase independently produced cogenerated power.

Summary and Evaluation

A free-market Reagan Revolution has not occurred in energy despite the improvements over the Carter administration. The philosophical underpinnings were not quite right: the administration accepted intervention in the beginning (synfuel and R&D subsidies, the Strategic Petroleum Reserve, sanctions on oil exports, regulation of interstate oil and gas transmission) and acquiesced in broader government involvement once in office (DOE and the windfall profits tax). The revolution was also stymied by Congress and the courts, which slowed free-market reforms and pushed interventionist initiatives.

Neither has there been a revolution away from Carter's energy policies. Oil deregulation was as much Carter as Reagan, and Reagan's failure to decontrol gas left Carter's Natural Gas Policy Act of 1978 to run its quasi-deregulatory course. Moreover, ironically, it was Reagan who nurtured some of Carter's infant energy programs. This has been particularly true with the Strategic Petroleum Reserve and the Synthetic Fuels Corporation but also applies to the windfall profits tax and DOE.

There are different ways to judge the Reagan energy record. An easy grading would favorably compare the Reagan administration with the Carter administration (and previous administrations in this interventionist century) and give extra credit to account for an often inhospitable Congress and courts. High marks in any case should be given for accelerated oil decontrol, which sped changes in the energy market that have so handsomely benefited consumers; rejection of standby price and allocation regulation, which closed out the Carter energy era; and rejection of major oil tariffs, which would have put the industry on a political basis for the first time

317

since 1980. The absence of proposed new federal energy programs is also impressive given the record of the Nixon, Ford, and Carter administrations. Yet, it is fair to say that more free-market reforms were expected, as indicated by charges of "backsliding" and a "fading energy agenda" from some market-oriented critics in Reagan's first term.[23] In fact, a close examination of the original agenda and resulting policies demonstrates that Reagan was far more successful in keeping his interventionist promises than achieving his market-oriented goals, as shown in Table 22.1. In this sense, the market received the worst of both worlds.

Still, the industry has been partly cleansed of the Carter debacle. The energy sector is predominantly free-market despite its being

Table 22.1

REAGAN ENERGY POLICY

Campaign Promise (1980)	Policy Type[a]	Carried Out	Resulting Policy[a]
Oil price & allocation deregulation	FM	Yes	FM
Wellhead natural gas deregulation	FM	No[b]	I
Windfall profits tax repeal	FM	No	I
Repeal nat. gas mktg. restrictions	FM	Yes	FM
Abolition of Department of Energy	FM	No[b]	I
Reduced monetary growth	M	Yes	M
Synthetic fuel subsidies	I	Yes	I
Energy R&D subsidies	I	Yes	I
Strategic petroleum reserve filling	I	Yes	I
Gasohol subsidies	I	Yes	I
Accelerated petroleum leasing on federal lands	M	Yes	M
Summary	5 FM	8 Yes	2 FM
	4 I	3 No	7 I
	2 M		2 M

[a]Free-market (FM), interventionist (I), and a mixture of free-market and interventionist (M).
[b]Attempted but no congressional support.

[23]See Joe Kalt and Peter Navarro, "Administration Backsliding on Energy Policy," *Wall Street Journal*, February 9, 1982, p. 24; and Milton Copulos, "Reagan's Fading Energy Agenda," Heritage Foundation Backgrounder (Washington, August 17, 1982).

the most taxed major industry in the United States. The intellectual climate fostered by Reagan has made intervention, not the free market, bear the burden of proof. But there remains a lengthy agenda of free-market proposals that would benefit consumers and industry alike and discourage new regulatory forays under a future administration with a different philosophical outlook.

23. Labor Reform: A Blip on the Radarscope

Morgan O. Reynolds

Ronald Reagan charged into Washington in January 1981 vowing to shrink the welfare state and install what the media labeled the most sweeping revolution in national economic policy since the New Deal. "If not us, who? If not now, when?" were the defiant questions. Now, in the autumn of the administration, the answers are in: "Not us and later, probably much later." The dictionary offers at least two meanings for the word "revolution," and apparently Reagan meant merely a rotation or whirling to nowhere instead of a drastic, wrenching change. His administration's tucking and trimming on labor regulations and spending added up to the same circumspect treatment we would expect from any Republican administration. A sea change? Hardly. More like a blip on the radarscope.

If policymakers were serious about enhancing the prosperity and independence of working men, women, and youth in America, they would move toward freer markets for labor services and away from the maze of federal restrictions that still rule hiring, firing, remuneration, and working conditions in U.S. labor markets. Government continues to hamper the economic opportunities of working people, especially the least advantaged, by direct interventions and by serving up indirect privileges and immunities to labor cartels. To be sure, labor contracts remain freer from government commands here than in the rest of the world, but our vast regulatory apparatus demands change rather than celebration. On labor issues, Republicans tacitly share an upside-down theory with Democrats—namely, that government is the source of progress and that working

The author wishes to thank Billy Lee Powers for research assistance.

people gain by removing labor-pricing decisions from the market-place and placing them in the hands of wise bureaucrats, labor chieftains, and the compassionate few.

The sad facts are that labor regulations, government-supported labor guilds, political wage-fixing, and the other paraphernalia of modern mercantilism do not create wealth for working people. Rather, capitalists, entrepreneurs, and a free-price system create wealth and improve living standards.

The question, "How's the Reagan record on labor?" brings to mind Henny Youngman's question, "How's your wife?" His answer was, "Compared to what?" We should compare Reagan's labor accomplishments to (1) his announced intentions, (2) what another Carter administration might have done, and (3) the available opportunities to deregulate labor markets.

The Reagan record looks good in terms of Reagan's intention and what Carter might have done, but not in terms of deregulation opportunities. Unlike what he did in other areas of the economy, Reagan never had a package to deregulate labor markets, even though federal restrictions on employment contracts are at the heart of the welfare state. Nothing ventured, nothing gained, mission accomplished. Compared to the labor activism and partially successful efforts to appease organized labor in the Carter administration, do-nothingism has undeniable merit. Some writers could argue that a Reagan administration earns its keep solely by preempting a Carter administration, but such mediocrity swells few hearts with pride. On labor policy, it was a story of lost opportunities. Labor policy was never entered on the Reagan menu, much less placed on the White House front burner.

Ideology and Intentions

The biggest minus of the Reagan administration was its complete and abject failure to make the ideological case for deregulation. Without this, no serious change in the labor framework is possible. Lack of conviction and principled discourse implies no lasting legacy.

It all was foretold on the 1980 campaign trail. Reagan, a former six-year head of an AFL-CIO union—the Screen Actors Guild—became the first former union president to win the U.S. presidency. Yet, the candidate initially suggested that the minimum wage and Davis-Bacon laws might be repealed, unions could be brought under the scope of antitrust law, the Occupational Safety and Health Administration (OSHA) might be dismantled, and a national right-to-work law could be passed. As the campaign wore on, however, aides toned down Reagan's remarks. Their "clarifications" included a teen pay differential instead of repeal of the minimum wage, no extension of antitrust to unions, no change in the Davis-Bacon Act, moderate changes to make compliance with OSHA commands easier, and no national right-to-work law. Carter's secretary of labor, Ray Marshall, charged "flip-flop," and a Reagan spokesman courageously responded that it was no such thing, merely "a pragmatic recognition of the facts of life."[1] Reagan's campaign chairman, William Casey, chimed in, "A Reagan administration would not approach the issue of labor law reform legislation with any hostility to labor institutions or their interests."[2] The Republicans sought and won an endorsement from the Teamsters and the National Maritime unions of America and promptly proclaimed, in effect, see, we're not anti-union at all; we're true blue-collars, just like our esteemed competitors.

What about the 1980 Republican platform on the issue of jobs and the workplace? It was the usual admixture of good sense, pious hopes, and buncombe for everybody. It declared that productive jobs grow through a dynamic private sector, and it pledged Republican support for, among other things, statist measures to "insure that [the unemployed] receive their rightfully earned unemployment compensation benefits," "assist workers threatened by foreign competition," "provide assistance, incentives for job retraining and placement, and job search and relocation allowances," create "comprehensive programs for disadvantaged youth," and provide for "governmental oversight of the health and safety of the workplace." Rather than propose an end to OSHA and a search for productive careers by its bureaucrats, the platform gently suggested that OSHA "consult with, advise, and assist businesses in coping with the regulatory burden." The platform had two items to offend AFL-CIO moguls, though: support of the states' option to adopt right-to-work laws under section 14b of the Taft-Hartley Labor Act

[1]Robert S. Greenberger, "Reagan Revises Tune in Bid to Harmonize with Unions; Carter Calls It a 'Flip-Flop,' " *Wall Street Journal*, October 13, 1980, p. 5.

[2]Suzanne Garment, "Labor on Electric Eve: Thinking the Unthinkable," *Wall Street Journal*, October 31, 1980, p. 28.

and opposition to the use of compulsory dues and fees for partisan political purposes.

In 1984, as if to verify that labor policy was a nonissue in the Reagan administration, the Republican platform neglected to include a labor section, although there were scattered references to a "youth opportunity wage," federal rules against home manufacture, protectionist legislation, welfare problems, discrimination, and the virtues of collective bargaining.

Plus Performances

All was not bleak on the labor front, however. The Reagan administration had several accomplishments.

Total Employment Growth

Following the severe downturns of 1980–82, the Great American Job Machine marched onward and upward. Employment grew by 15 million, and labor-force participation rates (65 percent) and share of working-age population with jobs (61 percent) rose to the highest on record. The operation of a relatively free price system for products, capital, and labor services in the United States explains this benign experience because only the pricing system can recoordinate employment and output. To its credit, the Reagan administration avoided new labor policies seriously inimical to recovery. Nonaction on the minimum-wage law, for example, has gradually rendered the $3.35 minimum a nonbinding constraint for entry-level jobs in many urban labor markets because market wage rates now exceed the minimum. As a result, the tragic job gap for black youths, with all of its devastating lifetime impacts, has begun to diminish, although it still remains far too high.

PATCO

Reagan's most stirring hour on the labor front was his willingness to uphold federal law in the 1981 strike by the Professional Air Traffic Controllers' Organization (PATCO). Among other useful effects, his action exposed the political popularity of resisting overweening union ambition in the public sector, a lesson largely forgotten since the days of Calvin Coolidge. Further, the incident probably boosted managerial resistance to union aggression in the private sector as well. Unfortunately, it was all a short-lived reaction by an actor who wished to be loved rather than to sustain sound managerial policies. Now the traffic controllers have re-unionized and there has been little progress toward modernizing or privatizing the troubled air traffic control system.

Diminished Department of Labor Budgets

While total federal spending nearly doubled between 1980 and 1988, Department of Labor outlays fell from $29.7 billion to $25.4 billion. Also, between 1980 and 1985, paid civilian employment in the federal government increased by 5 percent while Department of Labor employment declined from 23,400 to 18,200, or 22 percent. Employment was also reduced at most other labor agencies, including the Civil Rights Commission, Equal Employment Opportunity Commission, Federal Labor Relations Authority, Federal Mediation and Conciliation Service, National Labor Relations Board, and Railroad Retirement Board (the *Federal Register* lists 27 labor agencies). However, employment rose at the Pension Benefit Guaranty Corporation, at the Selective Service System, and at the U.S. Postal Service, where there was an eye-opening boost from 660,000 to 750,000 (all union jobs too, for which Reagan probably received little union thanks).

RIP CETA

In 1973 Congress gave birth to the Comprehensive Employment and Training Act (CETA) to succeed the Manpower Development and Training Act of 1962. David Stockman termed CETA a boondoggle.[3] That was apt because CETA was a scandal-ridden broth of on-the-job and classroom training, subsidized private- and public-sector job creation, and money for job search. This all-purpose gravy train, patronage, and vote-buying machine grew to $9 billion per year during the salad days of the Carter administration.

Economic studies find little or no social return in the form of higher labor earnings attributable to CETA.[4] At its unlamented death in 1982, however, the administration and Congress simultaneously spawned CETA's offspring, the Job Training Partnership

---

[3]David Stockman, *The Triumph of Politics* (New York: Harper & Row, 1986), p. 61.

[4]See Robert Moffit, "Symposium on the Econometric Evaluation of Manpower Training Programs: Introduction," *Journal of Human Resources* 22, no. 2 (Spring 1987): 149–56.

Act. This creature nominally dispenses with job creation, engages business and unions as "partners," focuses on training and job search subsidies, and spends a mere $4 billion per year. It bears all the earmarks of Republican socialism: Let's have the states allocate more of the money, let's not spend as much taxpayer wealth as the Democrats, let's be more businesslike, and let's work on an answer for critics who scream "welfare for corporations."

Minus Performances

The remaining Reagan policies either unambiguously failed to widen labor-market freedom or else narrowed it.

Draft Registration

The All-Volunteer Force was established by the Nixon administration in 1971, but the Selective Service Act remained in force as so-called permanent legislation. All that actually expired with the All-Volunteer Force was the president's authority to issue induction notices.[5] After the Soviets invaded Afghanistan in December 1979, President Carter resumed draft registration to belatedly show the Soviets that we took their aggression seriously.[6] Registration then became part of the 1980 presidential campaign and candidate Reagan pledged to repeal this Carter legacy.

Support for an All-Volunteer Force is a fundamental part of adherence to free-labor markets and a free society. In economic terms, reliance on military reserves is superior to an inefficient conscript mechanism. Yet, the primary Reagan legacy is that, between 1980 and 1985, the Selective Service System increased its staff from 97 to 301 employees.

Immigration

Free-labor markets include open borders. Immigrants obviously help themselves economically, but their employment and produc-

---

[5]Andrew J. Goodpaster, Lloyd H. Elliot, and J. Allan Hovey, Jr., *Toward a Consensus on Military Service: Report of the Atlantic Council's Working Group on Military Service* (New York: Pergamon, 1982), p. 286.

[6]Martin Anderson, "The All-Volunteer Force Decision, History, and Prospects," in William Bowman, Roger Little, and G. Thomas Sicilia, eds., *The All-Volunteer Force after a Decade* (Washington: Pergamon-Brassey's International Defense Publishers, 1986), pp. 10–14.

tion also benefit nearly everyone else.[7] Unions and other tribal groups remain unconvinced, of course. The 1984 Republican platform affirmed "our country's absolute right to control its borders" and that failure to "comply with our immigration laws . . . not only is an offense to the American people but it is fundamentally unjust to those in foreign lands patiently waiting for legal entry."

Between 1981 and 1985, the Reagan administration boosted the number of border patrol agents from 2,200 to 3,000 and their budget grew from $85.6 million to $141.9 million. For 1988, the administration requested that the Department of Justice receive nearly $1 billion more to "phase in new immigration laws, build more jails and enhance the Federal Bureau of Investigation."[8] Congress insisted that even more money be spent for border patrol and drug enforcement.

The Immigration and Reform Control Act of 1986 mandates that employers and new hires file a new form I–9 within three business days to verify that they are "U.S. citizens or aliens authorized to work." Illegal immigrants who cannot qualify for amnesty—probably a million people—are now bound to their current bosses in an even worse underground condition because above-ground employers legally can no longer hire them.[9]

Personnel

Revolutionary policies require revolutionaries with savvy and determination. The Reagan administration overlooked this little detail. To serve as secretary of labor, Reagan brought in Ray Donovan, a New Jersey fundraiser, labor relations construction executive, and political neophyte. This combination of qualifications proved lethal. Although Donovan removed the union label over Labor's front door by appointing conservatives, dutifully accepted budget cuts at Labor demanded by the Office of Management and Budget,

[7]See Jennifer Roback, "Immigration Policy: A New Approach," Cato Institute Policy Analysis no. 5, October 1981; Julian Simon, *The Ultimate Resource* (Princeton: Princeton University Press, 1981).

[8]"How President's Fiscal' 88 Budget Affects Programs: Education, Transportation, Housing Face Reductions," *Wall Street Journal*, January 6, 1987, p. 16

[9]Alfredo Corchado and Dianna Solis, "Immigration Law Creates a Subclass of Illegals Bound to Their Bosses and Vulnerable to Abuses," *Wall Street Journal*, September 2, 1987, p. 42

and initiated some labor deregulation such as allowing people to knit stocking caps at home, all of his efforts proved unsuccessful. By the end of 1981, Donovan was under criminal investigation (he was eventually found not guilty of all charges) and was rendered bureaucratically impotent thereafter in a series of events sometimes termed the "mugging of Donovan." The department remained adrift until Donovan's resignation in March 1985.

Donovan's industrial-homework decision is a good example of the rigors of labor deregulation. Following lengthy public hearings and comments, Donovan removed the restrictions on knitted-outerwear homework. The action was legally challenged by the International Ladies Garment Workers, Union and others. The court ordered the restrictions reimposed on May 24, 1984. Another rule of December 5, 1984, allowed homework provided that the contractor obtained a Department of Labor certificate authorizing the arrangement. In 1985, the land of the free and home of the brave was protected by 52 certificates issued by department functionaries.

In March 1985, Reagan appointed "pragmatist" Bill Brock as secretary of labor. A magazine headline accurately summed up this fence-mender's policies: "He has put teeth in OSHA, made peace with the unions and forged his own agenda despite the GOP's right wing."[10] Among Brock's many steps away from free-labor markets were his appointment of Steven Schlossberg of the United Automobile Workers as head of the Bureau of Labor-Management Relations and his failure to pay more than lip service to the White House's proposal of a $2.50-an-hour minimum summer wage for teenagers and to murmurings of possible changes in the Davis-Bacon law. So-called shrewd politicians such as Brock believe they will attract blue-collar and minority votes through big labor; they might ask why their "echo" policies contribute to solid Democratic majorities in both houses of Congress and to AFL-CIO lobbyists crowing, "We control the committees and the agenda on the floor." [11]

During the Reagan administration, big labor objected to anti-union appointments and rulings at the National Labor Relations Board (NLRB). Unions certainly lost some decisions, such as union contracts not being first among creditors in bankruptcy proceed-

[10]*Dun's Business Month*, July 1, 1986, p. 25.

[11]AFL-CIO executive Howard Samuel, quoted in *Nation's Business*, August 1987, p. 16

328

ings, but most of the adverse decisions occurred in the courts. The board tilted less than usual toward union demands, but this is perfectly normal.

Partisanship traces back to the National Labor Relations Act of 1935, a law passed at the urging of unions. A major purpose of NLRA was to appoint a political board that would be more sensitive to union political pressure than the courts were. So, fair's fair; if labor disputes are removed from the relative impartiality of the common law and put into politics, the unions will lose a few contests instead of most of them. NLRB history has been an extraordinary series of reversals and changes as Republican and Democratic administrations have come and gone. The Reagan board fit the pendulum pattern and was anything but radical.

In the twilight months of the Reagan administration, personnel failures continue. On September 1, 1987, Steven Schlossberg became the U.S. representative to the International Labor Organization to push for the absurd policies of international labor "standards." If this agenda should meet with any success, the world would grow poorer, the guilty would prosper, and the innocent would suffer.

Legislation

President Reagan's lack of interest in labor issues and the fiasco at the Department of Labor meant that nothing was accomplished by federal legislation. Nothing was attempted, yet serious deregulation in labor requires a great deal of undoing. It all remains undone.

Some legislators took the lead in trying to repeal the disastrous Davis-Bacon Act, which has been administered for 57 years to protect the monopoly wages and employment of the building trade unions on federally financed construction projects, and strengthen the Hobbs Act of 1945 to put union violence under federal law again, but these and many other reforms languished.[12] Although there was commotion over labor on Capitol Hill, nothing was accomplished. Pension reform, which should move toward defined contributions and individual retirement accounts instead of tax-

[12]On the Davis-Bacon Act of 1931, see Morgan O. Reynolds, *Power and Privilege: Labor Unions in America* (New York: Universe, 1984), pp. 134–39; on the Hobbs Act see Morgan O. Reynolds, *Making America Poorer: The Cost of Labor Law* (Washington: Cato Institute, 1987), pp. 22–24.

payer subsidies to defined-benefit plans for unionized retirees at bankrupt companies like LTV, ranks high on a long list of necessary changes. Liberalization of prison labor restrictions, relaxation of child care service rules, allowing borrowing from individual retirement accounts for training, an overhaul or outright repeal of NLRA, and many other measures await.[13]

A failure to seize the opportunities to deregulate labor contracts brought us to our current state: organized labor on the offensive. The solid Democratic majorities in both houses give unions a chance to pass much of their job-destroying and impoverishing agenda, including an increase in the minimum wage to $4.65 an hour, prohibition of companies with union and nonunion shops (so-called double-breasted companies in contract construction), newly extended unemployment compensation, a ban on polygraph tests by business firms, application of comparable-worth pay rulings, which has been administered for 57 years to protect the monopoly wages and employment of the building trade unions on federally financed construction projects, health benefits and paid parental leave, federal regulation of plant closings, protectionism in international trade, and much more.

Conclusion

Two anecdotes capture a lot about the Reagan administration's nonrevolutionary record in freeing people from federal restraints on voluntary acts of employment and production. First, in a 1984 interview, Jackie Presser, then an unconvicted Teamsters' president, said, "In some instances we received relief under President Reagan. We've had some concessions made at the Interstate Commerce Commission to help us sustain what we've got. We could have lost it all."[14] Inference: Rather than deregulating labor markets, Reagan sustained product market regulations to protect the labor-market status quo.

Second, when Reagan appointed Bill Brock as secretary of labor, the president earnestly announced that Brock's key tasks included

---

[13]Richard B. McKenzie, *U.S. Employment Opportunities in a Competitive World: Positive Approaches to a New Labor Policy Agenda* (St. Louis: Washington University, Center for the Study of American Business, 1987); Reynolds, *Making America Poorer*, and *Mandate for Leadership* (Washington: Heritage Foundation, 1980, 1981, 1984).

[14]Quoted in *U.S. News and World Report*, April 30, 1984, p. 87.

"rebuilding and maintaining" administration ties with organized labor and "attacking the serious endemic problem of youth employment, particularly minority youth."[15] To an economist, the juxtaposition is too delicious: union wage rates, barriers, and union-backed Department of Labor regulations are the major reasons black youths have dismal job prospects.

Billions of federal dollars spent on job programs, training, and placement have not and will never offset the tragic consequences of federal labor controls for the disadvantaged. Political programs serve those with political clout—middle-class administrators, union members and union officials, politicians, and corporate managers and shareholders—but not black youths. Many more billions will be wasted in the belief that the federal government is all-wise, all-knowing.

Less bad is not more good. The Reagan administration did not make a dent in the vast regulatory powers of the federal labor establishment. The entire apparatus is ready to be dialed up by the next administration. Today, OSHA, which is about as defunct as, the departments of energy and education, leads in harassing and raising the costs of nonunion and sometimes union companies.

After Ray Donovan's Don Quixote routine, no one wanted to confront labor policy. The game became back off, accommodate, and get back into the good graces of the AFL-CIO. Yes, the Reagan administration was less harmful than a Carter or Mondale administration would have been in labor markets. But there was no pro-capitalist rhetoric on labor markets from the White House, nor any effective leadership elsewhere. After some initial cutting on pork-barrel labor programs, breakfast sausages continued to roll to federal contractors, corporations, and unions. Certainly there was no tampering with federal labor law, nor its statist ideology. Instead, the labyrinth of federal obstacles to mutually profitable employment contracts stands tall. An old tax is a good tax; to get along, go along; Washington chortles.

The solution? In the long run, it is ideas, but in the short run, maybe Joseph Sobran was right: "Let somebody else be Reagan."[16]

---

[15]*Nation's Cities Weekly*, March 25, 1985, p. 9.

[16]*The American Spectator*, September 1987, p. 20.

And yet, why would a fake Reagan succeed where the real one failed? The Republicans won't get it right until they realize that what is wrong is the system of government control of labor contracts, not the people in charge.

24. What Environmental Policy?

Fred L. Smith, Jr.

In the environmental policy area, there was no Reagan Revolution. Such a revolution would not have been easy. Unlike such areas as tax policy or economic regulation, a consensus did not exist, even among free marketeers, that major reform of the environmental laws was either possible or desirable. Most people—even most conservatives—believed that the private voluntary and market solutions favored by the Reagan administration had little applicability to environmental problems. In economic jargon, pollution was an "externality" that would inevitably be ignored by market participants. Given this unfortunate state of affairs and the increasingly higher values placed on environmental amenities, ever more strict environmental laws were inevitable.

However, this approach to environmental concerns contained a hidden paradox. If it is indeed impossible for the market to address environmental problems, then the Environmental Protection Agency would have to regulate all economic activities having environmental consequences. But that requirement—given that all economic activities have *some* environmental effects—would mean that EPA would be forced to regulate the whole economy. By 1980, that logic had led to a massive expansion in the scale and scope of EPA. Environmental regulations had been extended to activities as disparate as whaling and microbiology, plant siting and ocean floor mining, housing design and forestry practices, and even land use. All were increasingly affected by EPA's decisions. This massive intervention was not without cost. Private firms found themselves spending tens of billions of dollars annually to meet the environmental goals established by EPA and other federal agencies. State and local governments spent billions more in constructing wastewater and solid waste disposal facilities.

Most of this structure was in place when Reagan took office. Approaches that had placed more reliance on state, local, and even private control efforts had long been abandoned in favor of direct federal regulation and spending. Continued environmental concerns were viewed as evidence that even tighter, more detailed controls were required. The U.S. economy had become, to a large degree, subject to environmental central planning. Few, however, had realized that any centralized effort to manage the economy entailed severe threats to civil and economic liberties. The road to serfdom, it turns out, can be paved with green or red bricks, but that fact, and what better alternatives should be explored, were not well understood by the Reagan team or outside observers.

But reality is what it is, regardless of whether one understands it or not, and thus the problems associated with centralized control had begun to emerge. First, EPA was finding that the information needed to direct the whole economy was not easily obtained. Indeed, as F.A. Hayek and others had pointed out in the 1930s, such information does not even exist in the absence of some system (for example, the market) whereby preferences can be expressed. Should, for example, EPA place greater emphasis on the removal of pesticides from the nation's rivers or on controlling the development of biotechnology? Lacking any information on what Americans actually preferred, EPA tended to leave such choices to the politicians.

EPA's second generic problem was how to encourage the citizenry to obey its directives. EPA had addressed this problem by reducing the number of control points (focusing on large point sources of pollution) and by enacting draconian enforcement laws. Nonetheless, the enforcement problem was increasingly difficult, and EPA was widely criticized for its enforcement laxity. Like any central control agency, EPA found it extremely hard to solve the information and incentive problems.

However, the central-control approach to the environment raised four additional problems peculiar to EPA's task. First, the environmental laws provide many opportunities for special interests to gain power. These special interests include both businesses and environmental ideologues. Businesses have found the environmental laws useful devices to restrict competition. The laws make it far harder to build a new plant, introduce a new product, or even use an old product in a new way. Such competitive innovations are inhibited by environmental laws: the new, the novel must demonstrate its virtue; the old, the familiar is accepted, warts and all.

334

This capture of environmental policy by business groups, however, is overshadowed by the success of environmental ideologues. Groups that call for "zero pollution" and "untouched nature" now largely dictate environmental policy. Their power is enhanced by the fact that many environmental laws include language encouraging EPA to finance public participation. Most of the public, however, have other demands on their time. Environmental issues are far too complex and demanding to capture the attention of the average citizen; thus, calls for public participation are answered only by committed activists. The values and goals of such individuals may (and in fact do) differ from those of most Americans. When such individuals operate in the private arena, they can play an important role in educating their fellow citizens on the value of prudent conservation. When environmentalists must persuade, they play a positive role. When, however, these same individuals operate in the political world—where coercion too often replaces persuasion—there is no guarantee that their actions will advance the public interest. Thus, the special power effectively made available to committed ideologues politicizes the policy debate.

A second factor making effective environmental policy difficult is the tendency not to place responsibility on individuals. Pollution, we seem to believe, results from a willful technology, rather than its use (or even misuse) by people. Despite Pogo's admonition, we seem to believe that the enemy is always someone else. Indeed, current environmental policy seems to regard individuals as irrelevant. Their only assigned role seems to be to lobby Congress for ever larger EPA budgets and ever more comprehensive EPA powers. This failure to enlist the individual in the pollution-reduction effort creates many problems. Since control is not required at the point where the pollution occurs, we are forced into costly attempts at remote-control pollution at some upstream point.

As the precision of the control effort declines, costs increase. Consider air-pollution control. Regions differ substantially in their sensitivity to air pollution—Chicago, the Windy City, enjoys frequent air changes, while Los Angeles swelters in air that may remain stagnant for weeks or longer. Variations among vehicles in the amount of pollution created are also great. Some vehicles emit far more pollution per mile than others; some vehicles are driven many miles, others only occasionally. A rational control strategy

335

would encourage a decreased use of the most polluting cars. Instead, we seek to force universal pollution reduction on all new cars. The result is much higher costs for newer cars because the total burden of cleanup is placed on this control point. The fact that older cars driven more miles may be far more significant is ignored. The focus on technology rather than the use of the technology forces us to spend ever larger sums to produce the "nonpolluting" (and increasingly unaffordable) car. Americans in rural Maine pay a heavy price for cars designed for pollution-sensitive regions of the nation.

Our environmental laws would reduce far more pollution if they addressed this problem and sought to control pollution at the stage where it is produced, rather than upstream. That fact was learned by most of us in childhood when we tried to grab a water hose five feet or so from the nozzle. In such situations, we generally got doused ourselves. Had the environmental laws focused on controlling pollution rather than controlling technology and sought therefore to enlist the individual, incentives would have been created both to develop cleaner cars and to use more-polluting cars only in periods or regions where pollution problems were less severe. Certainly, had such an approach been taken, we would be much further along the path to a cleaner environment. Such reforms, however, would make the costs of pollution control more visible to Americans—and might lead to a more rational allocation of effort among environmental programs. Many environmental leaders prefer their own priorities and enjoy the populist opportunity to blast business. Indeed, some seem far more anti-business than pro-environment.

The indirectness of current control strategies increases the overall costs of cleanup. This is not surprising. Although vast sums have been spent over the last several decades to reduce pollution, we still find that environmental quality gains are modest. Air quality has improved, but at the same time, oil and natural gas have been substituted for coal. As for water quality, the quality of our lakes and streams has changed very little despite increased expenditures. Some waters are improving, others deteriorating. The reasons for this lack of progress are unclear, but certainly include the clumsiness of the policies used to translate goals into reality.

A third reason why the command-and-control approach doesn't work results from a particularly pernicious defect in the current environmental laws: the inclusion in such acts of idealistic goals representing more pious hopes than attainable realities. Such utopian mandates do little more than provide environmentalists with a means of gaining power over policy. As political scientist Michael Greve argues:

> The EPA's inevitable failure to meet statutory goals and deadlines strengthens the environmental movement's ability to sustain its momentum. . . . It is very easy for the public to understand the environmentalists' point: once again, the government has failed to keep its promises. It is much harder for the other side to explain that the government could not possibly have kept these promises even under the most favorable of circumstances, and the assertion that the government is meant to fail at every twist and turn seems virtually unbelievable.[1]

Greve suggests that environmentalists use those failures to undermine the credibility of the bureaucracy and to shift power over EPA to themselves.

The fourth reason why the command-and-control approach fails is the increasing complexity of the environmental laws. When these laws focused on the simple issue of removing the bulk contaminants that fouled the air and water, their success or failure was observable, at least in principle. When the emphasis later shifted to the control of airborne and waterborne trace elements, however, extremely sophisticated analytical techniques were required to even detect such pollutants. Thus, individuals could no longer perceive the effects of actions taken by EPA and state agencies. Instead, they had to depend on media reports—reports that were, and are, selective in coverage and not always objective in analysis. Environmental policy had also gotten harder. The easy first-generation problems associated with removing bulk air and water pollutants had been replaced by something very different. In effect, having dealt with the haystack, the new problem was to find the needle.

With this focus on trace elements came a shift of emphasis from the control of discharges to the passage of regulations designed to

---

[1]Michael Greve, "Environmentalism and the Rule of Law," Ph.D. dissertation, Cornell University, 1987 (to be published in book form, 1989).

restrict—even ban—any process that might increase environmental risk. This shift now places a new form of risk—political risk—squarely on the shoulders of each regulating agency. If the agency approves a process or economic action, any subsequent "disaster" (a term itself subject to manipulation by environmental and media groups) will lead to a minute scrutiny of the agency's personnel and procedures. Hearings are likely in which the professional competence of the regulators will be attacked (data can always be found after the fact to suggest that a different decision was warranted) and their honesty questioned (major economic gains often result from the approval of a new product or process, and the regulators will certainly have talked to members of the firm promoting that innovation).

In contrast, the risks to the regulating agency that denies or delays the introduction of a new product or process are minor. Society may lose far more if a new product or process is mistakenly rejected.[2] After all, most safety gains result from the introduction of a product or process that, while still unsafe, is safer than the product or process it replaces. Yet the losses associated with such errors of omission are less likely to be voiced in the political process. Few people are aware of the safer, cleaner world that might have been, and the victims of technological stagnation are not likely to appear on the nightly news. The only party likely to raise these arguments is the entrepreneur promoting the product, and his comments have little credibility. The result is a strong bias toward the familiar risks of the status quo and against innovation.

Prospects for Change in 1981

When the Reagan administration took office, the approach taken to environmental programs had become one of the major barriers to environmental improvement. Few people within or outside of the administration, however, had any fully developed idea of what was wrong or of the extent to which environmental policy had become a central element of government's control over the economy.

Nonetheless, there were reasons to be moderately optimistic about the prospects for some gains when Reagan took office. Environ-

[2]See Aaron Wildavsky, *Searching for Safety* (New Brunswick, N.J.: Transaction Books, 1988).

mentalists, after all, were fully aware that Ronald Reagan had won overwhelmingly, sweeping in a Republican Senate. Moreover, Reagan, in his election campaign, had mentioned some goals, such as elimination of the Synthetic Fuels Corporation, that had attracted environmentalist support.

Environmentalists were even losing their halos. The mood of that time was discussed in a later *New York Times* article critical of environmental leaders. James Bovard suggested that "environmentalists have become good Washingtonians, more concerned about spending money for a good cause than actually solving a problem."[3] The placement of environmental policy in the Senate Environment and Public Works Committee had become an embarrassment and was creating some willingness on the part of more rational environmentalists to seek reform. An example of the greater willingness to scrutinize environmental spending was the critical media attention given to the federal grant program for construction of wastewater treatment plants.

Many billions of dollars had been spent on such plants under this very generous federal program. Local communities were entitled to 75 percent federal funding for all approved plants, and they were often able to have state programs pick up much of the remaining 25 percent. The program had also become an environmental pork barrel. Consequently, the media had begun questions as to whether the funds expended and plants built under this program effectively advanced environmental objectives.

A *Washington Post* series detailed the scandal.[4] The series noted that local officials had little reason to control costs. The program had weakly defined objectives—such as "clean up local waters"—and EPA found it very difficult to monitor the plans and construction schedules for the numerous projects approved under this program. Emphasis was placed on plant construction, with maintenance and operation receiving far less attention; plants were built, but whether or not they worked was not always clear. Some communities saw the "free funds" made available under this program as a "jobs" program, and they built plants far larger than required

[3]James Bovard, "Bankrupt Environmentalism," *New York Times*, July 10, 1985, p. A23.

[4]Patrick Tyler, "Dirty Water: A Federal Failure," *Washington Post*, May 10, 1981.

for local needs. Whole watersheds came to depend upon single plants that sometimes failed. Such concentration of waste management not only increased the risks to the waterways but also reduced natural flows in many areas of the country. Because the sewerage grant program was wasting money and threatening other environmental values, environmentalists seemed willing to consider substantive reform of—at least—that program.

Research also had begun on alternative strategies for environmental control. Historical research reexamining the reasons common-law remedies based on property rights and trespass had broken down suggested that such remedies might have been better able than government regulation to address pollution issues.[5] That work revealed that most environmental problems had emerged in situations where either common-law remedies had been suspended or the resources in question had been unowned (in some cases, such as wildlife, in which ownership had been made illegal). Markets cannot function without private property. Moreover, Public Choice researchers had found that some environmental laws had been heavily influenced by special interests. The Public Choice research is represented by such studies as that of the coal cleanup provision in the Clean Air Act that penalizes clean coal (produced by largely Western, nonunion labor) in favor of dirty coal (produced largely by Eastern union labor).[6]

Some environmentalists, moreover, were beginning to recognize instability of policies based on politics alone. That problem was made evident during the energy crisis, when even the avowedly pro-environment Jimmy Carter had sought to bypass environmental safeguards to encourage energy production. The fickleness of politics was dramatized by Carter's "fast-tracking" proposals and his decisions to launch the Synthetic Fuels Corporation, establish an energy mobilization board, and open more government-controlled lands to oil and gas drilling.

Thus, environmentalists were willing to consider some changes, although they largely retained their faith in federal action as the dominant means of preserving environmental quality. To persuade

[5]See Morton Horwitz, *Transformation of American Law* (Cambridge: Harvard University Press, 1977).

[6]See Bruce A. Ackerman and William T. Hassler, *Clean Air/Dirty Coal* (New Haven, Conn.: Yale University Press, 1981).

them of the values of market-oriented approaches, given their world view, would not have been easy under even the most optimistic of scenarios. The environmental movement had begun as an elitist, voluntary organization using the energies and wealth of its members to protect the environment. It remained elitist, but now saw morality only in the lobbying of Congress to expand the powers and funding of EPA.

The Superfund Wildcard

Into this modestly promising situation, Congress dealt the Superfund wildcard. The Comprehensive Environmental Response, Compensation, and Liability Act of 1980, known as CERCLA or Superfund, was passed after Reagan was elected but before he took office. Superfund was designed to solve the problems of abandoned hazardous-waste sites. For years, EPA officials and environmental activists had sought such a bill but had been unable to mobilize support. Then the Love Canal story, which broke in the media during the last months of the Carter administration, provided the "crisis" atmosphere needed to spur action. The Carter team and the environmental groups worked diligently to enact legislation prior to the bad guys taking over.

The Love Canal story is an interesting one deserving brief review.[7] Love Canal, in Niagara Falls, N.Y., was used in the post–World War II era as a storage location for chemical wastes from the Hooker Chemical Company. The site had been selected because it was clay-lined and thus largely impervious to leakage. After some years, Hooker was pressured to deed the land, under threat of condemnation, to the local school board, which wished to construct a school. That transfer took place for $1, with Hooker including a warning note in the transfer document that this site contained chemical wastes that might prove harmful. Still later, the school board sold a portion of this land to a developer who built a housing subdivision. During these construction periods, the integrity of the site was lost (sewer lines and roads were cut through the clay-capped site) and contaminants from the storage site began to percolate through the area. This leakage created noxious, unsightly

[7]Eric Zeusse, "Love Canal: The Truth Seeps Out," *Reason* 12, no. 10 (February 1981): 16–33.

seepage throughout the area and raised concern among the local residents. The chemical hysterics then entered the scene, reinforced by EPA (a pattern to be repeated throughout even the Reagan years), and the media trumpeted throughout the nation the message that chemical wastes threatened Love Canal residents.

The facts were and are that no health impacts have yet been observed from the Love Canal site, that the causes of the leakage itself were political, not economic, and that the proposed legislation would do nothing positive. None of this mattered. Superfund was to "provide for liability, compensation, cleanup, and emergency response for hazardous substances released into the environment and the cleanup of inactive hazardous waste disposal sites." Each of the words mentioned in the act was interpreted so as to maximize the scope and scale of EPA's power. Almost anything could be viewed as hazardous, almost anyone could be viewed as responsible. The emphasis of the act, however, was that business was largely responsible for any harms that might have occurred. That bias weakened dramatically the "polluter-pays" principle. Under Superfund, almost any site could be viewed as hazardous and almost anyone could be assigned responsibility for creating a hazard. Naturally, large firms would be picked more frequently for such assignments since they had money.[8]

President-elect Reagan might well have prevailed upon Senate Republicans to block this bill. For whatever reason, he did not. That omission was a mistake. The result was that all the evils of the environmental laws to date were repeated with a vengeance with Superfund. Superfund was funded initially at $1.8 billion over five years, a major increase in EPA's budget. Yet local communities had no cost-sharing responsibilities and states were to pay only 10 percent of total costs. Local communities saw Superfund money as "free." Not surprisingly, many communities requested assistance. Moreover, the standards for determining "hazard" were so poorly defined that a case could be made that almost any dump should

---

[8]For a more thorough review of Superfund, see Fred L. Smith, Jr., "Superfund: A Hazardous Waste of Taxpayers Money," *Human Events*, August 2, 1986, pp. 10–12, 19; James Bovard, "The Real Superfund Scandal," Cato Institute Policy Analysis no. 89, August 14, 1987; Richard Epstein, "The Principles of Environmental Protection: The Case of Superfund," *Cato Journal* 2, no. 1 (Spring 1982): 9–38; and Zuesse.

receive attention. Since the question "How clean is clean?" was not addressed in the legislation and since it was always possible (at a cost) to do better, EPA faced a no-win situation in which, no matter what it did, it would be castigated by the local community and the media. The fact that no costs were borne locally merely exacerbated this situation.

Then design problems created difficulties for the Reagan team. From the beginning, it was obvious that to run a program as ambitious and poorly designed as Superfund would require more staff. These would have to be new recruits or else transfers from other EPA programs. Yet EPA already had a full plate of air- and water-pollution problems. These older programs received less attention in the press, but all had strong political supporters who would swiftly mobilize if their program's staff were threatened with transfer. Nevertheless, the Reagan administration was determined to cut spending and thus new hires were not an option. The resulting new crunch was a major challenge to the incoming Reagan team. Superfund would inevitably absorb much of its energies, making it doubtful that Reagan's EPA would be able to take on any reform effort.

The Love Canal/Superfund publicity created another problem: it had terrorized large numbers of Americans suffering from various vague fears and had given them a target—hazardous waste. Superfund was supposed to address these fears, to make them go away. Since, however, these fears had little objective validity, it was hard to make them go away. To defuse the ticking time bomb of hysterical expectations that Superfund represented would have been very difficult in the most tactful and skillful of hands.

The Gorsuch Era

Tact and administrative expertise, however, were not the strong points of Anne M. Gorsuch, Reagan's choice to head EPA. Gorsuch came into office determined to clarify environmental policy, to eliminate unnecessary regulation, to reverse a perceived anti-business bias within EPA, and to show what careful attention to objectives could achieve. Gorsuch argued strongly and seemed to believe that she could "do more with less."

Certainly, Gorsuch was no free-market exponent. One event that indicates the conventionality of Gorsuch's approach was her response to a briefing by a group of environmental economists. The group discussed a range of economic approaches to pollution control such as emissions rights and pollution charges, but failed to interest Gorsuch. To her, challenges to the basic environmental laws were silly. Good management could make them work, and that was her task.[9]

Gorsuch's style was managerial, not conceptual. She and her entourage believed that the proper questions were those of timing, emphasis, and scope. Indeed, her program was the traditional progressive charter for good government—better science, regulatory reform, reduced backlogs and delays, strengthened federal-state-local relations, and improved management. It was not a particularly radical course, and it might have been feasible had the Superfund bill not been enacted. However, this strategy was very vulnerable to attack given the impossibility of EPA's overall charter and especially its new Superfund-mandated "make-people-feel-safe" task.

Like all tragedies, the story was painful but foreordained. The American people, we have since been told by most commentators, liked EPA. Reagan's efforts to cut budgets, reduce staff, favor business, and water down regulations wasn't acceptable, and Gorsuch was consequently doomed. Whether Gorsuch actually attempted these changes is somewhat beside the point. Certainly, there was no established constituency for the changes she proposed, and she did nothing to create it.

The Return to Normalcy

The return of William Ruckelshaus, a former EPA administrator and one acceptable to the environmentalists, resembled the return of Napoleon from Elba. The agency staff felt vindicated. In a blatant display of the arrogance of unelected bureaucrats, EPA staffers wore T-shirts proclaiming "I Survived the Ice Queen's Acid Reign" with lines drawn through the names of political appointees who had been forced out of EPA. The "Wicked Witch Was Dead," and

[9]An ironic element of Gorsuch's tenure was the extent to which she came to support and even initiate some of EPA's most foolish programs. It was the Gorsuch EPA that decided to purchase Times Beach, the Missouri town "contaminated" by dioxin—"that most toxic of all chemicals." Again, the facts of the case supported no such action, but facts have little to do with political decisions.

344

"normalcy" returned to the agency. Budgets began to grow again rapidly, along with staffing levels.

Ruckelshaus wasn't given carte blanche. For example, his efforts to move the acid-rain issue failed. In general, however, EPA was back in business and ready to take on any new challenge. Environmental policy might be foolish, but it is popular—and Ruckelshaus is not the last bureaucrat to relish control over a growth agency. Ruckelshaus was a media success and was able to handpick his successor, Lee Thomas. Appropriately enough, Thomas had directed the Superfund program. Neither Ruckelshaus nor Thomas had an easy time. Superfund didn't become a rational program with the transfer of authority. Hundreds of sites still clamored for attention—"free" money guaranteed that, as did the growing hysteria fanned in part by EPA itself. EPA never made any systematic effort to assure people of the true level (low to nonexistent) of environmental risk associated with hazardous wastes.[10] There may be no such thing as ghosts, but ghostbusters will never point that out. In other words, it should not come as a surprise to find a government agency reluctant to criticize its own raison dêtre.[11]

Under Gorsuch, Congress had viewed EPA's problem as bad management; under the Ruckelshaus-Thomas regime it came to see the problem as inadequate funding and authority. Over the initially strong opposition of the White House, Congress began to consider a greatly expanded Superfund bill. EPA worked behind the scenes to support this effort. The business community—the proximate loser in this charade—was split down the middle. The oil and chemical industry, which had borne the brunt of the earlier program (at $1.8 billion), decided to make everybody pay rather than fight the bill itself. An array of other firms—in other industries such as General Motors, Procter and Gamble, Caterpillar, and general associations such as the Grocery Manufacturers of America—fought to keep the tax burden focused on the oil and chemical industry. No group fought against the measure itself. As a result, the price tag of the program soared from the original $1.8 billion to an eventual

[10]See Bruce Ames, R. Magaw, and L. S. Gold, "Ranking Possible Carcinogen Hazards," *Science* 236 (1987): 271–80.

[11]One might note that James M. Buchanan received the Nobel Prize in economics during this period for his work demonstrating that self-interest persists even after an individual enters government.

$8.5 billion under the Superfund Amendments and Reauthorization Act of 1986.

The EPA leadership seemed to read newspapers eagerly, intent upon using every apparent new concern of the American people, or at least the American press, to justify expansion. EPA began to study indoor air pollution, the radon problem, and passive smoking. EPA was now responsible for all "bad air," at least of a certain kind, and began to spend funds to "protect" private homes. The notion that individuals might have adequate incentives to protect their own health did not dissuade the EPA from this empire-building course.

Environmental policy continues to expand. A totally new trend has been the globalization of environmental policy. The older trend toward emphasizing trace contaminants also continues. This expansion moves policy away from the observable and real, to the imaginary and foreign. Environmental policy mistakes become less observable. Increasingly, EPA policy can be discussed only by experts, and only environmental experts are believed. There has still been no effort to enlist individuals in the fight for environmental cleanup—we are still trying to reduce pollution by upstream controls even though the costs and technological problems associated with this approach become ever more obvious, like the hose held too far back that washes nothing but the holder. Indeed, in the air-pollution area, the recent trends are even more perverse in that efforts are being made to reduce pollution by controlling not engine technology but rather fuel itself. America now seeks to replicate the energy independence strategy that has destroyed the Brazilian economy. When will we ever learn?

EPA has also reactivated its former policy of providing grants to groups that will advance the agency's objectives. These so-called PIG (public interest group) grants play a strategic role in ensuring the growth of the agency over time. Another threat is posed by the so-called prenotification requirements, which would force firms to highlight the most disastrous event that might occur. This mandatory advertising for disaster is the equivalent of forcing firms to cry fire in a crowded theater.

One final innovation of the post-Gorsuch era deserves comment. That is the new emphasis being placed on the issue of risk assessment and risk management. Risk assessment is defined as the

346

"scientific" process to determine the level of a risk and its objective impact on mankind. Risk management then incorporates the political elements of the process. This effort to remove politics from risk management represents the traditional progressive, good-government approach to public policy. It assumes precise dividing lines and ignores the insights of the Public Choice school; but as an intellectual exercise, it can do no harm. Unfortunately, it continues to divert attention from the serious reform steps needed in the area.

There have been some minor successes during the Reagan years. Most occurred early—for example, oil deregulation, a move that encouraged Americans to reduce energy use, thus also producing beneficial environmental results. The Law of the Sea Treaty, which would have transformed two-thirds of the globe into a politicized disaster, had been moving along for many years, but was blocked at the last minute. Subsidies to destroy fragile coastal barrier islands (road and sewerage construction grants, flood insurance, federal housing subsidies) were curbed and steps were taken to increase the percentage costs borne by beneficiaries of federal water programs. Also the fifteenth annual Council on Environmental Quality report represented a first effort to indicate how voluntary arrangements might advance environmental objectives.[12] Chapter 9 of that report, "The Private Provision of Public Amenities," was especially valuable, containing a number of examples of situations in which environmental objectives were achieved by individuals, firms, and other nongovernment entities.[13]

Still, environmental policy has not yet done all the damage it can do. Proposed environmental laws are far more costly than those now in effect. The impact of Proposition 65 (California's effort to make the Superfund rules even more stringent) could be immense. Various "notification" requirements have been proposed that could easily terrorize the workplace and the neighborhood. Efforts to protect groundwater provide a convenient pretext for national land-use planning. The recommendations from the President's Commission on Americans Outdoors, if implemented, would restrict land use throughout the nation.

---

[12]See *Environmental Quality: 15th Annual Report of the Council on Environmental Quality* (Washington: Government Printing Office, 1984).
[13]Ibid.

The true costs of the Reagan administration's failure to gain control over environmental policy are only now becoming clear. A competing vision will be required to rationalize environmental policy.

Free-Market Environmentalism

It is critical that we seek environmental policy that preserves both the environment and a free society. Such policy should be less antagonistic to individual initiative and to entrepreneurship. Environmental policy must be purged of its antimarket bias—it must move away from policies that see auto pollution as the responsibility of Detroit but not the driver, water pollution as caused by industry but not publicly owned water-treatment plants, and the risks associated with dioxin but not those associated with peanut butter.

An alternative approach—referred to as free-market environmentalism—remains only partially developed.[14] The basis for this new approach flows from two basic observations: first, most of the environmental resources at risk are not owned and thus fall outside the marketplace; second, political risk-management strategies themselves entail serious risks. To address these problems, free-market environmentalists would extend private ownership to resources now managed in common and refocus liability laws in accordance with the polluter-pays principle. These reforms are radical. Still, they offer the promise of advancing both environmental and economic goals.

Conclusion

In these closing days of the Reagan administration, there seems little hope of any further positive action. The tally sheet so far is as follows. The environmentalists have advanced from simply enforcing measures over dirty water to asserting power over the economy and much of the country's natural resources. The lawmakers have learned to enjoy an unchallengeable source of pork-barrel handouts and vote-catching whipping boys (polluters, usually big business). The bureaucrats have settled comfortably into doing what they do

[14]Groups working to develop this concept include the Political Economy Research Center, the Cato Institute, the Heritage Foundation, the Manhattan Institute, the Foundation for Rational Environmental Economics, the Pacific Research Institute, and the Competitive Enterprise Institute.

348

best: obstructing new technologies and expanding their own empires. The opponents of this unholy coalition are in disarray. Business is divided against itself and is quite unready to mount any challenge to the serious threat that current environmental trends present. The media, which have served as watchdogs in the past, are too convinced of the threat posed by hazardous wastes to objectively assess current programs.

As for the administration, the White House is now being nursed by pollsters who desire only that the old actor gets one last good review before he leaves the stage. To that claque, there is no substance to policy, no principles, and no future; there is only appearance of the here and now. Thus, they coo over the "success" of EPA and the Department of State in negotiating a new global treaty regarding chlorofluorocarbons (CFCs), and in working toward comparable treaties dealing with other global problems. Former White House aide Michael K. Deaver lobbied to improve the prospects for acid-rain legislation. With attitudes like this in the White House, environmental policy reform was never likely.

PART VI

LAW AND THE COURTS

25. The Endangered Branch: The Judiciary Under Reagan

Stephen Macedo

This season of the bicentennial of our Constitution ought to be an occasion for serious reflection on the remarkable success of our founding document—a time to renew our understanding of constitutional institutions and values, a chance to resolve to strive harder to live up to constitutional ideals, an appropriate moment to reaffirm our confidence in this great experiment in "establishing good government from reflection and choice."[1]

Sadly, but perhaps not surprisingly, the official celebrations have been mainly glitz, hype, and platitude. But relief has come—right on time, and from an unexpected quarter. Whatever the shortcomings of Judge Robert H. Bork's judicial philosophy, his utterly unprecedented willingness to publicly expound and debate that philosophy before the Senate Judiciary Committee constituted a great public service. His confirmation hearings provided a kind of national seminar on constitutional first principles and the role of the judiciary in the constitutional order.

Judge Bork may not have convinced us, but we now all know something about judicial restraint, "original intentions," and what might be called the jurisprudence of the New Right. Even if Judge Bork had not been nominated to the Supreme Court, no discussion of the Reagan administration's judicial philosophy could neglect Bork's writings and speeches. More than any other person, he has articulated without inhibition the basic themes of this administration's vision of the Constitution. There can be no doubt that Judge Bork's writings and speeches have decisively shaped the judicial legacy of the Reagan administration.

This argument focuses on the difficulties of taking the administration's jurisprudence of original intent seriously. We need also to

---

[1]Alexander Hamilton et al., *The Federalist Papers*, no. 1.

consider the other ideas that, along with original intent, have but-
tressed the administration's narrow reading of individual rights
and its advocacy of judicial restraint. It is important to see that these
other ideas—namely, majoritarianism and moral skepticism—really
do underlie the administration's restraint philosophy because that
view is often wrongly portrayed as politically neutral.

The Politics of Judicial Restraint

One of the great attractions of Judge Bork's view of the judicial
role is its apparent modesty. Judicial restraint is portrayed as precisely the refusal to impose one's personal moral or political views
on the polity as a whole: "That abstinence from giving his own
desires free play, that continuing and self-conscious renunciation
of power, that is the morality of the jurist."[2]

Much of my argument, in contrast to the apparent modesty of
Bork, is going to sound terribly "political." Let me begin by affirming that any constitutional interpretation must be "political." This
is not to say, of course, that constitutional theories and arguments
must or should be influenced by political favors, bargains, or partisan advantage. Former senator Slade Gorton discovered that the
people of Washington State, to their eternal credit, would not tolerate political wheeling and dealing over votes on nominations to
the federal bench, such as that of Daniel Manion.

The argument about keeping politics out of the Supreme Court
is usually quite broad, including not only political bargaining but
also fundamental judgments of political principle—judgments, for
example, about the sorts of rights that people should have. But the
fact is that constitutional interpretation, or prescriptions about the
role of the judiciary, must rely upon fundamental political values;
the only question is whether these values are articulated and defended
or disguised by the rhetoric of neutrality and restraint.

And so it is wrong to suggest as, for example, Max Lerner did in
the *New Republic* that "Bork, at least in rhetoric, champions a restraint
philosophy that will be politically 'neutral.' "[3] It is as if judicial

[2]Robert H. Bork, *Tradition and Morality in Constitutional Law* (Washington: American
Enterprise Institute, 1984), p. 11.

[3]Max Lerner, "Bork's Progress," *New Republic*, September 14/21, 1987, p. 18.

restraint involves no more than judges refraining from imposing their values on society, in a kind of sublime act of modesty.

Judicial restraint is not politically neutral because, as the framers recognized, institutions have tendencies—the nature of the forum in which a decision is made influences the outcome. The Supreme Court's prophylactic remoteness from popular political interests and pressures makes it more receptive than the legislative and executive branches to claims to individual rights. The whole point of the Court's design was to make it more willing to fairly entertain arguments that the elected branches are exceeding their constitutional limits. This is precisely why Alexander Hamilton called the courts "bulwarks of a limited Constitution"; he defended the life tenure of Supreme Court justices, saying that

> nothing can contribute so much to [the Court's] firmness and independence as permanency in office; this quality may justly be regarded as an indispensable ingredient in its constitution, and, in great measure, as the citadel of the public justice and the public security.
>
> The complete independence of the courts of justice is peculiarly essential in a limited Constitution. . . . Without this, all the reservations of particular rights or privileges would amount to nothing.[4]

Given the institutional tendency of the Court, judicial restraint stands for a presumption in favor of the power of political majorities and against the claims of individual rights. That presumption is political because it embodies a set of political values: it elevates majority power at the expense of individual rights and the value of limited government. One need not endorse Justice Brennan's entire judicial record to recognize the validity of his charge that

> a position that upholds constitutional claims only if they were within the specific contemplation of the Framers in effect establishes a presumption of resolving textual ambiguities against claims of constitutional right. This is a choice no less political than any other; it expresses antipathy to the claims of the minority against the majority.[5]

---

[4]*The Federalist Papers,* no. 78.

[5]William J. Brennan, speech at Georgetown University, Washington, October 12, 1985; reprinted in the *New York Times,* October 13, 1985, p. 36.

The framers made the Supreme Court a coordinate branch, an equal branch, precisely to avoid any presumption against individual rights.

The idea of advocating judicial restraint but not executive restraint or legislative restraint is not only political but unconstitutional as well. The Constitution gives us three coordinate branches, three branches of equal constitutional status. This basic fact implies that the framers did not mean to slight the powers of the Court or the values represented by the Court. The fact that the framers, recognizing the institutional tendency of the Court, made it a coordinate branch indicates the basic value they attached to the protection of a broad sphere of individual rights. In the framers' scheme of values (as opposed to the Reagan administration's and Judge Bork's), the importance attached to protecting rights and individual liberty is just as basic as the value of democratic procedures.

When anyone advances an argument about the judicial role that he claims is nonpolitical, we need to be more than a little skeptical. Advocating either more or less power for judges is eminently political. Examples come from both ends of the political spectrum. The self-styled "Independent Citizens Committee to Keep Politics Out of the Court," for example, was formed to support California's liberal chief justice Rose Bird.[6] The deception is pretty transparent, at least from the outside.

The Jurisprudence of Original Intent

Any discussion of the Reagan administration's judicial philosophy (at least as pertains to the Constitution and the Supreme Court) must begin with the intentions of the framers, or original intent. As Attorney General Edwin Meese III put it in his widely noted address to the American Bar Association:

> It has been and will continue to be the policy of the administration to press for a Jurisprudence of Original Intention. In the cases we file and those we join as *amicus*, we will endeavor to resurrect the original meaning of constitutional provisions and statutes as the only reliable guide for judgment.[7]

[6]See Harold Meyerson, "Bork and Bird," *New Republic*, September 14/21, 1987, p. 21.

[7]"Address of the Honorable Edwin Meese III, attorney general of the United States, before the American Bar Association," Washington, D.C., July 9, 1985.

356

Or as Judge Bork has put it, "The Framers' intentions with respect to freedoms are the sole legitimate premise from which constitutional analysis may proceed."[8] When interpreting individual rights, says Bork, "the judge must stick close to the text and history."[9]

The jurisprudence of original intent raises a myriad of problems never adequately addressed by its proponents. Let us consider three types of problems: the who, the what, and the why of original intent.[10]

First, who are the "framers"? All the delegates to the Philadelphia convention? How do we make sense of the idea that this diverse group had a unified intent? The problem is even worse when we realize it was ratification that gave the Constitution the force of law; for it raises the issue. What about the 13 state ratifying conventions (over 1,600 delegates)? Or what about the 37 state ratifying conventions for the Fourteenth Amendment? If we rely only on the views of such leading men as Alexander Hamilton and James Madison, we have to realize that they were proponents of particular and (as it turned out later) different theories of the Constitution.[11]

The second problem is, What are intentions? The immediate expectations of the framers, or their long-term hopes and aspirations? Among the framers were men who recognized and lamented their inability to live up to their own ideals of human equality and liberty. Can we really believe that men such as Thomas Jefferson or George Mason meant to freeze the interpretation of their constitutional ideals and principles according to their actual practices? As Abraham Lincoln argued with regard to slavery, the founders saw no way to liberate their slaves but, in accordance with their ideals, they meant to place slavery on the course of ultimate extinction.

To read the framers' intentions from their practices and behavior

---

[8]Bork, *Tradition and Morality*, p. 10.

[9]Bork, "Neutral Principles and Some First Amendment Problems," *Indiana Law Journal* 47 (1971): 8.

[10]These issues are addressed at greater length in Stephen Macedo, *The New Right v. The Constitution*, 2d ed. (Washington: Cato Institute, 1987).

[11]My criticisms of original intent rely on two excellent discussions: Walter F. Murphy, "Constitutional Interpretation: The Art of the Historian, the Magician, or the Statesman?" *Yale Law Review* 87 (1978): 1752–71; Ronald Dworkin, "The Forum of Principle," in *A Matter of Principle* (Cambridge: Harvard University Press, 1985), pp. 33–71.

denies their genuine hopes that the country would progressively recognize and live up to the ideals embodied in the Declaration of Independence and the Constitution. Those who attempt to fix the Constitution's meaning by limiting it to the framers' actual behavior ignore the aspirational quality of the framers' project.[12] That the Constitution is law is undeniable. But it is law of a special sort. Unlike, for instance, traffic regulations, the law of the Constitution is hard to live up to.

Another aspect of the "what" problem is what counts as evidence of intent. Only public records, or private correspondence as well? Even if we stick to public evidence, we must face the fact that there is no public record of the Philadelphia convention; contrary to what Attorney General Meese has said, all we have are edited versions of the personal notes of several delegates.[13] Of these, only Madison's appear to approach completeness, and they were published after everyone who had been at the convention was dead.

The third problem is, Why read the Constitution in light of any sort of particular historical intentions when general language was actually chosen? The framers could be specific when they wanted to be. They said the president must "have attained to the age of thirty-five years," not that the president "must be mature." It seems to thwart, rather than honor, the project of the framers to read the sweeping phrases they wrote in light of narrow intentions, given that they could have used narrow language but chose not to. And as Justice Felix Frankfurter pointed out in *Adamson* v. *California*, what was voted on at each stage of the process of framing or amending the Constitution was the proposed language, not the speeches.[14]

The framers of the First Amendment could have said, "Congress shall make no law . . . abridging the freedom of *political* speech." That is how some proponents of original intent have said we should

---

[12]Sotirios A. Barber provides the best exploration (this side of Lincoln at least) of the Constitution as an aspirational document. See his *On What the Constitution Means* (Baltimore: Johns Hopkins University Press, 1984).

[13]Edwin Meese, address before the District of Columbia chapter of the Federalist Society Lawyers Division, November 15, 1985 (copies available from the U.S. Department of Justice).

[14]332 U.S. 46 (1947).

read the First Amendment.[15] But the intentionalists' First Amendment is much narrower than the amendment we have.

The framers of the Fourteenth Amendment could have said, "No state shall . . . deny to any person within its jurisdiction the equal protection of the laws *on grounds of race*." Before his confirmation hearings, Judge Bork said we should read the Fourteenth Amendment as barring only racial discrimination and not, for example, gender-based discrimination.[16] But again, Bork's interpretation was much narrower than the language that was adopted. That language speaks to the importance of equal protection as such, and not only in matters of race.

The proponents of original intent fail to take account of the crucial distinction between specific but ambiguous language and deliberately broad and abstract language. The First Amendment's freedom of the press could, conceivably, mean freedom for grape presses, or freedom to bench press, or freedom to put on the full-court press. That's ambiguity in a specific word: "press." References to original intentions seem to be at least a plausible way to clear up specific ambiguities of this sort.

But the difficulty in interpreting, for example, the Ninth Amendment has nothing to do with specific ambiguities. The Ninth says: "The enumeration in this Constitution, of certain rights, shall not be construed to deny or disparage others retained by the people." The Ninth doesn't tell us what other rights people have, so it is hard to interpret. But that difficulty stems from its deliberate breadth and abstraction, not its ambiguity. Of course, when proponents of original intent come across broad and open-textured parts of the Constitution such as the Ninth Amendment or the Fourteenth Amendment's "privileges and immunities" clause, they typically ignore them. That is what they mean by honoring the intentions of the framers. Throwing up your hands and walking away from the really hard parts of the Constitution—comparing the Ninth Amendment to an "inkblot," as Judge Bork did in his confirmation hear-

[15]Bork, "Neutral Principles," p. 20. It must be added, in fairness, that Bork has progressively abandoned his narrow reading of the First Amendment. What is not clear is how the "post-conversion" Bork can still claim to be taking original intentions seriously.

[16]Ibid., pp. 14–15.

ings—is as understandable as it is unacceptable. Nobody said interpreting the Constitution would be easy.

So the language of the Constitution, when it speaks broadly and abstractly, seems to defy narrow historical readings. And the framers' actions speak even louder than their words, for they conducted the Philadelphia convention in secret. If the framers had wanted us to be guided by their specific intentions, they chose an astounding strategy to convey those intentions to us.

A substantial historical argument now exists suggesting that the framers themselves did not intend us to be guided by their "intentions."[17] If the proponents of original intent are wrong about this, the original "interpretive intent" of the framers, the jurisprudence of original intent self-destructs.

On reflection, the jurisprudence of original intent is a singularly problematical way of reading the Constitution. The question, then, is why people are drawn to it. Original intent's attractions are partly products of the political values with which it is, in practice, associated. The jurisprudence of original intent is a political means of reading individual rights narrowly; it is a way of substituting narrow historical conceptions for the broad language of the Constitution— not with respect to government powers (to Congress's enumeration of powers, for instance) but only with respect to rights.

What the Constitution Stands For

To see the political nature of original intent, at least as deployed by Bork, Meese, and others, consider the way these New Right figures characterize the basic values of the founding document.

Bork has said that "the original Constitution was devoted primarily to the mechanisms of democratic choice. . . . The makers of our Constitution provided wide powers to representative assemblies and ruled only a few subjects off limits by the Constitution."[18] Bork reads the Constitution as basically or predominantly "democratic" as a way of supporting his narrow reading of individual rights. But by limiting judicially enforceable constitutional rights to

---

[17]H. Jefferson Powell, "The Original Understanding of 'Original Intent,' " *Harvard Law Review* 98 (1985).

[18]Bork, *Tradition and Morality*, p. 9.

those explicitly mentioned in the Constitution, Bork precisely reverses the logic of the framers and the Constitution.

Hamilton and Madison originally opposed the inclusion of a bill of rights because they feared that an enumeration of rights would lead precisely to the conclusion that Judge Bork has drawn: that it is rights that are specific and limited, and government powers that are broad and general. According to Hamilton, just the opposite is true: Congress's powers are specified and rendered as islands surrounded by a sea of individual rights.[19]

When the Bill of Rights was added, Madison insisted on the inclusion of the Ninth and Tenth Amendments to prevent precisely the sort of misreading that Bork expounds. The Ninth Amendment states clearly and straightforwardly that individual rights cannot be limited to those specifically listed in the Constitution. It is an "elastic clause" for individual rights that no conscientious interpreter can ignore. And it applies to the states through the Fourteenth Amendment to the Constitution.

Because constitutional rights cannot be limited to those specifically enumerated, Justice William O. Douglas's project for protecting privacy in *Griswold* v. *Connecticut* is entirely justified.[20] Justice Douglas sought, in effect, to discern and articulate the values underlying specified consitutional rights in order to discover what other rights could be justified by these implicit values.[21] The right to privacy announced in *Griswold*, even though it is not explicitly mentioned in the Constitution, is good law, and it should be understood as a way of using implicit constitutional values to flesh out the meaning of the Ninth Amendment. Bork, however, regards *Griswold* as a paradigm case of judicial tyranny.

Our founding documents not only signal the existence of unenumerated rights, they also suggest the proper way of thinking about what these rights are. The Declaration of Independence claims that governments are instituted to secure unalienable rights. The Con-

[19]*The Federalist Papers*, no. 84. See discussion in Herbert Storing, "The Constitution and the Bill of Rights," in *Essays on the Constitution*, ed. M.J. Harmon (Port Washington, N.Y.: Kennikat, 1978).

[20]381 U.S. 479 (1965).

[21]I have argued elsewhere that *Griswold*'s logic with respect to rights is essentially the same as the logic of *McCulloch* v. *Maryland* (4 Wheaton 316 [1819]) with respect to government powers; see Macedo, *New Right*, pp. 52–54.

stitution's Preamble spells out its purposes in broadly moral terms: establishing "justice," promoting the "general welfare," and securing "the blessings of liberty for ourselves and our posterity." The Ninth Amendment says unenumerated rights are "retained" by the people, which implies that they are moral, rather than created by government. The Declaration, the Preamble, and the Ninth Amendment all signal the importance of serious moral reflection about the sorts of rights and liberties that governments ought to respect.

Bork turns away from the moral and liberty-expanding purposes of the Declaration, the Preamble, and the Ninth Amendment and toward historical intentions because he—again, unlike the framers—is a deep moral skeptic. Cut loose from text and history, Bork fears, we find only a moral void governed only by personal taste. And the tastes of the greatest number should always win out, even when the right claimed is one closely related to private, intimate associations. For Bork, "moral and ethical values" have "no objective or intrinsic validity" of their own.[22] Chief Justice William H. Rehnquist and Edwin Meese have echoed similar skeptical sentiments.[23]

That Bork, Rehnquist, and company can advocate both respect for the framers and a radical moral skepticism displays just how selective they are about the intentions they are prepared to take seriously. Anybody who knows anything about the founders knows that they were not moral skeptics.

Bork's skepticism may seem healthy and "realistic," but it is, in fact, radically at odds with common-sense views of right and wrong. Nobody uninfected with a peculiarly intellectual skepticism could really say, as Bork has, that moral conflicts come down to conflicts of "gratification"—that the difference between individuals claiming a right to use contraceptives in *Griswold* and a state government opposing their claims is simply a question of two sets of gratifications. For Bork, moral "gratification" must be placed in the same scales with sexual gratification or economic gratification. Is that why we object to murderers, thieves, and rapists? Because their "gratifications" are outweighed by those of their victims?

[22]Bork, "Neutral Principles," p. 10.

[23]Meese, Federalist Society address, p. 11; William H. Rehnquist, "The Notion of a Living Constitution," *Texas Law Review* 54 (1976): 704.

Three elements compose the New Right's Constitution: original intent, majoritarianism, and moral skepticism. Each element is extremely doubtful on face and radically at odds with the project of the framers. The New Right's Constitution bears faint resemblance to the one we actually have. The Constitution we have makes the guarantee of broad individual rights just as important as democratic procedures. And so the jurisprudence promoted by the Reagan administration is so far out of line with the text, structure, and moral purpose of the Constitution that it is really not so much an exercise in constitutional interpretation as a surreptitious (though perhaps inadvertent) form of constitutional amendment.

The Constitution's broad protections for liberty should be taken as written, not artificially narrowed in light of arbitrary invocations of what is meant to pass for "history."

In practice, the invocation of original intent is becoming more and more arbitrary. Advocates of original intent are unwilling to bite the historical bullet and accept the fact the framers' particular original intentions, when they can be discerned, are often politically very unpleasant.

To take an example, Raoul Berger, in *Government by Judiciary*, finds "proof positive that segregation was excluded from the scope of the [1866 civil rights] bill."[24] The House manager of the bill, asked specifically about public schools, said that racially segregating public schools by race would remain. Since, according to Berger, the purpose of the Fourteenth Amendment was to "embody and protect" the Civil Rights Act of 1866, we must conclude that the framers of the Fourteenth Amendment's equal protection clause specifically intended to leave segregated public schools in place.

But for Bork, and others on the New Right, the results of taking particular historical intentions seriously are too embarrassing. And so Bork now says that a legitimate judicial interpretation must take as its premise, not a particular historical intention, but rather a "core value that the framers intended to protect."[25] Intentions are not to be read straight from history, they are to be constructed at

[24]Raoul Berger, *Government By Judiciary* (Cambridge: Harvard University Press, 1977), p. 119.

[25]Robert H. Bork, "Speech before the University of San Diego Law School," November 18, 1985. Reprinted in Federalist Society, *The Great Debate: Interpreting Our Written Constitution*, Occasional Paper no. 2 (Washington, 1987), p. 46.

some level of generality or abstraction. And so the equal protection clause prohibits all racial discrimination, even those examples (like segregated schools) that the framers intended to leave intact.

But the question Bork must face is this: If we are going to depart from the framers' specific intentions and include segregated schooling, why not include all discrimination? Why not read the equal protection clause the way it was written, in light of the Constitution as a whole, without the "racial" referent? Why isn't the "core value" of the equal protection clause the right of all people to be treated as equals?[26] Presumably, that would be going too far. We must depart from particular historical intentions, but only so far. Well, how far is too far? Until the proponents of original intent can specify the proper level of generality at which constitutional principles should be constructed, their view will appear arbitrary.

Gary McDowell, another important proponent and shaper of the New Right view, goes even further than Bork. By "intention," McDowell has said, he doesn't mean the "particular or subjective notions" of a particular time in the past, but the " 'postulates of good government' " that are gleaned from the "structural design of the government."[27] What McDowell seems to be saying is that when he says "historical," he doesn't mean the actual ideas of the past, and when he says "intention," he doesn't mean what people actually have in mind. McDowell wants the rhetoric of historical intention without the history and without the intentions; he wants it to mean a structural analysis of the Constitution. Why not say that instead? Structural analysis is not what Raoul Berger was up to. It is not what is commonly meant by the resort to historical intentions. McDowell, like Humpty Dumpty, seems to be trying to make words mean whatever he wants them to. But the proponents of original intent have a difficult brief, so we can sympathize with

[26]In his Senate confirmation hearings, the "post-conversion" Bork seemed to go all the way with the Fourteenth Amendment, admitting that it should be applied to gender-based and other forms of discrimination, reading the words of the amendment (in effect) as written. If he were prepared to apply this mode of constitutional interpretation across the board, there would be nothing left of his "original intent" philosophy and he would have a principled constitutional theory to stand on.

[27]See Gary McDowell and Stephen Macedo, "A Debate on Judicial Activism," in Macedo, *New Right*, p. 106.

efforts by Judge Bork and McDowell to distance themselves from that theory.

When we turn to the structure of the Constitution, as McDowell would have us do, what do we find? Support for a narrow reading of judicial power and individual rights? Far from it; rather, we find a Supreme Court whose constitutional status is coordinate with that of Congress and the president. Do we find a basically or predominantly democratic or majoritarian scheme of government? No, we find a government of limited powers and broad individual rights, in which elective processes are important but not basic. A host of limitations on popular power and the establishment of a broad sphere of individual rights are every bit as important to the Constitution as democracy.

And what we find when we look back to the ideas of the framers (and we should do that because they were wise statesmen from whom we can learn, not because they stand in authority over us) is a straightforward acknowledgment that a robust, independent judiciary is an essential element in the Constitution's scheme of limited government.

The presumption against the vigorous protection of individual rights that underlies the Reagan administration's deployment of original intent finds no support in either the Constitution itself or the views of the framers.

"The test of the moral quality of a civilization," Judge Jerome Frank observed, "is its treatment of the weak and powerless."[28] Judicial review expresses our commitment to be governed by more than power, prejudice, and narrow interests—it embodies our commitment to reasonable self-government.

The Constitution and the Court

The danger to constitutional government lies not in the judicial enforcement of constitutional rights, but in the mistaken notion that the Supreme Court is the final or ultimate interpreter of the Constitution for the polity as a whole. Supreme Court interpretations should be regarded as final only for the judicial branch of government. We should view the court politically as in a dialogue

[28]U.S. v. Murphy, 222 F.2nd 698 (1955) at 706; quoted in Henry Abraham, Freedom and the Court, 4th ed. (New York: Oxford University Press, 1982), p. 4.

with the other two branches about the best interpretation of our fundamental law, our basic political ideals.[29] All three branches have a right to interpret in performing their legitimate functions, and neither Congress nor the president should view Supreme Court interpretations as binding on them.[30]

What conservatives need to realize is that a vigilant judiciary is necessary to the health of our constitutional order. But a judiciary resolutely guarding the full range of legitimate constitutional rights need not be a liberal judiciary. A principled judiciary would give due weight to the Constitution's obvious concern with economic liberties and property rights.

The Constitution is, as I began by saying, a political document. Its interpretation is the province of all three branches of the federal government and, it must be added, of the citizenry as well. This is why the substantive Senate review of the judicial philosophy of Judge Bork is so salutary. Such debates invite not only elected officials but citizens themselves to deliberate upon the meaning of the founding document. Politicizing the Constitution, in this way, could help constitutionalize our politics. If the Constitution loses some of its nonpartisan luster, perhaps its ideals will also be taken more seriously in the polity as a whole. That would be a good trade-off because, in the long run, even the best Court cannot defend constitutional rights and liberties without the support of elected officials and citizens at large.

The constitutional spirit of the polity has been strengthened by its encounter with the Reagan administration's jurisprudence. The furor caused by Bork and the rejection of his nomination showed that the concern with constitutional rights is a political force to be reckoned with. This is good news, for the health of constitutionalism in America depends, finally, on what Madison called "the vigilant and manly spirit which actuates the people of America—a spirit which nourishes freedom, and in return is nourished by it."[31]

[29]This theme is developed and explored at greater length in Stephen Macedo's *Liberal Virtues: A Liberal Theory of Citizenship, Virtue, and Community* (Oxford: Oxford University Press, forthcoming).

[30]See the essays collected in Joseph M. Bessette and Jeffrey Tulis, eds., *The Presidency in the Constitutional Order* (Baton Rouge: Louisiana State University Press, 1981).

[31]*The Federalist Papers*, no. 57.

26. Civil Liberties: What Ever Happened to Limited Government?

Barry W. Lynn

The Reagan administration has been a staunch corrupter of the concept of individual rights. Ronald Reagan, as candidate and president, has managed, with considerable consistency, to get fundamental civil liberties issues backward. For example, instead of acknowledging that citizens have a right not to have their public schools promote religious practices, Reagan has claimed that Supreme Court decisions eliminating publicly sponsored school prayer violate the "right" of schoolchildren to decide to say grace before milk and cookies. In fact, these decisions did nothing but recognize that government prayer writing and officially sanctioned prayer periods violate the establishment clause of the First Amendment as applied to the states in the Fourteenth Amendment. They did not eliminate the individual and legitimate right of children to pray or not to pray on their own, even in a public building.

Similarly, Reagan has called for the recognition of the "rights" of crime victims, while criticizing the courts for giving too many "rights" to suspects. However, much as we might wish to construct ways to compensate victims, the Constitution does not secure rights to victims as such. It does clearly recognize that certain fundamental limits will be placed on government where it is seeking to enforce protective criminal laws, even if that means that law enforcement will be more difficult or that some who are guilty may go free. Reagan has likewise championed the "rights" of fetuses, but always at the expense of the acknowledged legal privacy and self-determination rights of women.

President Reagan has indeed suited up the troops to change the law to reflect his own theory of "rights," but he has been remarkably unsuccessful. From the beginning of his presidency, he has used as his principal commander Edwin Meese, first as counsel to the president and later as attorney general. Meese's actions are one of the best sources of evidence on the Reagan administration's civil liberties record. The following pages examine some of the major initiatives of the administration in abrogation of individual liberty.

The First Amendment

The guarantees of freedom of speech and the press create both a prohibition on government censorship and an affirmative obligation to keep government accessible to the citizenry. In both arenas, the Reagan administration has sought to expand government power at the expense of free debate by Americans on a variety of subjects.

Access to Government Information

From the beginning of this presidency, Reagan has tried repeatedly to amend the Freedom of Information Act to permit a variety of government agencies to have greater discretion to deny the public access to documents and to make the process of obtaining still available documents both more costly and more time-consuming.

Consistent with his interest in keeping the public informed only with the information he and his staff choose to release, the president has also tried to avoid disclosure of a great deal of information from current and former government officials. As part of his notorious National Security Decision Directive 84, he attempted to impose lifelong censorship agreements in the form of prepublication review on thousands of government workers.[1] Although congressional and public pressure derailed such a sweeping proposal, even existing contracts maintain a threatening tone for those employees seeking to obtain security clearances. Courts have consistently recognized that "the First Amendment limits the extent to which the United States, contractually or otherwise, may impose secrecy requirements upon its employees."[2] Nonetheless, the current agreement implies that the nondisclosure obligations of the contract reach "classifiable" material, material that has not been designated as "classified" (that is, reasonably expected to cause damage to the national security) nor derived directly from it (as the notes taken

[1] See "Administration Seeks a Stronger Lock on 'Classified' Files," *New York Times*, March 24, 1985, p. 5.

[2] *McGehee* v. *Casey*, 718 F.2d 1137, 1141 (D.C. Cir. 1983), citing *United States* v. *Marchetti*, 466 F.2d 1309, 1313 (4th Cir.); cert. denied, 409 U.S. 1063 (1972).

while reading a properly classified document). This places a chilling burden on employees, who are led to believe that they are supposed to recognize what material or information could be classified and are subject to penalties for mistaken assessments.

Notwithstanding this controversy, Attorney General Meese has gone even further, actually suggesting that reporters who obtain "leaked" information of a classified nature are criminals and could be prosecuted under federal law. In fact, any such effort would violate longstanding First Amendment principles.

Political Speech

Whatever else the First Amendment does or does not cover (and even Judge Bork does not know for sure), it certainly states an unequivocal protection for political debate. However, the Reagan administration has actively supported initiatives that curtail the right of Americans to advocate certain controversial political viewpoints, as well as the ability of Americans to hear such viewpoints from those outside the country.

Using restrictions in the hoary McCarran-Walter Act,[3] the administration has denied visitation rights to foreigners based on either their political beliefs or activities deemed to be "prejudicial to the public interest." Over the past seven years, people banned from entry have included Canadian naturalist writer Farley Mowat; Hortensia Allende, widow of the assassinated Chilean president; Nino Pasti, an Italian senator and former NATO general opposed to placement of cruise missiles in Europe; and several Cubans excluded because the purpose of their visits would be to "influence and exploit various groups in the United States . . . by encouraging them to accept a positive image of the Cuban Revolution and Cuban society."[4]

The administration has also used the Trading with the Enemy Act and the International Emergency Powers Act to bar travel to Cuba by prohibiting the expenditure of American funds "incident to" such travel. As a practical consequence, then, Americans cannot go unless they are guests of the Cuban government or are in the

[3]8 U.S.C. 1101 et seq.

[4]Letter, dated October 21, 1983, from Kenneth N. Skoug, Jr., director of the Office of Cuban Affairs, to Thomas H. Holloway, director of Cornell University's Latin American studies program.

369

narrow categories of citizens, such as relatives or journalists, exempt from the embargo. U.S. citizens are unable to independently gather information. Since the administration also reads these statutes as preventing the exportation of "anything of value," even the donation of books and magazines to Cuban libraries has been prohibited.

In perhaps the most naked assault on political speech so far, the State Department, with the blessing of the Department of Justice, recently ordered the closure of the Palestine Information Office in Washington. The office's sole purpose is to distribute information favorable to the cause of the Palestine Liberation Organization. Its director is an American citizen. There are no allegations that any terrorist activity is orchestrated by or participated in by the office. The State Department, which has had no contact with the office for seven years, announced in an Alice-in-Wonderland–like letter that (1) the PLO was to be designated a "foreign mission" under the Foreign Missions Act, but (2) since it was now a "mission," it could be closed by administrative decision made pursuant to a provision of the Foreign Missions Act. It is, of course, not like any foreign mission since it does not function diplomatically as an official representative of a foreign entity, nor indeed had it ever applied for that status. The power to designate has become the power to destroy. If this principle stands, the government will be able to select which American offices espousing ideas at the direction of foreign groups will be allowed to exist.

Curtailment of Sexual Speech

Midway through the Reagan years, the president met with leading religious opponents of sexually explicit materials and promised a new study commission on the subject, indicating unmistakably that "new" data would certainly repudiate the conclusions of a 1970 commission, which had found no link between pornography and antisocial conduct. Indeed, in May 1985, Attorney General Meese announced appointment of such a group, noting that its purpose was to find "more effective ways in which the spread of pornography could be contained," unequivocally staking out a position completely contrary to the 1970 commission, which had actually urged the repeal of all "obscenity" laws.[5]

[5]Charter of the Attorney General's Commission on Pornography (filed March 29, 1985), p. 1.

The commission, loaded with a stacked deck of largely compliant antipornography activists of one stripe or another, predictably called for a panoply of new federal initiatives against sexually oriented materials. Although the press treated the exercise as a somewhat humorous spectacle, the religious right insisted that some action needed to follow the issuance of the report. Meese complied just a week before the 1986 elections, announcing creation of an obscenity task force in the Department of Justice and noting that the administration would soon be sending a package of legislation to Congress. The legislation was to be a sweeping collection of some of the more radical proposals of the commission, including the creation of broad new forfeiture statutes directed at purveyors of sexually explicit materials, a crackdown on sexually oriented material on telephones and home computers, and drastic new record-keeping requirements for producers, distributors, and even retailers of sexually oriented materials. When the 99th Congress adjourned, however, no legislation had in fact been introduced.

The year following the commission's recommendations brought new law enforcement techniques that raise disturbing issues, aside from direct First Amendment interests. The Department of Justice authorized the first use of the federal racketeering and corrupt organizations statute to go after an alleged pattern of activity involving interstate transportation of obscene materials. Under RICO, a few previous convictions for a couple of magazines form the predicate offenses for a wholesale fishing expedition against a business that can result, for example, in the seizure of a bookstore's assets even before there is a determination that all seized items are legally "obscene."

As disturbing, the department recently announced a major "sting" operation that resulted in the indictment of close to 100 individuals for receiving child pornography through the mails. A dummy corporation was set up by the U.S. Postal Service, which, based on finding the names of individuals on the mailing lists of two actual child pornography dealers, then targeted them and solicited orders through letters and catalogues. The designer of the operation conceded, however, that over half of the targets did not in fact purchase any material. To some observers that looked like good evidence that such undercover operations should not be undertaken until a judge or other detached third party makes a judgment that there is a sufficient basis for issuing a warrant in the case. Indeed, in several past operations during this administration, defendants were successfully prosecuted under the Child Protection Act even though the only item found in their homes after execution of the search warrant was the single piece of child pornography sold to them by the government agency. As always, the more pernicious the underlying offense, the easier it is for law enforcement personnel to get away with using suspect tactics.

The Religion Clauses

It has sometimes appeared that this administration views itself as leading the charge to re-Christianize America. In spite of an absolutely dizzying level of religious freedom in this nation for those with essentially majoritarian religious sentiments, President Reagan and others have acted as if the forces of the American Civil Liberties Union, People for the American Way, and assorted other secular humanist collaborators have all but erased Christianity from the nation. This is all best encapsulated in the president's plaintive comment, uttered approximately every other September, that "God has been expelled from the public schools."

The president began his effort to return organized prayer to public schools in 1982 by endorsing a proposed constitutional amendment that read: "Nothing in the Constitution shall be construed to prohibit individual or group prayer in public schools and other public institutions. No persons shall be required by the United States or any state to participate in prayer." The Department of Justice memorandum that explained the proposal noted that its intent was to "reverse the effect of *Engle v. Vitale* and *Abington School District* v. *Schempp*, which held that it is an impermissible 'establishment of religion' . . . for a state to foster group prayer or Bible readings by students in public schools."[6] This proposal would actually have permitted the government to write prayers for children to recite. Even when the proposal was modified to prohibit the composition of these prayers by the state, governments would have been permitted to select prayers from those suggested by the community. This modified version failed its test in the Senate in 1984 even

[6]Statement of Edward C. Schmults, deputy attorney general, in *Voluntary School Prayer Constitutional Amendment: Hearing Before the Subcommittee on the Constitution of the Committee on the Judiciary, U.S. Senate*, 98th Cong., 1st sess., 1983.

though the White House pushed this proposal more vigorously than anything else on its "social agenda."

Following this congressional defeat, the administration moved into the Supreme Court, joining Alabama in its defense of a statute providing for a period of "meditation or voluntary prayer." A majority of the Court, however, found that the legislative history of the Alabama law demonstrated absolutely no secular purpose for the enactment, but was replete with claims that this would indeed return organized prayer to public schools. It was, concluded the Court, "intended to convey a message of state approval of prayer activities in the public schools."[7] The administration continued to claim that it sent no such message of approval. The noted constitutional scholar Walter Dellinger has quipped that if words like "or voluntary prayer" are not meant to lead to a specific result, we should see if the sponsors of such bills would insert the words "or sexual fantasy" in their future proposals.

In addition to the prayer controversy, the administration has regularly (and regularly unsuccessfully) floated voucher plans to give parents funds to spend at the schools of their choice. Although couched in the rhetoric of "choice" and "rights," these proposals have as their sole purpose the subsidization of private religious schools. The latest proposal involved Title I funds for education of the disadvantaged. Even though the First Amendment clearly requires that parents be allowed to set up alternative schools for their children, it affirmatively prohibits the bestowal of government financial benefits on such enterprises. Since the Constitution does not rely on cost-benefit analysis, it is irrelevant whether these schools could educate people more cheaply than public schools.

The administration also argued before the Supreme Court that it was proper to spend taxpayers' funds on teacher salaries in religious schools. In *Grand Rapids School District* v. *Ball*, the Court looked at the constitutionality of full-time employees of the school system providing classes of "remedial" and "enrichment" education in classrooms located in and leased from private, largely sectarian religious schools. Contrary to the Reagan administration's position, the Court ruled that this program violated the establishment clause because teachers could become intentionally or inadvertently involved

---

[7]*Wallace* v. *Jaffree*, 86 L.Ed.2d 29, 26 (1985).

in inculcating certain religious precepts, that the process represented a symbolic link between government and religion, and that it could have the direct effect of promoting religion by subsidizing the mission of these religious schools.[8] This case represented only too well the flip side of the problem of government subsidy: it posed a danger to the church's right to be secure from government influence. The private schools in this Michigan school district took down such items as religious pictures and crucifixes when the public school teachers arrived, desacralizing the institution for a few of Caesar's pieces of silver.

Reproductive Freedom

The Reagan administration has spoken with an unequivocal public voice about its desire to overturn *Roe* v. *Wade*, guaranteeing the right of a woman to choose to terminate a pregnancy through abortion.[9] During Reagan's first term, he supported a proposed constitutional amendment that stated that the Constitution does not secure the right to abortion, thereby permitting virtually any state regulation of the matter. He also embraced an equally expansive measure that would have declared that human life begins at conception and, collaterally, would have removed federal court jurisdiction to enjoin state limitations on abortion decisions. Both of these measures failed to achieve legislative approval. Some critics on the right have suggested that Reagan himself did not personally participate actively enough to push the measures. On the other hand, the breadth of these measures has had very limited public support in polls.

The second term has seen more focus on the courts. The Department of Justice's unsolicited amicus curiae brief in *Thornburgh* v. *American College of Obstetricians and Gynecologists* argued that *Roe* v. *Wade* was "so far flawed and is such a source of instability that this Court should reconsider that decision and on reconsideration abandon it."[10] Both Reagan and Meese have ridiculed the privacy concept in *Roe* as "judicially created." The Supreme Court declined the administration's suggestion.

[8] 87 L.Ed.2d 267 (1985).
[9] 410 U.S. 113 (1973).
[10] 106 S.Ct. 2169 (1986).

The administration has routinely supported restrictions on the federal funding of abortion, most recently prohibiting use of federal funds for prison inmate abortions, an effort effectively eliminating the opportunity for prisoners to obtain them. Moreover, in a twist representing a fundamental misunderstanding of both the right of free expression and privacy, Reagan has even endorsed legislation and undertaken administrative action to limit participation in the federal family-planning program to organizations that neither do abortions nor even do abortion counseling or referral with private funds. This domestic policy parallels the policy adopted in 1984 to cut off Agency for International Development funds for non-government family-planning organizations that "actively promote" (in fact, even mention the option of) abortion as a method of family planning. It is clearly unconstitutional to use the federal taxing and spending authority to suppress accurate information about the availability of a lawful medical procedure implicated in a fundamental freedom.

Criminal Laws

At every opportunity, the Reagan Department of Justice has been willing to trade away basic constitutional freedoms in the quest for a solution to the problem of crime. Perhaps the most visible arena is the so-called drug war, a conflict that erupted in earnest primarily on the floor of Congress just before the 1986 elections.

One cornerstone of the policy was Executive Order 12564, which required federal agencies to design drug-testing programs for a large percentage of their current employees and all new applicants. Essentially, the design was to test all employees in sensitive positions and then require either rehabilitation or firing. As an adjunct to that policy, the department sought unsuccessfully to include in the 1986 drug bill the language needed to eliminate some of the administrative protections in the Civil Service Act for those found to be using drugs.

Indeed, mandatory testing is now the subject of a variety of lawsuits, and courts are split on the issue of whether compulsory urinalysis without an objective, individualized suspicion of use is a violation of the Fourth Amendment's guarantee against unreasonable search and seizure. Serious due process rights are implicated as well in the extraordinarily high levels of unreliability in the tests.

Other antidrug initiatives focused on convicting those who traffic in the goods. The administration has supported, in the context of drugs and elsewhere, the erosion of the "exclusionary rule," the legal doctrine that requires that evidence obtained during unlawful (warrantless or otherwise impermissible) police searches shall not be admissible in court. This has proven to be the single most effective guarantor of proper police procedure; it imposes a real penalty on improper conduct. The administration has nevertheless urged that police officers with a subjective good-faith belief that probable cause exists be allowed to search for evidence of any federal crimes without the review of any detached judge or magistrate.

The administration has also sought to begin recrafting a federal death penalty that would pass muster under current Supreme Court standards.[11] A provision eventually deleted from the 1986 drug bill would have imposed the death penalty for drug dealers who engage in murder. The 1986 defense authorization bill, however, included a reintroduction of capital punishment for peacetime espionage by military personnel, a provision of dubious constitutionality.

The electronic age has ushered in further possibilities for highly intrusive surveillance of personal data. Several million federal and state arrest records, along with indexes of missing persons and stolen cars, are kept in the National Crime Information Center computers maintained by the Federal Bureau of Investigation. In spite of overwhelming evidence that a significant percentage of these data are inaccurate, the administration has resisted efforts to clean up the system. Moreover, it has announced intentions to implement a "test" in which non-law-enforcement agencies in a few jurisdictions will be able to obtain information for the purpose of making hiring decisions. Arrest records alone do not prove that an individual has actually committed a crime, and the ready release of such inflammatory data poses great privacy problems.

Two other areas have been the subject of Reagan cutback efforts: federal habeas corpus and the Miranda Rule. The former is primarily a legislative battle in which the administration seeks to curb access to the federal courts by state criminal defendants. The evidence

[11]See, for example, *Furman* v. *Georgia*, 408 U.S. 238 (1972).

376

suggests that federal court access has proven essential in the vindication of constitutional rights for some defendants, notwithstanding the putative commitment of state courts to these same rights. Administration efforts have centered around creation of a rigid one-year statute of limitations on the filing of claims, as well as elimination of appeals where there has been "full and fair adjudication" in state court. These alterations would insulate serious deprivations of liberty from federal scrutiny, without significantly cutting down on the workload of the federal judiciary.

Edwin Meese has adopted as his personal crusade the erosion of the Miranda Rule under which an individual must be told (prior to custodial police questioning) that he has a right to remain silent, that any statement he makes could be used in court, and that he has a right to retained or appointed counsel. It is simply one of the best ways to breathe life into the Fifth Amendment protection against self-disclosure of incriminating information. The Department of Justice has labeled the doctrine in *Miranda* "radical" and is still actively seeking a case in which the department can urge its essential nullification before the Supreme Court.[12]

Meese's logic in this regard is best evidenced by a statement he made to a major magazine that *Miranda* was a bad idea because "you don't have many subjects who are innocent of a crime. That's contradictory. If a person is innocent of a crime, then he is not a suspect."[13] In other words, since a high percentage of people who are suspects have committed crimes (almost certainly true), it is not necessary to tell any suspects, unless you know them to be innocent, that they have a right to remain silent or obtain an attorney. Besides turning the presumption of innocence on its head, this preposterous approach equates government-sanctioned ignorance of rights with justice. Aside from the clear knowledge of the framers of our Constitution that the system of justice they created would allow some guilty to escape punishment as a cost of protecting other individual freedoms, it is also true that empirical evidence shows that only 1.3 percent of all cases on the criminal dockets of 38 U.S. attorneys' offices involved the exclusion of evidence obtained

[12]Department of Justice, "The Law of Pre-Trial Interrogation," Truth in Criminal Justice Report no. 1, released January 1987.

[13]Howard Kurtz, "Meese Says Few Suspects Are Innocent of Crime," *Washington Post*, October 11, 1985, p. A6.

through an unlawfully obtained confession.[14] Principle aside, then, this is hardly a "loophole" through which hordes of criminals ride out of America's prisons.

Conclusion

All in all, the Reagan civil liberties record is a poor one. There is little sensitivity to the notion of a restrained government that needs compelling justification to abridge the freedom of the people. The good news, of course, is that most of the Reagan world of civil liberties remains a fantasy, yet to be approved by the Congress, the courts, or the American people themselves.

[14]Comptroller General of the United States, *Impact of the Exclusionary Rule on Federal Criminal Proceedings* (Washington, 1979).

27. One Cheer for the Reagan Years: Economic Liberties and the Constitution

Randy E. Barnett

In 1942, the Supreme Court of the United States held that a farmer in Montgomery County, Ohio, who had raised wheat on his own land to feed his own chickens and livestock was engaging in interstate commerce and, consequently, was subject to federal regulation under the commerce clause of the U.S. Constitution. That case, *Wickard* v. *Filburn,* along with countless other New Deal–era decisions, sounded the death knell for constitutionally protected economic liberty in the United States.[1]

The purpose in citing *Wickard* v. *Filburn* is not to engage in an analysis of this particular decision or of the commerce clause generally. Rather, *Wickard* v. *Filburn* symbolizes a mode of constitutional interpretation that justifies a virtually unlimited government power over citizens in the economic sphere. It also dramatically symbolizes the post–New Deal philosophy that the judiciary has no role to play in protecting the economic liberties of the people.

Assessing whether the Reagan years have advanced the cause of economic liberty is not an easy task. Within the sphere of constitutional law, however, we could do worse than to adopt what may be called the *Wickard* v. *Filburn* test. The test is this: Have the Reagan years brought us any closer to the day when courts would decide this type of case differently?

My guess is that in the past seven years we have edged a very slight bit closer to that day, but that at best, the Reagan administration deserves a single cheer for its efforts in reaching this goal. And at worst, it has seriously retarded the effort toward economic liberation.

---

[1]See *Wickard* v. *Filburn,* 317 U.S. 111 (1942).

The Prelude to the Reagan Years

An appreciation of the developments during the Reagan years requires some familiarity with the evolution of constitutional thinking.

Necessity Is the Mother of Constitutional Invention

Post–New Deal jurisprudence placed heavy reliance on two principles of constitutional analysis to support decisions such as *Wickard* v. *Filburn*. The first principle is that "necessity is the mother of constitutional invention." This is the view that changing circumstances require a "flexible" interpretation of constitutional prohibitions; that if we need an economic policy badly enough, it must be constitutional.

Whatever their true motives, supporters of New Deal legislation—indeed, advocates of economic legislation of every era—consistently offer economic necessity as a justification for their policies. This is done in much the same way that the "needs" of national security were used to justify the internment of citizens of Japanese origin during the same period.[2] Until the Public Choice school of economics revived historical American skepticism of public officials, these assertions of necessity invariably won out.

Perhaps it is too much to expect a handful of judges to consistently protect individual liberties, both economic and noneconomic, in the face of an overwhelming public outcry to deal with a perceived national economic or military catastrophe. But to their credit, the pre-court-packing-scheme Supreme Court tried to do just this. Six years before *Wickard* v. *Filburn*, in *United States* v. *Butler*, the Court held that the Agricultural Adjustment Act of 1933 was unconstitutional.[3] The Court first addressed the issue of congressional power. It said:

> From the accepted doctrine that the United States is a government of delegated powers, it follows that those not expressly granted, or reasonably to be implied from such as are conferred, are reserved to the states or to the people. To forestall any suggestion to the contrary, the Tenth Amendment was adopted. . . . The same proposition, otherwise stated, is that powers not granted are prohibited. None to regulate agricultural production is given,

[2]See *Korematsu* v. *United States*, 323 U.S. 214 (1944).
[3]See *United States* v. *Butler*, 297 U.S. 1 (1936).

380

and therefore legislation by Congress for that purpose is forbidden. . . .

Congress has no power to enforce its commands on the farmer to the ends sought by the Agricultural Adjustment Act. It must follow that it may not indirectly accomplish those ends by taxing and spending to purchase compliance. The Constitution and the entire plan of our government *negative* any such use of the power to tax and to spend as the act undertakes to authorize.[4]

The Court then directly addressed the issue of economic necessity:

It does not help to declare that local conditions throughout the nation have created a situation of national concern; for this is but to say that whenever there is a widespread similarity of local conditions, Congress may ignore constitutional limitations upon its own power and usurp those reserved to the states.[5]

Cases such as *Wickard* v. *Filburn*, then, represent the triumph of pragmatic or utilitarian concerns over constitutional constraints.

Judicial Restraint

But such a utilitarian approach was aided and abetted by another principle of constitutional analysis loudly urged by New Dealers and other enlightened social reformers of the day: judicial restraint. Ardent advocates of judicial restraint such as President Roosevelt accused the Supreme Court of "assuming the power to pass on the wisdom of these acts of the Congress."[6]

By 1936, the Supreme Court was feeling the heat. The justices who struck down the Agricultural Adjustment Act of 1933 in *United States* v. *Butler* felt the need to defend their actions against just such criticism:

There should be no misunderstanding as to the function of this court in such a case. It is sometimes said that the court assumes a power to overrule or control the action of the people's representatives. This is a misconception. This Constitution is the supreme law of the land ordained and established by the people. All leg-

---

[4]Ibid., pp. 68, 74. The Tenth Amendment declares: "The powers not delegated to the United States by the Constitution, nor prohibited by it to the States, are reserved to the States respectively or to the people."

[5]297 U.S. 1 (1936), pp. 74–75.

[6]Radio address, March 9, 1937, as quoted in Gerald Gunther, *Constitutional Law*, 9th ed., rev. (Mineola, N.Y.: Foundation Press, 1975), p. 247.

islation must conform to the principles it lays down. When an act of Congress is appropriately challenged in the courts as not conforming to the constitutional mandate the judicial branch of the Government has only one duty—to lay the article of the Constitution which is invoked beside the statute which is challenged and to decide whether the latter squares with the former.[7]

The Court then responded to the accusation that this was an illegitimate exercise of judicial power:

> All the court does, or can do, is to announce its considered judgment upon the question. The only power it has, if such it may be called, is the power of judgment. The court neither approves nor condemns any legislative policy. Its delicate and difficult office is to ascertain and declare whether the legislation is in accordance with, or in contravention of, the provisions of the Constitution; and having done that, its duty ends.[8]

It is worth noting that this era of judicial vigilance was not confined to economic liberties. Several landmark cases protecting other liberties are still good law today. For example, in 1923, in the case of *Meyer* v. *Nebraska*, the Court struck down a state statute prohibiting the teaching of foreign languages to students—in this case the teaching of German.[9] In 1925, in *Pierce* v. *Society of Sisters*, the Court upheld the right of parents to send their children to private schools against the wishes of the legislature.[10] In both these cases, the Court found that the state had not fulfilled its burden of showing the necessity of its restriction of liberty.

This type of judicial scrutiny of legislation eventually succumbed to the Court-packing scheme, the "switch in time that saved nine," and the nine Roosevelt appointments to the Court. From then until the Warren Court, no liberties were secure from legislative usurpation. From then until today, the economic liberties of people such as Mr. Filburn were left entirely at the mercy of the majority in Congress or in state legislatures. They could turn to the courts in vain.

[7]297 U.S. 1 (1936), p. 62
[8]Ibid., pp. 62–63.
[9]See *Meyer* v. *Nebraska*, 262 U.S. 390 (1923).
[10]See *Pierce* v. *Society of Sisters*, 268 U.S. 510 (1925).

What the Reagan Years Have Wrought

We have made some progress since *Wickard* v. *Filburn* in obtaining judicial protection of economic liberty. Most of this progress lies outside constitutional discourse. Thanks largely to economists associated with the Chicago school of economics and more recently with the Public Choice theorists, economic regulation is more likely today to be viewed as "special interest" as opposed to "public interest" legislation than it was 20 years ago. Whatever deregulation has occurred during the Carter and Reagan administrations is testimony to this influence.

The Reagan administration will have its most discernible and lasting impact on economic liberties, however, by its appointments to the judicial branch. Can its campaign to reform the judiciary pass the *Wickard* v. *Filburn* test? Are we any closer to the day when such a case would be decided differently? My thesis is that the Reagan years improved how we think about the question of constitutional interpretation, while retarding how we think of judicial review.

Interpretivism

In constitutional discourse, the most beneficial change has surrounded the much-discussed theory of original intent. Here the one cheer I have for the Reagan administration probably results from an unintended consequence. For a strict originalist position that attempts to tie interpretations of the text to the specific opinions of identifiable framers is an impractical nonstarter for all the obvious and much-discussed reasons.[11] Moreover, the philosophy of originalism can be used to restrict rather than enhance economic liberties.

Robert Bork, for example, had all but abandoned the original restrictive meaning of the enumerated powers even before his nomination to the Court. "A new, sharp-edged definition of national powers, such as commerce, taxing, and spending," he said in 1986, "would create chaos, politically, economically, and socially."[12]

---

[11] A useful summary of these defects can be found in Ronald Dworkin, *Law's Empire* (Cambridge, Mass.: Harvard University Press, 1986), pp. 313–37, 359–63. See also David Lyons, "Constitutional Interpretation and Original Meaning," *Social Philosophy and Policy* 4 (1987): 75.

[12] Robert Bork, "Federalism," speech at the attorney general's conference, Williamsburg, Virginia, January 24–26, 1986.

Once the precedents such as *Wickard* v. *Filburn* that so greatly expanded the scope of federal power are accepted as settled, however, a narrow interpretation of protected liberties and rights dangerously undermines economic and other liberties.

If the enumerated and unenumerated rights mentioned in the Constitution were inserted, as James Madison put it, "as actual limitations of such powers, or . . . for greater caution,"[13] then these rights assume added rather than reduced importance when the original limitations on enumerated powers are eroded. Originalists who cling to specific 18th-century conceptions of rights in the face of 20th-century government powers underestimate the caution of the framers. They steal from the people the very liberty that the Constitution was enacted to preserve.

Still, their rhetoric notwithstanding, all but a scant few who call themselves originalists quickly retreat to a level of abstraction that is far more congenial to economic liberty. Most professed originalists early on are forced to abandon the specific intentions of the particular framers as their guide and interpret provisions of the Constitution by referring to the general principles that animated their adoption. At the very least, the originalists have moved the rest of the profession to take more seriously the concept of the Constitution as a set of constraints and as a text whose provisions must be taken seriously as they are written.

In short, originalists have resurrected what John Ely has called interpretivism—that is, taking the text and its underlying principles of limited government seriously. By these remarks, I intend neither to unqualifiedly endorse a pure interpretivist approach nor by this caveat to disparage it. Rather, my more limited thesis is that the reemergence of interpretivism could be beneficial to economic liberties, since the rights to life, liberty, and property were central to the framers' political vision—a vision they deliberately embodied in a written Constitution.

A perspective that takes the constitutional text and its underlying principles of limited government and private property seriously would be suspicious, for example, of any interpretation of interstate commerce that would include a farmer who raises crops to feed his own chickens. Even as fervent a nationalist as John Marshall said

---

[13]*Annals of Congress*, vol. 1 (1834; ed. J. Gales and W. Seaton), p. 452.

in *Gibbons* v. *Ogden* that "the enumeration [of powers] presupposes something that is not enumerated."[14]

Economic liberty can be protected by restricting government power, by enforcing constitutional rights, or by doing both. To the extent that it is once again permissible to discuss limits on government regulation based on a serious reading of the commerce clause, the contracts clause, the takings clause, the Ninth Amendment, and other provisions, the arguments made by originalists or interpretivists have been helpful.

Whoever is responsible, the best evidence of progress occurred on the last day of the 1987 term of the Supreme Court in the case of *Nollan* v. *California Coastal Commission*.[15] In *Nollan*, the Court, led by Reagan appointee Justice Antonin Scalia, held that the commission's attempt to condition a building permit on the concession of a public easement across the Nollans' beach without providing just compensation violated the Nollans' Fifth Amendment rights.

To defend California's actions, the minority in *Nollan* employed the "necessity is the mother of constitutional invention" rationale.[16] In language reminiscent of the *Butler* decision of 1936, the Court rejected this argument, stating that:

> Had California simply required the Nollans to make an easement across their beachfront available to the public on a permanent basis in order to increase public access to the beach, rather than conditioning their permit to rebuild their house on their agreeing to do so, we have no doubt that there would have been a taking.[17]

The Court concluded that

> The lack of nexus between the condition [imposed on the Nollans] and the original purpose of the building restriction converts that purpose to something other than what it was. The purpose then

[14]9 Wheat. 1 (1824), p. 195.

[15]107 S.Ct. 3141 (1987).

[16]See, for example, ibid., p. 3163 (Blackmun, dissenting): "The easement exacted from appellants and the problems their development created are adequately related to the governmental interest in providing public access to the beach"; and also ibid., p. 3163 (Stevens, dissenting): "The public interest is served by encouraging state agencies to exercise considerable flexibility in responding to private desires for development in a way that threatens the preservation of public resources."

[17]Ibid., p. 3145.

becomes, quite simply, the obtaining of an easement to serve some valid governmental purpose, but without payment of compensation. In short, unless the permit condition serves the same governmental purpose as the development ban, the building restriction is not a valid regulation of land use but "out-and-out plan of extortion."[18]

The Court's treatment of the issue of judicial review of state economic regulation was probably the most significant part of the opinion. It rejected the standard that "the State *'could rationally have decided'* the measure adopted might achieve the State's objective"—the so-called rational basis test that accepts at face value virtually any reason asserted by the legislature and invariably justifies state action. Instead, the Court insisted on a more realistic test: that the regulation "substantially advance" the "legitimate state interest" sought to be achieved.[19] The Court found that the state action in this case failed to meet this standard.

Judicial Restraint

What the originalists have given, however, advocates of judicial restraint threaten to take away. Ronald Reagan likes to compare himself with Franklin Roosevelt. This, of course, is intended by conservatives primarily to rub salt into liberal wounds. Yet, on the issue of judicial philosophy, President Reagan is indistinguishable from his purported mentor. Like Roosevelt, he has gone out of his way to find nominees who are small "d" democrats—in the case of Robert Bork, born-again democrats—who espouse the philosophy of judicial restraint.

The problem with judicial restraint is twofold. First—and most obvious—judicial restraint leaves individual citizens at the mercy of the political process. Don't go crying to the courts when your liberty is infringed, say advocates of judicial restraint. Write your congressman. In short, Mr. Filburn need not have filed suit.

Second—and ironically—judicial restraint forces interpretivists to abandon their hard-won progress to bind judges to the Constitution. For to justify a hands-off posture toward legislatures, advocates of restraint are forced to ignore inconvenient passages of the

[18]Ibid., p. 3148.
[19]Ibid., p. 3147 n. 3.

Constitution. Furthermore, they have to ignore the insight of the framers, who were more concerned with the tyranny of faction than they were with the tyranny of judges.

Advocates of judicial restraint adopt a strange interpretive technique—strange, at least, for those who also profess respect for the framers' intentions. They impose upon the text their own standards of interpretation and find that whole passages of the Constitution fall short of their standards.

The first of their standards is that of certainty of meaning. Unless a provision of the text is virtually self-explanatory—as is, for example, the age restriction on who may run for president—they deny that the provision provides adequate guidance for judges. Letting judges interpret ambiguous principles, they say, is to let them roam the fertile fields of their imagination and to thwart the democratic process. Therefore, they urge us to ignore, for example, the public use clause of the Fifth Amendment or the privileges and immunities clause and due process clauses of the Fourteenth Amendment. And as for the Ninth Amendment's explicit reference to rights "retained" by the people—well, the framers ought to be ashamed of themselves for having written such meaningless nonsense.

The second standard of interpretation used is to equate judicial review with illicit judicial lawmaking. If the president vetoes an act of Congress, no one thinks the president is usurping the legislative function of Congress. No one thinks the president is making law. On the contrary, by exercising his veto power, the president is denying the statute the force of law.

If, however, a judge strikes down a statute as unconstitutional, she better have a very specific textual justification or she will be accused of illicit lawmaking—of "substituting her policy judgment for that of the legislature." Entirely forgotten is the original theory of enumerated powers, which forbids any exercise of legislative power that is beyond those specified in the Constitution. In short, judicial restraint places the burden of proof on the people to justify their liberty, not on the government to justify its assumed power. When judges refuse to evaluate the citizen's claim of right against a statute, the legislature is allowed to judge the propriety of its own action. In sum, judicial restraint makes the legislature the judge in its own case.

This mind set of judicial restraint was manifested in the 1984 case of *Hawaii Housing Authority* v. *Midkiff*.[20] In this case, the Supreme Court upheld a state statute compelling the forced transfer of property titles from their private owners to private leaseholders. Although the statute did provide for compensation to the property owners, at issue in the case was whether the taking of property from one person to give to another could be considered a taking for "public use" as required by the Fifth Amendment.

Speaking for a unanimous court, Reagan appointee Justice Sandra O'Connor explicitly adopted the post–New Deal philosophy of judicial restraint by quoting with approval the following passage from the 1946 case of *United States ex. rel. TVA* v. *Welch*:

> Any departure from this judicial restraint would result in *courts deciding on what is or is not a governmental function* and in their invalidating legislation on the basis of their view on that question at the moment of decision, a practice that has proved impractical in other fields.[21]

Consequently, she accepted a standard of review that would uphold the legislation "where the exercise of the eminent domain clause is *rationally related to a conceivable public purpose*"[22]—the rational-basis test that no statute can fail.

Moreover, the Court accepted the proposition that the Fifth Amendment requirement of "public use" was satisfied upon the enunciation of a legitimate "public purpose," concluding that "redistribution of fees simple to correct deficiencies in the market attributable to land oligopoly is a rational exercise of the eminent domain power."[23]

In short, in the name of judicial restraint, the Supreme Court of the United States could not inquire as to whether there was an actual problem to be solved, whether any alleged problem was the genuine motivation of the legislation, whether the means chosen were likely to accomplish the end, or whether there might have

[20]467 U.S. 229 (1984).

[21]327 U.S. 546 (1946), pp. 240–41 (emphasis added).

[22]Ibid., p. 241 (emphasis added).

[23]Ibid., p. 243. For a detailed description of the difference between these two approaches to the takings clause of the Fifth Amendment, see R. Epstein, *Takings: Private Property and the Power of Eminent Domain* (Cambridge, Mass.: Harvard University Press, 1985).

been less-restrictive alternatives available to the state. Imagine the hue and cry if, instead of being a Fifth Amendment takings case, the Supreme Court applied this see-no-evil approach to the First Amendment. In this manner has economic liberty become the bastard child of the Constitution.

The Constitutional Alternative: Judicial Vigilance

The theory of the Constitution before the adoption of the Bill of Rights was that the people retain their rights while delegating specific powers to their agents in government—in the same manner that principals delegate to their agents the power to act on their behalf while retaining their rights. Without meaningful judicial scrutiny of assertions of governmental authority or power, the people or the principals in this relationship would be at the mercy of their agents, who could then define their mandate in any manner they choose. Only violent revolution would be available to police the relationship.

The Bill of Rights was demanded because sole reliance on the strategy of securing liberty by restricting government powers was thought by many to be far too risky. Constitutional rights were needed to supplement a scrutiny of powers as a kind of redundant safety system for the protection of liberty. Certain rights were enumerated in what became the first eight amendments. But to counter any later argument that these were the only rights retained by the people, James Madison drafted the Ninth Amendment.[24]

His version originally read:

> The exceptions here or elsewhere in the Constitution, made in favor of particular rights, shall not be construed to diminish the just importance of other rights retained by the people, or as to enlarge the powers delegated by the Constitution; but either as actual limitations of such powers, or as inserted merely for greater caution.[25]

In other words, the enumerated rights serve two functions: They are a redundant safeguard against an expansion of government power and they further restrict federal power by regulating the

[24]See Randy E. Barnett, "Reconceiving the Ninth Amendment," *Cornell Law Review* 75 (forthcoming).

[25]*Annals of Congress*, vol. 1, p. 452.

means by which certain permissible government ends may be pursued. In neither case did their enumeration reflect a belief by the framers that the people retained no other rights than those listed.

If Congress is held within a narrow conception of its powers, we can expect the conflict between legislative powers and individual rights to be rare (though still possible). As government powers begin to expand, however, the need to protect individual rights also expands. In short, the enumerated and unenumerated rights of the people assume increased importance as the scope of government begins to increase.

Moreover, the original Constitution prohibited the states from impairing the obligations of contract—a provision that was swiftly rendered functionless. The enactment of the Fourteenth Amendment in the 19th century, however, brought an end to the complete autonomy of state legislatures. Like those of Congress, their enactments became the proper subject of federal judicial scrutiny.

The abdication by the judiciary of its role in restricting the scope of government powers threatens liberty and impinges on individual rights. When this occurs, the abdication of judicial protection of individual rights eliminates any check on the political process. It is no accident that Mr. Filburn's lawyers challenged the Agricultural Adjustment Act of 1938 as being beyond the enumerated powers of Congress and in violation of Mr. Filburn's Fifth Amendment rights.

What Lies Ahead?

What lies ahead in the post-Reagan years is anybody's guess. Much, of course, depends upon the judicial appointments made by the next president. But the real uncertainty comes from the judicial and constitutional philosophy promoted during the Reagan years—a philosophy that is, to borrow a phrase from Judge Bork, "at war with itself."[26] Which strain wins out—interpretivism or judicial restraint—will determine whether we rediscover and enforce the provisions in the Constitution that safeguard economic liberties or whether we continue to turn our backs on the constitutional rights of those who—to the great benefit of us all—find their sustenance and fulfillment in the marketplace.

[26]Robert R. Bork, *The Antitrust Paradox: A Policy at War with Itself* (New York: Basic Books, 1978).

28. Civil Rights as a Principle Versus Civil Rights as an Interest

Clarence Thomas

My comments on civil rights will take a broad perspective, which reflects my experiences in seven years in the Reagan administration.[1] In 1980 I was confident that great strides could be made on behalf of individual liberty. Now, I take comfort in having made several relatively modest but significant reforms.[2] Although we are able to take credit for much good, I believe that the administration's efforts did go awry, in both rhetoric and substance.[3] Perhaps its faults can best be examined if I focus on one particular theme: our failures to enunciate a principled understanding of what we were about and to articulate the meaning of individual rights and how we might best defend them.

Let me begin with a quotation from that august journal of learning, the *New York Review of Books.* Professor Ronald Dworkin, who rivals the sainted John Rawls in some circles, concludes his trashing of Robert Bork as follows:

> Our constitutional tradition is jeopardized as much by that policy of stagnation as by outright repeal [of civil rights laws], because the heart of that tradition is the idea of constitutional integrity—that the freedom and dignity recognized for one group of Americans, in one set of decisions, must be available to all other

[1] I wish to acknowledge the research assistance of Ken Masugi and John Marini.

[2] I am still amazed that the *Washington Post*, of all sources, praised the Equal Employment Opportunity Commission (EEOC) in a recent editorial. "The EEOC Is Thriving," *Washington Post*, August 1, 1987, p. A22.

[3] Another examination of my experiences in the Reagan administration can be found in my remarks at the Heritage Foundation, "Why Black Americans Should Look to Conservative Policies," June 18, 1987.

groups with equal moral claims. So long as Bork rejects that ideal of constitutional integrity, that tradition is not safe in his hands.[4]

Let me dissent. It reflected disgracefully on the whole nomination process that Judge Bork is not now Justice Bork.

But the issue of Judge Bork aside, Dworkin does go to the core of the civil rights debate today. Dworkin correctly notes the primacy of the principle of freedom and dignity, but I think he misunderstands the substance of that principle. He reveals his error by applying his principle to groups, rather than to individuals. For it is above all the protection of *individual* rights that America, in its best moments, has in its heart and mind.

To develop and implement a just civil rights policy, the Reagan administration had first to make clear its principled understanding of this issue. Simply put, we failed to do so—not because we lacked commitment to equal justice under law, but because we did not present our case for civil rights on the highest possible plane. In this way, we complemented the failure of the Supreme Court to deal adequately with race-related issues. It is nowhere clearer than in the field of jurisprudence how distant the Court and the political branches remain from an understanding of the principles of equality and liberty that make us one nation. Thus has civil rights become entrenched as an interest-group issue rather than an issue of principle and universal significance for all individuals.

The Foundation of Civil Rights

Let me attempt to recover that foundation of individual liberties and indicate how such an approach might have benefited the administration. It is easy enough to blame the Court for "voodoo jurisprudence," but Congress must share a great deal of the blame. I begin by sketching very briefly the development of civil rights law since *Brown* v. *Board of Education,* in 1954.[5] The main problem with the Court's opinions in the area of race is that it never had an

[4]Ronald Dworkin, "The Bork Nomination: An Exchange," *New York Review of Books*, October 8, 1987, p. 61. Dworkin was replying to M. B. E. Smith, who had written in response to Dworkin's original piece, "The Bork Nomination," *New York Review of Books*, August 13, 1987, pp. 3–10.

[5]349 U.S. 294 (1954). I have developed some of these themes more fully in "Toward a 'Plain Reading' of the Constitution—The Declaration of Independence in Constitutional Interpretation," *Howard Law Journal* 30, no. 4 (1987): 691–703.

392

adequate principle in the great *Brown* precedent to proceed from. Psychological evidence, compassion, and a failure to connect segregation with the evil of slavery prevented the Court from ending segregation as a matter of simple justice. Then, 14 years later, in the *Green* v. *County Board of Education* case,[6] we discovered that *Brown* not only ended segregation but required school integration. And then began a disastrous series of cases requiring busing and other policies that were irrelevant to parents' concern for a decent education. The Court appeared in these and many other cases to be more concerned with meeting the demands of groups than with protecting the rights of individuals. I could go into other cases, but the principle, or rather the lack of principle, is clear enough. In a good cause, the Court was attempting to argue *against* what was best in the American political tradition.

I must now turn to Congress, for it compounded the Court's errors, especially following the great expansion of national power and the development of the administrative state in the 1960s. These distinct but related developments go far toward explaining the present status of civil rights. Despite the changes in the civil rights movement, much of the fervor remains. It must never be forgotten that men and women gave their lives for the cause of civil rights. No other domestic issue of this century compares with it, so conservatives should not be surprised at the ferocity with which the heirs of the civil rights movement react when they are attacked.

When Congress ceases to function as a representative and a deliberative body—with the principal task of general lawmaking—the unorganized public is the great loser. No other institution in democratic society can perform the task of deliberation and representation. Congress is the only place where a reasonable attempt can be made to reconcile public and private interests with a view to the common good. In fact, no other institution can bring about the kind of consensus that occurs when majorities are created in support of particular measures.

In turning our attention to the case of civil rights legislation, perhaps it can be said that we get the kind of enforcement of civil rights laws—including race and gender preferences—that powerful members of Congress desire. This is not to say that Congress as an

---

[6]391 U.S. 430 (1968).

institution has been willing or able to pass laws that explicitly mandate affirmative action. On the contrary, Congress as a body is rarely able to get support for specific, controversial policies that benefit some and harm others. Typically, Congress enacts laws that are quite general, noncontroversial, and apparently beneficial to all. There is the expectation, however, that the bureaucracy charged with administering the laws will be responsive to the demands of interested parties and their spokesmen, whether committee members or special-interest groups. In doing so, policy implementation reflects the interests of the few taking precedence over the interests of the many. The outcome can be administration of the laws in a manner that produces results that are diametrically opposed to the language of the law itself. I need only point, once again, to the case of policies of gender and race preference. Here we have the 1964 Civil Rights Act administered and interpreted by the bureaucracy and the courts in a manner far different from the law as passed by the legislature. Yet, it is hard to believe that the bureaucracy can flaunt the clear intent of the law and the lawmaking body without the support of critical members of the political communities—public and private—as well as important committee members concerned with such legislation. The bureaucracy and courts appear to have provided the institutional means by which members of Congress can be insulated from a hostile public when public policy has little popular support. When laws are administered or interpreted in dubious or controversial ways, the bureaucracy or the courts get the blame. On the other hand, by strategic intervention, members of Congress can get credit from those who benefit from the law or its implementation.

The courts, however, have proved less than satisfactory as the final arbiters in the administrative process. There is no question that courts have entered the policymaking process in an important way. But the founders purposely insulated the courts from popular pressures, on the assumption that they should not make policy decisions. The judiciary was protected to ensure justice for individuals. This required insulating judges from other groups or interests in society, even the interests of a majority. However, it was unthinkable that courts would take the side of particular groups in the policymaking arena. This, incidentally, was a major error in the strategy of the civil rights establishment in opposing Judge Bork.

By turning Supreme Court nominations into power struggles, they transform the Court into another majoritarian institution. How, then, can it protect the rights of politically unpopular minorities?

The Politicization of Civil Rights

When political decisions have been made by judges, they have lacked the moral authority of the majority. Courts have played a small part in policymaking until recently, precisely because they were not thought to be suited to the task of policymaking. When they have made important political and social decisions in the absence of majority support, they have only exacerbated the controversies they have pronounced on. Despite the supposed neutrality of the courts, few people would suggest that judges' training makes them better suited than elected officials to make *political*—as opposed to judicial—decisions. The dignity of the judiciary is not enhanced by its politicization.

Let us look once more at the Civil Rights Act of 1964 as an example of the way this process has worked. We note that Congress passed a general law in relatively clear language. Subsequently, though, as in the case of Title VII of the act, the law was interpreted in a very different way.

The Court has made rather creative interpretations of equal protection and legislative intent in a number of civil rights cases beginning with *Regents of the University of California* v. *Bakke*. The egregious example was *United Steel Workers* v. *Weber*, back in 1979, followed by recent decisions such as *Local 28 of the Sheet Metal Workers' International Association* v. *EEOC* and *Johnson* v. *Transportation Agency, Santa Clara County*.[7] In each case, Congress could have reinterpreted its legislative intent to rebut the interpretation of Justice Brennan in *Weber*. But of course it demurred, some members throwing blame on the Court and others praising the Court for recognizing what Congress intended all along. Does any of this cause great concern to members of Congress? Not really. Congress is not held accountable by the general public for the manner in which a law is implemented or interpreted. Rather, Congress, as a body, was generally credited with passing a reasonable and noble law, which had the

[7]*Bakke* 438 U.S. 265 (1978); *Weber* 443 U.S. 193 (1979); *Local 28* 106 S. Ct. 3019 (1986); *Johnson* 107 S. Ct. 1442 (1987).

support of the majority. It no longer bore responsibility for the Court's interpretation.

Once a law is passed, the action shifts to implementation—or Congress as administrator. Here, individual members get credit by pleasing those interested groups who have a stake in certain policy outcomes. Perhaps that is why the most controversial questions concerning contemporary politics have been decided in the administrative and judicial arena and also why the bureaucracy and the courts have been placed at the center of politics and public policymaking. And, interestingly enough, it has been with the blessing of Congress itself. Congress has put itself in the position of not only being able to take all the credit for the good laws it passes but also being able to blame the courts or the bureaucracy whenever the interest groups provide enough pressure.

Not that there is a great deal of principle in Congress itself. What can one expect of a Congress that would pass the ethnic set-aside law the Court upheld in *Fullilove* v. *Klutznick*?[8] What the two branches were saying is this: the Court can reinterpret civil rights laws to create schemes of racial preference where none was ever contemplated. And Congress can devise laws justifying racial and ethnic set-asides on the basis of its powers to regulate interstate commerce. Any "equal protection component" of the Fifth Amendment due process clause is irrelevant. Thus the Court sweeps aside any limits on its powers over individuals, including the ethnic minorities this legislation allegedly benefits. It is interesting to note that Drew S. Days, III, assistant attorney general for civil rights in the Carter administration and one who argued the case before the Court, has criticized the decision in a reflective essay in the *Yale Law Journal*.[9] Days attacked the sloppiness of that legislation as well as that of other affirmative action schemes that make crude distributions of goods such as contracts or jobs. Whether this criticism represents more a virtual abandonment of a bad principle or a shift in tactics remains to be seen. But it is reassuring to see that the crudity of such legislation is evident even to those who once supported it. The tragedy for civil rights is that it has become confused with pork barrel, as even its partisans now concede. And when that confusion

[8] 448 U.S. 448 (1980).
[9] "Fullilove," *Yale Law Journal* 96 (January 1987): 453–85.

takes place, civil rights can be bartered and sold by Congress, the bureaucracy, and even the courts.

Having been critical of the overemphasis on "affirmative action," I am hesitant to say more about it at this time. Let me say for now that what is known as affirmative action arose precisely because of the congressional and bureaucratic attitudes I have sketched above. And they have been abetted by lazy businesses, especially large corporations. I am confident it can be shown, and some of my staff are now working on this question, that blacks at any level, especially white-collar employees, have simply not benefited from affirmative action policies as they have developed. Therefore, it is wrong for politicians to focus implicitly on blacks when attacking "affirmative action." Such an attack, however justified on the principle of color-blindness, places the blame primarily on blacks, who have not been helped. No one in this country should be made the fall guy for some other person's easy way of solving problems. And this resentment is what hiring-by-the-numbers policies have produced. A positive civil rights policy would aim at reducing barriers to employment, instead of trying to get "good numbers." Those who have been in the government know the artificial barriers to hiring someone you want. That is the sort of practice we should be seeking to eliminate. That is the sort of affirmative action I practice at my agency.

Congress, a political scientist recently observed, reflects "great individual responsiveness, equally great collective irresponsibility."[10] I have attempted to elaborate on a few reasons why Congress as an institution has not succeeded in its responsibility to govern in the full light of day. I have tried to make clear why so much of its day-to-day activity involves oversight of the executive branch bureaucracy and why it has become necessary, in the administrative state, for individual members of Congress to be especially responsive to organized special interests. I have also tried, briefly, to indicate why this situation poses problems for good, effective, and constitutional government.

Thus we return to the old, fundamental issue of the separation of powers. To understand properly the problem with civil rights

[10]Gary C. Jacobson, *The Politics of Congressional Elections* (Boston: Little, Brown, 1983), p. 189.

today, one must keep in mind the rise of the administrative state and the transformation of Congress. To focus exclusively on the Supreme Court is to miss the point. Quick-fix solutions, such as the appointment of another justice with the right views, are not enough to ensure protection of our freedoms.

Thus, I cannot resist adding a note here to the recent discussion of the meaning of the Ninth Amendment. ("The enumeration in the Constitution, of certain rights, shall not be construed to deny or disparage others retained by the people.") It relates directly to our theme of civil rights and the courts. Some senators and scholars are horrified by Judge Bork's dismissal of the Ninth Amendment, as others were horrified by Justice Arthur Goldberg's discovery, or rather invention, of it in *Griswold* v. *Connecticut*.[11] But the Ninth Amendment has to be considered in its context at the founding.

We should recall that Alexander Hamilton, later the architect of early American national prosperity, argued against a bill of rights. This was not due to a hostility toward individual rights, as some commentators later insisted. Rather, he maintained that the entire Constitution was itself a bill of rights, which limited government power. To add a series of amendments that would explicitly deny to the national government certain powers over various subjects would imply that those subjects, and perhaps others besides, could be regulated in other, unspecified ways. But in government of limited powers, each use of political power would have to be approved under the Constitution. That President Reagan had to speak out on behalf of an "economic bill of rights" is a point in Hamilton's favor. After all, we have today ignored economic liberties as a vital part of the rights protected by constitutional government. Once a bill of rights was required for the passage of the Constitution, it would appear that the Ninth and Tenth amendments meet Hamilton's original objection. If we understand the Ninth Amendment thus, it has a great significance in that it reminds us that the Constitution is a document of limited government. And I daresay the great majority of those who were berating Judge Bork for slighting the Ninth Amendment were scarcely proponents of limited government.

A major question remains: Does the Ninth Amendment, as Justice

[11]381 U.S. 479 (1965).

398

Goldberg contended, give to the Supreme Court certain powers to strike down legislation? That would seem to be a blank check. The Court could designate something to be a right and then strike down any law it thought violated that right. And Congress might also use its powers to protect such rights—say a "right" to welfare. But the Court is the more interesting case for our speculation, because Congress already has virtually unlimited power, as the *Fullilove* case indicates. Must not the Court be able to check Congress? Let's say the Court did discover a right to welfare. Then one can imagine it requiring Congress to raise taxes to enforce this right. And one can readily imagine Congress acquiescing. After all, a congressman can plead, the Court did it, and they are simply obeying the requirements of the Constitution, and we are obeying the Court. In a nutshell, this is the problem with using the Ninth Amendment. Maximization of rights is perfectly compatible with total government and regulation. Unbounded by notions of obligation and justice, the desire to protect rights simply plays into the hands of those who advocate a total state. The rhetoric of freedom (license, really) encourages the expansion of bureaucratic government. Readers of this volume should know F. A. Hayek's distinction between freedom and freedoms, between a fundamental principle and various benefits found in free societies.[12] Far from being a protection, the Ninth Amendment will likely become an additional weapon for the enemies of freedom.

The Revival of Limited Government

The always arduous task of preserving freedom was a simpler task when limited government was respected. The question now becomes, How do we achieve this great object? That its defense is still possible is seen in the testimony of Oliver North before the congressional Iran-contra committee. Partly disarmed by his attorneys' insistence on avoiding closed sessions, the committee beat an ignominious retreat before North's direct attack on it and, by extension, on all of Congress. This shows that the people, when not presented with distorted reporting by the media, do retain and act on their common sense and good judgment, and that members of

---

[12]See, for example, F. A. Hayek, *The Road to Serfdom* (Chicago: University of Chicago, 1944).

Congress can listen if their attention is grabbed. Self-government need not be an illusion!

Americans first proclaimed this desire for self-government in the Declaration of Independence. Here, as Lincoln put it, lies "the father of all moral principle" in Americans. Equality means equality of individual rights, an equality resting on the laws of nature and of nature's God. Among those rights are life, liberty, and the pursuit of happiness. Because no man is the natural ruler of another, government must proceed by consent. And that, in turn, requires representation, elections, and separation of powers. These are the requirements of free government, and they rest on a moral conception of human worth, based on human nature.

Perhaps the most powerful contemporary statement defending freedom based on our founding principles comes from an address more noted for its controversial couplet, "Extremism in the defense of liberty is no vice. . . moderation in the pursuit of justice is no virtue."

If one reads Barry Goldwater's 1964 speech accepting the Republican nomination for the presidency, one sees how little the political world has changed, even after two terms of Ronald Reagan. The threats to freedom remain as strong as ever, both at home and abroad. The power of the central government has grown dramatically since 1964, as has the Soviet menace. But the speech's most famous words implied to many listeners—it certainly did to me then, a high school student—an endorsement of extremist groups, such as the Ku Klux Klan and the John Birch Society, which were so hotly disputed during the convention. But one must reread the whole speech to see that such a conclusion is wrong.

Allow me to recall some of the stirring passages from Goldwater's speech:

> We Republicans see in our constitutional form of government the great framework which assures the orderly but dynamic fulfillment of the whole man, and we see the whole man as the great reason for instituting orderly government in the first place.
>
> We can see in private property and in economy based upon and fostering private property the one way to make government a durable ally of the whole man rather than his determined enemy.
>
> We can see in the sanctity of private property the only durable foundation for constitutional government in a free society.
>
> And beyond that we see and cherish diversity of ways, diversity

400

of thoughts, of motives, and accomplishments. We don't seek to live anyone's life for him. We only seek to secure his rights, guarantee him opportunity, guarantee him opportunity to strive with government performing only those needed and constitutionally sanctioned tasks which cannot otherwise be performed.[13]

This eloquence and good sense notwithstanding, the Goldwater nomination was a decisive step in a longstanding estrangement of the black vote from the Republican party. The Arizona senator's defense of freedom was not enough to persuade black Americans to stay with the party of Lincoln—not after his opposition to the 1964 Civil Rights Act, the major modern legislative development in the assurance of equality of rights for black Americans. But what would happen if conservatives were to prove their embrace of the civil rights revolution, through their steadfast support of the 1964 and 1965 acts? Wouldn't conservatism and the cause of civil rights then be on the same side, the right side? There is nothing in Goldwater's speech that conservatives today, black Americans, and others affected by civil rights laws could not wholeheartedly agree upon. And unless Americans begin to take seriously Goldwater's warning, our troubles may prove overwhelming.

To illustrate my point about reinforcing the cause of civil rights, let me quote briefly from another widely cited address:

> The glory of this land has been its capacity for transcending the moral evils of our past. For example, the long struggle of minority citizens for equal rights once a source of disunity and civil war is now a point of pride for all Americans. We must never go back. There is no room for racism, anti-semitism or other forms of ethnic and racial hatred in this country. . . . Use the mighty voice of your pulpits and the powerful standing of your churches to denounce and isolate those in our midst.

You may recognize the speaker of these lines from his later reference to the Soviet Union as "an evil empire."[14] President Reagan's speech to the National Association of Evangelicals is not remembered for its words about civil rights. But his point, as I take it, is that we must continue to recognize evil and call it for what it is, whether

---

[13]July 16, 1964; reprinted in *Vital Speeches of the Day*, August 15, 1964, p. 644.

[14]Ronald Reagan, "Remarks of the President to the 41st Annual Convention of the National Association of Evangelicals," March 8, 1983, pp. 6, 8.

we find it abroad or at home. The zeal needed to fight tyranny abroad is the same quality of soul needed to fight for freedom at home. For freedom is an indivisible cause. And it can once again, in another administration, reunite Americans.

A civil rights policy based on principle, replacing the one based on interest-group advantages, would be a blessing not only for black Americans but for all Americans. That is what I have been working for as chairman of the EEOC. Partisans of freedom should be alert to seizing the opportunities as well as warning of obstacles awaiting them.

PART VII

THE REAGAN LEGACY

29. A Record of Success

Malcolm S. Forbes, Jr.

Given the realities of the world and the frailties of human beings, the Reagan administration's economic policy to date has to be judged an enormous success. The chief achievement of the Reagan presidency is the massive reductions in individual income-tax rates. The benefits that have resulted from those tax reductions outweigh all of the shortcomings and missed opportunities in other areas of the administration's economic policy.

Taxes are not simply a means of raising revenue; they are also a price. The taxes on our income, capital gains, and corporate profits are the price we pay for the privilege of working, the price we pay for being productive, and the price we pay for being innovative and successful. If the price of those things is too high, we get fewer of them. If the price is lowered, we'll get more of them.

The Kemp-Roth bill of 1981 and the tax reform bill of 1986 reduced individual income-tax rates to levels we hadn't seen in 60 or 70 years. Too many of our policymakers ignore the simple fact that *people* make an economy run—*people* manage companies, not investment tax credits or accelerated depreciation schedules.

To see evidence of that, all we have to do is look at Japan and Britain. Japan's corporate income taxes are about twice as high as ours. By contrast, for almost 30 years Britain had some of the most liberal business depreciation investment incentives and laws in the Western world. Which country has invested more in the past 30 years, Japan or Britain? Which country has had more economic growth? To ask those questions is to answer them. If people have an incentive to get ahead—if they're able to keep enough of what they earn through their labor and innovation—then the economy as a whole benefits, even if some of the traditional business incentives aren't in force.

The tax reforms of 1981 and 1986 are forcing states to reduce their marginal rates, and they're going to force other industrialized countries to reduce their onerous rates as well. We live in an age of mobility. Brains and money are mobile; they go where the opportunities are. Today the opportunities are more likely to be found in the United States than in most other industrialized nations. Why do we have a capital inflow? It's not because we are big spenders. Nor is it because we have high interest rates—if that were the reason, money would have been going to the Philippines or Zaire. Capital has been coming to this country because there are more opportunities here.

Our tax rate reductions will force other industrialized countries to lower their tax rates not because of anything we might say but because of the sheer pressure of events. In fact, several countries have already begun to compete with each other to do so. The Canadians have made a halting start; the British have said that they will be reducing their rates; the other Europeans are taking small steps; the Japanese are stumbling in that direction. So it's not just the United States that will benefit from our recent rate reductions; other nations will benefit from them as well—assuming, of course, that Congress doesn't tamper with the tax code again, which is an awfully big assumption. But if the debate in 1988 goes well, the reduced rates will remain in force, and that's going to have a powerful impact on our economy and on those of the Western world.

One of the shortcomings in the economic policy of the Reagan years is that the administration did not push privatization, in every area from the Postal Service to Pentagon procurement, as early or as persuasively as it should have. In terms of cutting back programs or eliminating bad programs and curbing the growth of spending, the administration's record, to be charitable, is very mixed. Its monetary policies have been rather erratic, its approach to Third World debt rather disappointing. The administration doesn't seem to realize that Third World countries are in trouble not because of their indebtedness—which is not much worse than, say, that of Canada or Australia at the turn of the century—but because of being overtaxed, overbureaucratized, and overregulated. The Baker plan showed promise, but unfortunately there was very little effective follow-through on it. But in an imperfect world, the administration can be excused for those shortcomings, grave though they may be, because of what it has done on the tax front.

Economic Hypochondriacs

The success of the administration's tax reforms is evident from the vitriol of its opponents. Certain scholars, policymakers, and politicos seem to be prone to a kind of hypochondria when it comes to looking at the U.S. economy. From what those people write about trade, for example, you would think that America was in the red and Japan was in the black. What gets overlooked is that a trade deficit or surplus is simply a number and that its significance depends upon the particular situation. During the first 100 years of its existence, for example, the United States routinely ran trade deficits. Fortunately, in those days we didn't have an IMF or a World Bank to tell us that we were doing the wrong thing. As a result of our ignorance, we became a great industrial nation.

Japan ran big trade deficits in the 1950s and the early 1960s. It's very amusing to read what some of our experts wrote about Japan in the 1950s. They didn't write about the emergence of a giant that would humble many of our traditional industries. They wrote about what a hopeless basket case Japan was, and they often cited its large trade deficits. The Japanese were wise enough not to translate that analysis into their language, and we can see what being unaware of it did for them. By contrast, Mexico and Brazil have trade surpluses, but I doubt that even Louisiana or Texas would trade its economy for that of Mexico or Brazil.

Our large trade deficit is a sign of our strength, not our weakness. In the past four or five years our economy has grown more than those of most other nations. We've had enough money and credit to buy more goods and services from them than they have been able to buy from us. If it had not been for the American market, Europe's economy would be even more stagnant than it is, the Third World would be in even worse financial shape, and even Japan would have had considerably lower growth rates.

We've done what a great power is supposed to do: we've carried the rest of the world with us, and we've benefited from doing so as well. If the economies of other nations had grown as much as ours has, if they had done to their tax codes what we have done to ours, and if they had pushed deregulation the way we, at least sometimes, have, they would now be in a position to buy more goods and services from us, and our trade deficit would go the way of the oil shortage.

In short, a trade deficit is neither a good thing nor a bad thing per se; it depends on the circumstances. Look at West Germany. Its economy is weak in many critical respects. Its unemployment rate is high, its job-creation record is unimpressive, and it trails the United States in many areas of technology. But West Germany does have a trade surplus, and it sometimes acts as if it were the Tarzan of the international economy. Because of that one number, the West Germans think they're doing very well.

The chief reason for our budget deficit is not that we have had insufficient revenues but that until two years ago there was a rip-roaring increase in government spending. However, our revenues have grown considerably in the past four or five years. Moreover, if you look at what might be called the net government deficit—the combined federal, state, and local deficits and surpluses—as a proportion of GNP, you'll find that we've probably done better than the Japanese and not much worse than the West Europeans. That doesn't mean that we've done a good job; it just means that almost everyone else in the world has done as bad a job as we have.

In addition, the federal, state, and local governments' combined investment is very high. (Of course, that raises the question of whether governments should be making those kinds of investments. Much of that investing should probably be done by the private sector.) So if you compare the net government deficit with the net government investment, you'll find that our books are almost in balance on an expense level.

The economic hypochondriacs claim that we are a spendthrift nation. You'd never know it from reading what they write, but the net wealth of the American people in real terms is higher today than it's ever been. Our assets have been growing much faster than our liabilities. They also claim that we don't invest enough, but as Alan Reynolds, George Gilder, and others have pointed out, whereas our investment rate has been going up in recent years, those of Japan and Western Europe have been going down.

Contrary to the economic hypochondriacs, manufacturing is the same proportion of our economy today as it was 30 years ago. What we make and how we make it have changed, but our ability to make things has remained basically unchanged. Since the 1982 recession 13½ million jobs have been created, a very large percentage of which have been high-paying jobs. Even though we really misused and abused the economy during the 1970s, in the past 18 years or so we've created over 30 million jobs—more jobs than exist in West Germany, which has the largest economy in Western Europe.

The Intellectual Debate

The administration has failed not in the areas to which the economic hypochondriacs point but in the intellectual debate—the ideological battle. Its opponents have raised the concern that we lack compassion. In our inner cities, we see more illegitimacy, more illiteracy, more crime, more broken families, and more members of a permanent underclass today than ever before. Those conditions, as Charles Murray and others have demonstrated, can be traced directly to social engineering on the state and federal levels. And yet the policies that have had such miserable results remain in effect because they reassure us that we are compassionate. If a law has a "compassionate" purpose, we overlook the fact that the people it was intended to help have actually been hurt by it.

The administration's opponents have been allowed to get away with promoting that way of thinking. It's sort of the equivalent of the days of religious wars, when they would burn you at the stake and you weren't supposed to mind that because it was going to save your soul. The administration has given its opponents a free ride in the intellectual debate.

Unfortunately, even in circles that should know better, people have been buying the notion that the prosperity we've enjoyed during the past few years is the result of selfishness and therefore lacks moral legitimacy. They read about the Ivan Boeskys of the world, and somehow those incidents seem to cast aspersions on our economic gains.

If we're going to succeed in preserving our recent gains and making new gains, we must get across the notion that the free enterprise system does not appeal to the worst part of human nature but brings out the best in people. We must get across the notion that free enterprise gives basic rights to the individual and that letting people develop their talents to the fullest so as to meet the needs and wants of others, whether perceived or unperceived, is moral as well as productive. We must get across the notion that the free enterprise system encourages people to channel their energies into constructive paths instead of the destructive paths that we see being followed in other nations' economies. Some progress has been made in those areas, but not nearly enough.

When people say that we can't let things be determined by the market, we've got to ask, "What is the market?" The market consists of people. When we talk about the discipline of the market, we're talking about individuals deciding whether to buy what's being offered to them. The nation is a democracy in terms of economics as well as politics, but until we get that point across to the public, we're going to be vulnerable to counterattacks by our ideological opponents.

Members of the administration have been weak on attacking mercantilism and beggar-thy-neighbor policies. They know that the proposed trade bill would probably have bad results. They know how much damage the Smoot-Hawley tariff did in the 1930s. But they've allowed their opponents to set the terms of the debate, and they've failed to refute the argument that we need protectionism in order to preserve jobs. We have to start pointing out that protectionism is a tax and that a protectionist trade policy would make it a crime for working people to buy a VCR. We have to bring it down to the individual level.

Progress and Change

Change, not stability, is the chief characteristic of the U.S. economy. Progress always involves change, and change is sometimes unsettling. Throughout American history there have been periods that seemed like a hurricane of change, yet the nation has always emerged from those periods the stronger for having weathered the storm.

If we learn to cope with change, virtually all of us will have a chance to advance. If we interfere with change in an attempt to preserve a mythical past, we will diminish not only our present opportunities but our future ones. What makes that fact so difficult to get across is that people don't know what they will miss if they succeed in preventing change. If we had blocked the development of the automobile, we wouldn't know that it could have increased our mobility and transformed society. The real danger is that we will fail to make people understand that they will deprive themselves of future benefits if they keep change from happening.

410

I'm an optimist. I believe that if the debate is properly framed—
if the right people take up the right cudgels—we will have an
environment in which we can build on the administration's success
in reducing tax rates and make more progress in promoting free
enterprise. My feeling is that when historians look back on this
period, they will conclude that the nation's economy and political
system had once again confounded the critics, the skeptics, and the
crepe-hangers, thus enabling America to reassume its rightful role
as the leader and inspiration of the world.

30. The Intellectual Debate

Paul H. Weaver

When my friends at the Cato Institute asked if I would talk about the intellectual debate in the age of Reagan, I quickly said yes. Now that I've had a chance to ponder the subject for a while, I wonder if I shouldn't have been slower to agree. For the intellectual debate in the Reagan years, as a phrase, doesn't summon forth an abundance of large and invigorating thoughts. On the contrary, it sounds like the answer to a bad joke that begins, What's the shortest, dullest book in the world?

There is an important exception to this statement that I'll get to later, but in broad outline, the public discourse in the eighties has been pretty much a zero. Not since the political black hole that was World War II—not since the mindless 1920s—has political debate been so drab and dishonest. In the White House and on Capitol Hill, among the agencies and on the hustings, at the think tanks and in the magazines, I believe the past seven years will be remembered not for illuminating debate or galvanizing new ideas, but for hustling, hypocrisy, lying, sleaze, and stasis. It has been an era in which our leaders have sucked the last drops of life out of the dying ideas and concerns of earlier decades. It has been an era in which institutions have avoided and fuzzed up issues, not defined and confronted them. It has been an era in which technique has flourished and substance has withered.

The fifties, by contrast, were a period of political ferment beneath a placid Republican surface. The sixties brought an explosion of ideas and movements—civil rights, antiwar activism, student rebellion, black power, poverty, and redistribution. The seventies were, if anything, even more interesting and consequential. Suddenly Americans were grappling with issues of personal morality, from feminism to bioethics; the market idea returned in a blaze of glory after almost a century's eclipse; isolationist and Wilsonian concepts of foreign policy made comebacks as liberal globalist interventionism crumbled; there was growing debate over the roles of Congress, the president, the courts, and the press; and our historic national commitments to economic and demographic growth were reconsidered. Over the course of these rich and fascinating decades, the rise, flowering, and collapse of the political movement we call liberalism occasioned a veritable torrent of ideas, debate, and intellectual ferment.

In Ronald Reagan's America, the great debates have dealt with the deficit, terrorism, sleaze, Teflon, how little the president knows and how long his naps are, morning in America, AIDS, adultery, Soviet cheating on treaties, and whether Miller Lite has more taste or is less filling. The best-selling books have described Jane Fonda's viewpoint on aerobic exercise, how to be a 60-second manager, and the life and times of the chief executive officer of the smallest car company in the United States as told to William Novak. In recent years, how have we spelled the intellectual debate? B-O-R-I-N-G, that's how.

The reason public discussion has been so mindless is not that there are no ideas or currents of change abroad in the land. To the contrary, beneath the surface, a lot is going on in the political culture. But this ferment has been largely hidden from public view by the interesting and depressing phenomenon called Ronald Reagan.

Reagan swept into Washington as the leader of what both friends and enemies believed would be a conservative revolution. Looking back as he prepares to depart, it's clear that President Reagan dominated the scene like no one since Franklin Delano Roosevelt, but there was no revolution. He kept the nation from reverting to liberalism, but he had little impact on its policies and made little contribution to its sense of direction.

Reagan was a brilliant political leader, articulating the beliefs of groups that had been disaffected from liberalism and rallying them to his cause. He believed in traditional values, the free market, and anticommunism, and through the warmth of his personality and sincerity of his conviction, he crystallized a new public mood. And it wasn't just talk. Unlike his Republican predecessors, Reagan appointed any number of true believers to important positions. In the 1980s, anti-Communists, free-marketeers, and supporters of traditional values were no longer pariahs inside the beltway. The

Reaganites, many of whom were extremely talented, did well in the Washington community, and more than a few of them are now to be found throughout the upper and middle levels of the capital's law firms, public relations consultancies, think tanks, lobbying groups, and news organizations.

But Reagan's striking rhetoric led to few changes in policy or political culture. This was partly because, beneath the common opposition to liberalism, the viewpoints assembled under the banner of Reaganism were wildly at odds with one another. There was Christian fundamentalism, which was far from neoconservatism, and neither the fundamentalists nor the neoconservatives had the least bit in common with the libertarians, ethnic Catholics, or country club Republicans. Since there wasn't much the president's constituents actually agreed on besides throwing the liberal rascals out, it was hard for the administration to do much of anything.

The incredible internal diversity of the administration has turned Reagan's winning personal qualities—the aw-shucks, all-American charm, the unintense, nonanalytical intellectual style, the breezy moralism—into a crippling liability for a president. This was one administration that really required a firm hand at the helm and a clear mind and penetrating vision at the top if it was to get anywhere. Ronald Reagan has many virtues, but they don't include the intellectual power and moral insight needed to pull the complex strands of the nation's politics together in a coherent political whole. Thus, instead of boldly putting forward a broad, sweeping program of political reform and national renewal, the administration, with a few exceptions, has been immobilized. As a result, an administration that should have been a source of new ideas and a stimulator of public debate has been a giant wet blanket smothering our political and cultural life.

The administration's ineffectuality is the result not just of its extraordinary diversity and its leader's limitations, but also of the Reaganites' extraordinary talents for that powerful set of arts and techniques called public relations. It would take a book to define and explore this important and little-understood subject, so suffice it to say that the Reagan administration not only practiced PR, but raised the technique to new heights. The effect of its PR-mindedness was to erect an almost impenetrable barrier between one thought and another, between one action and another, and between thought

415

and action. The result was that the administration was mostly incapable of taking positive and coherent steps in any policy area.

As the president and his people reckoned it, one could denounce big government and simultaneously preside over a 20 percent increase in the share of gross national product accounted for by federal spending. One could attack overregulation (Reagan did) and disband one's regulatory-reform task force after two years of inactivity (this also happened, in 1983). One could declare war on terrorism and sell weapons to the world's leading terrorist government. One could tout the free market and free trade, yet slap quotas on steel and car imports, more than doubling the share of the economy protected from foreign competition. One could make historic cuts in the personal and business income tax, yet also preside over growing spending that puts the tax achievements at risk.

Reaganism adds up to little in policy terms because it represents not the dawn of a new era, but the twilight of an old one. Behind the talk of free markets and traditional values, Reaganism in practice has consisted mostly of career advancement for administration members and the usual interest-group politics. It differed from what had gone before because the president ran against liberalism, not on it, and, of course, because Reagan himself is the most naturally talented American leader since Lincoln. Ronald Reagan helped a nation of scoffers regain lost faith. Like Roosevelt, he effected a new reconciliation between the American people and the welfare state. It was a cool, grudging reconciliation, based not on respect for the welfare state (on the contrary, Reagan taught disrespect) but on personal trust of Reagan. Yet it worked. The arrangement kept political dissent to a low level and gave people new faith in the future. It also kept the welfare state intact. Liberals who put down the "Teflon presidency" are putting down the leadership that added years to the dwindling life expectancy of liberalism's greatest creation.

So what comes next? God only knows. But concealed in the cheesy murk that has been the public discourse during the Reagan years are some clues that tell us something about the logic and direction of our times, and thus about the shape of the future. For as we contemplate the farcical and bitter end of the Reagan years, not all the disparate elements that make up Reaganism have fared equally well. Some elements have done worse than others.

The defense buildup and Reagan's globalist, interventionist foreign policy have fared very badly, I think. Not only has the Iran-contra mess done for aggressive anti-Communist foreign policy what $600 toilet seats did for Pentagon spending (both of which remind me of what Watergate did for the reputation of Richard Nixon), but we are hearing from a widening range of quarters, including any number of conservatives, the idea that the time has come for the United States to withdraw from exposed, costly foreign entanglements such as NATO. The United States will continue to preach democracy, individual rights, and other liberal values, as we have historically done and as we always should. But if Ronald Reagan with his incredible persuasiveness and enormous electoral majorities cannot sustain an interventionist foreign policy, no one can. The postwar anti-Communist/interventionist/globalist foreign policy is on its deathbed. Its day has come and gone.

Like Pat Robertson's meteoric failure in the GOP primaries, the morass into which the Bork nomination ran shows that traditional morality and the neotheocratic element of Reaganism have little staying power on the national stage. Yes, secularism and expanded personal freedom will go on offending a lot of Americans, and this in turn guarantees that modernist morality will remain a contentious issue. But it is utterly certain that secularism and individual freedom are here to stay. There is no workable alternative to modernism, at least not in national politics.

The part of Reaganism that has fared best in the policy arena and public discussion is its commitment to markets and individual freedom. After seven years of Reagan, public mistrust of big government remains intense, deregulation continues (though at a much-reduced pace), tax cutting and loophole closing retain broad public appeal, user fees and privatization are still coming on strong, and the strength and influence of markets continue to grow. The dominance of the market idea in the realm of regulation and economic policy is firmly established, and individualist approaches have made headway in the once-sacrosanct realm of social policy. Today, everyone accepts the volunteer army; a growing number of Americans agree that a minimum wage is a pernicious policy; practically no one thinks that welfare is desirable, and even Democrats argue for workfare; and incentives are accepted in health insurance.

When you look at the policy debate today, the ideas that are fresh and that hold real promise, politically and practically, are free-market ideas. The only candidates who can persuasively address our important public problems are the ones who go at them from a free-market vantage point. Only one presidential candidate dared speak about our coming social security crisis—Pete du Pont, who took a pro-market, pro-choice viewpoint. The people saying useful things about education problems are the ones offering demonopolization strategies.

To me, this signifies that the classical liberalism piece of the Reagan experience—the part that stresses a modest foreign policy, limited government, the free market, and individual freedom—is the part that emerges from the Reagan years in the best shape. I personally welcome that, and I believe that the nation's libertarian future can be discerned in other features of the public discussion.

At the beginning of this essay, when I was describing what a dark and boring time the Reagan years have been in terms of the public discourse, I said there was an exception to this generalization that I wanted to get to later. That time has come—and actually I want to talk about two exceptions to the rule.

The few sparks that have illuminated the political culture of the Reagan years have been struck not by philosophers, novelists, or political leaders, but by policy analysts and satirical journalists.

As for the policy analysts, who populate dozens of think tanks, academic schools, and departments, they have been increasingly active, and their work has been increasingly dominated by the discipline of economics and the market idea. Pro-market policy studies, virtually nonexistent just 15 years ago, have been a growth industry, and they have flowered in the Reagan years. Scores of interesting studies of topics from schools to welfare to taxation to industrial policy to eminent domain and so on down a long, long list have cast fresh light on old topics and begun to establish a new intellectual orthodoxy that will influence lawmakers for years to come. The vitality of market ideas has been apparent not just in Ronald Reagan's America, nor yet only in Maggie Thatcher's Great Britain, but also in François Mitterrand's France, and even among the Scandinavian worthies who hand out the Nobel Prizes in economics.

The other signs of life in the public discourse during the age of Reagan have come from satirical journalists such as Mark Alan

Stamaty, the creator of "Washingtoon," and Michael Kinsley, the irrepressible bubble popper of the *New Republic*. This, to be sure, is a personal sort of judgment, but for me Stamaty is the nation's funniest cartoonist, and Kinsley's *New Republic* is the only magazine that seems fresh and alive and intellectually engaging—the only publication to which I turn eagerly and greedily each week, rather than dutifully as a conscientious observer of this and that.

Stamaty and the *New Republic* are, of course, slashing, scathing, freewheeling assassins of the modern corporate or welfare state. Their rapiers and meat axes respond almost involuntarily to the hypocritical posturings, dishonest idealism, and self-serving pretentions of the men and women who dominate politics and journalism in Reagan's Washington. They are enemies of PR-think, media babble, and political hype in all its sophisticated modern forms. They are enemies not just of Reaganism, but of the entire political system as it has evolved in the last decades. They are enemies of the state. I think they're wonderfully funny. I love their work.

Most of my conservative and neoconservative friends hate Stamaty and the *New Republic* and cannot understand what I could possibly see in them. The last time I praised Kinsley's work in public, a distinguished supply-side economist walked up to me in a rage and asked in a loud voice when I had joined the *New Republic*'s staff, that being the only reason he could think of why anyone might praise what he said was the most "despicable" publication in America. He for one thought the editorial page of the *Wall Street Journal* (for which he actually did once work) was the best publication in America, and didn't I agree, etc.? My neoconservative friends say that Stamaty not only isn't funny to them, but that reading him literally turns their stomachs.

These different responses to "Washingtoon" are partly a reflection of temperament. But they also reflect fundamentally different views of the nation's political institutions. Conservatives and neoconservatives generally are put off by today's adversarial, cynical, and satirical political humor and criticism ("Kinsleyism," I've heard one young "neocon" call it) because at bottom they like our political, economic, and other institutions in something like their current form. They would like to see the corporate state become more conservative (or neoconservative), but they have no problem with—

419

indeed, they quite accept—the modern presidency, the tutelary and interventionist state, managerialist ideas of public law, majoritarian approaches to individual rights, the modern corporation, the modern university (which, although they criticize it now, they tried to "defend" against the New Left in the sixties), and so on. They think of themselves as cosmopolitan and sophisticated people, and they believe that hypocrisy, lying, and wire-pulling are endemic to politics.

To them, then, Kinsleyism, which attacks people for hypocrisy, lying, and cynical wire-pulling, represents a giant lie about the basic nature of our institutions. It is running down good institutions they are trying to defend. If it continues indefinitely, they fear, America itself will be fundamentally damaged or changed. If our journalists are intolerant of liars or adulterers and make an issue of their lies and adultery, they fear, we are going to be eliminating from our political life many of the best potential political leaders, and our complex national political institutions just won't have the capacity to sustain so many large and beneficent interventionist programs and projects.

There is another view of Kinsleyism, which is that it is essentially destructive and, therefore, a positive and highly beneficial phenomenon. That's my view.

Kinsley and Stamaty are attacking a real problem that has been growing for years and that in the Reagan years established itself as perhaps our biggest political problem. The natural distortions of the press, which in the Reagan years was the dominant milieu for conducting politics, and the essential nihilism of public relations, which was raised to new heights by the Reagan administration, have combined to empty our politics of meaning, coherence, or answerability. In other words, the hypocrisy, lying, and cynical wire-pulling that Kinsleyite assassins are taking aim at are real and consequential. They are what have turned the public discourse into a desert. They are what made the Reagan administration such a bitter disappointment to so many. They are what protects the corporate state from the profound disaffection and building wrath of the American people.

For those who take a protective, conserving posture toward our society and institutions as they stand today, Kinsleyism is offensive and dangerous. But for the rest of us who believe that fundamental changes are needed and overdue, it is welcome, funny, and desirable. The "Washingtoon's " clever horselaugh and the *New Republic*'s rapierlike attacks on frauds left and right are signs of health and vigor in the political culture. They represent a rejection of the fraudulent tutelary, therapeutic, and other justifications claimed by institutions looking for fresh ideological fig leaves with which to conceal their political privates—their contempt for democracy, their indifference to individual rights, their habit of expropriating the broad mass of the American people for the benefit of the self-appointed few. They are the psychological preamble to a declaration of independence from the corporate state.

In short, the few bright spots in the public discourse of the Reagan years are, I believe, signs of nascent individualist self-respect. From such aggressive, negative, despairing public perceptions can grow large and good things.

31. Who Will Lead?

Edward H. Crane

The failure of the Reagan administration is, in my view, ultimately a failure of leadership.

I don't want to spend time here arguing the merits of my position that the Reagan administration has failed, both in terms of its stated objectives in 1980 and in terms of the more ambitious goals my classical liberal or libertarian principles call for. By way of shorthand, though, let me suggest that if you had asked a typical Reagan supporter what his or her goals were back in 1980, it would not have been an increase in federal spending from 22 percent of gross national product to 24 percent of GNP; nor would it have been an increase in the civilian federal workforce of some 159,000 bureaucrats. Yet that and much more like it is what has happened. The Department of Education has not only not been abolished, but its budget has been increased by a billion dollars a year since Ronald Reagan was elected.

The question is, Why has this happened? To blame President Reagan alone is clearly not fair. Obviously there are powerful forces at work in Washington that facilitate the seemingly inexorable growth in the size and power of government. These can best be described as systemic forces and, despite the fact that they've been analyzed and explained by some brilliant thinkers, they remain greatly underestimated in terms of their power over the course of events in Washington.

To begin with, there is the almost clichéd but very important observation that governments confer concentrated benefits and pay for them through diffused costs. The billions of dollars that are wasted through pork-barrel legislation, as documented by the Grace Commission, are just part of the problem. The special interest that stands to make millions of dollars testifies before Congress while the average taxpayer, for whom the program may cost 50 cents, opts not to fly to Washington. And the media, with unblinking innocence, report "overwhelming" public support for the program.

Then there are the insights of James Buchanan and the Public Choice school—namely, that like the rest of us, government bureaucrats are self-interested. One of the main reasons for the need for institutes such as Cato, in fact, lies in the proclivity of bureaucrats to spend a great deal of their time thinking up rationales for new government programs or for expansion of existing programs. There are, quite literally and I suppose somewhat unconsciously, thousands of bureaucrats and billions of dollars of taxpayers' money devoted to this phenomenon on an ongoing basis. It, too, is an underappreciated force for government growth.

To cut short this outline of the systemic causes of government growth, let me just point to Milton Friedman's phrase, the "tyranny of the status quo," by which he refers to the fact that a given program may be debated for years—decades even—only to be passed by a single vote in Congress. From that point forward, however, the only debate centers on whether the program's budget should be increased by 5 percent or 15 percent. And Friedman points to what he calls the "Iron Triangle" as an explanation for why this occurs. A distinctly unholy alliance is formed by the direct beneficiaries of the program, the bureaucracy administering it, and its congressional oversight committee. As defenses go, the Redskins should have it so good.

I could go on, of course, about the systemic forces that generate government growth here in Washington. Certainly the inexplicable disregard for the economic liberties guaranteed in the Constitution—in Article I, section 10, and the Fifth and Fourteenth amendments—is an important additional example. But the point I hope to make in concluding these essays is that proper leadership can overcome these obstacles. For all the entrenchment of systemic government growth that's occurred over the past decades, it's really not that much compared to the centuries of government oppression—dating back, really, to the beginning of recorded history—that the leaders among our forefathers were able to overcome. I'm a great believer in methodological individualism—the idea that individual human beings can make a difference and that we are not the victims of some kind of irresistible force of historical determination.

I should say, parenthetically, that I would prefer to live in a world

424

in which political leadership was not required. Perhaps we approached that kind of society in our colonial period when the British were too far away to do much effective ruling and we hadn't yet conceived our own central government. But that was then and this is now, and I fear we're going to need some serious political leadership if we ever hope to regain the kind of society in which government plays a limited and minor role in our lives.

There are three important attributes that this kind of leadership requires. First and foremost, a leader needs vision and the ability to articulate a vision of the kind of free, pluralistic, and prosperous society that is our rightful heritage as Americans. It is here that Ronald Reagan scores best as a leader, and here where advocates of limited government owe the president a debt of gratitude. Reagan virtually single-handedly restored the philosophical backbone of the Republican party, recently the party of Nixon and Rockefeller and Jerry Ford, of me-tooism and the corporate state. To do this was no small task, for we had gotten to the point that to invoke the thoughts of the founders or to speak of the principles of free enterprise and individual liberty was to invite ridicule. You have to have lived in Washington to realize how thoroughly confused and shocked were the *Washington Post* and the rest of the political establishment here—in both parties—over the enormously positive response Mr. Reagan received from the American people as he articulated those principles in his powerful speeches.

I don't want to drift into politics here, but I do think, given the Reagan legacy, it is depressingly ironic that the two leading candidates in the race for the 1988 Republican presidential nomination were each disdainful of political philosophy, one having told reporters (with a straight face) that his handlers, whom he said he greatly respected, believed that it was too early in the campaign for him to articulate a vision for America, but that they'd work one up for him as the race heated up.

In any case, vision is not in itself adequate. The second attribute that is required of a modern-day leader of the kind we should be seeking is the intelligence and the courage to recognize that this vision of America requires challenging the status quo that Milton Friedman warned us about. In a sense, many prominent Democrats are willing to do that, but only in ways that would make matters worse, through higher taxes and new industrial policy schemes.

425

On this second attribute, President Reagan scores badly, indeed. By giving carte blanche to the Pentagon and by taking so-called entitlements off the table, the president essentially gave up the battle to control federal spending before it began. In his speeches, the president has bragged that his administration has spent more on food stamps, education, farm subsidies, and social security than any administration in history. As Bill Niskanen points out in the opening essay of this book, after its incredibly inept attempt to cut social security benefits, the administration was afraid to challenge any issue it felt it might lose on. It adopted a conscious policy of not challenging the status quo, with the one exception of tax reform. That issue, by the way, is a good example of how the status quo can be successfully challenged, and I would point to Sen. Bill Bradley as a good example of how a politician can play a proper leadership role on such an issue.

Finally, the third attribute our prospective leader requires is the administrative ability to get the job done. I've never understood why conservatives were always bragging about the hands-off management style of Ronald Reagan. You can't fight the status quo, the entrenched bureaucracy, and the Iron Triangle with a laissez-faire management style. What you must do above all else is take care in your appointments, make sure that those people are committed to your vision, and demand to know each morning what they plan to do to help achieve that vision.

If you want to abolish the Department of Education, you don't appoint Terrel Bell, a man committed to an increased federal role in education, to head the department. If you want a reduced federal role in health care delivery, you don't appoint Otis Bowen, a man who had written articles calling for an expansion of Medicare, to head the Department of Health and Human Services. If you're opposed to federal jobs programs, you don't appoint Bill Brock, an advocate of a billion-dollar federal jobs program, to head the Department of Labor.

Individuals do matter. You appoint Mark Fowler to head the Federal Communications Commission, and Jim Miller or Dan Oliver to head the Federal Trade Commission, and you make some progress in rolling back the intrusions of the federal government. But unfortunately, these men are exceptions to the rule in the hands-off Reagan administration.

426

Whether we can find a leader who combines Ronald Reagan's vision with a recognition that such a vision requires challenging the political status quo and the administrative ability to get the job done is problematic. The preselection process is not encouraging. F.A. Hayek wrote about why the worst get on top in politics. And Bergen Evans in his book, *The Spoor of Spooks and Other Nonsense,* wrote:

> There is no necessary connection between the desire to lead and the ability to lead, and even less to the ability to lead somewhere that will be to the advantage of the led. . . . Leadership is more likely to be assumed by the aggressive than by the able, and those who scramble to the top are more often motivated by their own inner torments than by any demand for their guidance.

Senators Gary Hart and Joe Biden somehow come to mind. But it is true. Most people who want to be political leaders want to run other people's lives. People who want to be career legislators tend not to be great champions of the private sector. Never trust anyone who was elected to the student council in high school.

And, when someone does come along and presents a principled view of the world, he or she can count on the media to scoff. Consider the mind-set of the media when a reporter for the *New York Times,* Gerald Boyd, ended a news story on the campaign (dated September 19, 1987) with this editorial comment: "Following Mr. Bush, Mr. Kemp and Mr. du Pont, who both trail the Vice President, called on the party to emphasize principle over political expediency, a plea traditionally made by political underdogs."

But Ronald Reagan proved that appeals to political principle don't have to be limited to underdogs. In 1986, a CBS News–*New York Times* poll showed that a remarkable 83 percent of the American people would like to see the budget balanced through federal spending cuts. Eighty-three percent. And is it any wonder? As recently as 1920, spending at all levels of government amounted to only 10 percent of national income. By 1950, spending had risen to 26 percent. In 1986, spending by government at all levels amounted to 43.6 percent of national income.

It seems clear enough to me that Americans are seeking the kind of leader I'm talking about. And it's vitally important that we find that person. The key is that he or she must be willing to challenge the status quo; be willing to lose some battles with Congress, and then go back for more; and have the good sense to build an administration team with the guts, brains, and commitment to get the job done. Now, I don't approve of what Ollie North did with his covert machinations, but I think it's fascinating to witness how a clear-eyed, strong-willed person with a commitment to a cause and a little courage can intimidate a bunch of weak-kneed politicians.

Unfortunately, the politicians ultimately intimidated Ronald Reagan and his advisers. It didn't have to be that way. As I've tried to demonstrate, it would be wrong for supporters of limited government to throw up their hands in dismay and say, "If Reagan couldn't do it, nobody can." It definitely won't be easy, but somebody can. Somebody must. The American experiment in limited government and individual liberty is too important to leave in the hands of those not totally committed to preserving it.

Contributors

Doug Bandow, special assistant to the president in 1981–82, is a senior fellow at the Cato Institute.

Randy E. Barnett is an associate professor at Illinois Institute of Technology, Chicago-Kent College of Law; director of the Law and Philosophy Program at the Institute for Humane Studies at George Mason University; and an adjunct scholar of the Cato Institute.

David Boaz is vice president for public policy affairs at the Cato Institute.

Robert L. Bradley, Jr., is the author of *The Mirage of Oil Protection* (University Press of America, 1988) and *Oil, Gas, and Government: The U.S. Experience* (Cato Institute, forthcoming) and an adjunct scholar of the Cato Institute.

Ted Galen Carpenter is director of foreign policy studies at the Cato Institute.

Robert W. Crandall is a senior fellow at the Brookings Institution.

Edward H. Crane is president of the Cato Institute.

Catherine England is director of regulatory studies at the Cato Institute.

Roger D. Feldman, senior economist at the Council of Economic Advisers in 1984–85, is a professor of health services research and economics at the University of Minnesota.

Peter J. Ferrara, a senior staff member in the White House Office of Policy Development in 1984–85, is a professor of law at George Mason University, John M. Olin Fellow in Political Economy at the Heritage Foundation, and an adjunct scholar of the Cato Institute.

Malcolm S. Forbes, Jr., is president and chief operating officer of Forbes, Inc., and deputy editor-in-chief of *Forbes*.

429

James L. Gattuso is McKenna Senior Policy Analyst in Regulatory Affairs at the Heritage Foundation and from 1986 to 1988 was co-editor of the *Washington Antitrust Report*.

Kevin R. Hopkins, director of the White House Office of Policy Information in 1982–84, is a senior research fellow at the Hudson Institute.

Jerry L. Jordan, a member of the Council of Economic Advisers in 1981–82, is senior vice president and chief economist at First Interstate Bancorp.

Lawrence J. Korb, assistant secretary of defense in 1981–84, is program director for the Center of Public Policy Education at the Brookings Institution.

Laurence J. Kotlikoff, a senior economist with the Council of Economic Advisers in 1981–82, is the chairman of the Department of Economics at Boston University.

Christopher Layne, a Los Angeles attorney, is an adjunct scholar of the Cato Institute.

Mickey D. Levy is chief economist at First Fidelity Bancorporation.

Barry W. Lynn is a legislative counsel at the American Civil Liberties Union.

Stephen Macedo is an assistant professor of government at Harvard University and an adjunct scholar of the Cato Institute.

William A. Niskanen, a member of the Council of Economic Advisers in 1981–85, is chairman of the Cato Institute.

William Poole, a member of the Council of Economic Advisers in 1982–85, is a professor of economics and director of the Center for the Study of Financial Markets and Institutions at Brown University and an adjunct scholar of the Cato Institute.

Richard Rahn is vice president and chief economist of the U.S. Chamber of Commerce.

Earl C. Ravenal is Distinguished Research Professor of International Affairs at the Georgetown University School of Foreign Service and a senior fellow at the Cato Institute.

430

Morgan O. Reynolds is a professor of economics at Texas A&M University and an adjunct scholar of the Cato Institute.

Fred L. Smith, Jr., is president of the Competitive Enterprise Institute.

Clarence Thomas has been chairman of the Equal Employment Opportunity Commission since 1982.

Robert L. Thompson, assistant secretary for economics at the U.S. Department of Agriculture in 1985–87, is dean of the School of Agriculture at Purdue University.

Norman B. Ture, undersecretary of the treasury for tax and economic affairs in 1981–82, is president of the Institute for Research on the Economics of Taxation and an adjunct scholar of the Cato Institute.

Paul H. Weaver is John M. Olin Media Fellow at the Hoover Institution.

Murray L. Weidenbaum, chairman of the Council of Economic Advisers in 1981–82, is Mallinckrodt Distinguished University Professor of Economics and director of the Center for the Study of American Business at Washington University in St. Louis.

431

Cato Institute

Founded in 1977, the Cato Institute is a public policy research foundation dedicated to broadening the parameters of policy debate to allow consideration of more options that are consistent with the traditional American principles of limited government, individual liberty, and peace. Toward that goal, the Institute strives to achieve a greater involvement of the intelligent, concerned lay public in questions of policy and the proper role of government.

The Institute is named for *Cato's Letters*, pamphlets that were widely read in the American Colonies in the early 18th century and played a major role in laying the philosophical foundation for the revolution that followed. Since that revolution, civil and economic liberties have been eroded as the number and complexity of social problems have grown.

To counter this trend the Cato Institute undertakes an extensive publications program dealing with the complete spectrum of policy issues. Books, monographs, and shorter studies are commissioned to examine the federal budget, Social Security, regulation, NATO, international trade, and a myriad of other issues. Major policy conferences are held throughout the year, from which papers are published thrice yearly in the *Cato Journal*.

In order to maintain an independent posture, the Cato Institute accepts no government funding. Contributions are received from foundations, corporations, and individuals, and other revenue is generated from the sale of publications. The Institute is a nonprofit, tax-exempt, educational foundation under Section 501(c)3 of the Internal Revenue Code.

CATO INSTITUTE
224 Second St., S.E.
Washington, D.C. 20003